HUMAN RELATIONS

From Theory to Practice

University of Oklahoma Press : Norman

By George Henderson

Foundations of American Education (with William B. Ragan) (New York, 1970)

Teachers Should Care (with Robert F. Bibens) (New York, 1970)

America's Other Children:Public Schools Outside Suburbia (editor) (Norman, 1971)

To Live in Freedom: Human Relations Today and Tomorrow (Norman, 1972)

Education for Peace: Focus on Mankind (editor) (Washington, D.C., 1973)

Human Relations: From Theory to Practice (Norman, 1974)

Library of Congress Cataloging in Publication Data

Henderson, George, 1932–
    Human relations: from theory to practice.

    Bibliography: p.
    1. Interpersonal relations.   2. Group relations training.   I. Title
HM132.H46   301.11   73–19387
ISBN 0–8061–1184–4

Copyright 1974 by the University of Oklahoma Press, Publishing Division of the University. Composed and printed at Norman, Oklahoma, U.S.A., by the University of Oklahoma Press.

To my students,
who encouraged me to write this book

PREFACE

This book is written for professionals and nonprofessionals actively involved in efforts aimed at improving human relationships. Specifically, this book is meant to supplement the many fine textbooks in education, sociology, psychology, social work, and social welfare which focus on strategies and programs for social change. It is built on the belief that humane relationships need not be left to chance.

From my review of the literature in human relations training, it is clear that much more can be done to improve the various activities described as "the helping professions." On the other hand, there are many good programs in operation today. It is my intention to accentuate the positive, humane programs and practices and to discourage further use of inhumane programs and practices.

It is also my hope that other writers will improve upon this attempt to present an overview of the rapidly growing field of study called "human relations." As the world moves into the twenty-first century, it could be valuable if we could also improve upon the disciplines related to human behavior. If we fail, self-destruction and genocide seem more than a remote possibility.

Many people contributed to the completion of this book. My special appreciation goes to John Douglas and Marcia Trachtenberg, who assisted in writing Chapter 2, and Cheryl Kienholtz, who assisted in writing Chapter 15. Others who helped in some important manner include Connie Bleck, Sarah Burns, Michele Henderson, Alfreda Lawson, Zahea Nappa, Marilyn Rycroft, and Nancy Waters. Sheridan Wood added the refining touches to the rough manuscript. His critical eye and constructive suggestions account for much that is good about this book.

Finally, I am grateful to the authors and publishers who granted us permission to reprint their materials.

GEORGE HENDERSON

January 2, 1974

CONTENTS

Part One **FOUNDATIONS**

*Think of what it is like to have most of your life ahead
and be told you are obsolete! . . . That you are not
a person but a joke.*—ZOE MOSS

Americans are a collection of many kinds of people. They come in all colors, sizes, shapes, and philosophies. Above all else, most of them exhibit a burning desire for peace, freedom, and justice. And they expect their government to make these desires come true.

Perhaps, some writers say, we expect too much of our government. But is it too much to believe that America can become a nation where all citizens may walk in dignity, eat wholesome meals, sleep in decent houses, live in economic and social freedom, and, finally, be able to die timely deaths unhurried by malnutrition and inadequate social services?

Peace, justice, and freedom are not much to ask. A just government and its people will meet the moral challenges of racial strife, of callousness to suffering and death, of hate and greed.

Who or what will give positive images to the millions of hungry, angry, tired, and alienated citizens? In the quest for an answer to this question, many citizens are asked to participate in various community and organization-oriented programs which focus on human relations training.

THE SEARCH FOR IDENTITY

We cannot fully understand the development of human relations training without examining the post–World War II years, the time and the setting in which it developed. Americans had lived through World War I and the depression of the 1930's, and many people were tired of the long-range global goals that had characterized the period preceding

3

World War II. At war's end most persons turned their attention to the material goods they had been deprived of during the 1930's and early 1940's. That change in direction signaled the genesis of William H. Whyte's "organization man."[1] Whyte observed that the social ethic of the organization man reflected the decline of the Protestant ethic, especially its emphasis on personal independence. Two principal tenets of the new social ethic were belief in belonging to a group as the ultimate need of the individual and belief in the group as the ultimate source of creativity.

The organization man of the 1940's and 1950's was preoccupied with his appearance, image, and role in significant organizations. He joined groups to enhance his prestige. Most successful organization men achieved some sense of community but had little control over the dominant values and goals which characterized their organizations. Their task was to do what was necessary to belong, to fit into the social order. They worked for their families instead of themselves; their future was laid out by society.

David Riesman called the organization men and women "the other-directed"—unable to distinguish thoughts from feelings and unable to express feelings even when recognizing them.[2] Today, more than twenty-five years later, the organization men are still with us, most of them unable to distinguish between what they want and what they ought to want. Decisions of this nature are left to a few leaders. The other-directed people are attuned to the attitudes and opinions of others and have insatiable psychological needs for approval. They find fulfillment only when they are accepted as members of a valued group. It is difficult for well-indoctrinated members of an organization to assert much autonomy. In many instances they become generally helpless, passive, indecisive, and lacking in self-esteem.

Erich Fromm's conception of the typical mid-twentieth-century person, the "marketer," is similar to Riesman's other-directed man.[3] Persons fitting the marketer category derive their self-esteem from their value or salability as a commodity or an investment ("I am what I do"). According to Fromm, the responsibility of freedom is too frightening for them, and so they live by conforming to social pressures and seeking approval from others; they have no self-identification. In spite of economic or professional success, there is a sense of emptiness among those who fit Fromm's marketer category. They feel impotent within the bureaucratic organization, and ultimately they turn into passive

1 William H. Whyte, Jr., *The Organization Man*, 7.
2 David Riesman, *The Lonely Crowd: A Study of the Changing American Character.*
3 Erich Fromm, *Man For Himself: An Inquiry into the Psychology of Ethics.*

consumers. In socioscientific terms they become alienated—they lose touch with themselves and join the "lonely crowd."

In looking at the passive, alienated man, we find it easy to understand the appeal of existential philosophy and its influence on the human relations movement. In emphasizing one's own feelings in the "here and now" and living one's own life, human relations has existential implications and reflects the appeal of such existential thinkers as Rollo May. Existential thought which gives human relations a philosophical base is devoted to discovering basic human conditions and recognizing the despair, insecurity, and alienation of urban dwellers.

May is convinced that a crucial problem of our times is that of identity, "a coherent sense of self, . . . a sense of wholeness, of integration, of knowing what is right and what is wrong and of being able to chose."[4] This crisis of identity also means the loss of significance of the self. Behavioral scientists note the likelihood that persons will feel impotent when they are surrounded by systems of mass production and their related economic, political, and social movements. Along with a feeling of powerlessness, alienated people also lose their sense of worth and dignity. May also writes about the value crisis of modern man. In our rapidly changing Western society many of the old values and behavior patterns no longer apply.

This was the conditions in which many persons found themselves during the 1950's and 1960's. Sensing that something was wrong, they sought new directions. Because existentialism stressed personal growth and understanding, it paved the way for training and encounter groups where a person could be himself, where he could choose and decide for himself. The group thus became a means to lessen an individual's alienation from himself and others. For a growing number of people, human relations training became a suitable means to meet the isolation and alienation of contemporary life.

Another reason for the rise of human relations training has been the willingness of young persons to question existing socialization processes. There is a lack of touch among most persons and an absence of affection in both intra- and interpersonal activities. Various youth movements have challenged the older adult fear of close personal relationships which might call for some type of commitment requiring individuals to express their feelings. Non-Americans frequently chide Americans for being cold, isolated, and ruthless. Intimacy and warmth are missing in almost all formal organization relationships. Sensing their aloneness and isolation, various groups have sought conditions which require more awareness of feelings and communication with others. For those with this need, personal-growth groups are attractive

[4] Quoted in Allen Wheelis, *The Quest for Identity*, 19.

because they provide the warmth and security often absent in their relations with their families and in their jobs.

With increased reliance on science and technology, bureaucratization and mechanization (especially in communication systems), and computerization of industry, government, and education, a dehumanized culture has developed in which the individual does not seem to be of any worth. A deterministic-behavioristic view prevails in which man is seen as only a cog in a larger machine.

Fromm called attention to the need of people to develop wholesome personalities through socialization. The personality, Fromm noted, is shaped by the way in which persons relate to each other, and this relationship is determined by the socioeconomic and political structure of a nation. In most instances individual needs are not being satisfied. Fromm concluded that there is a conflict between human needs and the social structure; the middle-class life of prosperity, while satisfying material needs, leaves most people with a feeling of intense boredom.[5] The poor are also unfulfilled in basic psychological needs. Increased mobility compounds this situation. Mobility detaches the individual from permanent significant relationships which provide identity and values. When this detachment happens, occupational specialization adds to mobility because it forces persons to follow jobs instead of friends.

In many instances increased urbanization has meant a decline in community life and the absence of meaningful social activities. Each year more people find themselves trapped in an impersonal techno-structure in which their desires to meet, exchange ideas, and develop close relationships and in which their needs to express feelings and emotions spontaneously are unfulfilled. Most social institutions seem to have lost their ability to provide people with ways of finding these satisfactions. Traditional organizations are not providing the mechanisms for closeness. If the number of people attending human relations training programs is an indication, there is a growing hunger for intimacy, relatedness, care, affection, and understanding which our major institutions of employment, religion, and family are not providing.

Members of traditional organizations have been forced to seek or establish new forms of human interaction. One alternative is human relations training. Proponents of such training believe that they have the answer to the question: Can intimacy and community be re-created in today's mechanized and alienated society? Human relations training is an attempt to counter the dehumanization of our culture.

Traditional therapy programs have not come to terms successfully with the problems of individuals in rapidly changing societies. Arthur

5 Erich Fromm, *The Sane Society*, 19.

Burton concluded: "Those whom society labeled 'average' or 'normal' frequently resented their being placed in that existential limbo, resented the fact that their alienation, their loneliness, their despair, their anxiety were ignored *because* they were normal."[6] The framework and references of traditional psychoanalysis do not correspond to the requirements of persons in a technological society. Rollo May wrote: "There is plenty of evidence that the sense of isolation, the alienation of one's self from the world is suffered not only by people in pathological condition but by countless 'normal' persons as well in our day. Individual psychotherapy is at a loss of how to deal with this person."[7] This is another reason for the appeal and rise of human relations training. Groups can make a person realize that he is not alone; he loses his sense of uniqueness, isolation, and guilt when he sees that his conflicts and problems are shared by others:

> In the 1960's . . . something was dreadfully wrong with the state of the nation. A sense of wholeness, which healthy men and healthy societies have, was missing in urban America. Everything . . . was fractured, compartmentalized and contradictory. . . . The spiritual hunger was aggravated, in the mid-1960's, by a growing awareness that the entire social-political structure was somehow out of control.[8]

TOWARD HUMAN RELATIONS TRAINING

The 1960's brought a radical change in the behavior of a significant number of high school and college youths. They were angry about what they believed to be the meaningless and emptiness of their society. Rich in education and material security, they were bewildered by their loneliness and isolation. Some of them demanded change; unlike most of their parents, they rejected delaying social gratifications. Others de-emphasized the future focus and need for security. Still others looked to groups in hopes of finding themselves.

The young were not, of course, the only ones attracted to human relations training activities. Many adults were, too. As they rejected their parents' values, older adults often realized that many things they had struggled and sacrificed for were void of meaning. Thus they sought to bring some meaning to their struggles and sacrifices. Human relations training is akin to a revolution against the denigration of an individual feeling of self-worth. Through human relations the individual is brought back into center focus.

Like individuals, institutions are also affected by human relations training. For example, before the emphasis on human relations the

[6] Arthur Burton, ed., *Encounter: Theory and Practices of Encounter Groups*, 9.
[7] Quoted in Hendrik Ruitenbeek, *The New Group Therapies*, 29.
[8] Rasa Gustaitis, *Turning On*, xii–xiii.

field of education almost always overlooked the affective aspect of the teaching-learning process. This neglect partly accounted for the youth rebellion and the so-called generation gap:

During the 1960's, public education discovered the emotions. Cognitive learning and skill training, the traditional components of education, no longer satisfied the needs of a generation that had experienced the civil rights revolt, the widening generation gap, and the increasing confusion of teachers, administrators and school board members about ends and means in education. The result was a growing interest in various approaches to affective learning. . . . Among these approaches the most enthusiastically embraced has been the so-called sensitivity training.[9]

The psychological and social conditions that generated the movement toward sensitivity training are still with us. When our material needs are largely satisfied, our attention usually turns to psychological needs, and we seek greater authenticity and fulfillment: "When one is scrambling for a living, uncertain as to where the next meal will come from, there is little time or inclination to discover that one is alienated from others in some deep sense."[10]

Just as psychotherapy has never reached the lower classes or ghetto residents, human relations training is largely an activity of the middle-class, affluent society. Human relations professionals spend an inordinate amount of time in training middle-class Americans who have already bought their homes, cars, and television sets. By and large, trainees in human relations programs are themselves members of a successful economic unit. They have bought their consumer goods and are now seeking ways to buy back their togetherness.

Late in the 1960's, with the help of the mass media, the popularity of "going to groups" caught on. Human relations training became the fashionable thing to do. To be "with it," for example, affluent people began attending weekend workshops. Some participants were seeking growth, but others were simply seeking social status. Human relations had become a fad. Training groups and encounter groups became chic; their weekend, short-term nature accorded with the fast-paced, fast-changing characteristics which pervade so many aspects of American life. The early training and encounter groups were designed as temporary experiences.

Despite its negative aspects, human relations training is a poignant illustration of the increasing discomfort and turmoil in today's society.

---

[9] Robert W. Siroka, Ellen K. Siroka, and Gilbert A. Schloss, *Sensitivity Training and Group Encounter*, 181.
[10] Carl R. Rogers, *On Becoming a Person: A Thrapist's View of Psychotherapy*, 106.

8

In looking at the reasons for the growth of permanent organizations in the 1960's, it is clear that the inability of those organizations to combat alienation was an overpowering reason for public acceptance of human relations training. Abraham Maslow gave a good summary:

I believe that the tremendous and rapid increase in T-groups and other personal growth groups and intentional communities may in part be motivated by this unsatisfied hunger for contact, for intimacy, for belongingness and by the need to overcome the widespread feelings of alienation, aloneness, strangeness and loneliness, which have been worsened by our mobility, by the breakdown of traditional groupings, the scatterings of families, the generation gap, the steady urbanization and disappearance of village face-to-faceness and the resulting shallowness of American friendship.[11]

It is ironic that, while trying to find themselves and escape from "other-directedness," many persons failed to realize that personal growth groups offer another form of external control. Encounter groups, for example, tend to develop certain rigid norms of behavior and jargon. Group members foster conformity by exerting pressure on an individual to behave in accordance with group standards. In some instances group leaders have definite expectations of how group members should interact or what the result of the interaction should be. Sometimes it is difficult to distinguish between what evolves and what is staged.

Just as changes in an individual participant can reflect conformity to group pressures instead of freedom from anxiety and frustration, other hazards and shortcomings may be detected in human relations programs. Some dismiss human relations training as "brainwashing," "communism," or "sexual promiscuity." Other critics say: "The individual's privacy is invaded. His psyche is ruthlessly exploited,"[12] or, "Too much emphasis on human relations encourages people to feel sorry for themselves, makes it easier for them to slough off responsibility, to find excuses for failure, to act like children."[13] While much of such criticism reflects the fear of individuals who oppose change and want to maintain the status quo, those concerned with human relations training should heed the following points:

1. The human relations movement is characterized by a lack of professional training, responsible leadership, and codified standards.

[11] Abraham H. Maslow, *Motivation and Personality*, 44.
[12] Siroka, Siroka, and Schloss, *op. cit.*, 178.
[13] M. P. McNair, "What Price Human Relations?" *Harvard Business Review*, Vol. 35 (March–April, 1957), 20.

Thus, some human relations programs are conducted by opportunists and charlatans who can do a great deal of psychological damage to participants. It is necessary to protect both responsible leaders and the public by establishing program criteria, certification for qualified leaders, codified standards for groups, and effective methods for screening participants. The lack of professionalism is one of the more glaring inadequacies in the human relations movement. A professional organization would establish guidelines for the groups and leaders to prevent the human relations movement from turning into a parasitic game operated for the psychological and economic benefit of incompetent trainers.

2. As noted above, human relations training can do psychological damage if participants are left unprotected and without the necessary insight to understand their experiences. Participants in human relations training activities often become deeply involved in revealing themselves and are left with unsolved conflicts or, if stripped of their defenses, with emotional problems. Albert Ellis wrote: "The movement may be psychologically irresponsible, because it helps break down the defenses of some disturbed individuals, opens them up without closing them, and may lead to more harm than good."[14] For example, participants in race relations workshops frequently do not acquire the skills needed to counter racism. The result is that the participants are both frustrated and left with personal guilt. Few trainers provide for follow-up counseling, and, if problems arise, few participants are able to use their trainers as consultants for back-home problems. Perhaps this kind of agreement should be part of the original contract between group leaders and participants.

3. Many human relations programs are advertised or conceived of as instant cures. Frederick Perls cautioned that humanistic psychology is now entering what he called "a new and more dangerous phase, . . . the phase of the turner-onners: turn on to instant cure, instant joy. . . . We are entering the phase of the quacks and the con-men, who think if you get some breakthrough, you are cured—disregarding any growth requirements, disregarding any of the real potential. . . ."[15] Maslow also described "the long, slow, painful effort to use and apply insights." Individuals *can* gain insight during human relations training, but it takes time, effort, and usually professional help to assimilate and integrate the new experiences. There are no easy answers or instant cures. The public has become aware of the fact that some training or encounter programs proclaim universal panaceas just as other quack cures are foisted on the public.[16]

[14] Burton, *op. cit.*, 123.
[15] Frederick Perls, *Gestalt Therapy Verbatim*, 1.

4. Too often follow-up studies or evaluations of results are lacking. Most of the few studies that have been conducted have shown positive results. The National Training Laboratories (NTL) claim that less than 1 per cent of their clients have suffered psychological damage.[17] In a study by William Schutz, 83 per cent of the respondents reported that the group was a "good experience."[18] Other results have been negative. In an article entitled "How Sensitive Is Sensitivity Training?" Ralph Crawshaw discussed three cases of emotional disturbance aggravated by a group experience.[19] It is generally recognized by human relations professionals that more and better-designed research studies are desperately needed.

5. Another important question to be asked is whether the changes people experience during human relations programs are lasting. NTL claims that two-thirds of its clients have improved their interpersonal skills.[20] Elizabeth Mintz found participants less enthusiastic after an intervening period of time but still reporting permanent gains.[21] Other researchers hypothesize that the benefits of group activities are short-lived and the effects not valid because behavior change does not last—in short, that group learning cannot be transferred to daily living and is, therefore, useless. Further research is urgently needed in this area. Until then the unanswered question is, "The shortcuts provided by the new group therapies are there (and for many fortunately so), but in the long run how long do they last?"[22]

Responsible persons involved in human relations training should consider these shortcomings. Until recently professionals have been reluctant to examine critically the theory and practice of the various human relations programs. However, if the human relations movement is to be more than a fad, the problems and deficiencies must be remedied. The risks and pitfalls of the human growth movement are frightening. The potentials and promise are great.

MOVE TO HUMANISM

Human relations training draws from humanism, the philosophies emphasizing the values of love, creativity, and self-fulfillment. Departing from the nineteenth-century mechanistic model, human relations pro-

[16] Burton, *op. cit.*, 23.
[17] Robert Buckhout et al., eds., *Toward Social Change: A Handbook for Those Who Will*, 313.
[18] William Schutz, *Here Comes Everybody*, 257.
[19] *Psychological Abstracts*, Vol. 44 (July, 1970), 1298.
[20] Buckhout et al., *op. cit.*, 313.
[21] Elizabeth Mintz, "Marathon Groups: A Preliminary Education," *Psychological Abstracts*, Vol. 44 (August, 1970), 1298.
[22] Ruitenbeek, *op. cit.*, 240.

11

grams characterize man as a feeling, thinking person whose goals are fulfillment and self-realization. Such a view is antithetical to both the Freudian and the behavioristic schools of psychology. Psychoanalysis defines man as a creature of instinct and a prisoner of his past who can hope for no more than adjustment, while behaviorism defines man as a mechanistic programmable organism. Human relations programs, especially those drawing on humanistic psychology, emphasize man's potential for growth.

Table 1. Three Approaches to Interpersonal Feelings

Theory	Source of Conflict	Source of Anxiety	Goal
Instinct theory.........	Man/Nature	Lack of impulse control	Adaptation, pleasure
Interpersonal theory.........	Man/Man	Lack of consensual validation	Valid communication
Existential theory.........	Man/Self	Lack of meaning and/or integrity	Identity

SOURCE: Warren G. Bennis et al., eds., *Interpersonal Dynamics* (Homewood, Ill., Dorsey Press, 1964), 29. Reproduced by permission.

Human relations programs deal not so much with the neurotic or psychotic aspects of the individual as with possibilities for his "normal" emotional, intellectual, and spiritual growth. The primary area of focus is not sickness but health, growth, and transcendence. Humanistic psychology best illustrates the direction in which human relations training has moved: "Humanistic psychology, from whose passionate forehead the encounter group has sprung, tends to talk about emotional growth, fulfillment of one's potential, feeling, contact, and the participative experiencing of oneself and others with honesty, awareness, freedom and trust."[23]

Maslow, often called the father of humanistic psychology, stressed the holistic nature of human beings, emphasizing growth and development of one's potential rather than dwelling on neuroses and seeking cures. Because Freud mainly looked at the sick half of society, Maslow

[23] Even though the movement is young, it does draw on older, more traditional theorists such as Carl Jung and Otto Rank, both early followers of Freud. Jung believed the goal of growth was to become a responsible person who has found meaning or purpose in his existence—what he termed "the attainment of self-hood." Otto Rank emphasized individuality and affirmation of one's will. He described the healthy personality as having the courage to become a separate person who can assert himself and act in an antonomous, creative manner.

wanted to fill the void by looking at the healthy half. Maslow believed that we cannot understand mental illness until we understand mental health. Consequently, he devoted himself to studying positive psychology concerned with the healthful, fully functioning individual:

Human life can never be understood unless its highest aspirations are taken into account. Growth, self-actualization, the striving toward health, the quest for identity and autonomy, the yearning for excellence must now be accepted beyond question as a widespread and perhaps universal human tendency.[24]

Maslow was convinced that each human being is an organized, integrated whole, motivated by a number of basic needs which are species-wide, apparently unchanging, and genetic or instinctual in origin.[25] He further theorized that each person's needs are arranged in a hierarchy according to their urgency. According to Maslow, as our basic survival needs are met, we become motivated by higher-order needs. However, Maslow also believed that most persons only partly satisfy their basic needs, and the unsatisfied needs have the greatest influence on their behavior. Thus most persons react to the deprivation of their needs and fail to develop their psychological potential:

The average individual is motivated by deficiencies—he is seeking to fulfill his basic needs for safety, belongingness, love, respect and self-esteem. The healthy man is primarily motivated by his need to develop and actualize his fullest potentialities and capacities.[26]

Once a person has coped with the lower-order deficiency needs (D-needs), his energies are freed for socially meaningful pursuits, being needs (B-needs),[27] and self-actualization.[28] The traits of a self-actualized person are:

1. An adequate perception of reality
2. An acceptance of others, self, and human nature
3. A resistance to enculturation
4. A close degree of autonomy
5. Close relationship with a few friends and loved ones
6. A strong ethical sense
7. An unhostile sense of humor
8. Creativity, inventiveness, and spontaneity

[24] Everett Shostrom, "Group Therapy: Let the Buyer Beware," *Psychology Today*, Vol. 2 (May, 1969), 39.
[25] Maslow, *op. cit.*, xii–xiii.
[26] Frank Goble, *The Third Force: The Psychology of Abraham Maslow*, 38.
[27] *Ibid.*, 32.
[28] Kurt Goldstein, *Human Nature in the Light of Psychopathology*, 140.

Self-actualization is not a goal in itself but a means to achieve a fully functioning self. In seeking his full potential, the healthy individual encourages growth and fosters actualization.

Like Maslow, Carl Rogers has explored health as a positive problem.[29] Rogers believes that if human beings have a chance they will move in the direction of personal growth and social cooperation (contrary to Freud's emphasis on the dark, evil side of man). Rogers bases his theory of man on the concept of self-image. Ideally a person should have a realistic, flexible self-image built on honest observations of experience, behavior, thoughts, and feelings. This kind of person, Rogers concluded, moves away from façades and "oughts," away from meeting expectations and pleasing others, and moves toward self-direction and openness to experience, acceptance of others, and trust of oneself. Such a person Rogers calls "fully functioning." Most human relations programs draw heavily from Rogers' concept of fully functioning people.

Another humanistic psychologist, Sidney Jourard, has concluded that there is a connection between positive health and self-disclosure. Freud discovered that when a person avoids knowing and being himself he becomes ill. Expanding on Karen Horney's concept of the "self-alienated," Jourard has defined a healthy person as one who has the ability to make himself known to at least one other person significant to him. Only in letting himself be known to another does he really begin to know himself.

Jourard has described many persons considered "normal" who are not living satisfying, meaningful lives. He has concluded that behavior can be typical but not healthful and that "normal" personalities are not necessarily healthy ones. In modern-day American society a person is considered normal if he can enact an expected role. Thus life can become a process of putting on an act. We present ourselves as acceptable, admirable, and employable and hide our real selves.[30] Human relations programs focus on person-to-person relationships instead of role-to-role relationships. Sterile role conformity can lead to physical or mental illness:

We are discovering, and soon will demonstrate with more rigorous scientific proofs, that one of the reasons why people fail to grow, why they fail to fulfill many of their potentialities as persons, why they frequently fall ill, is because their daily mode of existence among people is characterized by impersonality, by playing roles, by self-manipulation and manipulation of others, by failure or inability to be and dis-

[29] Rogers, *loc. cit.*
[30] Sidney M. Jourard, *The Transparent Self: Self-Disclosure and Well-Being,* 26–28.

close themselves to respond in personal emotional honesty to them.[31]

The existential philosophers of the nineteenth century, such as Sören Kierkegaard and Friedrich Nietzsche, and those of the twentieth century, such as Martin Heidegger, Jean Paul Sartre, Paul Tillich, and Martin Buber, have also described their concepts of the healthy personality. To summarize their views, such a person:

1. Is aware of his being. He has the capacity to choose his own behavior.

2. Assumes responsibility for his behavior. Life is what he makes it.

3. Displays the "courage to be." He makes decisions, asserts himself, and accepts the consequences.

4. Looks at himself and others as human beings and not as things or actors of many roles. He relates to others not at a distance but in an affirming sense. To use Martin Buber's words, he enters into an I-Thou relationship.[32]

Maslow, Rogers, Jourard, and the existentialists have provided us with a humanistic picture of the ideal, healthy person—a self-actualizing, fully functioning individual who is able to disclose himself to others and relate honestly to them. This is the kind of person human relations training attempts to nurture. The basis of such training lies in the belief that persons are capable of developing their potential for humaneness. A well-designed group is one of the best settings in which to achieve such growth. Let us now look briefly at a few theories of interpersonal relations which are crucial to developing a science of human relations.

Human relations training borrows much from such "conventional" psychologists as Alfred Adler, Karen Horney, and Harry Stack Sullivan. After breaking with Freud, Adler focused on the significance of social interest or social feeling. He emphasized interpersonal relations as basic to a healthy personality.[33] Sullivan extended Adler's ideas and developed the "interpersonal school" of psychiatry.[34] He studied individuals in relation to other persons. Sullivan, like Horney, realized that emotional problems cannot be understood or abated without examining the interpersonal relationships between the individual and other people in his life.

"Growth" is a core concept in human relations. According to Herbert

[31] Episcopal Church, *Basic Reader in Human Relations Training, Part II,* 28.
[32] Sidney M. Jourard, *Personal Adjustment: An Approach to the Study of Healthy Personality,* 11.
[33] Alfred Adler, *The Practice and Theory of Individual Psychology.*
[34] Henry Stack Sullivan, *The Interpersonal Theory of Psychiatry.*

A. Otto and John Mann, growth is increasing the depth and validity of communication with others and is therefore essentially a social, interdependent process.[35] In order to better understand this interpersonal process, William Schutz developed a theory of how people relate to each other. His system, called Fundamental Interpersonal Relations Orientation (FIRO), measures how individuals act in interpersonal situations.[36]

Schutz's system focuses on three expressed and wanted interpersonal needs—inclusion, control, and affection. Inclusion (in or out) is the degree of belongingness, recognition, and individuality. It encompasses the person's concept of himself as a significant, worthwhile human being. This need is generally the most deeply felt need of group members. Control (top or bottom) refers to power relations and decision making in the group. Control means competency and responsibility. Affection (close or far) takes in the individual's need to feel lovable and the emotional close feelings of group members. Knowing an individual's orientation in these three dimensions will help one understand individual behavior as well as group interaction.

GROUPS REVISITED

Ferdinand Tönnies was one of the early theorists to make a significant contribution to the study of groups.[37] In the late 1880's he coined the terms *Gesellschaft* (an impersonal bureaucratic hierarchy) and *Gemeinschaft* (a closed, more personal community). George Herbert Mead's ideas of "social behaviorism" are also important in this context. Mead spoke of "self" as being socially formed, capable of arising only in a social setting where there is a social communication or interaction.[38]

In the early 1900's group methods were practiced by Joseph Pratt, who used supportive therapy while working with tuberculosis patients. At the same time, psychiatrists E. W. Lazell, L. C. Marsh, and Trigant Burrow used group methods to work with emotionally disturbed patients. In the 1920's, Paul Schilder and Louis Wender applied psychoanalytic concepts to group psychotherapy. In Europe, Alfred Adler was using group concepts with the Viennese working class. It is important to note that many Germans, Danes, and Russians were using group methods before 1930.

Those interested in encounter groups attach significant meaning to the work of Jacob L. Moreno in Vienna in the early 1900's. Through his

[35] See Herbert A. Otto and John Mann, eds., *Ways of Growth: Approaches to Expanding Awareness.*

[36] William C. Schutz, *FIRO: A Three-Dimensional Theory of Interpersonal Behavior.*

[37] Ferdinand Tönnies, *Community and Society.*

[38] George Herbert Mead, *Mind, Self, and Society: From the Standpoint of a Social Behaviorist.*

interest in group dynamics while working with prostitutes, Moreno developed the technique of psychodrama. The role playing employed in psychodrama brought insight and catharsis for individuals playing the roles and empathetic identification for observers. Describing his work with groups of children, Moreno wrote, "The general aim of the classes was on the one hand to train the whole organism of the child and not merely one of its functions, on the other hand, to lead them into the experience of 'wholes.' "[39] Moreno saw people as willing, creative participants in society and their creativity growing out of the continuous process of interaction with others.

In 1912, Moreno published a series of poetic writings called *Einlad-ung zu einer Begegung* ("Invitation to an Encounter").[40] It was the first definition and description of encounter. He defined encounter as the "intuitive reversal of roles," "the realization of self through others," "total reciprocity." Encounter is "in the here," "in the now," "extemporaneous, unstructured, unplanned and unrehearsed." It was then, as it is now in human relations training, "a hodge-podge of discussion, analysis, evaluation, growth, role-playing, role-testing, and role-training, physical tenderness, joy of being and joy of life."[41]

What is the future of human relations training? The current popularity of such training emphasizes the fact that each year more people acknowledge that our society lacks meaningful natural groups in which people can meet on an intimate, informal basis. Certainly the technologically advanced nations are not providing an abundance of ways for people to find satisfaction in unstructured, spontaneous settings. As we have noted earlier, the need to exchange ideas and share something meaningful is not being met through traditional institutions and organizations. Human relations programs provide opportunities for people to share their confusion and insecurity and form interdependent bonds. In embracing human relations, "ordinary" people have discovered that their loneliness is alleviated and they are freed to grow, to risk, to change. They move into new relationships with other persons.[42] Carl Rogers has said that the personal-growth aspect of human relations is one of the most successful modern inventions for dealing with the feeling of unreality, of impersonality and of distance and separation that exists in so many people in our culture.[43]

If human relations as a profession promises more than it can deliver,

[39] Jacob L. Moreno, "The Viennese Origins of the Encounter Movement," *Group Psychotherapy*, Vol. 22 (March, 1969), 13.
[40] *Ibid.*, 9.
[41] *Ibid.*, 7.
[42] Carl Rogers, "Interpersonal Relationships: USA 2000," *Journal of Applied Behavioral Science*, Vol. 4 (July–September, 1968), 269.
[43] Carl Rogers, *Carl Rogers on Encounter Groups*, 116.

it probably will be nothing more than a vogue and will fade away when a new and more glamourous fad emerges. However, human relations training has great potential for our society. Jourard and Fromm believe there are two paths that the United States can take in the future: it can become a fascist nation, or it can become a pluralistic, humanistic society in which human growth occupies the central focus. By facilitating both individual and social change, human relations professionals can play an important part in helping the country's leaders choose the road toward humanism.

Many organizations currently employ some form of human relations training to resolve antagonisms. In helping develop interpersonal competencies and helping organizations to change, human relations training has become a much-used tool in intergroup conflict. When people are regarded superficially, their differences are accentuated—white and nonwhite, male and female, rich and poor—but as we learn to understand each other, differences fade, and the commonality of human beings emerges.

Yet even if the human relations movement continues to grow, it is only a partial answer to our social problems. Human relations training is not an absolute cure for intrapersonal and interpersonal problems; it is not the only way to help persons, nor is it always an immediate and painless solution. Nevertheless, as modest as the achievements have been to date, human relations as an academic discipline has been established. Human relations training has "profound significance for both today and tomorrow. Those who may have thought of [it] as a fad or phenomenon affecting only a few people temporarily would do well to reconsider. It is a profoundly significant movement, and the course of its future will for better or worse, have a profound impact on all of us."[44]

THE GOOD HUMAN BEING

The "good human being" is given many different names by various theorists, depending in some cases upon whether he has a humanistic or some other philosophical orientation. Some characteristics ascribed to the good human being are healthy personality, self-actualization, creativity, love, growth, individualism, freedom, choice, being, transcendence, power, and self-preservation. One can see the movement along this continuum from psychology and nonviolence through humanism and power elitism.

The only theorist who speaks of "the good life" and who uses that term to describe it is Carl Rogers.[45] To him the good life is the process, not the content, of interaction. It is a direction to move toward, not a

[44] *Ibid.*, 167–68.
[45] See Rogers, *On Becoming a Person.*

18

destination to arrive at. Specifically, Rogers describes the good life as the process of movement in a direction which the human organism selects when it is inwardly free to move in any direction.

Rogers' definition has a quality of the independence involved in freedom of choice. It is similar to Maslow's hierarchy of needs and Schutz's three basic areas of development for the fully functioning man. According to Maslow, however, self-actualization cannot be sought as a goal in its own right; rather, it is a by-product of the active commitment of one's talents to some cause outside the self, such as the quest for beauty, truth, or justice. Jourard, on the other hand, describes the healthy personality in terms of a healthy self-structure: "The individual with a healthy self-structure can face and admit all of his motives and feelings and all of his past and present actions. . . . he is not afraid to be 'transparent,' to be known by others as he authentically is."[46] Being known to others and open to experience in oneself is also a characteristic of Rogers' fully functioning person. The healthy personality in Freudian terms is the genital character who is mature and normal. Concomitants of the definitions of the healthy personality among the psychotherapists are the qualities of creativity, capacity for growth, capacity for love, acceptance of self and others, individual freedom, and capacity for work.[47]

The nonviolent theorists tend to equate the good person with one who lives by the dictates of the Bible, specifically those of the Sermon on the Mount. An essential part of the definition is love for mankind, particularly for one's enemies. This quality is evidenced in Gandhi's definition of the vow of *ahimsa*, or nonkilling: "It is not enough to take the life of any living being. One may not even hurt those whom he believes to be unjust; he may not be angry with them, he must love them. Conquer the tyrant by love. Suffer punishment even unto death for disobeying his will."[48] Henry David Thoreau's definition includes the concept of individualism: "I desire that there be as many different persons in the world as possible; but I would have each one be very careful to find out and pursue *his own* way, and not his father's or his mother's or his neighbor's instead."[49] For the nonviolent theorists the means for the realization of the goals of the good human being are based on the "peaceable revolution" of Thoreau or the "revolutionary nonviolence" of Gandhi and Martin Luther King, Jr.

The good society for King was characterized by freedom and human

[46] Jourard, *Personal Adjustment*, 181.
[47] Fromm, *The Sane Society*, 90.
[48] Romain Rolland, *Mahatma Gandhi: The Man Who Became One with the Universal Being*, 117.
[49] Henry David Thoreau, *Walden and On the Duty of Civil Disobedience*, 53.

dignity.[50] For him nonviolence was more than a strategy that one uses simply because it is expedient at the moment; it is ultimately a way of life that men live by because of the sheer morality of its claim. This, then, was the central ingredient in King's conception of the good society. In the statement of his "dream" King emphasized that unarmed love and unconditional love would have the final word.

The good society for Gandhi would be the realization of *satyagraha*, the truth ethnic. The power of truth as "that which is" was Gandhi's strategy in his revolution for love.[51] In his application of the "love ethic of Jesus" to the social realm, Gandhi's goal was its application to the morals of group and nation as well as the individual—the moral universe is one.

For Thoreau the good society was equivalent to a good government: "That government is best which governs not at all—and when men are prepared for it, that will be the kind of government which they will have."[52] His view of Utopia was one in which the state comes to recognize the individual as a higher and independent power, from which all its own power and authority are derived, and treats him accordingly:

> *I please myself with imagining a State at last which can afford to be just to all men, and to treat the individual with respect as a neighbor; which even would not think it inconsistent with its own repose, if a few were to live aloof from it, not meddling with it, nor embraced by it, who fulfilled all the duties of neighbors and fellowmen. A State which bore this kind of fruit, and suffered it to drop off as fast as it ripened, would prepare the way for a still more perfect and glorious state, which I also have imagined, but not yet anywhere seen.[53]*

The power elitists, as represented by Karl Marx, see a violent revolution as necessary for the replacement of the bourgeoisie by the proletarian state, through which justice for the worker could be attained.[54]

As the descriptions of the good human being are most relevant to the psychotherapists, humanists, and nonviolent theorists, so to some extent is the concept of the good society most pertinent to the power elitists, and also to the nonviolent theorists. The good society, as defined by C. Wright Mills, is a result of knowledge properly used under the moral leadership of "the relatively free intellectuals" of the present

[50] Martin Luther King, Jr., *Stride Toward Freedom: The Montgomery Story*, 68.

[51] E. Stanley Jones, *Mahatma Gandhi: An Interpretation*, 81.

[52] Thoreau, *op. cit.*, 222.

[53] *Ibid.*, 240.

[54] Robert C. Tucker, *The Marxian Revolutionary Idea*, 152.

society.[55] The good society visualized by Marx is one in which "productive labor, instead of being a means to the subjection of men, will become a means to their emancipation, by giving each individual the opportunity to develop and exercise all his faculties, physical and mental, in all directions; in which, therefore, productive labor will become a pleasure instead of a burden."[56]

Thus the good society is one wherein people are paramount. Human productivity in such a climate of free choice is supplemented with faith in oneself and in mankind, a faith that will overcome the emotional and mental anguish, the sense of emptiness and alienation, characterizing group life. To counter the prophecies of doom which focus on human relations training, I offer Buber's concept of the attainability of community: "The primary aspiration of all history is a genuine community of human beings—genuine because it is community all through. A community . . . based on the actual and communal life of big and little groups living and working together, and on their mutual relationships. . . . A community of faith truly exists only when it is a community of work."[57]

If human relations programs can assist participants in finding peace within themselves and with other persons, such programs will certainly assist in raising our nation to a higher level of humanity.

It Hurts to Be Alive and Obsolete: The Aging Woman[58]

ZOE MOSS

What, fat, forty-three, and I dare to think I'm still a person? No, I am an invisible lump. I belong in a category labelled a priori *without interest to anyone. I am not even expected to interest myself. A middle-aged woman is comic by definition.*

In this commodity culture, we are urged and coerced into defining ourselves by buying objects that demonstrate that we are, or which tell us that they will make us feel, young, affluent, fashionable. Imagine a coffee table with the bestsellers of five years ago carefully displayed. You giggle. A magazine that is old enough—say, a New Yorker *from 1944 with the models looking healthy and almost buxom in their*

[55] Robert C. Tucker, "C. Wright Mills," in *Encyclopedia of the Social Sciences,* Vol. 10, 362.

[56] Tucker, *The Marxian Revolutionary Idea,* 18.

[57] Martin Buber, "In the Midst of Crisis," in *The Writings of Martin Buber* (ed. by Will Herberg), 127, 129.

[58] By Zoe Moss. Copyright © 1970 Robin Morgan. Reprinted from *Sisterhood is Powerful: An Anthology of Writings from the Women's Liberation Movement* (ed. by Robin Morgan), New York, Random House and Vintage Books, 1970, 17075. Reprinted by permission.

padded jackets—or a dress that is far enough gone not to give the impression that perhaps you had not noticed fashions had changed, can become campy and delightful. But an out-of-date woman is only embarrassing.

The mass media tell us all day and all evening long that we are inadequate, mindless, ugly, disgusting in ourselves. We must try to resemble perfect plastic objects, so that no one will notice what we really are. In ourselves we smell bad, shed dandruff, our breath has an odor, our hair stands up or falls out, we sag or stick out where we shouldn't. We can only fool people into liking us by using magic products that make us products, too.

Women, especially, are commodities. There is always a perfect plastic woman. Girls are always curling their hair or ironing it, binding their breasts or padding them. Think of the girls with straight hips and long legs skulking through the 1890's with its women defined as having breasts the size of pillows and hips like divans. Think of the Rubens woman today forever starving and dieting and crawling into rubber compression chambers that mark her flesh with livid lines and squeeze her organs into knots.

If a girl were to walk into a party in the clothes of just five or six years past, in the make-up and hairstyle of just that slight gap of time, no one would want to talk to her, no man would want to dance with her. Yet what has all that to do with even a man and women in bed? This is not only the middle class I am talking about. I have seen hippies react the same way to somebody wearing old straight clothes.

It is a joke, but a morbid one. My daughter has a girlfriend who always laughs with her hand up to her mouth because she is persuaded her teeth are yellow, and that yellow teeth are hideous. She seems somber and never will she enjoy a natural belly laugh. Most young girls walk around with the conviction that some small part of their anatomy (nose, breasts, knees, chin) is so large or so small or so misshapen that their whole body appears to be built around that part, and all of their activities must camouflage it.

My daughter is a senior in college. She already talks about her "youth" with a sad nostalgia. She is worried because she is not married. That she has not met anyone that she wants to live that close to, does not seem to figure in her anxiety. Everything confirms in her a sense of time passing, that she will be left behind, unsold on the shelf. She already peers in the mirror for wrinkles and buys creams and jellies to rub into her skin. Her fear angers me but leaves me helpless. She is alienated from her body because her breasts are big and do not stand out like the breasts of store mannequins. She looks twenty-one. I look forty-three.

I want to beg her not to begin worrying, not to let in the dreadful daily gnawing already. Everyone born grows up, grows older, and ages every day until he dies. But every day in seventy-thousand ways this society tells a woman that it is her sin and guilt that she has a real living body. How can a woman respect herself when every day she stands before her mirror and accuses her face of betraying her, because every day she is, indeed, a day older.

Everything she reads, every comic strip, every song, every cartoon, every advertisement, every book and movie tells her that a woman over thirty is ugly and disgusting. She is a bag. She is to be escaped from. She is no longer an object of prestige consumption. For her to have real living sexual desires is obscene. Her touch is thought to contaminate. No man "seduces" a woman older than him: there is no conquest. It is understood she would be "glad for a touch of it." Since she would be glad, there can be no pleasure in the act. Either this society is mad or I am mad. It is considered incredible that a woman might have had experiences that are valuable or interesting and that have enriched her as a person. No, men may mature, but women just obsolesce.

All right, says the woman, don't punish me! I won't do wrong! I won't get older! Now, if a woman has at least an upper-middle-class income, no strong commitments such as a real career or a real interest in religion or art or politics; if she has a small family and hired help; if she has certain minimal genetic luck; if she has the ability to be infinitely fascinated by her own features and body, she may continue to present a youthful image. She can prolong her career as sexual object, lying about her age, rewriting her past to keep the chronology updated, and devoting herself to the cultivation of her image. Society will reward her greatly. Women in the entertainment industry are allowed to remain sexual objects (objects that are prestigeful to use or own—like Cadillacs) for much of their lives.

To be told when you have half your years still to wade through and when you don't feel inside much different than you did at twenty (you are still you!—you know that!), to be told then that you are cut off from expressing yourself sexually and often even in friendship, drives many women crazy—often literally so.

Don't tell me that it is human nature for women to cease to be attractive early. In primitive society a woman who is still useful—in that by all means far more humane definition than ours—will find a mate, whom she may share as she shares the work with his other wives. Black women are more oppressed on the job and in almost every other way in this society than white women, but at least in the ghetto men go on assuming a woman is sexual as long as she thinks so too.

Earlier mythology in which "the widow" is a big sex figure, French

23

novels in which the first mistress is always an older woman, the Wife of Bath, all reinforce my sense that there is nothing natural about women's obsolescence.

I was divorced five years ago. Don't tell me I should have "held on to my husband." We let go with great relief. Recently he has married a woman in her late twenties. It is not surprising he should marry someone younger: most people in this society are younger than my ex-husband. In my job, most of the people I meet are younger than I am, and the same is true of people who share my interests, from skiing to resistance to the war against Vietnam.

When my daughter was little I stayed home, but luckily for me I returned to work when she entered school. I say luckily, because while I believe my ex-husband has an obligation to help our daughter, I would never accept alimony. I can get quite cold and frightened imagining what would have happened if I had stayed home until my divorce, and then, at thirty-eight, tried to find work. I used to eat sometimes at a lunchroom where the rushed and overworked waitress was in her late forties. She had to cover the whole room, and I used to leave her larger tips than I would give someone else because to watch her made me conscious of women's economic vulnerability. She was gone one day and I asked the manager at the cash register about her. "Oh, the customers didn't like her. Men come in here, they want to see a pretty face."

I have insisted on using a pseudonym in writing this article, because the cost of insisting I am not a cipher would be fatal. If I lost my job, I would have an incredible time finding another. I know I will never "get ahead." Women don't move up through the shelves of a business automatically or by keeping their mouths shut. I could be mocked into an agony of shame for writing this—but beyond that, I could so easily be let go.

I am gregarious, interested in others, and I think, intelligent. All I ask is to get to know people and to have them interested in knowing me. I doubt whether I would marry again and live that close to another individual. But I remain invisible. I think stripped down I look more attractive on some abstract scale (a bisexual Martian judging) than my ex-husband, but I am sexually and socially obsolete, and he is not. Like most healthy women my face has aged more rapidly than my body, and I look better with my clothes off. When I was young, my anxiety about myself and what was to become of me colored all my relationships with men, and I was about as sensual as a clotheshanger. I have a capacity now for taking people as they are, which I lacked at twenty; I reach orgasm in half the time and I know how to please. Yet I do not even dare show a man that I find him attractive. If I do so, he may react

24

as if I had insulted hims with shock, with disgust. I am not even allowed to be affectionate. I am supposed to fulfill my small functions and vanish.

Often when men are attracted to me, they feel ashamed and conceal it. They act as if it were ridiculous. If they do become involved, they are still ashamed and may refuse to appear publicly with me. Their fear of mockery is enormous. There is no prestige attached to having sex with me.

Since we are all far more various sexually than we are supposed to be, often, in fact, younger men become aware of me sexually. Their response is similar to what it is when they find themselves feeling attracted to a homosexual : they turn those feelings into hostility and put me down.

Listen to me! Think what it is like to have most of your life ahead and be told you are obsolete! Think what it is like to feel attraction, desire, affection toward others, to want to tell them about yourself, to feel that assumption on which self-respect is based, that you are worth something, and that if you like someone, surely he will be pleased to know that. To be, in other words, still a living woman, and to be told every day that you are not a woman but a tired object that should disappear. That you are not a person but a joke. Well, I am a bitter joke. I am bitter and frustrated and wasted, but don't you pretend for a minute as you look at me, forty-three, fat, and looking exactly my age, that I am not as alive as you are and that I do not suffer from the category into which you are forcing me.

SUMMARY

Human relations education necessarily draws its curriculum from relevant aspects of psychiatry, psychology, social work, sociology, community organization, urban affairs, political science, religion, history, business management, philosophy, literature, and the arts. It is also important to note that human relations education contributes to these disciplines.

Human relations education is offered in a wide variety of settings, including community centers, schools, places of religious worship, hospitals, and military installations. Basic to a professional human relations approach is the belief that all individuals are potential social change agents, each capable of being an active party in solutions to interpersonal and intergroup problems which affect them personally. Thus a major objective of human relations education is to provide resources through which people become better able to identify, describe, and abate individual, group, organizational, and governmental problems.

Chapter 1
SUGGESTED READING

Adler, Alfred. *The Practice and Theory of Individual Psychology.* New York, Harcourt, Brace, Inc., 1925.

Back, Kurt W. *Beyond Words: The Story of Sensitivity Training and the Encounter Movement.* New York, Russell Sage Foundation, 1972.

Bennis, Warren G., and Philip E. Slater. *The Temporary Society.* New York, Harper & Row, Publishers, Inc., 1968.

Buber, Martin. *The Knowledge of Man.* New York, Harper & Row, Publishers, Inc., 1965.

Buckhout, Robert, et al, eds. *Toward Social Change: A Handbook for Those Who Will.* New York, Harper & Row, Publishers, Inc., 1971.

Bugental, James F. T. *Challenges of Humanistic Psychology.* New York, McGraw-Hill Book Company, 1967.

Burton, Arthur, ed. *Encounter: Theory and Practices of Encounter Groups.* San Francisco, Jossey-Bass, Inc., 1969.

Dewey, John. *Problems of Men.* New York, Philosophical Library, 1946.

English, Oliver, and G. Pearson. *Emotional Problems of Living.* New York, W. W. Norton & Company, Inc., 1955.

Etzioni, Amitai. *Modern Organizations.* Englewood Cliffs, N.J., Prentice-Hall, Inc., 1964.

Fromm, Erich, *The Art of Loving.* New York, Harper & Row, Publishers, Inc., 1956.

———. *Escape from Freedom.* New York, Holt, Rinehart & Winston, Inc., 1941.

———. *Man for Himself: An Inquiry into the Psychology of Ethics.* New York, Fawcett Publications, Inc., 1967.

———. *The Sane Society.* New York, Fawcett Publications, Inc., 1968.

Goble, Frank. *The Third Force: The Psychology of Abraham Maslow.* New York, Pocket Books, Inc., 1971.

Goldstein, Kurt. *Human Nature in the Light of Psychopathology.* New York, Schocken Books, 1940.

Greening, Thomas C., ed. *Existential Human Psychology.* Monterey, Calif., Brooks/Cole Pub. Co., 1971.

Gustaitis, Rasa. *Turning On.* New York, The New American Library, Inc., 1969.

Herberg, Will, ed. *The Writings of Martin Buber.* New York, Meridian Books, Inc., 1958.

Hoffer, Eric. *The True Believer.* New York, Harper & Row, Publishers, Inc., 1951.

Jones, E. Stanley. *Mahatma Gandhi: An Interpretation.* New York, Abingdon-Cokesbury Press, 1958.

Jourard, Sidney M. *Personal Adjustment: An Approach to the Study of Healthy Personality.* New York, The Macmillan Company, 1958.

———. *The Transparent Self: Self-Disclosure and Well-Being.* Princeton, N.J., Van Nostrand Reinhold Company, 1961.

King, Martin Luther, Jr. *Stride Toward Freedom: The Montgomery Story.* New York, Harper & Row, Publishers, Inc., 1958.

Levy, Ronald. *Human Relations: A Conceptual Approach.* Scranton, Pa., International Textbook Company, 1969.

Maslow, Abraham H. *New Knowledge in Human Values.* New York, Harper & Row, Publishers, Inc., 1954.

———. *Motivation and Personality.* New York, Harper & Row, Publishers, Inc., 1954.

May, Rollo, ed. *Existential Psychology.* New York, Random House, Inc., 1961.

Mead, George H. *Mind, Self, and Society: From the Standpoint of a Social Behaviorist.* Translated by C. W. Morris. Chicago, University of Chicago Press, 1934.

Mintz, Elizabeth. "Marathon Groups: A Preliminary Education," *Psychological Abstracts,* Vol. 44 (August, 1970).

Moreno, Jacob L. "The Viennese Origins of the Encounter Movement," *Group Psychotherapy,* Vol. 22 (March, 1969).

Osborne, Ronald E. *Humanism and Moral Theory.* Buffalo, N.Y., Prometheus Books, 1969.

Otto, Herbert A., and John Mann, eds. *Ways of Growth: Approaches to Expanding Awareness.* New York, Grossman Publishers, 1968.

Perls, Frederick S. *Gestalt Therapy Verbatim.* Lafayette, Calif., Real People Press, 1969.

Reich, Charles A. *The Greening of America.* New York, Random House, Inc., 1970.

Riesman, David. *The Lonely Crowd: A Study of the Changing American Character.* New Haven, Yale University Press, 1950.

Rogers, Carl R. *Carl Rogers on Encounter Groups.* New York, Harper & Row, Publishers, Inc., 1970.

———. "Interpersonal Relationships: USA 2000," *Journal of Applied Behavioral Science,* Vol. 4 (July–September, 1968).

———. *On Becoming A Person: A Therapist's View of Psychotherapy.* Boston, Houghton Mifflin Co., 1961.

Rolland, Romain. *Mahatma Gandhi: The Man Who Became One with the Universal Being.* New York, Century Company, 1924.

Royce, Joseph R. *Encapsulated Man.* Princeton, N.J., D. Van Nostrand Co., 1964.

Ruitenbeek, Hendrik. *The New Group Therapies.* New York, Avon Books, 1970.

Schutz, William C. *FIRO: A Three-Dimensional Theory of Interpersonal Behavior.* New York, Holt, Rinehart & Winston, Inc., 1958.

———. *Here Comes Everybody.* New York, Harper & Row, Publishers, Inc., 1971.

Shostrom, Everett L. "Group Therapy: Let the Buyer Beware," *Psychology Today,* Vol. 2 (May, 1969).

———. *Man, The Manipulator: The Inner Journey from Manipulation to Actualization.* Nashville, Abingdon Press, 1967.

Siroka, Robert W., Ellen K. Siroka, and Gilbert A. Schloss. *Sensitivity Training and Group Encounter.* New York, Grosset & Dunlap, Inc., 1971.

Skinner, B. F. *Beyond Freedom and Dignity.* New York, Bantam Books, Inc., 1971.

———. *Walden Two.* New York, The Macmillan Co., 1948.

Sullivan, Henry Stack. *The Interpersonal Theory of Psychiatry.* New York, W. W. Norton & Company, Inc., 1953.

Thoreau, Henry David. *Walden and On the Duty of Civil Disobedience.* New York, The New American Library, Inc., 1963.

Tönnies, Ferdinand. *Community and Society.* Translated and edited by Charles P. Loomis, East Lansing, Michigan State University Press, 1957.

Tucker, Robert C. *The Marxian Revolutionary Idea.* New York, W. W. Norton & Company, Inc., 1969.

Wheelis, Allen. *The Quest for Identity.* New York, W. W. Norton & Company, Inc., 1958.

Whyte, William H., Jr. *The Organization Man.* New York, Simon and Schuster, Inc., 1956.

Wilde, Jean T., and William Kimel, eds. *The Search for Being.* New York, Twayne Publishers, Inc., 1962.

More common among most whites are the false
understandings and images whch they retain about
Indians. For many, the moving pictures, television, and
comic strips have firmly established a stereotype
as the portrait of all Indians: the dour, stoic,
warbonneted Plains Indian.—ALVIN M. JOSEPHY

The humanities contribute much to understanding human relations: they express people's life experiences and promote understanding through this expression. It is in this respect that the humanities are considered a means of communication. They communicate through various media, directly and indirectly connecting human emotions. Albert Levi summarized this contribution as follows: "The social function of the humanities is to unify society through the development of a common emotional and intellectual framework within its individual members."[1]

THE ARTS AND HUMAN RELATIONS

Dance, the theater, and music are areas in the humanities which contribute to improving human relationships. In their dances, music, and plays artists relay their experiences to others: they communicate.

To understand the arts, it is necessary to define art, the artist, and a work of art, for all of these contribute to the process of human communication. Curt Sachs wrote: "Art is the re-creating of things seen and heard, the giving of form and substance to the intangible and irrational perceptions."[2] In *The Art of Enjoying Music*, Sigmund Spaeth gave his definition of artist:

An artist is a person who succeeds in transferring his own thoughts, moods and emotions to other people. If beauty and truth are the same,

[1] Albert W. Levi, *The Humanities Today*, 83.
[2] Curt Sachs, *World History of the Dance*, 6.

*as has been claimed, then an artist arrives at beauty by expressing his
own feelings in such a way that others will recognize their truth.*

*Insincerity is generally easy to detect in art. But sincerity alone does
not make an artist. There must also be the command of a medium of
expression that will inevitably transfer the feelings of the artist to
others.*[3]

Finally, the artist's work needs to be examined. It is the form and substance of his expression. A work of art or an expression of thought,
whether it is literary, musical, or plastic, whether it is old or new,
whatever its standards of formal structure, merits our consideration
because it can provide a key to the broader Gestalt of life. John Gassner
pinpoints the contribution of the arts:

*All the arts are means of communication, and their history is at its
best a record of men communicating their observations and perceptions, their insight into humanity and their aspirations for humanity,
to other men. Nor has the process been a simple case of the creators
giving and the public receiving the bounties of the creative soul. In
all but the most singular cases of an artist withdrawn from life and
spinning gold out of a unique personality, the history of art is an
account of the artist taking his materials and his outlook, his knowledge
and ideals, from his time and place; highlighting and sharpening that
which is already present in his environment; making distinctively
visible or articulate that which his fellowmen see less clearly or express
less articulately. It is this interchange between the creator and the
community that makes possible the effectiveness of the arts.*[4]

Arnold Graeffe stated that a distinct property of art is its address to
the human essence in all of us.[5] He concluded that the arts elevate us
above the primitive rationalism of our immediate existence and help
establish a true scale of value:

*To learn how to select and enjoy a great symphony, to purchase or
produce and appreciate a great painting, to read, write, understand,
interpret, or enjoy great literature, to comprehend the elements of the
history of thought, and to learn how to trace the cultural development
of man through great philosophical and religious systems is different
from learning how to build a bridge or perform an appendectomy . . . ,
but [these] first mentioned . . . are just as functional in human conduct
in our complicated society as are the latter. Indeed, it is to the former*

[3] Sigmund Spaeth, *The Art of Enjoying Music*, 6.
[4] John Gassner, *Human Relations in the Theatre*, 5.
[5] Arnold D. Graeffe, *Creative Education in the Humanities*, 34, 195.

abilities that we look in order to give meaning and significance to the more practical concerns of life.[6]

DANCE

At first glance it seems that the division of the humanities known as the dance makes few contributions to the field of human relations. However, there is a strong suggestion of a relationship in Rudolf Laban's article "The Educational Therapeutic Value of the Dance."[7] Laban argued that there is a thing called "charm of behavior" which anyone, dancer or not, can acquire, and that the pursuit of it has educational and remedial possibilities:

Ordinary people do not associate their charm of behavior with any acknowledged or unacknowledged stage technique. They would never dream of dancing in a ballet and yet, I am sure, they are quite conscious of and probably cherish and love the particular charm of their movement. They may even cultivate it. Now, if this is not the quintessence of dance I do not know what else it can be. Everybody who dances strives after this "something" even if sometimes unconsciously perhaps clumsily. Dancers are often trapped by external skill which is indispensable for a theatrical career, but their guiding star is, without doubt, the charm of movement. . . .

If one can call the humble striving after this radiant quality "dancing," I would have to refute my initial statement. I should have to affirm that the dance has the most eminent educational and remedial possibilities.[8]

Dance is a means of expression using the body as a medium moving in space and time. Dance is related intimately to man's basic need to communicate through movement what he is and how he feels. Indeed, it is a means of communciation, for it is a way of formulating and exchanging feelings and thoughts on a nonverbal level, person to person.

Doris Humphrey, a pioneer in modern dance, explained that the essential purpose of modern dance "is to reveal something about people, to each individual some emotional state, idea or situation which he can identify with his own experience."[9] According to Lloyd, Ms. Humphrey felt that she should reveal something about her own particular experiences in relation to others, something she knows

[6] *Ibid.*, ix.

[7] Rudolph Laban, "The Educational Therapeutic Value of the Dance," in Walter Sorell, ed., *The Dance Has Many Faces*, 113–27.

[8] *Ibid.*

[9] Doris Humphrey, "America's Modern Dance," *Theatre Arts*, Vol. 34 (September, 1950), 45.

herself. Lloyd quoted her as saying, "I wish my dance to reflect some experience of my own in relationship to the outside world; to be based on reality illumined by imagination; to be organic rather than synthetic; to call forth a definite reaction from my audience; and to make its contribution toward the dream of life."[10]

José Limón, a great modern dancer and choreographer, was a student of Ms. Humphrey at one time. Concerning his relationship with her, he said, "In Doris Humphrey I found a master who knew that every dancer, being an individual, was an instrument unique and distinct from any other, and that in consequence this dancer must ultimately find his own dance, as she has found hers." About himself as an individual he continued: "I was by origin a Mexican, reared in the United States. I must find the dance to say what I had to say about what I was."[11]

A few years later Limón choreographed *Danzas Mexicanas*, a dance relating Limón's own life experiences. It is a suite of solos of five virile images in native costumes. Concerning this composition, *Dance Observer* noted: "The surface of these passionate evocations is now as solid as glass and as transparent. What each says about Indio, Conquistador, Peon, Caballero and Revolucionario is fully stated and once for all, they are that powerful in their fusion of large gesture and magnificent dance, that affirmative in feeling and meaning."[12]

Limón observed that modern dance must be not only personal and unique but also timely: "The artist's function is perpetually to be the voice and conscience of his time. It was Doris Humphrey who first taught me that man is the fittest subject for choreography. And Martha Graham continues triumphantly to prove that his passions, grandeurs, and vices are the ingredients of great dance, great theater, and great art."[13] If by "dance" we mean a state of mind, a recognition of the necessity of the art of the dance to come to terms with our time, then dance cannot be relegated to the position of a merely transitory influence.

MUSIC

Otto Deri, in *Exploring Twentieth-Century Music*, makes an effort to universalize human experience by showing how the "new" music of this century is closely related to earlier styles. Music can be a universal

[10] Margaret Lloyd, "Doris Humphrey: Yesterday and Today," *Dance Magazine*, Vol. 28 (November, 1954), 38.

[11] José Limón, "An American Accent," in *The Modern Dance: Seven Statements of Belief* (ed. by Selma Jeanne Cohen), 23.

[12] *Dance Observer*, Vol. 10 (April, 1943), 45.

[13] Limón, *op. cit.*, 24.

form of expression which can unite and arouse large numbers of people.

Alan Walker observed, in *An Anatomy of Musical Criticism*, that musical communication is complete in itself. In this regard he quoted a letter from Mendelssohn written to Marc-André Souchay in 1842: "There is so much talk about music, and yet so little is said. . . . Words seem to me so ambiguous, so vague, so easily misunderstood in comparison to genuine music. . . . The thoughts expressed to me by music that I love are not too indefinite to be put into words, but on the contrary, too definite." In much the same vein Edward Dickinson wrote: "To appreciate music, therefore, is to respond impulsively to the human element in it, finding there an echo of our own humanity. This element, in order to make itself intelligible, employs a language which it has devised out of its own peculiar needs."[14]

In *The World of Soul: Black America's Contribution to the Pop Music Scene*, Arnold Shaw explained verbally what Soul communicates musically:

Soul is black nationalism in Pop. Stylistically it can be imitated, as it has been by white singers and instrumentalists. But the native expression derives from people whose ancestors reached these shores in chains, who cooked soul food as a matter of survival, who attended religious services in storefront gospel churches, and who have a long history of deprivation, exploitation, and segregation behind them.[15]

The essence of Soul is a degree of personal involvement emanating from the musician's feelings of outrage at the adversities of an oppressive world, from his need to shout out grievances, and from his need to get rid of injustices. Projection into song of black dignity, self-respect, and militancy is Soul. Projection of humaneness into our relationships is good human relations.

ART

There are abundant examples of the contribution art can make to human relations. Among the obvious are the works of William Hogarth and Honoré Daumier, who pioneered social criticism in art. James Abbot McNeill Whistler stated that it is the duty of the artist to project beauty onto nature:

That nature is always right, is an assertion, artistically, as untrue as it is one whose truth is universally taken for granted. Nature is very rarely

[14] Alan Walker, *An Anatomy of Music Criticism*, 4; Edward Dickinson, *The Spirit of Music*, 6.

[15] Arnold Shaw, *The World of Soul: Black America's Contribution to the Pop Music Scene*, 6.

right, to such an extent even, that it might almost be said that nature is usually wrong: that is to say, the condition of things that shall bring about the perfection of harmony worthy of a picture is rare, and not common at all.[16]

Paintings have much to tell us about the relationships among human beings if we will but look. An example is *The Bellelli Family,* by Edgar Degas, a family portrait of his aunt, the Baroness Bellelli, the baron, and his two cousins. John Canaday suggested that we must look at the picture carefully before learning anything about the family: "In that case ask yourself what the relationship of the father to the rest of the family might be, what the emotional tie of each of the little girls is to each of the parents, and what the difference is, temperamentally, between these two children."

By carefully studying the portrait, we discover that the father is separated from the rest of the family by a series of vertical lines and that he sits with his back to us, his head half-turned. He is also painted indecisively, and one has the feeling that he is a stranger to us and even to his family. The wife dominates the rest of the picture, enclosing the entire figure of her younger daughter within her silhouette. The other daughter is seated almost midway between the mother and younger daughter and her father, and her gaze toward her father tells us of her sympathy for him. And the composition of the picture does not depend on the particular family or artist, as Canaday pointed out:

If the identity of the painter and the family were unknown to us, any meaning "The Bellelli Family" might lose would be superficial. . . . The picture's greatness lies in its ability to stir us to thought beyond the limited considerations of a single family's not unusual circumstances. And it does so because Degas has crystalized his material into the forms of perfect order, rid of all confusions, incidentals, vagaries, and distractions. In the resultant clarity our sensibilities and understanding may expand.[17]

THEATER

The theater offers many contributions to human relations. Social scientists have taken such techniques as role playing and psychodrama from the theater, and they have also learned to appreciate the direct benefits from the aesthetic experience of the theater. John Ciardi calls it "Esthetic Wisdom": "To assert that there is something called Esthetic Wisdom is to make a general claim for the arts as a special kind of

16 John W. McCoubrey, *American Art: 1700–1960,* 185.
17 John E. Canaday, *Metropolitan Seminars in Art,* Vol. 7 (New York, Metropolitan Museum of Art, 1958), 11, 13.

human experience; it is to say that such a body of knowledge exists and that art is the one means of acquiring it."[18]

Ciardi cited the instance when psychiatrist Frederick Werthm interviewed an illiterate young man charged with matricide. What the young man told Wertham sounded familiar. He turned to *The Oresteia* and *Hamlet*, where he found much of what he had just heard, in terms of feelings, from that young man, who undoubtedly had not read either work. "Wertham need not have felt surprise," Ciardi wrote. "He had located in the plays that ability to project oneself vicariously into an emotional situation, which is exactly what we expect of great artists and is what lesser artists try to achieve."[19]

Aeschylus and Shakespeare were able to record the reactions and the order of reactions of matricides not because they themselves were matricides but because they were special men capable of understanding what is human. "That body of knowledge and experience that shapes the world as Aeschylus and Shakespeare sensed it is Esthetic Wisdom. Art is not its ornament but its way of knowing," Ciardi concluded.

The effect of drama on the viewer is matched and sometimes perhaps surpassed by its impact on the actor. David Alan Shafter described it in this manner:

For example, would an actor who played Dr. Stockman in Ibsen's Enemy of the People *find the virtues of that character were his if he were faced with a similar situation? Conversely, how does the actress who portrays Hedda Gabler deal with boredom and frustration? Just how strong is the effect of portraying a character on the actor? Whatever the answer to this question, perhaps it is not unreasonable to assume that every actor carries away something of the character he portrays, and of these characters—experiences each helps in some way to fashion a frame of reference through which the individual sees the world he lives in. If this is so, there is a great need for plays written specifically for delinquent boys [to act in] in which good, strong, positive character identifications can be made.*[20]

The "unity of opposites" approach of Lajos Egri provides valuable insight into human motivation. Egri argued that a fine play is condensed human experience which offers the participants (audience, actors, director, writer) catharsis and vicarious understanding of those who have lived differently from them. He reasoned that the technique

[18] John Ciardi, "Esthetic Wisdon," *Saturday Review*, April 8, 1972, 22.
[19] *Ibid.*
[20] David A. Shafter, "Drama for Delinquents" (Masters thesis, Department of Theatre, Southern Illinois University, 1964), 22.

of unity of opposites is one of the tools used to condense this experience: "It is a phrase that many people apply wrongly or misunderstand in the first place. Unity of opposites does not refer to any opposing forces or wills in a clash. Misapplication of this unity leads to a condition in which the characters cannot carry a conflict through to the finish. . . . The real unity of opposites is one in which compromise is impossible."[21] Egri gives the example of Nora and Helmer in Ibsen's *A Doll's House*:

Nora and Helmer were united by many things: love, home, children, law, society, desire. Yet they were opposites. It was necessary for their individual characters that this unity should be broken, or that one of them should succumb completely to the other—thus killing his individuality . . . the unity could be broken and the play ended only by the "death" of some dominant quality in one of the characters—Nora's docility, in the play.[22]

Egri observed that when a real unity of opposites exists it can be broken only if a dominant trait or quality in one or more characters is fundamentally changed. This approach can help people to endure painful but brief relationships, and it can help them determine whether they will have to change some trait in themselves or strive for a change in the other person before they can have a strong relationship that will not require the complete subjugation of one to the other.

The concept of unity of opposites sheds considerable light on interpersonal conflicts. George Bernard Shaw observed in "The Problem Play: A Symposium" that a truly good problem play, which deals with social issues, will deal with unity of opposites and genuine human motivations.[23] Shaw presented four points:

1. Every social question provides material for drama because it arises from conflict between human feelings and circumstances.

2. Dramatists have generally preferred to deal with conflicts between man and his fate because of their own political ignorance and that of their audiences.

3. Our complex civilization discourages dramas that arise out of comprehensive philosophies.

4. The tendency is to drive social questions onto the stage and to call on the other arts to help improve our social organizations.

In his introduction to *Aristotle's Theory of Poetry*, John Gassner explains the longevity of the principles of Aristotle's *Poetics*—the philoso-

21 Lajos Egri, *The Art of Drmatic Writing: Its Basis in the Creative Interpretation of Human Motives*, 119.
22 *Ibid.*, 119–20.
23 In James B. Hall and Barry Ulanov, eds., *Modern Culture and the Arts*, 345–56.

pher's treatise on drama—by the existence of social problems: "[Drama's] survival can, indeed, be truly jeopardized only by the triumph of a philosophy that would abolish concepts of right and wrong and of individual responsibility, deny the possibility of free will, and reduce life to pure mechanism or to nihilistic meaninglessness."

Gassner explicitly defined the humanitarian role in his book *Human Relations in the Theatre*:

Humanitarianism has been a matter of record ever since the classic Greek playwrights made themselves spokesmen for Athenian enlightenment, and it is common knowledge that the modern theatre, inaugurated by Ibsen and sustained by Checkhov, Shaw, Galsworthy, O'Casey, O'Neill and their many minor colleagues has been firmly wedded to enlightened principles. When the professional theatre declines from its standards we can instantly sense that something catastrophic is happening to a nation, as was the case when racism and chauvinism infiltrated the German drama with the rise of National Socialism.[24]

Contemporary plays depicting the plight of racial minorities, women, and economically underprivileged people have sparked a new sense of public awareness throughout the world.

PHILOSOPHY

Few writers would argue that one's philosophy of life has little to contribute to human relations. Albert Memmi, writing in *Dominated Man*, studied six cases of dominated human beings: the black person, the colonized, the Jew, the proletarian, the woman, and the domestic servant. Memmi concluded that all are victims of racism, which he defined as "the generalized and final assigning of values to real or imaginary differences, to the accuser's benefit and at his victim's expense, in order to justify the former's own privileges or aggression."[25]

Existential philosophy has had the greatest impact on the theoretical foundation of human relations training. Most existentialists believe that human beings are unique beings, able to reflect, make free decisions, and set goals. Furthermore, existentialists believe that in order for us to exist and realize our fullest human potential, each person must learn to act as a free person rather than as a member of a crowd.

Now let us examine the writings of six existential writers—Jean-Paul Sartre, Fëdor Dostoevski, Franz Kafka, Friedrich Nietzche, and Hermann Hesse.

[24] John Gassner, "Introduction," in *Aristotle's Theory of Poetry; Human Relations in the Theatre*, 9.
[25] Albert Memmi, *Dominated Man*, 185.

37

JEAN-PAUL SARTRE (1905–)

The most common premise of existentialism is that *existence precedes essence*. In brief, persons exist first; afterward, they encounter and define themselves and become only what they make of themselves. Men and women consciously drive themselves toward a future. If existence precedes essence, Sartre reasoned, individuals are responsible not only for what they are but also for what other people are. To choose a direction implies affirming the value of what one chooses:

What we choose is always the better; and nothing can be better for us unless it is better for all. If, moreover, existence precedes essence and we will to exist at the same time as we fashion our image, that image is valid for all and for the entire epoch in which we find ourselves. Our responsibility is thus much greater than we had supposed, for it concerns mankind as a whole.[26]

Thus anguish, abandonment, and despair are natural responses to our societal responsibilities. Most persons cannot help but feel a profound sense of guilt—even anxiety—when they choose destinies for others. Of course, some persons do not exhibit such anxiety; perhaps they are hiding or running from it. Sartre reasoned that one must always ask himself what would result if everyone did as he does. Sartre then asks: "Who then can prove that I am the proper person to impose, by my own choice, my conception of man upon mankind? If a voice speaks to me, it is still I myself who must decide whether the voice is or is not that of an angel." According to Sartre, every man ought to ask, "Am I really a man who has the right to act in such a manner that humanity regulates itself by what I do?"[27] This anguish is well known to those who have borne responsibilities associated with leadership.

As Fëdor Dostoevski wrote, "If God did not exist, everything would be permitted." With this premise as a starting point for existentialism, man has no excuse; he is condemned to freedom—responsible for everything he does. "While he recognizes society as one's situation, he admits of no conditioning by society that could excuse one's conforming to that situation."[28] There are no rules of general morality to show man what he ought to do—no signs are warranted—man must interpret them. We ourselves decide our acts.

Sartre has declared that there is no reality other than action. Man is the sum of his actions; he is what his life is. For those who have not made a "success" of their lives, this thought seems dreary, and yet it

[26] Walter A. Kaufmann, ed., *Existentialism from Dostoevsky to Sartre*, 292.
[27] *Ibid.*, 293.
[28] Maurice Friedman, ed., *To Deny Our Nothingness*, 251.

allows us to acknowledge that reality is reliability and that our humanity consists of a thousand interpretations.

In essence, Sartre's belief is that all that we are is the result of what we dare to do:

All man's alibis are unacceptable; no gods are responsible for his condition; no original sin, no heredity and no environment; no race, no caste, no father, and no mother; no wrong-headed education, no governess, no teacher; not even an impulse or a disposition, a complex or a childhood trauma. Man is free; but his freedom does not look like the glorious liberty of the Enlightenment; it is no longer the gift of God. Once again, man stands alone in the universe, responsible for his condition, likely to remain in a lowly state, but free to reach above the stars.[29]

Existentialism has been accused of being a plea to dwell in the "quietism of despair." Such introspective philosophies as existentialism may develop when there are no effective solutions. Furthermore, quietism is the attitude of people who say, "Let others do what I cannot do": "For many have but one resource to sustain them in their misery, and that is to think, circumstances have been against me. I was worthy to be something much better than I have been."[30] There is in all of us a wide range of abilities and potentialities which are unused but still viable and which cannot be inferred from the history of one's actions. Existentialism has also been accused of depicting what is mean or sordid while neglecting the brighter side of human nature. When characters are depicted as cowardly, they are responsible for their cowardice. But to Sartre existentialism is an optimistic rather than a pessimistic doctrine, for people are responsible for their destiny. They are not discouraged from action. Indeed, from this perspective, hope lies in action.

Existentialists are accused of confining us within our individual subjectivity. Sartre admits to this charge for purely philosophical reasons, beginning with the Cartesian *cogito*: "I think, therefore I exist." Sartre claims that only this awareness gives us dignity—an immediate sense of ourselves. The *cogito* theory does not make man into an object, but rather aims at establishing the human region as a model of values separate from the material world. This subjectivity includes not only self-discovery but also the discovery of others as the condition for our own existence: "I cannot obtain any truth whatsoever about myself, except through the mediation of another. The other is indispensable to

[29] Kaufmann, *op. cit.*, 46–47.
[30] *Ibid.*, 300.

my existence, and equally so to any knowledge I can have of myself."[31]

One may accept the characterization of humanism as a philosophy that holds man to be the supreme value. This characterization implies that value is attributed to man according to distinguished deeds of certain men. Sartre's humanism characterizes man as being his own master. Man is truly human when he accepts the human condition; we exist, we work, we die, we are involved, and in choosing we invent ourselves and assume complete responsibility for our lives. We give life meaning, and we choose the meaning of value.

Existentialism is not meant to plunge human beings into despair nor to exhaust itself with proving that God does not exist. If God did exist, it would not matter. The problem is that people must discover themselves once more without a valid proof of the existence of God. Existentialism is a knowledge of action that is inclusive of integrity, distinction, courage, and effort.

Sartre's short story "The Wall," written in 1939, is recommended as an introduction to the crux of his thought. In that story Sartre, treating confrontation with death, wrote with painful awareness of the moral issues of the time and contributed a wealth of psychological impressions comparable to Dostoevski's *Notes from the Underground*.

FËDOR DOSTOEVSKI (1821–81)

Dostoevski's *Notes from the Underground* is one of the most radical and original works of world literature. Whether or not one considers Dostoevski an existentialist, Part One of *Notes* stands out as perhaps one of the finest statements on existentialism ever written. There Dostoevski presented the theater of the mind—self-sufficient, conscious of its every infirmity and yet resolved to exploit the mind. He portrayed individuality as wretched and revolting but nonetheless as the highest good: "The man whom Dostoevski has created in this book holds out for what traditional Christianity has called depravity; but he believes neither in original sin nor in God, and for him man's self-will is not depravity: it is only perverse from the point of view of rationalists and others who value neat schemes above the rich texture of individuality."[32]

FRANZ KAFKA (1883–1924)

Franz Kafka's writings illustrate that an individual's life lends itself to many different interpretations. Although it has been said that ambiguity is the essence of his art, Kafka is not obscure; his intelligence is

[31] *Ibid.*, 303.
[32] *Ibid.*, 13.

bright, critical, and clear—he did not want his work to be reduced to one exclusive meaning:

The key to Kafka, perhaps, is that sense of caricature which is borne in on us again and again. If one feels that one recognizes reality in Kafka, one always feels at the same time that it is somehow caricatured. Though this caricature is one of the nature of an abstraction from concrete reality, it does not point afterward to some still more abstract concept but back to an altogether concrete way of seeing—a perception of reality that again and again lays bare the absurdity inherent in Kafka's particular relationship to it.[33]

Kafka portrayed the absurdity of modern man by questioning whether there can be a positive way to resolve this tension. Human existence means suffering; yet suffering is positive and necessary for progression. Paths to love must encounter misery and hardship, and if one avoids the road, he misses the goal. Kafka trusted existence—the world beckons. "Life's splendor lies forever in wait," wrote Kafka, "veiled but not hostile, reluctant, or deaf. If you summon it by the right word, by its right name, it will come."[34]

Kafka captured the human being in the midst of confusing social order, and he found personal meaning in the thick of the absurd:

Kafka . . . is . . . the man who more than any other has sought the way forward through the very heart of the absurd. . . . If we see Kafka only in terms of his problematic, we shall join those who regard him as "an end"—a neurotic, a nihilist, an enemy of culture, or a desperate believer "fleeing humanity." But if we see in Kafka the humor and the trust and the steady movement toward meaning in the teeth of contradiction and despair, we shall glimpse the sense in which Kafka is "a beginning" for modern man.[35]

The Trial and *The Penal Colony* are two of Kafka's works which illustrate the above points. *The Trial* is the story of a respectable banker who is suddenly arrested and spends his life fighting a charge whose nature and the reason for which he never learns. Bureaucracy crushes his reality without a trace of justice. Kafka develops the theme of the absurd world that breaks in on the self, imposing a demand that the self must meet in order to find meaning in its existence. *The Penal Colony* contains the works that Kafka allowed to be published during his lifetime. It represents the full range of his talent and allows a wide range of interpretation to the reader.

[33] Maurice Friedman, "The Problematic Rebel," in Friedman, *op. cit.*, 343.
[34] *Ibid.*, 345.
[35] *Ibid.*, 46.

FRIEDRICH NIETZSCHE (1844–1900)

On the title page of *Thus Spoke Zarathustra* are these words: "A Book for Everyone and No One." Zarathustra was the founder of the ancient Persian religion Zoroastrianism, and the book he is credited with, the *Zend-Avesta*, is its Bible. The heart of the religion was a conflict between good and evil. To Nietzsche, Zarathustra was the first to see in this struggle the translation of morality into the realm of metaphysics. He created morality, and thus he must recognize it. Zarathustra was, in Nietzche's view, more truthful than any other thinker, and his teaching upheld truthfulness as the highest good: "The self-overcoming of morality through truthfulness, the self-overcoming of the moralist into his opposite—into me—that is what the name Zarathustra means in my mouth."[36]

Nietzsche held to no fixed position, doctrine, or picture of the world. He questioned the viability of philosophies which tried to make the whole truth communicable. Knowledge, like thought, is interpretation, and for Nietzsche existence is capable of infinite interpretation. His ultimate value was honesty. In addition, to him truth was self-understanding. He pointed out a valuable warning to human relations practitioners when he said that free, creative self-understanding can be replaced by slavish rotation about one's own empirical existence. We should not, in short, become obsessed with our own lives. He expressed it as follows:

> *Among a hundred mirrors*
> *before yourself false . . .*
> *strangled in your own net*
> *self-knower!*
> *self-executioner!*
> *crammed between two nothings,*
> *a question mark. . . .*

He did not wish to be exemplary, and he turned away from those who would follow him with the command, "Follow not me, but you!" He tried to awaken the deepest suspicion of himself, explaining that a teacher has the duty of warning his students against him. Nietzsche wrote: ". . . there is nothing in me of the founder of a religion. . . . I want no believers. . . . I have terrible anxiety that some day they will speak reverently of me. I will not be a saint, rather a Punch. Maybe I *am* Punch."[37]

Nietzsche was conscious of the meaning, sense, and necessity of what happened to him. He was concerned with chance, for to him

[36] Friedrich Nietzsche, *Thus Spoke Zarathustra*.
[37] Friedrich Nietzsche, "Ecce Homo," in Kaufmann, *op. cit.*, 179.

"sublime chance" ruled existence: "What you call chance—you yourself are that which befalls and astonishes you."[38]

HERMANN HESSE (1877–1962)

Hermann Hesse's novel *Steppenwolf* represents Harry Haller's sickness of the soul, as well as the sickness of the times. Perhaps these illnesses parallel each other. If so, does one cause the other, or are they simultaneous? Haller's sickness is the sickness of today—one that strikes strong-spirited people. Although Hesse was filled with despair, he survived through faith in the meaningfulness of life: "And even the unhappiest life has its sunny moments and its little flowers of happiness between sand and stone. So it was, then, with the Steppenwolf too."[39]

Steppenwolf deals with suicide as a way of coming to terms with harsh reality:

As every strength may become a weakness (and under some circumstances must), so, on the contrary, may the typical suicide find a strength and a support in his apparent weakness. As thousands of his like do, he found consolation and support, and not merely the melancholy play of youthful fancy, in the idea that the way to death was open to him at any moment.[40]

Perhaps the most important theme of *Steppenwolf*—one with which people can identify and find comfort in—is the notion that we are many people, some good, some bad.

From the brief preceding review of existential thought, it should be easy to understand why human relations training has borrowed much from existential philosophers. The act of placing each participant in the center of focus and the belief that each person should live his own life are two illustrations of the existential foundations of human relations training.

RELIGION

In forming an expression of religion's contributions to human relations, we find examples in the humane tenets common to most religions. Two sermons delivered in 1893 by the Reverend Samuel M. Crothers stressed the ideal of universality as the greatest charm of the Roman Catholic Church: "It will yield at last only to catholicity larger than its own."[41] In the sermon "Calvinism," Crothers discussed the problem of

---

[38] *Ibid.*, 178.

[39] Hermann Hesse, *Steppenwolf*, 43.

[40] *Ibid.*, 48.

[41] Samuel M. Crothers, "Roman Catholicism" (sermon preached at Unity Church, St. Paul, Minn., 1893).

43

facing an awesome, uncertain future armed only with faith: "The world has yet work for men who, facing the worst, yet believe in the best, and who, looking up to the Eternal, can say, 'Though he slay me, yet will I trust him.' "[42]

Duncan Howlett, in *The Fourth American Faith*, offered a new look at Adam and Eve, calling them pioneers in religion. Howlett points out that Adam and Eve were expelled from the garden of Eden not because they sinned, but because of God's fear of what they might do next: "Then the Lord God said (after Adam ate the fruit), 'Behold, the man has become like one of us, knowing good and evil; and now, lest he put forth his hand and take also of the tree of life, and eat, and live forever'—therefore the Lord God sent him forth from the garden of Eden, to till the ground from which he was taken."

Traditionally Adam's expulsion from Eden has been considered punishment for his sin of disobedience. But, Howlett says, if we take a new look at Adam, he can be seen as a hero:

And so I would take Adam out of the role in which Christianity has cast him. I would take off his back the burden of the world's sin which Pauline theology has placed there. I would instead offer Adam as a hero, and his wife Eve as a heroine greater than he. Both are pioneers. Both—in the biblical context—brought us the knowledge we have to have in this sordid world—knowledge of the difference between good and evil.[43]

Howlett's view offers a contribution to human relations in general and to women's liberation in particular.

HISTORY

In *The Conquistadors*, Hammond Innes illustrated how cultural differences allowed a small force of Spaniards, whose culture taught them to fight wars to kill, to subdue a much larger force of Mexican and Peruvian Indians, whose cultures taught them to capture rather than kill so that their foes could be used as victims of ritual sacrifice. The book also teaches us that the cost in human misery is high when the protagonists are convinced of the "God-givenness" of their own cultures.

History can also provide case studies for human relations students. Marion L. Starkey's *The Devil in Massachusetts* fills this bill admirably. The book offers carefully documented accounts of the Salem witch trials, and it offers a good "laboratory" for those interested in applying

---

[42] Samuel M. Crothers, "Calvinism" (sermon preached at Unity Church, St. Paul, Minn., 1893).

[43] Duncan Howlett, *The Fourth American Faith*, 117.

44

various interpersonal interaction theories to known cases. Those interested in Gestalt group theories will find much support for the notion that groups display characteristics which cannot be explained by their constituent parts. On the surface the events of the trials seem incredible: nineteen persons, many of whom were what we would now call upstanding members of the community, were hanged, and one was pressed to death, solely on the word of hysterical young girls who in their more rational moments admitted that "we must have our sport."

Aldous Huxley succinctly summed up the importance of the work: "In this admirable book, [the author] has made it easy for a modern reader to grasp the local and parochial realities of an isolated outbreak of witch-hunting. In the process she has made it possible for us to understand those dark, those truly diabolic forces which lurk in the recesses of the human mind, ready, whenever history gives them their opportunity, to break out into the open."[44]

A historical study like this one gives students of human relations not only a chance to study the dynamics of the group hysteria that allowed the atrocities to be commited but also, more importantly, a chance to explore the dynamics of the group efforts of wiser men who stopped the Salem witch trials and tried to see that reparations were made to the families of those who were executed.

Biographies and autobiographies also offer rich historical materials for gaining insight into human relations problems and solutions.

SKETCHES FROM LIFE

Much of the content of the humanities evolves around slices of life which grow out of pleasant and unpleasant human relationships. Supplementing and sometimes surpassing behavioral science literature are humanists' studies of language, humor, essays and letters, and novels.

LANGUAGE

The study of language qualifies as a division of the humanities. Dorothy L. Seymour has contributed much to a better understanding of language in human relations.[45] Ms. Seymour discussed the West African language foundation of "Black English," or ghetto speech, and argued methodically that it is not sloppy talk or bad English but a dialect with a form and structure of its own. To support her position, she quoted Kenneth Johnson, a black linguist, who maintained that as long as disadvantaged black children are confined to their own sub-

---

[44] Quoted in Marion L. Starkey, *The Devil in Massachusetts*, xxi.
[45] Dorothy L. Seymour, "Black English," *Intellectual Digest*, Vol. 2 (February, 1972), 78–80.

culture they will not substitute their functional nonstandard dialect for a nonfunctional standard dialect.

To those who would argue that the nonstandard dialect is "deficient," Ms. Seymour pointed out that they may find standard English even more open to the charge:

Linguists have made it clear that language systems that are different are not necessarily deficient. A judgment of deficiency can be made only in comparison with another language system. Let's turn the tables on Standard English for a moment and look at it from the West African point of view. From this angle, Standard English (1) is lacking in certain language sounds; (2) has a couple of unnecessary language sounds for which others may serve as good substitutes; (3) doubles and drawls some of its vowel sounds in sequences that are unusual and difficult to imitate; (4) lacks a method of forming an important tense (habitual); (5) requires an unnecessary number of ways to indicate tense, plurality and gender; and (6) doesn't mark negatives sufficiently for the result to be a good strong negative statement.[46]

She proposed an official "bidialectism" for teachers as well as for students and concluded that if we do not provide for diverse language there will be continued estrangement of a large segment of the minority population. Lest anyone fear the diversity of more than one dialect in a nation, we take special heed of the words of Kenneth E. F. Watt, an anthropologist who argued that diversity is essential for survival: "The rapid loss of diversity in the world is a serious and pervasive phenomenon. Everywhere we look, we see examples of a large number of diverse entities being replaced by a small number of similar entities."[47]

HUMOR

Without a doubt, humor is a branch of the humanities. Harvey Mindess concluded that the sense of the ridiculous to be found in humor offers an antidote to emotional distress.[48] He wrote: "The extent to which our sense of humor can help us to maintain our sanity is the extent to which it moves beyond jokes, beyond wit, beyond laughter itself. It must constitute a frame of mind, a point of view, a deep-going, far-reaching attitude to life."[49]

Mindess suggested a cluster of qualities that characterize a thera-

[46] *Ibid.*, 80.

[47] Kenneth E. F. Watts, "Man's Efficient Rush Toward Deadly Dullness," *Natural History*, Vol. 81, No. 2 (February, 1972), 75–82.

[48] Harvey Mindess, "The Sense of Humor," *Saturday Review*, August 21, 1971, 10–12.

[49] *Ibid.*, 10.

peutic frame of mind pertaining to humor: flexibility, spontaneity, un-conventionality, shrewdness, playfulness, humility, and an enjoyment of the ironies that permeate our lives:

In order to command a therapeutic sense of humor, we must become acutely aware of the anomalies that run through all human affairs. We must come to know, not theoretically but practically, that the happiest relationships are laden with suffering, that the greatest accomplishments are anticlimactic, that rational acts are motivated by irrational drives, that psychotic thinking makes excellent sense. We must know that assertiveness is the mask of fearfulness, that humiilty is a kind of pride, that love is a euphemism for lust, that truth is the pawn of fashion, that we cherish our misery, and that we all are more irrational than we acknowledge.[50]

An example of the efficacy of humor to change social conditions by making social injustice humorously evident is illustrated in the poem "The Golf Links," by Sarah Cleghorn. Ms. Cleghorn's short poem is credited with accelerating the movement to abolish child labor in the United States. The poem was written shortly after she toured a spinning mill which employed children and which was surrounded by a golf course:

> *The golf links lie so near the mill*
> *That almost every day*
> *The laboring children can look out*
> *And watch the men at play.*

That's serious humor, but humor nevertheless, and it is the irony of this kind of humor that often brings certain injustices to the full attention of those who, when aroused, can do something about it.

ESSAYS AND LETTERS

In "Of Ego," John Ciardi examined ego from two viewpoints: macro and micro. Of the macro, he stated that we have become very proficient at projecting order in chaos and that the ego is easily persuaded to accept confusion. Ciardi suggested that we might be better off to give up the search for universal truths and focus on the less grandiose goal of interpersonal unity:

For without such eternal sanctions to be mean about, man is forced back upon himself. His ego still needs to feel that sense of importance, but it finds it in giving itself to others, in that exchange of needs we may reasonably hope to call mercy and reasonably hope to use as the

[50] *Ibid.*

47

cornerstone of a possible civilization. It is, after all, something (and more than something—much) to realize we don't matter except to one another, for then we can matter mightily, if only for a while.[51]

In another essay, "Hanging Around Words," Ciardi discussed the poet's use of words as instruments not only of denotation but also of connotation, and particularly the basic qualities which give words "history": "For [poets] words are entities that involve roots, textures, histories, associations, levels of usage, shape, taste, their particular demands upon the speech muscles. In good poetry those intrinsic qualities of words often determine what the poem is and how it gets to be what it is."[52]

Human relations practitioners without a knowledge of history are unable to understand the past and are consequently unable to appreciate fully the present. In his book *The Age of Aquarius* (pages 268–69) William Braden offers a historical perspective of diversity which supports Kenneth Watts's pleas for diversity:

We are now witnessing in America a reassertion of ethnic identity, and—while it no doubt conceals a certain degree of white backlash— the overall development is probably a healty one. But . . . such enclaves are not bound together by a common American culture which effectively transcends them. The problem is not to assimilate these enclaves or subcultures into the emerging technological superculture, which is not really a culture at all but rather a mechanical and inhuman nonculture. The problem is to integrate them into a viable American culture. They would enrich it by their very diversity; at the same time they would be preserved as functioning parts of an organic whole. What is wanted is harmony, not homogeneity.[53]

A broader essay of societal evolution and its human relations prospects is found in William Glasser's "The Civilized Identity Society." Glasser outlined four easily discernible phases of human existence: (1) the *primitive survival society*, in which the major preoccupation was to cooperate and survive in a hostile environment; (2) the *primitive identity society*, in which people gained leisure and pleasure in a less hostile world so that they had time for rituals, symbols, and religion as ways in which to identify themselves; (3) the *civilized survival society*, which came with increased population, a decrease in wild game, and the discovery of agriculture and which made land valuable enough for human beings to fight one another to win and exploit it;

[51] John Ciardi, "Of Ego," *Saturday Review*, January 22, 1972, 25.
[52] John Ciardi, "Hanging Around Words," *Saturday Review*, March 11, 1972, 14.
[53] William Braden, *The Age of Aquarius*, 268–69.

48

and (4) the *civilized identity society*, which has begun emerging in the past twenty years as our attention turns again to a role-dominated society in which human concern centers on self-identity, self-expression, and cooperation. According to Glasser, the new identity society is a regeneration of cooperation and involvement.[54]

The field of letters is an aspect of the humanities whether those letters are written by "professional humanists" or by persons some might classify as behavioral scientists. An example of a letter which contributes to human relations can be found in Stanley A. Freed's review of Rosalie H. Wax's book *Doing Fieldwork*. Ms. Wax, an anthropologist, gave advice on some of the human relations problems young anthropologists face when they go into the field: "I have no advice on how to live graciously through the experience of being exploited, hoodwinked, shortchanged, blackmailed, robbed, or fooled, except by bearing in mind that every fieldworker could furnish examples."[55] Freed highlighted the significance of the book by quoting a few brief but well-chosen words: "The great feat in most field expeditions, as in life, says Wax, 'is to find the areas in which a mutual or reciprocal trust may be developed. That these areas will be new or odd to both hosts and fieldworker is very likely. But it is in these areas of mutual trust and, sometimes, affection, that the finest fieldwork can be done.' "[56]

Letters can afford intimate glimpses of human relations in action.

NOVELS

In *Twelve Great American Novels*, Arthur Mizener presents interpretative studies of a dozen outstanding novels. They give excellent examples of how American writers handle inner and outer reality. Although the book was written for the unspecialized or "common reader," human relations students will find it of interest. They may be especially interested in Mizener's attitude toward literary criticism:

Dr. Johnson once said that he "rejoiced to concur with the common reader" in his admiration for Gray's "Elegy." It is not an easy attitude to take without sounding condescending, and not many critics in our time appear interested even to try. Yet it is difficult to understand how anyone can have been a teacher without recognizing how necessary it is to try, how much the intelligent untrained reader—what Dr. Johnson meant by "the common reader"—needs that concurrence, and how futile and finicking in its overspecialized way the critic's own work

[54] William Glasser, "The Civilized Identity Society," *Saturday Review*, February 19, 1972, 26–31.

[55] Stanley A. Freed, "Person to Person," *Natural History*, Vol. 81, No. 4 (April, 1972), 82–88.

[56] *Ibid.*, 87–88.

becomes if he fails to achieve it. The humanistic discipline that has lost its desire to concur with the common reader ceases to be human.[57]

Carle Levi's *Christ Stopped at Eboli* is a novel treatment of the year Levi, an Italian artist, spent in political custory in southern Italy during Mussolini's reign before World War II. The place of Levi's "exile" was Gagliano, a town bypassed by Christianity because it lay beyond Eboli, where "Christ stopped." Levi's book is a convincing picture of a pagan enclave which lacks the religious influence of Christianity.

In Hazard, by Richard Hughes, is a novel based on the actual ordeal of a British freighter caught in a giant hurricane in the Caribbean in the 1920's. Hughes's account of how the captain of the storm-battered *Archimedes* dealt with the captain of the rescuing salvage ship illustrates the contribution a novelist can make to the understanding of human conflicts. Edwardes, captain of the wrecked ship, refuses to let Captain Abraham put any of his own men aboard the wreck to conduct towing operations:

"I'll have you know, Captain, that anything needful on this ship my own men can do, We don't need any help from strangers to work our own ship, thank you—*what do you think my men are? Passengers?"*

This was no ordinary situation to be dealt with by cold logic. Such high-pitched emotion could only be answered in the same key. Captain Abraham rose from his seat, moved into the centre of the cabin, and there fell on both his knees. He lifted his right hand above his head, fixed his wordly, hatchet-face in as otherworldly an expression as he could manage.

"Captain!" he said, "I swear by Almighty God, that if I have my own men on board to fix tow it shall not affect the salvage question not by one jot nor one tittle! Nor it don't derogate any from your crew! I swear by Almighty God that it's just the usual procedure!"

"Very well," said Captain Edwardes, a tear in his eyes "Mr. Buxton, let them come up."[58]

Stereotypes and the Real Indian[59]
ALVIN M. JOSEPHY, JR.

For almost five hundred years the American Indian has been one of the principal symbols of the New World.

[57] Arthur Mizener, *Twelve Great American Novels*, xi.

[58] Richard Hughes, *In Hazard*, 201–202.

[59] From Alvin M. Josephy, Jr., *The Indian Heritage of America*. Copyright © 1968 by Alvin M. Josephy, Jr. Published by Alfred A. Knopf, Inc., and Bantam Books, Inc. Reprinted by permission.

To many persons, the mention of Brazil, Peru, Bolivia, or almost any South American state evokes an image of its original native inhabitant, whether a river dweller in a dugout in the jungle basins of the Orinoco and Amazon, or a ponchoed descendant of the Incas tending llamas in the highlands of the Andes. Mexico, Guatemala, and the other countries of Central America are still synonymous in the popular mind with visions of the Mayan, Aztec, and other glittering pre-Columbian civilizations and with the present-day arts and handicrafts of their inheritors. And in Washington, D.C., the United States Travel Service of the Department of Commerce, established to attract visitors from other countries to the modern, industrialized U.S., testifies to the great interest foreign tourists have to this day in the storied Iroquois, Apaches, and Sioux of other times by using the symbol of the war-bonneted Plains Indian on much of its official travel literature. Even the Eskimo and his igloo and kayak come readily to mind at the thought of Alaska and parts of Canada.

In truth, the beliefs, ways of life, and roles of the American Indians are interwoven so intimately with the cultures and histories of all the modern nations of the Americas that no civilization of the West Hemisphere can be fully understood without knowledge and appreciation of them. And yet, from the time of the Europeans' first meeting with the Indians in 1492 until today, the Indian has been a familiar but little known—and, indeed, often an unreal—person to the non-Indian. What has been known about him, moreover, frequently has been superficial, distorted, or false.

What the white man calls him is itself the result of an error. When Christopher Columbus reached the New World, he had no idea that a land mass lay between Europe and Asia; the islands at which he touched he thought were those known at the time as the Indies, which lay off the coast of Asia, and the people he found on them he called los Indios, *the people of the Indies, or the Indians. Other early navigators and chroniclers used the same name mistakenly for the various peoples they met at the end of each western voyage, and by the time the Europeans discovered their error and realized that they were still far from Asia, it was too late. The name had taken hold as a general term of reference for all the inhabitants of the newly found lands of the Western Hemisphere.*

Errors of far greater significance—and seriousness—stemmed from fundamental cultural differences between Indians and non-Indians. Deeply imbedded in the cultural make-up of the white man with a European background were the accumulated experiences of the Judeo-Christian spiritual tradition, the heritages of the ancient civilizations of the Near East, Greece, and Rome, and the various political, social, and economic systems of western Europe. The Indians did not share any of these but, on their part, were the inheritors of totally different traditions and ways of life, many of them rooted in Asia, some of them thousands of years old, and all as thoroughly a part of Indian societies as European ways were a part of the white man's culture.

Meeting peoples with such different backgrounds led white men to endless misconceptions. Beginning with Columbus, the whites, with rare exceptions, observed and judged natives of the Americas from their own European points of view, failing consistently to grasp the truths and realities of the Indians themselves or their backgrounds and cultures. In the early years of the sixteenth century educated whites, steeped in the theological teachings of Europe, argued learnedly about whether or not Indians were humans with souls, whether they, too, derived from Adam and Eve (and were therefore sinful like the rest of mankind), or whether they were a previously unknown subhuman species. Other Europeans spent long years puzzling on the origin of the Indians and developing evidence that they were Egyptians, Chinese, descendants of one of the Lost Tribes of Israel, Welshmen, or even the survivors of civilizations that had once flourished on lost continents in the Atlantic and Pacific oceans.

In the lands of the New World, white men who came in contact with Indians viewed Indian cultures solely in terms that were familiar to themselves, and ignored or condemned what they did not understand. Indian leaders were talked of as "princes" and "kings"; spiritual guides and curers were called wizzards, witch doctors, and medicine men, and all were equated as practitioners of sorcery; Indian societies generally —refined and sophisticated though some of them might be—were termed savage and barbaric, often only because they were strange, different, and not understood by the whites.

Many of the differences brought friction and, on both continents, fierce, interracial war. Conflicts resulted from misconceptions of the nature of Indian societies, the limits of authority of Indian leaders, and the non-hostile motives of certain Indian traits. Differing concepts concerning individual and group use of land and the private ownership of land were at the heart of numerous struggles, as were misunderstandings over the intentions of Indians whose actions were judged according to the patterns of white men's behavior rather than those of the Indians.

Through the years, the white man's popular conception of the Indian often crystallized into unrealistic or unjust images. Sometimes they were based on the tales of adventurers and travelers, who wove myths freely into their accounts, and sometimes they were reflections of the passions and fears stirred by the conflicts between the two races.

Described by early writers as a race of happy people who lived close to nature, the Indians of the New World were first envisioned by many Europeans as innocent, childlike persons, spending their time in dancing and equally pleasurable pursuits. From this image in time sprang Jean Jacques Rousseau's vision of the natural man, as well as arguments of liberal philosophers in Europe who influenced revolutionary movements, including those of the United States and France, with comparisons between the lot of Europeans "in chains" and Indians who lived lives of freedom.

This idealistic version of the Indian as a symbol of the naturally free man persisted into the nineteenth century, sometimes being advanced by admiring observers like the artist George Catlin who visited many tribes and found much to admire in their ways of life, but generally being accepted only by persons who had no firsthand contact with Indians. On each frontier, beginning along the Atlantic coast, settlers who locked in conflict with Indians quickly conceived of them as bloodthirsty savages, intent on murder, scalping and pillage. As the frontier moved west, and the Indian menace vanished from the eastern seaboard, generations that did not know Indian conflict at first hand again thought of the native American in more tolerant terms. James Fenimore Cooper's version of the Noble Red Man helped gain sympathy among easterners for Indians who were hard pressed by the whites elsewhere. Thus, throughout much of the nineteenth century people in the northeastern cities often gave support to movements for justice for the southern and western tribes.

But as long as conflicts continued, the border settlers regarded the Indians in terms that had been familiar to the New England colonists during King Philip's war in the seventeenth century, and echoed the sentiment that "the only good Indian is a dead Indian." Only with the defeat of tribes did that point of view change—and then, inevitably, it was succeeded by still another image, which also moved from one border to another as settlers took over lands from which they had dispossessed the natives. It was the cruel conception of the Whisky Indian, the destroyed and impoverished survivor who had lost his home, tribal life, means of sustenance, and cultural standards, and lacking motivation—and often even the will to live—sought escape in alcohol. Unfeeling whites, failing to recognize the causes of the Indians' degradation, forgot their past power, pride, and dignity, and regarded them as weak and contemptuous people.

Only rarely did astute observers try to understand Indian life and depict Indians realistically. One of them, Edward R. Denig, an American fur trader living among still-unconquered tribes on the upper Missouri River during the first half of the nineteenth century, wrote angrily on the white man's lack of knowledge about Indians at that time.

It would be well for the public if everyone who undertook to write a book was thoroughly acquainted with the subject of which he treats. . . . This is particularly the case in most of the works purporting to describe the actual life and intellectual capacity of the Indians of North America; much evil has been the consequence of error thus introduced, bad feelings engendered, and unwise legislation enforced, which will continue until our rulers are enlightened as to the real state of their Government, character, organization, manners and customs, and social position . . . a hastily collected and ill-digested mass of information form the basis of works by which the public is deceived as to the real state of the Indians. Even foreigners who have possibly passed a winter at some of the trading posts in the country, seen an Indian dance or two or a buffalo chase, return home, enlighten Europe if not America with regard to Indian character; which is only the product of their brains and takes its color from the particular nature of that organ. Hence we find two sets of writers both equally wrong, one setting forth the Indians as a noble, generous, and chivalrous race far above the standard of Europeans, the other representing them below the level of brute creation.

It might be assumed that much has changed since the time when Denig wrote. But despite vast study by scientists and a voluminous literature of modern knowledge about Indians, still common are ignorance and misconceptions, many of them resulting from the white man's continuing inability to regard Indians save from his own European-based point of view. Today most Indians on both continents have been conquered and enfolded within the conquerors' own cultures; but the span of time since the various phases of the conquest ended has been short, and numerous Indians still cling to traits that are centuries, if not millennia, old and cannot be quickly shed. Many Indians, for instance, still do not understand or cannot accept the concept of private ownership of land; many do not understand the need to save for the future, a fundamental requirement of the economies of their conquerors; many find it difficult, if not impossible so far, to substitute individual competitiveness for group feeling; many do not see the necessity for working the year-round if they can provide for their families by six months of work, or the reason for cutting the earth-mother with a plow and farming if they can still hunt, fish, and dig roots. Many yet feel a sacred attachment to the land and a reverence for nature that is incomprehensible to most whites. Many, though Christian, find repugnance in the idea that man possesses dominion over the

54

birds and beasts, and believe still man is brother to all else that is living.

Such ideas, among a multitude that continue to hold numerous Indians apart from non-Indians, are either unrecognized or frowned upon by most whites today. Those who are aware of them are more often than not irritated by their persistence, yet the stubbornness of the white critics' own culture to survive, if a totally alien way of life, like that of the Chinese Communists, were to be forced upon them, would be understood.

More common among most whites are the false understandings and images which they retain about Indians. For many, the moving pictures, television, and comic strips have firmly estabished a stereotype as the true portrait of all Indianss the dour, stoic, warbonneted Plains Indian. He is a warrior, he has no humor unless it is that of an incongruous and farcical type, and his language is full of "hows," "ughs," and words that end in "um." Only rarely in the popular media of communications is it hinted that Indians, too, were, and are, all kinds of real, living persons like any others and that they included peace-loving wise men, mothers who cried for the safety of their children, young men who sang songs of love and courted maidens, dullards, statesmen, cowards, and patriots. Today there are college-trained Indians, researchers, business and professional men and women, jurists, ranchers, teachers and political office holders. Yet so enduring is the stereotype that may a non-Indian, especially if he lives in an area where Indians were not commonly seen, expects any American Indian he meets to wear a feathered headdress. When he sees the Indian in a conventional business suit instead, he is disappointed!

If Indians themselves are still about as real as wooden sticks to many non-Indians, the facts concerning their present-day status in the societies of the Americas are even less known. Again, stereotypes, like those of "the oil-rich Indian" or "the coddled ward of Uncle Sam," frequently obscure the truth. A few Indians have become wealthy, but most of them know poverty, ill health, and barren, wasted existences. Some have received higher education, but many are poorly educated or not educated at all. Some are happily assimilated in the white man's societies; others are in various stages of acculturation, and many are not assimilated and do not wish to be anything but Indian. In the United States, in addition, it often comes as a surprise to many otherwise well informed whites to learn that the Indians are citizens and have the right to vote; that reservations are not concentration camps but are all the lands that were left to the Indians, and that are still being guarded by them as homes from which they can come and go in freedom; that the special treaty rights that they possess and that make them a unique minority in the nation are payments and guaran-

55

tees given them for land they sold to the non-Indian people of the United States; that Indians pay state and federal taxes like all other citizens, save where treaties, agreements, or statutes have exempted them; and that, far from being on the way to extinction, the Indian population is increasing rapidly.

Finally, there are facts that should be obvious to everyone after five hundred years but are not, possibly because Columbus's name for them, Indians, is to this day understood by many to refer to a single people. Despite the still commonly asked question, "Do you speak Indian?" there is neither a single Indian people, with different racial characteristics, different cultures, and different languages. From Alaska to Cape Horn, in fact, the Indians of the Americas are as different from each other as are Spaniards, Scots, and Poles—and, in many cases, as will be seen, they are even more different.

SUMMARY

It should be obvious from this overview of the humanities that they do indeed make a contribution to human relations by condensing the vital aspects of interpersonal relationships so that they can be vicariously experienced, and therefore understod, by those who would never be able to have those experiences otherwise, and by doing it in a multitude of ways, which often seem "useless" to unimaginative people.

Chapter 2
SUGGESTED READING

Albright, H. D., *et al. Principles of Theatre Art.* Boston, Houghton Mifflin Co., 1968.

Avey, Albert E. *Handbook in the History of Philosophy.* New York, Barnes & Noble, Inc., 1964.

Barthel, Joan. "Dancers Are Chosen People," *New York Times,* July 31, 1966.

Braden, William. *The Age of Aquarius.* New York, Simon & Schuster, Inc., 1971.

Canaday, John E. *Metropolitan Seminars in Art,* Vol. 7. New York, The Metropolitan Museum of Art, 1958.

Ciardi, John. "Esthetic Wisdom," *Saturday Review,* April 8, 1972.

———. "Hanging Around Words," *Saturday Review,* March 11, 1972.

———. "Of Ego," *Saturday Review,* January 22, 1972.

Cohen, Selma Jeanne, ed. *The Modern Dance: Seven Statements of Belief.* Middletown, Conn., Wesleyan University Press, 1965.

Crothers, Samuel McChord. "Calvinism." Sermon preached at Unity Church, St. Paul, Minn., 1893.

———. "Roman Catholicism." Sermon preached at Unity Church, St. Paul, Minn., 1893.

Deri, Otto. *Exploring Twentieth-Century Music.* New York, Holt, Rinehart & Winston, Inc., 1968.

Dickinson, Edward. *The Spirit of Music.* New York, Charles Scribner's Sons, 1925.

Egri, Lajos. *The Art of Dramatic Writing: Its Basis in the Creative Interpretation of Human Motives.* New York, Simon & Schuster, Inc., 1960.

Freed, Stanley A. "Person to Person." *Natural History,* Vol. 81, No. 4 (April, 1972).

Friedman, Maurice, ed. *To Deny Our Nothingness.* New York, Dell Publishing Company, Inc., Delta Books, 1967.

Garza, Daniel. "Saturday Belongs to the Palomía," *Harper's Magazine,* July, 1962.

Gassner, John. *Human Relations in the Theatre.* New York, Freedom Pamphlets, 1949.

Glasser, William. "The Civilized Identity Society," *Saturday Review,* February 19, 1972.

Graeffe, Arnold D., *Creative Education in the Humanities.* New York, Harper & Row, Publishers, Inc., 1951.

Hall, James B., and Barry Ulanov, eds. *Modern Culture and the Arts.* New York, McGraw-Hill Book Company, 1967.

Heilbrone, Robert. *The Worldly Philosophers.* New York, Simon & Schuster, Inc., Clarion Books, 1967.

Hesse, Hermann. *Steppenwolf.* New York, Holt, Rinehart & Winston, Inc., 1963.

Howlett, Duncan. *The Fourth American Faith.* Boston, The Beacon Press, 1968.

Hughes, Richard. *In Hazard.* New York, Time-Life Books, 1966.

Humphrey, Doris. "America's Modern Dance," *Theatre Arts,* Vol. 34 (September, 1950).

Innes, Hammond. *The Conquistadors.* New York, Alfred A. Knopf, Inc., 1969.

Kaufmann, Walter A., ed. *Existentialism from Dostoevsky to Sartre.* New York, Meridian Books, Inc., 1956.

Levi, Albert W. *The Humanities Today.* Bloomington, Indiana University Press, 1970.

Levi, Carlo. *Christ Stopped at Eboli.* Translated by Frances Frenage. New York, Time-Life Books, 1964.

Lloyd, Margaret. "Doris Humphrey: Yesterday and Today," *Dance Magazine,* Vol. 28 (November, 1954).

Martin, John. "The Dancer as an Artist," *New York Times Magazine,* April 12, 1953.

McCoubrey, John W. *American Art: 1700–1960.* Englewood Cliffs, N.J., Prentice-Hall, Inc., 1965.

Memmi, Albert. *Dominated Man.* Boston, The Beacon Press, 1968.

Mindess, Harvey. "The Sense in Humor," *Saturday Review,* August 21, 1971.

Mizener, Arthur. *Twelve Great American Novels.* Cleveland, World Publishing Co., 1969.

Nietzsche, Friedrich. *Beyond Good and Evil.* Translated by Walter Kaufmann. New York, Random House, Inc., 1966.
——. *Thus Spoke Zarathustra.* Translated by R. J. Hollingdale. Great Britain, Penguin Books, 1961.
Sachs, Curt. *World History of the Dance.* New York, W. W. Norton & Company, Inc., 1937.
Schwartz, Elliott, and Barney Childs. *Contemporary Composers on Contemporary Music.* New York, Holt, Rinehart & Winston, Inc., 1967.
Seymour, Dorothy L. "Black English," *Intellectual Digest,* Vol. 2 (February, 1972).
Shafter, David A. "Drama for Delinquents." Masters Thesis, Department of Theatre, Southern Illinois University, 1964.
Shaw, Arnold. *The World of Soul: Black America's Contribution to the Pop Music Science.* New York, Cowles Book Co., Inc., 1970.
Sorell, Walter, ed. *The Dance Has Many Faces,* 2d ed. New York, Columbia University Press, 1966.
Spaeth, Sigmund. *The Art of Enjoying Music.* New York, Garden City Publishing Co., 1938.
Starkey, Marion L. *The Devil in Massachusetts.* New York, Time-Life Books, 1963.
Tillich, Paul. *The Courage to Be.* New Haven, Conn., Yale University Press, 1952.
Toynbee, Arnold. *A Study of History,* abr. ed. 10 vols. Ed. by D. C. Somervell. New York, Oxford University Press, 1946.
Trilling, Lionel, ed. *The Experience of Literature: a Reader with Commentaries.* Garden City, N.Y., Doubleday & Co., Inc., 1962.
Walker, Alan. *An Anatomy of Music Criticism.* Philadelphia, Chilton Book Co., 1966.
Watts, Kenneth E. F. "Man's Efficient Rush Toward Deadly Dullness," *Natural History,* Vol. 81, No. 2 (February, 1972).
Williams, Sherley. *Give Birth to Brightness: A Thematic Study in Neo-Black Literature.* New York, The Dial Press, 1972.
Winch, Peter. *The Idea of a Social Science and Its Relation to Philosophy.* New York, Humanities Press, Inc., 1958.

MANAGEMENT OF HUMAN RESOURCES

Another version of obtaining commitment is to gain
the new member's acceptance of very general ideas like
"one must work for the good of the company," or
"one must meet the competition."—EDGAR H. SCHEIN

Human relations training began in the field of business management. Management of people has always been a controversial issue in industry, as well as in government. Some authorities have defined managers as "those who use formal authority to organize, direct, or control responsible subordinates (and therefore, indirectly, the groups or complexes which they may head) in order that all service contributions be coordinated in the attainment of an enterprise purpose."[1] Herbert J. Cruden and Arthur W. Sherman have referred to management as the process of planning, organizing, staffing, directing, and controlling the activities and the personnel within an organization in order that its objective may be accomplished.[2] Therefore, management is the process of getting things done with and through the efforts of people.

From a human relations standpoint, management received its impetus in 1927 when Elton Mayo and his associates, Fritz Roethlisberger, William J. Dickson, and T. North Whitehead, launched the now-famous Western Electric program. Even earlier, Frederick W. Taylor had been called the "father of modern management." We will discuss five persons who attempted to conceptualize management in varying degrees of totality—Frederick W. Taylor, Elton Mayo, Fritz J. Roethlisberger, William J. Dickson, Chester I. Barnard, and Douglas McGregor. We will also discuss the contributions of present-day management theorists who focus on organizational strategies for achieving

---

[1] Robert Tannenbaum, Irving R. Weschler, and Fred Massarik, eds., *Leadership and Organization: A Behavioral Science Approach*, 263.

[2] Herbert J. Cruden and Arthur W. Sherman, eds., *Personnel Management*.

goals by maximizing the human resources: Chris Argyris, Robert R. Blake, Jane S. Mouton, and Matthew Miles.

FREDERICK W. TAYLOR (1865–1915)

While working as an assistant foreman at the Midvale Steel Company in Pennsylvania, Frederick W. Taylor noticed several gross patterns of inefficiency which he decided to measure. With a stopwatch he measured the amount of time actually taken for a given operation and the amount of physical motion involved. These time-and-motion studies became the basis for Taylor's theory of "scientific management." The principles he developed are sometimes referred to as a "physiological organization theory" because of their relation of human to industrial operations. Thus, the field of industrial relations was begun.

The human relations aspects of Taylor's industrial relations were relegated to a focus on increased labor output and productivity. For Taylor, greater efficiency meant an increase in prosperity and a diminution in poverty, not only for the workers but for the whole community as well. Although working conditions did not improve appreciably with scientific management, the "profit-motive" concept did gain greater importance. Strategies used by Taylor were: (1) identifying the job (what is the job and how is it being performed?) (2) calling attention to and elimiating wasteful motions, (3) timing the job and worker in order to achieve better and ideal performance, and (4) incentive plans or payments. It was obvious to Taylor that maximum prosperity, in reality, meant production.

The central problem which concerned Taylor was elevating wage systems to a scientific plane. He criticized the older forms of piecework wage plans because they did not result in the desired motivational outcomes. Taylor observed: "The ordinary piece-work system involves a permanent antagonism between employer and men. . . . even the best workmen are forced continually to act the part of hypocrites to hold their own in the struggle against the encroachment of their employers."[3] Taylor sought exactly the opposite for his system, trying to make each workman's interests the same as that of his employer. Taylor's plan was designed to give workers monetary rewards in direct relation to time saved in the performance of jobs.

Taylor established "scientific management" as a new approach which sought to accomplish two goals: (1) higher industrial efficiency through improved management practice and (2) greater collaboration among those working in industry. Testifying before a congres-

[3] Quoted in William G. Scott, *Organization Theory: A Behavioral Analysis for Management*, 23.

sional committee, he had the following to say about scientific management:

Scientific management is not an efficiency device, . . . not a system of figuring costs, . . . not a piece-work system, . . . not a bonus system, . . . not a premium system. . . . it is not holding a stop watch on a man and writing things down about him. . . . it is not time study, it is not motion study. . . . it is not any of the devices which the average man calls to mind when scientific management is spoken of.

In its essence scientific management involves a complete mental revolution on the part of the workingman, . . . and it involves an equally complete mental revolution on the part of those on the management's side. . . .

The great revolution that takes place in the mental attitude of the two parties under scientific management is that both sides takes their eyes off of the division of the surplus as the all-important matter, and together turn their attention toward increasing the size of the surplus until this surplus becomes so large . . . that there is ample room for a large increase in wages for the workmen and an equally large increase in profits for the manufacturer.[4]

Taylor's testimony revealed that scientific management was more than techniques; it was a way of thought. His ideas attempted to reconcile the paradox of the need for cooperation among people in industry with the philosophy of individualism prevailing at that time. The mechanisms of his approach included such matters as specific wage plans and motion-and-time studies. The "right wage" was an explosive issue that came out of the new industrial economy. He felt that the wage paid must be related to the work done. To find the relation, he formulated time-study experiments to measure work. He considered the analysis of work and the payment of wages crucial elements of business harmony. In essence he believed that, given a fair wage, scientifically set in relation to a far amount of work, an employee would be induced to work harder.

Other concepts that Taylor introduced included "functional foremanship," which was a view of organizing personnel in the most effective way: "Functional foremanshp allowed concentration on a few specializations within a job toward which each foreman had some individual bent . . . the concept could be applied to higher levels of management as well. The result would be a high degree of standardization and specialization in all managerial positions."[5]

Taylor stressed the importance of strong personal cooperation be-

[4] *Ibid.*, 24–25.
[5] *Ibid.*, 27.

tween manager and worker. Because he saw management as an art, he stressed the need for functional foremanship with a de-emphasis on more authoritarian management. (It is important to note that when referring to management, Taylor was speaking of task management—the responsibiilty of the supervisor or foreman.) He also suggested ways of coping with natural and systematic "soldiering," or loafing on the job, and the necessity of scheduling job activities.

Although not directly opposed to labor unions, Taylor was more interested in devising ways to avoid strikes without union intervention. And he was relatively successful in this endeavor. A great part of the success in avoiding strikes was a result of the high wages which the best men were able to earn with differential rates. But there were two important things in terms of human feelings and interaction which Taylor failed to deal with: communication was still only one way, and working conditions were not appreciably altered. In short, the motive for cooperation was still profit, not human relations. Through the insight and direction of men like Henry Towne, Pierre Janet, and Elton Mayo, these conditions began to change.

Taylor, an engineer, had described his approach toward management as an engineering approach; it was concerned with the techniques of arranging work forces and their activities to achieve the maximum output at the lowest cost. His assumption was that the speed, cost, and quality of goods and services are dependent variables that can be maximized by adjustments of a number of independent variables, including division of labor, patterns of supervision, financial incentives, flow of materials, and physical methods and conditions of work performance. As noted earlier, Taylor failed to focus on sociopsychological determinants of morale and efficiency. It was Elton Mayo who added "human factors" in management.

ELTON MAYO (1880–1949)

The writings of Elton Mayo are of great historical significance as well as being an enormous influence upon the development of industrial psychology and sociology. Mayo was more interested in individual counseling problems than in social organizational changes with an industrial environment. He saw in the modern industrial civilization many human problems which social scientists seemed to be ignoring because they did not fit their conceptions of problems that science should study or the techniques and methods it should use.

Influenced by Pierre Janet, Mayo became concerned with two basic ideas: (1) the nature of society and (2) the problems of the individuals. It was his feeling that the industrial revolution had destroyed traditional society and established routines. He became involved with industrial sociology and psychology at the Harvard Graduate Business School, and in 1927, with the aid of Lawrence J. Henderson, he launched a human relations program there. Mayo specialized in the personal and social determinants of productivity and cooperative behavior. He has been called the "father of research on the human relations problems of industry."

Probably one of the most important studies to call attention to the significance of informal groups in a large organizational setting was Mayo's pioneering work at the Western Electric Plant at Hawthorne, Illinois.[6] Beginning in 1927, he tried to find relationships between physical conditions of work and the productivity of employees at the plant. He set up a control group and an experimental group and proceeded to vary systematically the physical variables of light, heat, and humidity. Production rose as these conditions improved, but when he restored the original conditions, he was surprised to find that worker output remained at a high level. Only then did the researchers probe the attitude of the groups of workers. They found morale to be high, partly because the workers were relieved of the usual supervision and partly because they enjoyed being singled out for special attention by the experimenters. The term *Hawthorne effect* came to be used to describe this phenomenon. The change in attitude among the workers seemed to be more important than changes in physical conditions. The results called attention to the significance of small-group processes which exist informally outside the formal structure and organization of the plant.[7]

It was to the great credit of Mayo and his associates that they were alert to effects they had not anticipated, for the important changes actually produced by these experiments turned out to occur in interpersonal relations among workers and between the managers and the managed, on informal standards governing the behavior of members of the work group, and on the attitudes and motives of workers existing in a group context.[8]

Mayo proposed that "it must be possible for the individual as he works [to see] that his work is socially necessary; he must be able to see beyond his group to the society. . . . The workman is still conceived [by the employers] as a mere item in the cost of production rather than as a citizen fulfilling a social function. No increase in wages or improvement of working conditions can atone for the loss of real autonomy and all sense of social function."[9]

[6] Elton Mayo, *The Human Problems of an Industrial Civilization.*
[7] Cruden and Sherman, *loc. cit.*
[8] See Dorwin Cartwright and Alvin Zander, eds., *Group Dynamics: Research and Theory.*
[9] Elton Mayo, *Democracy and Freedom: An Essay in Social Logic*, 37.

63

Much of what Mayo perceived concerning management is found in current sociological perspectives of societal change and its effect upon "responsible living." Progress, for Mayo, has its seamy side, and, like Emile Durkheim, he believed that human progress is often stunted by technological progress, resulting in social disunity or in the inability of indivduals to identify with the interests of a larger group. According to Mayo, social disunity creates two continuous problems for management: (1) the satisfaction of material and economic needs and (2) the maintenance of spontaneous cooperation throughout the organization.

Mayo stated that any organization must be *effective* and *efficient*. By this he meant that economic theory must provide solutions for problems created by social disunity. In order to find such solutions, managers must have firsthand knowledge of and acquaintance with the human problems in their organizations.

Mayo asserted that managers need skills for the management of "responsible living." When these skills are obtained, he concluded, management-labor distance will be minimized, if not erased. Thus, the ultimate goal of management for responsible living is to provide opportunities for people to live together in peace and amity. It should be noted that Charles Horton Cooley "discovered" some of the assumptions associated with Mayo as early as 1902.

The main conclusions that can be drawn from Mayo's researches are the following: (1) work is a group activity; (2) the social world of the adult is basically patterned around work activity; (3) the need for recognition, security, and a sense of belonging is more important in a worker's morale and productivity than the physical conditions in which he works; (4) a complaint is not necessarily an objective reflection of facts but is often a symptom of other problems; (5) each worker's attitudes and effectiveness are conditioned by social demands from both inside and outside the work plant; (6) informal groups on the job exercise strong social controls over the work habits and attitudes of the individual worker; (7) the change from an established to an adaptive society tends to disrupt continually the social organization of a work plant and of industry in general; and (8) group collaboration does not occur by accident; it must be planned for and developed.

FRITZ J. ROETHLISBERGER (1898–) AND WILLIAM J. DICKSON (1904–)

Two of the outstanding members of the Hawthorne Research group were Fritz Roethlisberger and a Western Electric executive, William J. Dickson, who wrote the authoritative account of the studies, *Management and the Worker*. Although Mayo directed the Western Electric program, the principal fruits of that program bear little relation to Mayo's ideas about social integration and psychotherapy. These results deal with informal relations among workers, with worker-management relations, and with the methods for gathering systematic observational and interviewing data upon behavior in organizations.

Roethlisberger and Dickson were the researchers who discovered that a simple study of working conditions and employer efficiency actually culminated in an elaborate sociopsychological interpretation of employee and management behavior within the organizational setting.

Their main hypothesis was that the social function of the informal organization serves to protect the group from outside interference by manifesting a strong resistance to change or threat of change. This study and evaluation by the Mayo group was the beginning of research into the human relations factors in business. Until their study, researchers thought that the incentive to work was based only on the amount of pay and the conditions of work.

Several conclusions were drawn which helped develop subsequent personnel counseling programs. It was shown that increased group cohesiveness leads to increased productivity and that cohesiveness in the small group reduces turnover in the larger organization. The positive "Hawthorne effect" was established as a variable that must be accounted for in terms of attitude and labor output. Today it is recognized that adequate understanding of the latter proposition is a major human relations task in industry. Roethlisberger and Dickson are credited with emphasizing the role of the counselor in helping the worker relate to his job and the organization.

In their book *Counseling in an Organization: A Sequel to the Hawthorne Researches*, Roethlisberger and Dickson described the personnel counseling program instituted at the Hawthorne plant, using their research findings related to the personnel problems that confronted them. They were reluctant to make simple generalizations in their 1927 research work, partly because they were impressed by the complexity of human behavior and by the uniqueness of each situation. Rather than teaching them a broad theory, Roethlisberger and Dickson trained managers by having them study and analyze individual cases.[10]

Roethlisberger later became involved in yet another project at Harvard that involved the training of counselors in human relations for industry. He was particularly interested in the skills and techniques in human relations specifically connected with communication. By "human relations" Roethlisberger meant the conscious development and practice of a skill by which people learn to relate themselves better

[10] See also William W. Haynes and Joseph L. Massive, eds., *Management: Analysis, Concepts and Cases.*

to their human, social surroundings. Implicit in this concept is the notion of "task orientation," coupled with mutual cooperation and understanding. He was interested in bridging the gap between theory and practice and took special pains to choose trainers and to select the kinds of skills they should acquire.

CHESTER I. BARNARD (1886–1961)

Chester I. Barnard's works, especially his *Functions of the Executive,* exerted an important influence on the human relations movement. Barnard placed great emphasis on informal organization, as well as on the complexity of human motivation, with stress on the limited nature of financial incentives. Barnard also greatly influenced the current development of organization theory with his emphases on communication, status, and ethical influences.

A contemporary of Mayo, Barnard took an interest in labor and management relations. He served as the first president of the New Jersey Bell Telephone Company (1927–48) and was chief administrator of the New Jersey Relief Administration during the depression. These experiences, along with his work with Mayo and Lawrence Henderson at Harvard University, enabled him to gain a more humanistic perspective, not only toward industrial relations but also on society as a whole.

Barnard outlined several stages in understanding a problem-solving situation: "The fine art of executive decision consists in not deciding questions that are not now pertinent, in not deciding prematurely, in not making decisions that cannot be made effective, and in not making decisions that others should make."[11]

The executive, according to Barnard, does work which consists of maintaining the operation of the organization. Broadly speaking, the organization may be defined as that group which results from the modification of the action of individuals through control of or influence upon them to achieve common goals. In brief, the executive function is to provide a "system of communication to promote the securing of essential efforts and to formulate and define organizational goals."

The specific task of the executive function is to continuously obtain a coalition of the establishment and maintain a system of communication. In order to do this, the executive must secure personnel and position. The process employed to accomplish these functions may be viewed as a matter of judgment. In the first place, these functions and the process must be analyzed scientifically. Moreover, the executive, with scientific knowledge, must exhibit faith, responsibility, and

[11] Chester I. Barnard, *The Functions of the Executive.*

morality. The underlying motivation may be stated as a belief in the efficacy of cooperation among people of free will.

The executive, then, is not just a manager of production. In a sense he creates a productive system which allows for free persons to cooperate with one another to fulfill a certain function.

Barnard advocated less emphasis by management on material rewards to employees and more emphasis on "ideal benefactions." These benefactions included

pride of workmanship, sense of adequacy, altruistic service for family or others, loyalty to organization in patriotism, etc., aesthetic and religious feeling, . . . opportunities for the satisfaction of the motives of hate and revenge, . . . customary working conditions and conformity to habitual practices and attitudes, . . . the opportunity for the feeling of enlarged participation in the course of events, . . . and the condition of feeling personal comfort (communion) in social relations.[12]

Barnard outlined the importance of stratification within organizations. He advocated this social arrangement as one of great potential in motivating employees to work harder. He reasoned that the desire to reach the top of the organizational ladder would lead to greater work commitment and greater individual effort which would facilitate the organization's achievement of its goals. He argued that the main purpose of stratification was to provide lower-rewarded members with a clear line of promotion with ever-increasing rewards. It would motivate such workers to work harder but would at the same time discourage suggestions for change.

Barnard analyzed organizations as "cooperative systems," that is, open-ended "natural dynamic systems of cooperative effort that had to meet two conditions in order to survive . . . : they must secure both their objectives and the cooperation of their individual contributors."[13] Thus they must be effective and efficient. According to Barnard there are three "givens" in any cooperative system: (1) a common impersonal organizational purpose must be established, (2) individual motives must be satisfied in order to secure the individual's contribution, and (3) the processes of communication must be developed whereby these opposite poles of the system of cooperative effort must be brought into dynamic equilibrium.

One of Barnard's major contributions to administrative behavior was a theory of the growth and survival of organizations based on the interaction of individual motivational mechanisms. According to Barnard, each participant in an organization is both positively and negatively

[12] *Ibid.*, 215.
[13] Ernest Dale, ed., *Readings in Management: Landmarks and New Frontiers.*

motivated to remain in the system. He called the positive motivations the "inducements" provided to the participant by the organization. Each participant, then, will remain in the organization as long as his inducements (money, pleasant associates) outweight his contributions (work performed) on his personal scale.

Barnard also studied the concept of authority in organizational structures. He pointed out that authority is significant for administration to the extent that it has behavioral consequences. He proposed that we speak of an authority relation between two persons only when the commands of the superior are generally obeyed by the subordinate.

Barnard concluded that it is up to managers, the executives of an organization, not only to give purpose and leadership to their subordinates but also to communicate their authority in a dyad of understanding. He emphasized the connection between authority and communication of orders or ideas. Good leadership, he felt, is a product of *insight* into the human problems involved. Authority implies an understanding of the orders issued by an executive. Ultimately, the functions of the executive, and of the workers, are seen as basically connected with the functions of the organization. Along with Herbert Simon, Barnard developed the theory of "organizational equilibrium," which holds that the principle of "satisfactory exchange" always benefits the giver, commensurate with the harmony of the manager-worker-organization function.

In the final analysis, perhaps Barnard's greatest contribution to management was his idea of the corporation as a cooperative system that includes not only the executives and employees but also the investors, the suppliers, and the customers. He stressed the informal organizations within a company—an essential aspect of the human relations movement.

DOUGLAS McGREGOR (1906–64)

Any book on human relations in management would be incomplete if it excluded Douglas McGregor. Two important suppositions form the basis of McGregor's approach: Theory X (the assumptions upon which traditional organizations are based) is inadequate for the full utilization of human potentialities, and Theory Y (the assumptions consistent with current research knowledge) leads to higher motivation and greater realization of both individual and organizational goals.[14]

Theory X is the traditional negative view of man in a work situation. The worker inherently dislikes work. The managers must force, punish, and reward workers to produce. Most workers want to be led by the

[14] Douglas McGregor, *The Human Side of Enterprise.*

nose and have little responsibility or ambition. Without this active intervention (controlling, rewarding, and so on) by management, workers will be passive or resistant to organizational needs. In other words, management consists of getting things done through other persons.

Theory Y challenges this whole set of beliefs about man and human nature and about the task of management. Theory Y is McGregor's real contribution to the study of management; it draws its basic assumptions from Abraham Maslow's hierarchy of needs. McGregor felt that Theory X has been observed to be true by management not as a consequence of man's inherent nature but rather because of the nature of industrial organizations, of management policy and practice.

McGregor proposed the following as the broad dimensions of Theory Y:

1. Management is responsible for organizing the elements of productive enterprise—money, materials, equipment, people—in the interest of economic ends.

2. People are not by nature passive or resistant to organizational needs. They have become so as a result of experience in organizations.

3. The motivation, the potential for development, the capacity for assuming responsibility, and the readiness to direct behavior toward organizational goals are all present in people. Management does not put them there. It is a responsibility of management to make it possible for people to recognize and develop these human characteristics for themselves.

4. The essential task of management is to arrange organizational conditions and methods of operation so that people can achieve their own goals best by directing their own efforts toward organizational objectives.[15]

Job enlargement, a term pioneered by International Business Machines (IBM), encourages the acceptance of responsibility at the bottom of the organization; it provides opportunities for satisfying social and egoistic needs. Its principle is based on McGregor's Theory Y. In the final analysis Theory Y encourges the individual to take greater responsibiilty for planning and appraising his own contribution to the company's objectives and the effects on his self-actualization needs.

The most important aspect of Theory Y is that McGregor's assumptions are dynamic rather than static in that they indicate the potential for human growth and development. They stress the necessity for

15 Dale, *op. cit.*, 315.

"selective adaption" rather than absolute control in one form. His theory places the problems of human management right where they belong—on the manager. If the workers are lazy or indifferent, Theory Y implies, the causes lie in management's methods of control and organization.[16]

When McGregor applied Theory Y to management strategy, he envisioned four phases in what he called "management by integration and self-control." The steps are (1) clarification of the broad requirements of the job, (2) establishment of specific "targets" for a limited time period, (3) management of process during the target period, and (4) appraisal of the results.[17]

In conclusion, McGregor described the essential task of management as the arrangement of organizational conditions so that methods of operation enable people to achieve their own goals by directing their own efforts toward organizational objectives.

OTHER THEORISTS

The "scientific management" movement had pioneers other than Taylor. They include Frank and Lillian Gilbreth, Morris L. Cooke, Henry Gantt, and Harrington Emerson. Gantt and the Gilbreths were disciples of Taylor. They labored extensively in analyzing work and setting up the "right" wage. Taylor's work was refined and expanded by the Gilbreths' method analysis and Gantt's task-and-bonus system. Gantt was interested in standardization for establishing "habits of industry," by which he meant conditioning workers for industrial life. Emerson assigned a major role to standardization in the efficiency principles which he established as guides for management. Cooke applied the concept of standardization to public administration.[18]

To some degree the area of management is concerned with the system of rewards in industry. Taylor, Barnard, and McGregor all spoke to concepts of rewards and incentives. Karl Marx characterized piece rates as the form of wages most in harmony with the capitalistic mode of production.[19] Incentive systems are recorded as having been used as early as 400 B.C. by the Chaldeans and probably by the Romans in the first century A.D.

Henri Fayol was a successful French industrialist who developed some universal generalizations about management.[20] Colonel L. Ur-

[16] See David R. Hampton, Charles E. Summer, and Ross A. Webber, eds., *Organizational Behavior and the Practice of Management*.

[17] McGregor, *op. cit.*, 62.

[18] Scott, *op. cit.*, 27.

[19] Karl Marx, *Capital*, 608.

[20] Henri Fayol, *General and Industrial Management*.

wick, a well-known British management expert, is an exponent of the "traditional principles" of management.[21]

A contemporary of Barnard was Herbert A. Simon.[22] Barnard greatly influenced Simon in the latter's organization theory. Simon incorporated some of the findings of small-group research into his theory. He emphasized the rational features of decision making, as opposed to the stress on emotions from human relations research. He also emphasized the consequences of intended rationality rather than unconscious motivation.

Daniel Bell severely criticized Mayo's and Roethlisberger's human relations movement. Bell's individualistic cast of mind was repelled by Mayo's "sense of belonging." He saw the social skills Mayo advocated as merely a means of manipulating employees so that managers might continue to devote their efforts to the old game of money and power. His fundamental point was that "the goals of production are taken as 'given' and that the worker is to be 'adjusted' to his job so that the human equation matches the industrial equation."[23]

Frederick Herzberg held a management point of view similar to McGregor's. He felt that the most important source of job satisfaction was the sense of achievement or accomplishment. He felt that the Mayo human relations approach, at its best, "can do no more than remove sources of dissatisfaction. If a manager is really to motivate his subordinates, he must look to factors in the job itself."[24]

Elton Mayo's and Fritz Roethlisberger's human relations approach, sound as it appears, did not work too well in a great many cases. It may be that the approach was too narrow or improperly applied by other theorists. The employee satisfactions that the Hawthorne group identified are important, but they appear to be wanting. Some writers believe that Mayo's approach was misinterpreted by his advocates and that this may have been the reason for several major failures. Supporters of Mayo say that the "faulty practitioners" of the human relations approach fail to implement five steps: (1) take a personal interest in their men; (2) provide the worker with information about his job and his company; (3) recognize the status of the individual; (4) listen to what the worker has to say; and (5) give the worker a sense of participation.

Critics of Mayo add that these five steps failed to go far enough to make any important difference: "You have to think and act in terms of introducing significant changes into such critical areas as managerial

[21] Haynes and Massive, op. cit., 48.
[22] Herbert A. Simon, The New Science of Management Decision.
[23] Dale, op. cit., 145.
[24] Ibid., 305.

decision making, the organization of technology, and the structure of the organization itself."[25]

Another criticism of the Hawthorne approach was that it omitted an important source of job satisfaction: the sense of achievement.

One criticism of Taylor's "mental revolution" is that it never happened as he predicted. Although the criticism is valid, in some ways Taylor's system did produce a revolution in management thinking that led to greater productivity. Managers were helped to see the need for more careful preplanning of work and the benefits of systematic study rather than chance inspiration. Today few humanistic writers agree with Taylor's basic assumption that the fundamental motivating force for the "economic man" is the chance to earn more money.

Barnard was considered the first person to depart from the classical approach to management. He spoke from experience and not from an "ivory tower" university setting. One focal point in Barnard's "stratification" scheme is the idea that the greater the stratification the less change is possible in an organization. Those at the top of the hierarchy, the ones with the most rewards, are likely to be the most affected by any change, and so they tend to support the status quo. However, if the people at the top decide that change is needed, it comes more quickly in a highly structured organization than in one which is relatively unstructured.

McGregor's Theory Y stresses the importance of commitment— commitment to organizational objectives and individual objectives. The real crux of the matter for management is to instill commitment in its employees. A limiting factor in instilling commitment is that it must be earned and cannot be commanded. Theory Y provides a functional way to achieve commitment. Although he cannot force commitment, a manager can provide good examples of management that might spark commitment. Another criticism of McGregor's humanistic approach is the pragmatic aspect of Theory X. It works on a short-term basis, whereas Theory Y tends to take longer to accomplish. The military, for example, could not function effectively by either Theory X or Theory Y —it employs some aspects of both, depending upon the situation.

DATA COLLECTION FEEDBACK

Data collection feedback is an important aspect of management. The criteria for useful, humanistically oriented feedback are excellent guidelines for the process. Data collection feedback can be defined as the process by which observable facts, after having been effectively collected and analyzed, are fed back to the system (individual, group, organization, system of organizations) by a disinterested (in the ob-

[25] *Ibid.*, 304.

jective sense) observer in a way that facilitates the health and well-being of the system.

The feedback process is an integral part of the organizational process. Whatever the formal structure of the organization, the adaptive behavior of the employees has a cumulative effect. It feeds back into the formal organization and reinforces itself. The feedback process exists where the adaptive mechanisms become self-maintaining. How this behavior manifests itself in terms of activity by the employees is dependent upon manager-worker relationships and the complexity of organizational structure.

The characteristics of helpful feedback can be summarized as follows:

1. It is descriptive rather than evaluative.
2. It is specific rather than general.
3. It takes into account the needs of the receiver and of the giver.
4. It is directed toward behavior about which the receiver can do something.
5. It is solicited rather than imposed.
6. It is well timed.
7. It is checked to ensure clear communication.

Chris Argyris, Robert R. Blake, Jane S. Mouton, and Matthew Miles are four experts in this area of interest. Each has contributed to the development of a human relations orientation for the process of data collection feedback. For a broader view of feedback as it relates to organization development, see Chapter 12.

CHRIS ARGYRIS (1923–)

Chris Argyris developed the concepts "interpersonal competence" and "competence acquisition" activities. He defined interpersonal competence as the ability to cope effectively with interpersonal relationships. Competence acquisition is a learning process, applied in organizational settings, in which the intent is to provide the participants with opportunities to diagnose and increase their interpersonal competence.[26]

Information and feedback are essential in Argyris' organization consultant activities. He noted that information can be helpful in creating behavioral change if it meets two requirements: it must be directly verifiable and it must be minimally evaluative. Directly verifiable information used in the learning situation is composed of mutually agreed upon categories. The greater the dependence of the indi-

[26] Robert Golembiewski and Arthur Blumberg, eds., *Sensitivity Training and the Laboratory Approach*, 221.

viduals on the conceptual scheme, the more they must verify the information they are using. Information, therefore, should be as far as possible directly verifiable and remain as close as possible to observable data.[27]

The second major characteristic of helpful information is that it should be minimally evaluative of the recipient's behavior. Such information describes behavior without labeling it "good" or "bad." This is important for two reasons. First, such information reduces the probability of making the receiver defensive, thereby creating conditions favorable to an increase in accurate listening. Second, minimally evaluative information places the responsibility for evaluation, if there is to be any, on the individual trying to learn about himself.

A third major characteristic of helpful information is that its meaning should be consistent. Information that contains contradictory messages will tend to decrease the effectiveness of interpersonal relations. Communication should, Argyris noted, be two-way, between consultant and client and between client and consultant. The feedback thus derived provides a way to increase meaningfulness of research to the clients and to the consultant. While feedback may be threatening at times to both parties, it also provides a substantive basis for an effective relationship. This relationship, if nurtured properly, may also become the basis for effective communications between the worker and management or between management and the organizational hierarchy.

It is important also to note the distinction between feedback and "feed-upon." The latter is a negative, often manipulative form of feedback which blocks communication instead of facilitating it. Argyris made this distinction to indicate the complexity of communication. Complexity, he concluded, must be respected, but we can never be completely certain what criteria are relevant to the communication patterns in an organization. At any rate, the attitudes of the individual workers comprise the substance of change in the total system, and their impact cannot be minimized. Management and the functional hierarchy must be made aware of the importance of such data collection feedback in terms of their organizational development and intra-communications.

The aforementioned characteristics describe what Argyris refers to as competence-oriented feedback (minimally distorted, directly verifiable, and minimally evaluative). This kind of feedback is to be distinguished from survival-oriented feedback, which tends to be highly distorted, difficult to verify, and highly evaluative.[28]

The giving and receiving of competence-oriented feedback depends

[27] Chris Argyris, *Intervention Theory and Method*, 110.
[28] Golembiewski and Blumberg, *op. cit.*, 242.

partly upon self-awareness and self-acceptance, and finally these factors depend upon helpful feedback. The giving and receiving of helpful feedback is essential in competence acquisition activities.

With respect to intervention activities—games, questionnaires, and so on—Argyris stated that valid interventions are necessary for the client to learn and for the consultant to help. Argyris defines valid intervention as that which describes the factors, plus their interrelationships, that create the problem for the client system. There are several tests possible to check the validity of interventions: public verifiability, valid prediction, and control over the phenomena.[29]

It is important that the consultant obtain minimally distorted information, that is, information which closely approximates reality. Minimal distortion involves acceptance, trust, and an awareness of one individual's effect upon others—ultimately, an awareness of self. Further, minimal distortion relies on verifiable information. Information can be divided into two kinds: observable and inferred. To put this theory into an organization perspective: if a consultant were to tell a manager that the primary problem of the organization is communication, this would be inferred information, since the manager is not aware of the consultant's frame of reference. It would set up a dependency relationship and would inhibit confidence and trust. Therefore, to achieve effective competence, observable information is preferred. The client-manager must be trained to perceive effect, to observe information as it is given and received, and to be aware of self in order to clarify what is actually occurring. In addition to obtaining minimally distorted information, the consultant needs to obtain as much data as possible that can become the basis for change and increased competence on the part of the client in problem solving.[30]

Argyris stresses the importance of Maslow's notion of self-actualization as a product of good feedback in organizational behavior. His approach is essentially that of an observer, utilizing diagnostic procedures to analyze his findings. These procedures include a semi-structured research interview, a participant-observer, and a non-participant role for himself in conducting his interviews and "check questions" to test the validity of certain statements made by the employees during the course of the interviews. A difficult problem for the consultant to overcome is the attitude of many of the clients toward him. The clients' attitudes toward the consultant invariably influence the data they will provide, so that there is something of a Hawthorne effect in the compilation of research data.

The potency of predisposition is only one variable in collecting re-

[29] Argyris, *op. cit.*, 17.
[30] *Ibid.*, 110.

search data for effective organizational feedback. Many implied as well as many obvious factors are also connected with the interview process. For one thing, to obtain a clear understanding of the interviewees' attitudes, the researcher must be aware of the questions which the research questionnaire does *not* ask and which the interview might not reveal.

Research involved in such data collection may take many forms. For example, the diagnostic procedures outlined above may be supplemented by small-group interaction involving the presence of a human relations "trainer." Whereas the survey feedback process is essentially objective in nature, human relations training is often highly subjective. Process analysis is an important function of this procedure, with clarification and positive feedback the mainstays of effective communication.

MATTHEW B. MILES (1926–)

Matthew B. Miles's contribution to this area centers around his survey feedback method of consultation. Survey feedback is defined as "a process in which outside staff and members of the organization collaboratively gather, analyze and interpret data that deal with various aspects of the organization's functioning and its members' work lives, and, using the data as a base, begin to correctively alter the organization structure and the members' work relationships."[31]

The process aspect of this method is more important than the precision of the data. Client involvement is characteristic of this intervention method. From the beginning, the client system is involved in the data collection activities, not only in the data collection, but also in the formulation of survey questions.

After objective data are collected within an organization, they are analyzed and summarized and fed back to the organization. Survey feedback takes place through an interlocking set of conferences. Through the examination of the data, plans of action are formulated in response to the problems revealed by the data. Presenting the data may have the following three effects: the data may corroborate the client's feelings; they may have a disconfirming effect if they contradict beliefs; and they may have further inquiry effects. The discussion may lead to related problems not dealt with directly in the data.

Miles suggests that there are certain characteristics necessary for feedback to be helpful for learning: the feedback must be clear and undistorted; it should come from a trusted, nonthreatening source; and it should follow as closely as possible the behavior to which it is a

[31] Warren G. Bennis, Kenneth D. Benne, and Robert Chin, eds., *The Planning of Change*, 408.

reaction.[32] With quick, accurate, trusted evidence, the learner can proceed to correct his behavior effectively. Miles suggests three broad methods of gathering data: observation, interviewing, and paper-and-pencil techniques. Direct observation of behavior is too often unsystematic and recorded carelessly. All the usual limitations of biased, selective perception usually apply. To be worthwhile, observation must be guided and supported by some sort of paper-and-pencil recording method, such as a checklist or rating sheet. Observational data are only as good as the recording procedure. Standardized performance tests can be useful for direct observation.

Interviewing probably provides the most complete and practical data. Interviews can elicit systematic responses to a preplanned set of questions and are also vastly more flexible than any prestructured questionnaire. But when conducting an interview, the consultant must devise some kind of systematic interview guide. As with observation, an adequate recording method is essential. The interview method may be applied individually or in groups. However, group interviewing may bias the answers since the individuals may be influenced by what the other group members say.

Paper-and-pencil techniques can be administered individually or in a group. The data are recorded directly by the client in this method; consequently, such techniques allow for anonymity or confidentiality if desired. There are five basic types of paper-and-pencil techniques: open-end, questionnaire, rating, sociometric, and projective methods.

ROBERT R. BLAKE (1918–) AND JANE S. MOUTON (1930–)

The most significant contribution of Robert R. Blake and Jane S. Mouton to improving human relations within formal organizations is the management tool called the Managerial Grid®.[33] ' The two variables studied in the Grid approach are concern for *production* and concern for *people*. Feedback is given to the managers so that they can ascertain where they stand in terms of their concerns for people and production and how these concerns influence each other.

The Managerial Grid approach involves forms of analysis in which each individual involved can assess his managerial style. The investigation includes self-evaluating instruments, self-administered learning quizzes, in-basket procedures, and organizational simulations. An evaluation of team effectiveness is made, along with a diagnosis of major organization problem areas. This approach to organization de-

[32] Matthew B. Miles, ed., *Learning to Work in Groups*, 43.
[33] Robert R. Blake and Jane S. Mouton, *Building A Dynamic Corporation Through Grid Organization Development*.

velopment is self-administered by management except for occasional consultation.

The Grid (illustrated in Figure 1) is explained as follows:

9, 1: Supervisor places heavy emphasis upon getting the job of the organization done. He is pessimistic about his subordinates, and he believes in control and relies heavily upon formal authority.

1, 9: Supervisor's style suggests a state of bliss and happiness. He relies heavily on personal diplomacy and hopes to obtain compliance because he is a nice guy and his subordinates owe it to him to do the job.

1, 1: Supervisor has low concern for achievement of organizational goals combined with low concern for human relationships.

5, 5: Supervisor is middle-of-the-road in both areas of concern above. He believes that emphasis on organizational goals and on the

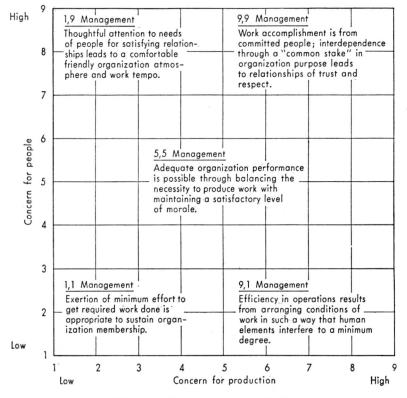

Figure 1. The Managerial Grid®

SOURCE: *The Managerial Grid*, p. 10, by Dr. Robert R. Blake and Dr. Jane S. Mouton. Copyright © 1964 by Gulf Publishing Company, Houston, Texas. Used by permission.

welfare of the workers are equally important, and he works to maintain a balance between the two.

9, 9: Supervisor attempts to get the work accomplished from committed people who are interdependent through a common stake in the relationships among the organization's purposes, a climate of trust, and a climate of request.

Throughout the Grid model, information is collected and fed back to the clients, who are continually involved in all aspects of the process. The analysis of the data provides the impetus for change.

In summary, the Blake and Mouton Managerial Grid offers a perspective for understanding and assessment. The Grid allows a visual portrayal of any person in a management role in relation to his concern for people and for production. It enables comprehension and analysis of the inaction of these two concerns. In each facet of the Managerial Grid, behavioral science information and approaches dominate. Methods of team development, confrontation meetings, and intergroup conflict are introduced after educational (Grid) input.

In the final stage the model method is introduced. The model is designed by the organization itself after the assessment with behavioral science methodology, and it is believed to be the best model to maximize the use of resources in redesigning the culture of the organization.

OTHER THEORISTS

Ralph White and Ronald Lippitt adhere to the philosophy that Miles uses in his survey-feedback method.[34] Motivational forces for change operating from within the organization are preferable to induced motivation.

Richard Beckhard developed the "confrontation meeting" as a technique to allow a top management team to assess its state of health in a very short amount of time.[35] Data collection and sharing are essential in his process. This technique is similar to Blake and Mouton's Management Grid in some aspects.

John Mann also uses the survey-feedback method of organizational change; his theory is complementary to Miles's theory. Roy M. Whitman emphasizes the importance of feedback as a learning process in T-groups.[36] He extends the idea of feedback to include not only the understanding of the information but also the utilization of the feedback to create a new thought or insight.

[34] Ralph White and Ronald Lippitt, *Autocracy and Democracy: An Experimental Inquiry.*

[35] Richard Beckhard, *Organization Development: Strategies and Models.*

[36] Roy M. Whitman, "Psychodynamic Principles Underlying T-Group Processes," in *T-Group Theory and Laboratory Method* (ed. by Leland P. Bradford et al.), 310–35.

Organizational Socialization and the Profession of Management[37]

EDGAR H. SCHEIN

Some basic elements of organizational socialization. *The term social-ization has a fairly clear meaning in sociology, but it has been a difficult one to assimilate in the behavioral sciences and in management. To many of my colleagues it implies unnecessary jargon, and to many of my business acquaintances it implies the teaching of socialism—a kiss of death for the concept right there. Yet the concept is most useful because it focuses clearly on the interaction between a stable social system and the new members who enter it. The concept refers to the process by which a new member learns the value system, the norms, and the required behavior patterns of the society, organization, or group which he is entering. It does not include all learning. It includes only the learning of those values, norms, and behavior patterns which, from the organization's point of view or group's point of view, it is necessary for any new member to learn. This learning is defined as the price of membership.*

What are such values, norms, and behavior patterns all about? Usually they involve:

1. The basic goals *of the organization.*

2. The preferred means *by which these goals should be attained.*

3. The basic responsibilities *of the member in the role which is being granted to him by the organization.*

4. The behavior patterns *which are required for effective perform-ance in the role.*

5. A set of rules or principles *which pertain to the* maintenance of the identity and integrity *of the organization.*

The new member must learn not to drive Chevrolets if he is working for Ford, not to criticize the organization in public, not to wear the wrong kind of clothes or be seen in the wrong kind of places. If the organization is a school, beyond learning the content of what is taught, the student must accept the value of education, he must try to learn without cheating, he must accept the authority of the faculty and be-have appropriately to the student role. He must not be rude in the classroom or openly disrespectful to the professor.

By what processes does the novice learn the required values and norms? The answer to this question depends in part upon the degree of prior socialization. If the novice has correctly anticipated the norms

---

[37] By Edgar H. Schein. Reprinted from *Industrial Management Review*, Winter, 1968, by permission of the Industrial Management Review Association.

*of the organization he is joining, the socialization process merely in-
volves a reaffirmation of these norms through various communication
channels, the personal example of key people in the organization, and
direct instructions from supervisors, trainers, and informal coaches.*

*If however, the novice comes to the organization with values and
behavior patterns which are in varying degrees out of line with those
expected by the organization, then the socialization process first involves a destructive or unfreezing phase. This phase serves the function
of detaching the person from his former values, of proving to him that
his present self is worthless from the point of view of the organization
and that he must redefine himself in terms of the new roles which he is
to be granted.*

*The extremes of this process can be seen in initiation rites or novi-
tiates for religious orders. When the novice enters his training period,
his old self is symbolically destroyed by loss of clothing, name, often
his hair, titles and other self-defining equipment. These are replaced
with uniforms, new names, and titles, and other self-defining equipment consonant with the role he is being trained for.*

*It may be comforting to think of activities like this as being charac-
teristic only of primitive tribes or total institutions like military basic
training camps, academies, and religious orders. But even a little
examination of areas closer to home will reveal the same processes both
in our graduate schools and in the business organizations to which our
graduates go.*

*Perhaps the commonest version of the process in school is the im-
position of a tight schedule, of an impossibly heavy reading program,
and of the assignment of problems which are likely to be too difficult
for the student to solve. Whether these techniques are deliberate or not
they serve effectively to remind the student that he is not as smart or
capable as he may have thought he was, and therefore, that there are
still things to be learned. As our Sloan Fellows tell us every year, the
first summer in the program pretty well destroys many aspects of their
self-image. Homework in statistics appears to enjoy a unique status
comparable to having one's head shaved and clothes burned.*

*Studies of medical schools and our own observations of the Sloan
program suggest that the work overload on students leads to the development of a peer culture, a kind of banding together of the students
as a defense against the threatening faculty and as a problem-solving
device to develop norms of what and how to study. If the group solutions which are developed support the organizational norms, the peer
group becomes an effective instrument of socialization. However, from
the school's point of view, there is the risk that peer group norms will
set up counter-socializing forces and sow the seeds of sabotage, re-*

*bellion, revolution. The positive gains of a supportive peer group gen-
erally make it worth while to run the risks of rebellion, however, which
usually motivates the organization to encourage or actually to facilitate
peer group formation.*

    *Many of our Sloan Fellow alumni tell us that one of the most power-
ful features of the Sloan program is the fact that a group of some 40
men share the same fate of being put through a very tough educational
regimen. The peer group ties formed during the year have proven to
be one of the most durable end-results of the educational program and,
of course, are one of the key supports to the maintaining of some of the
values and attitudes learned in school. The power of this kind of social-
ising force can be appreciated best by pondering a further statement
which many alumni have made. They stated that prior to the program
they identified themselves primarily with their company. Following
the program they identified themselves primarily with the other Sloan
Fellows, and such identification has lasted, as far as we can tell, for the
rest of their career.*

    *Let me next illustrate the industrial counterpart of these processes.
Many of my panel members, when interviewed about the first six
months in their new jobs, told stories of what we finally labeled as
"upending experiences." Upending experiences are deliberately
planned or accidentally created circumstances which dramatically and
unequivocally upset or disconfirm some of the major assumptions
which the new man holds about himself, his company, or his job.*

    *One class of such experiences is to receive assignments which are so
easy or so trivial that they carry the clear message that the new man
is not worthy is being given anything important to do. Another class of
such experiences is at the other extreme—assignments which are so
difficult that failure is a certainty, thus proving unequivocally to the
new man that he may not be as smart as he thought he was. Giving
work which is clearly for practice only, asking for reports which are
then unread or not acted upon, protracted periods of training during
which the person observes others work, all have the same upending
effect.*

    *The most vivid example came from an engineering company where
a supervisor had a conscious and deliberate strategy for dealing with
what he considered to be unwarranted arrogance on the part of engi-
neers whom they hired. He asked each new man to examine and
diagnose a particular complex circuit, which happened to violate a
number of textbook principles but actually worked very well. The new
man would usually announce with confidence, even after an invitation
to double-check, that the circuit could not possibly work. At this point
the manager would demonstrate the circuit, tell the new man that they*

had been selling it for several years without customer complaint, and demand that the new man figure out why it did work. None of the men so far tested were able to do it, but all of them were thoroughly chastened and came to the manager anxious to learn where their knowledge was inadequate and needed supplementing. According to this manager, it was much easier from this point on to establish a good give-and-take relationship with his new man.

It should be noted that the success of such socializing techniques depends upon two factors which are not always under the control of the organization. The first factor is the initial motivation of the entrant to join the organization. If his motivation is high, as in the case of a fraternity pledge, he will tolerate all kinds of uncomfortable socialization experiences, even to extremes of hell week. If his motivation for membership is low, he may well decide to leave the organization rather than tolerate uncomfortable initiation rites. If he leaves, the socialization process has obviously failed.

The second factor is the degree to which the organization can hold the new member captive during the period of socialization. His motivation is obviously one element here, but one finds organizations using other forces as well. In the case of basic training there are legal forces to remain. In the case of many schools one must pay one's tuition in advance, in other words, invest one's self materially so that leaving the system becomes expensive. In the case of religious orders one must make strong initial psychological commitments in the form of vows and the severing of relationships outside the religious order. The situation is defined as one in which one will lose face or be humiliated if one leaves the organization.

In the case of business organizations the pressures are more subtle but nevertheless identifiable. New members are encouraged to get financially committed by joining pension plans, stock option plans, and/ or house purchasing plans which would mean material loss if the person decided to leave. Even more subtle is the reminder by the boss that it takes a year or so to learn any new business; therefore, if you leave, you will have to start all over again. Why not suffer it out with the hope that things will look more rosy once the initiation period is over.

Let us summarize thus far. Organizations socialize their new members by creating a series of events which serve the function of undoing old values so that the person will be prepared to learn the new values. This process of undoing or unfreezing is often unpleasant and therefore requires either strong motivation to endure it. The formation of a peer group of novices is often a solution to the problem of defense against the powerful organization, and, at the same time, can strongly *enhance the socialization process if peer group norms support organizational norms.*

Let us look next at the positive side of the socialization process. Given some readiness to learn, how does the novice acquire his new learning? The answer is that he acquires it from multiple sources—the official literature of the organization; the example set by key models in the organization; the instructions given to him directly by his trainer, coach, or boss; the example of peers who have been in the organization longer and thus serve as big brothers; the rewards and punishments which result from his own efforts at problem solving and experimenting with new values and new behavior. . . .

Of course, sometimes the values of the immediate group into which a new person is hired are partially out of line with the value system of the organization as a whole. If this is the case, the person will learn the immediate group's values much more quickly than those of the total organization, often to the chagrin of the higher levels of management. This is best exemplified at the level of hourly workers where fellow employees will have much more socializing power than the boss.

An interesting managerial example of this conflict was provided by one recent graduate who was hired into a group whose purpose was to develop cost reduction systems for a large manufacturing operation. His colleagues on the job, however, showed him how to pad his expense account whenever they traveled together. The end result of this kind of conflict was to accept neither the cost reduction values of the company nor the cost inflation values of the peer group. The man left the company in disgust to start up some businesses of his own.

One of the important functions of organizational socialization is to build commitment and loyalty to the organization. How is this accomplished? One mechanism is to invest much effort and time in the new member and thereby build up expectations of being repaid by loyalty, hard work, and rapid learning. Another mechanism is to get the new member to make a series of small behavioral commitments which can only be justified by him through the acceptance and incorporation of company values. He then becomes his own agent of socialization. Both mechanisms involve the subtle manipulation of guilt.

To illustrate the first mechanism, one of our graduates went to a public relations firm which made it clear to him that he had sufficient knowledge and skill to advance, but that his values and attitudes would have to be evaluated for a couple of years before he would be fully accepted. During the first several months he was frequently invited to join high ranking members of the organization at their luncheon meetings in order to learn more and how they thought about things. He was so flattered by the amount of time they spent on him, that he worked extra hard to learn their values and became highly committed to the organization. He said that he would have felt guilty at the thought of not learning or of leaving the company. Sending people to expensive training programs, giving them extra perquisites, indeed the whole philosophy of paternalism, is built on the assumption that if you invest in the employee he will repay the company with loyalty and hard work. He would feel guilty if he did not.

The second mechanism, that of getting behavioral commitments, was beautifully illustrated in Communist techniques of coercive persuasion. The Communists made tremendous efforts to elicit a public confession from a prisoner. One of the key functions of such a public confession, was that it committed him publicly. Once he made the commitment, he found himself under strong internal and external pressure to justify why he had confessed. For many people it proved easier to justify the confession by coming to believe in their own crimes than to have to face the fact that they were too weak to withstand the captor's pressure.

In organizations a similar effect can be achieved by promoting a rebellious person into a position of responsibility. The same values which the new member may have criticized and jeered at from his position at the bottom of the hierarchy suddenly look different when he has subordinates of his own whose commitment he must obtain.

Many of my panel members had very strong moral and ethical standards when they first went to work, and these stood up quite well during their first year at work even in the face of less ethical practices by their peers and superiors. But they reported with considerable shock that some of the practices they had condemned in their bosses were quickly adopted by them once they had themselves been promoted and faced the pressures of the new position. As one man put it very poignantly—"my ethical standards changed so gradually over the first five years of work that I hardly noticed it, but it was a great shock to suddenly realize what my feelings had been five years ago and how much they had changed."

Another version of obtaining commitment is to gain the new member's acceptance of very general ideals like "one must work for the good of the company," or "one must meet the competition." Whenever any counter-organizational behavior occurs one can then point out that the ideal is being violated. The engineer who does not come to work on time is reminded that his behavior indicates lack of concern for the good of the company. The employee who wears the wrong kind of clothes, lives in the wrong neighborhood, or associates with the wrong people can be reminded that he is hurting the company image. . . .

The final mechanism to be noted in a socialization process is the

85

transition to full fledged member. The purpose of such transitional events is to help the new member incorporate his new values, attitudes, and norms into his identity so that they become part of him, not merely something to which he pays lip-service. Initiation rites which involve severe tests of the novice serve to prove to him that he is capable of fulfilling the new role—that he now is a man, no longer merely a boy.

Organizations usually signal this transition by giving the new man some important responsibility or a position of power which, if mishandled or misused, could genuinely hurt the organization. With this transition often come titles, symbols of status, extra rights or prerogatives, sharing of confidential information or other things which in one way or another indicate that the new member has earned the trust of the organization. Although such events may not always be visible to the outside observer, they are felt strongly by the new member. He knows when he has finally "been accepted," and feels it when he becomes "identified with the company."

The Function of Leadership[38]
T. R. McCONNEL

Faculty participation in policy formation and university government is here to stay. In colleges and universities—and in business and industry as well—there is a new emphasis on democratic processes. One of the great spokesmen for humane and democratic management was Douglas McGregor, who served as president of Antioch College and also as professor of industrial management at MIT. It was he who wrote:

The motivation, the potential for development, the capacity for assuming responsibility, the readiness to direct behavior toward organizational goals are all present in people. Management does not put them there. It is a responsibility of management to make it possible for people to recognize and develop these human characteristics for themselves.

The essential task of management is to arrange organizational conditions and methods of operation so that people can achieve their own goals best by directing their own efforts toward organizational objectives.[39]

Perhaps among all of the colleges and universities in the United

[38] Condensed from T. R. McConnel, "The Function of Leadership in Academic Institutions," *Educational Record*, Vol. 1 (Spring, 1968). Reprinted by permission of the American Council on Education.

[39] Warren G. Bennis and Edgar H. Schein, eds., *Leadership and Motivation: Essays of Douglas McGregor*, 15.

States, Antioch College is best known for its emphasis on community participation and responsibility. Its administrative committee, which is formally only advisory to the President but which actually exercises a strong influence on institutional policy and operation, has long been composed of administrative officers, faculty members, and students. At Antioch, McGregor found a laboratory in which he could test his theories of democratic management. An Antioch faculty member is reported to have said of him that, "If there was anything he was trying to overcome or destroy, it was the institutional habit of talking about the virtues of democracy while running affairs autocratically."[40]

McGregor nevertheless discovered that administrators must make decisions. Just before his resignation at Antioch took effect, he made the following confession:

Before coming to Antioch I had observed and worked with top executives as an adviser in a number of organizations. I thought I knew how they felt about their responsibilities and what led them to behave as they did. I even thought that I could create a role for myself that would enable me to avoid some of the difficulties they encountered. I was wrong! . . .

I believed, for example, that a leader could operate successfully as a kind of adviser to his organization. I thought I could avoid being a "boss." Unconsciously, I suspect, I hoped to duck the unpleasant necessity of making difficult decisions, of taking the responsibility for one course of action among many uncertain alternatives, of making mistakes and taking the consequences. I thought that maybe I could operate so that everyone would like me—that "good human relations" would eliminate all discord and disagreement. . . .

I could not have been more wrong. It took a couple of years, but I finally began to realize that a leader cannot avoid responsibility for what happens to his organization. In fact, it is a major function of the top executive to take on his own shoulders the responsibility for resolving the uncertainties that are always involved in important decisions. Moreover, since no important decision ever pleases everyone in the organization, he must also absorb the displeasure, and sometimes severe hostility, of those who would have taken a different course.

A colleague recently summed up what my experience has taught me in these words: "A good leader must be tough enough to kick a man when he is down." This notion is not in the least inconsistent with humane, democratic leadership. Good human relations develop out of strength, not of weakness.[41]

[40] *Ibid.*, 56.
[41] *Ibid.*, 67, 68.

College and university administrators should not act without con-
sulting or fully involving those who may be affected or who will have
to carry out a policy or decision in day-to-day operation. Nevertheless,
administrators must act. To do so often requires quiet and unpreten-
tious courage.

Many administrators, whether from lack of courage or failure to
comprehend their roles, do everything possible to avoid making de-
cisions or taking initiative. Hutchins once observed that many admin-
istrators busy themselves with so many activities that they should leave
to subordinates that they have no time to do anything important; they
conscientiously take their salaries and never administer at all. He re-
ferred to these functionaries as mere office holders.[42] *A former vice*
chancellor on one of the University of California campuses has said
that:

At the present time not less than 60 percent of all academics in the
universities in this country have so profound a distaste for the classroom and for the pains of genuine scholarship or creative thought that
they will seize upon anything—curriculum iconography, faculty politics, bureaucratized research, *anything*—to exempt themselves re-
spectably from each.[43]

The same psychological mechanism, if my observation is correct,
characterizes 60 per cent, if not more of all academic administrators.

SUMMARY

The use of data collection and feedback measures to initiate change is
often an effective technique not only for the obvious reason that the
data often show the need for change but also for various nonrational
reasons. The collected data may very well justify and emphasize
needed areas of change; however, the very fact that someone has collected and analyzed data may point out to the clients that change is
necessary, even if the data are not valid.

Such strategies as Miles's survey feedback, which assume that the
data alone will not necessarily accurately identify causes or solutions
but will provide a basis for discussions between the individuals involved, are very useful in initiating change: the data are discussed by
the clients; the clients know immediately what is happening; group
norms are encouraged; and by beginning the process at the top of the
organization, legitimacy is established throughout the system.

[42] Robert M. Hutchins, "The Administrator," *Journal of Higher Education*, Vol. 17
(November, 1946), 395–407.
[43] Robert A. Nisbet, "What Is an Intellectual? *Commentary*, Vol. 40 (December,
1965), 93–101.

The strategies which rely heavily on the data collected must be concerned with the accuracy with which they identify the problems and the case made for alternative solutions. This kind of data-based strategy for initiating change relies heavily on the rationality of the organizational decision makers, for ultimately they are the ones who deal with the data. Data collection and feedback methods are especially applicable in human relations programs which focus on organization development.

The essential premise of the theorists discussed in this chapter is that there are data within human relations activities in business and industry which it is possible to collect. When collected, they may be fed back to concerned persons to clarify their understanding, enhance their knowledge, and provide guidance for problem solving.

Chapter 3
SUGGESTED READING

Adams, Joyce. *Managerial Psychology: Human Behavior in Business and Industry.* North Quincy, Mass., Christopher Publishing House, 1965.

Argyris, Chris. *Executive Leadership.* New York, Harper & Row, Publishers, Inc., 1953.

———. *Intervention Theory and Method: A Behavioral Science View.* Reading, Mass., Addison-Wesley Publishing Co., Inc., 1970.

Barnard, Chester I. *Dilemmas of Leadership in the Democratic Process.* Princeton, Princeton University Extension Fund, 1939.

———. *The Functions of the Executive.* Cambridge, Mass., Harvard University Press, 1938.

Beckhard, Richard. *Organization Development: Strategies and Models.* Reading, Mass., Addison-Wesley Publishing Co., Inc., 1969.

Bennis, Warren G., and Edgar H. Schein, eds. *Leadership and Motivation: Essays of Douglas McGregor.* Cambridge, Mass., M.I.T. Press, 1966.

Bennis, Warren G., Kenneth D. Benne, and Robert Chin, eds. *The Planning of Change.* New York, Holt, Rinehart & Winston, Inc., 1969.

Blake, Robert R., and Jane S. Mouton. *Building a Dynamic Corporation Through Grid Organization Development.* Reading, Mass., Addison-Wesley Publishing Co., Inc., 1969.

———, and ———. *The Managerial Grid: Key Orientations for Achieving Production Through People.* Houston, Tex., Gulf Publishing Co., 1964.

Blau, Peter, and R. Schoenherr. *The Structure of Formal Organizations.* New York, Basic Books Inc., 1971.

Bradford, Leland P., Jack R. Gibb, and Kenneth D. Benne, eds. *T-Group Theory and Laboratory Method.* New York, John Wiley & Sons, Inc., 1964.

Burns, Tom, and G. M. Stalker. *Management of Innovation.* Chicago, Quadrangle BooKs, Inc., 1962.

Caiden, Gerald. *Administrative Reform.* Chicago, Aldine Publishing Co., 1969.

Cartwright, Dorwin, and Alvin Zander, eds. *Group Dynamics: Research and Theory.* New York, Harper & Row, Publishers, Inc., 1960.

Carver, Fred D., and Thomas J. Sergiovanni, eds. *Organizations and Human Behavior: A Focus in Schools.* New York, McGraw-Hill Book Company, 1969.

Cruden, Herbert J., and Arthur W. Sherman, eds. *Personnel Management,* 2d ed. Cincinnati, Ohio, Southwestern Publishing Company, 1963.

Dale, Ernest, ed. *Readings in Management: Landmarks and New Frontiers.* New York, Richard D. Irwin, Inc., 1965.

Dickson, William J., and Fritz J. Roethlisberger. *Counseling in an Organization: A Sequel to the Hawthorne Researches.* Cambridge, Mass., Harvard University Press, 1966.

Dye, Thomas R., and Brett W. Hawkins, eds. *Politics in the Metropolis: A Reader in Conflict and Cooperation.* Columbus, Ohio, Charles E. Merrill Publishing Co., 1967.

Fayol, Henri. *General and Industrial Management.* Translated by Constance Storrs. New York, Pitman Publishing Corp., 1949.

Gardner, B. B. *Human Relations in Industry.* Chicago, Richard D. Irwin, Inc., 1948.

Golembiewski, Robert T., and Arthur Blumberg, eds. *Sensitivity Training and the Laboratory Approach: Readings About Concepts and Applications.* Itasca, Ill., F. E. Peacock Publishers, Inc., 1970.

Hampton, David R., Charles E. Summer, and Ross A. Webber. *Organizational Behavior and the Practice of Management.* New York, Scott, Foresman & Co., 1968.

Haynes, William W., and Joseph L. Massive, eds. *Management: Analysis, Concepts and Cases,* 2nd ed. Englewood Cliffs, N.J., Prentice-Hall, Inc., 1969.

Hunter, Floyd. *Top Leadership, U.S.A.* Chapel Hill, University of North Carolina Press, 1959.

Likert, Rensis. *New Patterns of Management.* New York, McGraw-Hill Book Company, 1961.

Marx, Karl. *Capital.* Translated by Samuel Moore and Edward Aveling. New York, International Publishers, Inc., 1948.

———. *The Communist Manifesto.* Translated by Samuel Moore. Chicago, Henry Regnery, 1954.

Mayo, Elton. *The Human Problems of an Industrial Civilization.* New York, The Macmillan Co., 1933.

McGregor, Douglas. *The Human Side of Enterprise.* New York, McGraw-Hill Book Company, 1960.

———. *Leadership and Motivation.* Cambridge, Mass., M.I.T. Press, 1969.

Miles, Matthew B., ed. *Learning to Work in Groups.* New York, Columbia University Press, 1959.

Roethlisberger, Fritz. *Counseling in an Organization.* Cambridge, Mass., Harvard University Press, 1966.

———, and William J. Dickson. *Management and the Worker.* Cambridge, Mass., Harvard University Press, 1939.

Scott, William G. *Organization Theory: A Behavioral Analysis for Management.* Homewood, Ill., Richard D. Irwin, Inc., 1967.

Simon, Herbert A. *The New Science of Management Decision.* New York, Harper & Row, Publishers, Inc., 1960.

Tannenbaum, Robert, Irving R. Weschler and Fred Massarik, eds. *Leadership and Organization: A Behavioral Science Approach.* New York, McGraw-Hill Book Company, 1961.

Taylor, Frederick W. *The Principles of Scientific Management.* New York, Harper & Brothers Publishers, 1916.

———. *Scientific Management.* New York, Harper & Brothers Publishers, 1947.

———. *Shop Management.* New York, Harper & Brothers Publishers, 1919.

Thompson, Clarence B. *The Theory and Practice of Scientific Management.* New York, Houghton Mifflin Co., 1917.

White, Ralph, and Ronald Lippitt. *Autocracy and Democracy: An Experimental Inquiry.* New York, Harper & Row, Publishers, Inc., 1960.

COMMUNITY CONTROL

The streets of my town are empty then, on Saturdays. It
does not have many people, most of the year. On
Saturday mornings you can see a few gringo children
waiting for the movie to open, and not much else. The
streets are empty, and the gringos sit in the restaurant and
the barber shop and talk about the money they made
or lost on the cotton crop that fall.—DANIEL GARZA

The major contribution of the social sciences to human relations training is found in studies that focus on the power elite. An analysis of the
term *power elite* must assume at least two propositions: (1) that *power*
is understood to be a form of social dominance of one group over
another and (2) that *elite* refers to the most prominent advocates and
possessors of that power. In most instances this power is essentially
political or economic in nature. It involves an implied social stratification, a set of ethics and rules, a hierarchy of authority, a high degree of
bureaucratization in technological societies, and a great propensity for
the perpetuation of established institutions. (By way of definition,
most references to the elite in this book are to the "ruling class," which
is variously defined by the men discussed below. It generally refers to
the holders of economic wealth rather than to those with status, for
reasons which will be discussed subsequently.)

Karl Marx is without question one of the most influential social
scientists of modern times. Among his many interpreters have been
Max Weber, who described in detail the bureaucracies which Marx
listed; C. Wright Mills, who attempted to delineate Marxism for the
modern-day society by continually reevaluating Marxist thinking; and
Floyd Hunter, who provided methods for identifying the power elite
in cities and communities.

KARL H. MARX (1818–83)

Karl Marx was at first a student of Georg Hegel but later was attracted
to the views of Ludwig Feuerbach and Friedrich Engels. Marx's pri-

mary concern was to present an interpretation of the historical trend in social structure. The social and economic system contemporary with his early life was capitalism, which had been furthered by the Industrial Revolution. Marx believed capitalism to be only a temporary phase which would pass away into socialism when the proletariat (the workers) rebelled against exploitation by the heads of industry. He thought that the working classes around the world should become conscious of their common interests and develop an international solidarity that would oppose traditional idealism by substituting an ideology centering in economic determinism and by recognizing the struggle among economic classes. This struggle would be a concrete, practical dialectic and would continue until it developed a classless society in which man was no longer a commodity and wherein the wholeness of each human life might be realized.

Marx sought to understand society well enough to influence and to change it. He was concerned with the social problems of the proletariat. His diagnosis was that misery and alienation engendered class struggle; his prognosis was that this struggle would culminate in revolution; his prescription was a classless society. Marx's approach to planned change was based on the violent aspects of a power-coercive method. The division of labor in the Industrial Revolution had led to the worker's alienation from the objects he produced, from his employer, and from his fellow workers. Marx believed that the cure for alienation lay in economic planning in which all men took part.

Thomas B. Bottomore has sought to explain Marx's ideas about the power elite or the ruling class.[1] Marx said that members of this class have access to the dominant material and are the intellectual forces in society. In other words, the class which controls material goods needed for production also tends to control the human resources needed for production.

Marx's materialist conception stated only that economic relationships are ultimately determining. He believed that the property system—the methods of production and exchange—is derived from the tools man has available in a particular historic epoch. The superstructure, including a man's family, the state, and the law, is in turn derived from these economic conditions. In short, Marx's theory made economics the single most important independent variable in his system.

Marx's power elite was made up of those who owned and controlled the means and processes of production of goods and services in the society. He was committed to a classless society in which political coercion would disappear because there would be no vested private interests to be rationalized and defended. His counterforce in society

[1] Thomas B. Bottomore, ed., *Karl Marx.*

93

was one which would challenge the elite status by educating the working class to a consciousness of their deprivation. Once this consciousness was achieved, a violent overthrow of the power elite would take place. The outcome of the struggle would be victory for those best able to maximize the power of the instruments of production.

Marx was committed to the revolutionary transfer of power because he doubted that the power elite could be re-educated, since re-education would mean loss of privileges and coercive power. Re-educative methods of changing would have to take place only after a change in power allocation. Thus, in essence, Marx's planned change in society could only take place if a counter power was built to offset and reduce the power of the economic elite. The simplistic Marxian view made the person with economic influence the real holder of power.

Marx's perspective on the power elite was best set forth in the opening remarks of his *Communist Manifesto*, written in collaboration with Engels. The title of the first chapter, "Bourgeois and Proletarians," is a key to the entire doctrine of Marxism, for it is built upon the history of class struggles: "By bourgeoisie is meant the class of modern capitalists, owners of the means of social production and employers of wage-labor. By proletariat, the class of modern wage-laborers who, having no means of production of their own, are reduced to selling their labor-power in order to live."[2] Accompanying the rise in power of the bourgeoisie was the industrial-trade movement, which Marx said had increased the capital of the bourgeoisie and made it more and more powerful in many areas, especially in politics. The result was that the bourgeoisie became the power elite of society. The intent of the *Manifesto* was to provide an economic interpretation of history in the context of the struggle between the classes of society. Marx expanded his ideas by describing the consequences of an unchallenged bourgeois production, property, and political structure. He argued that democracy merely substituted "ballots for bullets," ballots which imposed too many limitations on an all-out class struggle. He predicted that socialism was a logical consequence of a class war and would ultimately arrive at forms of communism which had no social classes. Marx offered arguments for the self-destructive tendencies inherent in any other form of government than "sociocommunism."

Warren Bennis, Robert Chin, and Kenneth Benne have offered a theory of the changing power elite which is relevant at this juncture. They note that, while Marx was not the first person to consider the idea of a ruling class, he made a unique contribution: "What was original with him was his way of relating these concepts to a process

[2] Karl Marx, *The Communist Manifesto*, 13.

94

and strategy of fundamental social change."[3] Marx, being a proponent of a classless society, advanced the theory that the workers of the world could overcome the power of the bourgeoisie, or ruling class. Bennis, Benne, and Chin call Marx's strategy of social change "power-coercive." It is essentially a strategy of determining the basic ingredients to bring about a desired change.

In answer to the question whether Marxist ideology is applicable today in our complex social systems, a few examples can be cited. In the United States, Marxism is associated with several organizations which have in recent times appeared in newspaper headlines: "The Black Panthers in America call themselves Marxist-Leninists"; "The students of the Free Speech Movement call upon Marx, Lenin, Guevara, and Mao."[4] Many other groups are committed to the Marxist strategy that power-coercive methods must be used to facilitate a change, after which more democratic processes may be incorporated.

Earlier political philosophers had seen power as related to the government and the organizations within it. Marx broke new ground in proposing that power originates primarily in economic production, that economic production influences all aspects of society, that the main wielders of social power are social classes, and that government is essentially a servant of the dominant social class. Marx took the concept of power away from the political realm and developed a theory of social process and social development based on the exercise of power. He adopted the fundamental postulate that all Western societies rest on a foundation of economic production. Within a society's dominant mode of production the "forces of production," the technological and physical aspects of economic activity, are important in determining how effectively surplus resources, or wealth, can be produced. But economic technology does not determine how these resources will be used and distributed in society. Especially crucial for social organization, therefore, is a second aspect of the economy, which Marx called the "social relations of production." Whoever controls the dominant mode of economic production in a society will determine how the existing technology will be utilized and how the resulting resources will be distributed, with the consequence that these persons will exercise power throughout the total society.[5]

Man, in Marx's image of him, is essentially a producing animal who has his historical being primarily in the realm of material production.

[3] Warren G. Bennis, Kenneth D. Benne, and Robert Chin, *The Planning of Change*, 55.

[4] Jean-François Revel, *Without Marx or Jesus: The New American Revolution Has Begun*, 216.

[5] Irving L. Horowitz, ed., *Power, Politics and People*, 71.

The growth process of the human species is in substance a process of man's production of the world of material objects that surrounds him. And history being chiefly a production process, human society itself is basically a society of production—a set of social relations that men enter in their productivity activity. Marx called these social relations of production the "basis" of society. All other institutions and forms of consciousness, including political institutions and political consciousness, he relegated to the social "superstructure" arising over this foundation:

Marx's theory goes on to assert that the human society of production has been deeply divided throughout recorded history. The social relations of production have been in many different forms of a "social division of labor" between a minority class of nonproducing owners of the means of production and a majority class of nonowning producers. Every social system based on the division of labor is necessarily, moreover, a conflictual system. The social division of labor is not simply a division but an antagonism, and class-divided society is society in conflict. What makes it so, according to Marx, is a rebelliousness of man as producer against his life-conditions in societies of production based on division of labor. The rebelliousness is explained by the inability of man as producer to develop his productive powers freely and to the full within any given social division of labor.[6]

Thus bourgeois man could not develop the new capitalist productive powers freely within the division of labor between lords and serfs and the feudal system of landed property. In modern times, in Marx's view, the proletarian man is increasingly restive because of his inability to develop freely the productive powers of modern machine industry.

Generalizing, we may say that, for classical Marxism, the rebelliousness of man as producer is a constant historical tendency which periodically rises to a peak of intensity, bursts out in a revolutionary upheaval, and then subsides—but not for long—with the resulting transformation of society. The envisaged destination of the historical process is a classless society, in which the social relations of production will no longer take the form of division of labor, and hence will not become again a fetter upon man's powers of production.[7]

Marx believed that dialectic change is never inevitable but that when major social changes do occur they tend to follow the dialectic process. Since the component sectors of a society are in continual conflict for control over the means of economic production (and, in turn, power and wealth), all societies contain within themselves potential

[6] Robert C. Tucker, *The Marxian Revolutionary Idea*, 61.
[7] *Ibid.*

seeds of change. The process of change is contingent on many factors, including the amount of control the ruling elites exercise over the rest of the society, the degree of organization existing among the nonelites, and the effectiveness of the leaders advocating social change.

Another of Marx's concepts was that of conflicting social classes. His thesis consisted of a definition of social classes, an analysis of the nature of capitalism, and an argument for class conflict and revolution. Marx defined a social class as a population of people within a society who stand in a common relation to the major means of economic production and who therefore exercise similar amounts of power in society and are in continual conflict with other classes.

Marx analyzed the capitalistic economic system in depth to discover why it produced the extreme exploitation of workers he observed in all industrialized societies. He concluded that dialectic social change would end only if social classes were completetly abolished and radically new kinds of societies were established.

The state, a key element in the social superstructure, is functionally defined by Marx (and Engels) in this theoretical context. The state institutionalizes the conflict situation in societies founded on division of labor in production and so is "simply the official form of the antagonism in civil society."[8] The state, according to this view, is an instrument for waging the class struggle *from above*. The "possessing class," as the beneficiary of an existing social order of production, will necessarily resist all efforts of the "producer class" to transform society. In doing so, it will freely make use of organized coercion. To curb the ever-rebellious producers and to protect the social order from the danger of overthrow, the state will use the police, the prisons, the standing army, the courts, and other organs. Marx saw the state as a weapon of class conflict, and thus in "classical Marxism" the state is seen as fundamentally a repressive force. Therefore, the weapon that is the state, in the hands of the economically dominant class, is employed to prevent the underlying antagonism in the society from exploding into revolutionary violence.

The Marxist view of the state is governed by an underlying assumption about society:

The repressive function that is assigned to state power arises logically out of the imperative needs of society as a conflictual system whose very persistence is always at stake. The state is the supreme defense mechanism of a threatened social structure, and a mechanism that is regularly having to be used, violently, because the internal threat to the system ... is continually manifesting itself in violent ways.[9]

[8] *Ibid.*, 62.
[9] *Ibid.*

Marx held that when class struggles grow in intensity they become political struggles. The possessing class is ready to call out the police or the army on the slightest provocation from the producers. By the same token the producers cannot fight their class struggles without pitting themselves against the existing state. Since the state is the social structure's defense mechanism, the producers cannot revolutionize the social order without overthrowing the state and taking political power —they cannot transform the social foundation without tearing down the old political superstructure. In Marxist political theory all social revolutions necessitate political revolutions.

Thus, struggles between government and its opponents are manifestations of class conflict. Marx wrote that "all struggles within the state, the struggle between democracy, aristocracy and monarchy, the struggle for the franchise, etc., are merely the illusory forms in which the real struggles of the different classes are fought out among one another."[10] Marx concluded that, before the proletariat could take action to alter its social condition, it must develop class-consciousness and class organization. He also maintained that if the proletariat was ever to wrest control of the means of production from the bourgeoisie it must do so through violent class conflict—total revolution.

Marx believed that eventually a truly classless society could be achieved, a society in which there would be no economic exploitation. Individual and collective social responsibility, not power and exploitation, would form the basis of organized social life.

MAX WEBER (1864–1920)

Max Weber is a monumental figure in the social sciences. A German political economist and sociologist, he was the founder of a mode of thought which C. Wright Mills later espoused.[11] Weber believed that the historical materialism of his day was one-sided, neglecting the interplay of economic forces with political, military, social, and psychological pressures. Weber attempted a synthesis of these factors. His effort to distinguish the character of social relationships has been particularly influential. He argued that the social relationship was the basic unit of society.[12]

The best known of Weber's writings are his studies in the sociology of religion. In *The Protestant Ethic and the Spirit of Capitalism*, Weber demonstrated the relationship of organized Protestantism to the development of capitalism. He argued that capitalism requires a particular kind of psychology in which people are willing not only to work

10 *Ibid.*, 65.
11 Seymour M. Miller, *Max Weber*, 9.
12 *Ibid.*, 10.

hard but also to innovate, to save the funds they have acquired, and to reinvest them in business enterprise. Protestantism was seen not as alone producing capitalism but rather as producing the necessary motivation so that the new economic form could emerge.

Weber's conceptualization of social stratification was the result of starting with a Marxian premise in a larger framework and adding political and social dimensions. Weber saw stratification as broader than the purely economic process. A status dimension was important over and above the economic "class" basis of stratification in society (which he saw as the workers' inability to compete successfully in the market with the capitalists). His status dimension brought about his discussion of the nouveau riche pattern, which he characterized as a group attempting to adopt a behavioral mode which the new rich hoped would win them high social position.

The political or power realm forms a third dimension of the stratification system. Power, as viewed by Weber, is the chance of an individual or of a number of persons to realize their own will in a society even against the resistance of others who participate in the action. While economic power is predominant in capitalist society, it is not the exclusive source of power. Weber believed the state, a legitimated organization which monopolizes military power and pursues national objectives, is the single most powerful bureaucracy. Weber concluded that the organization of a bureaucracy and the attitudes of both the officials and the employees in regard to its operation act in concert to sustain the most efficient use of resources ever to be employed. When at its optimum operation, the personal, irrational, and emotional elements of management are minimized and the organization members tend to work with speed and precision.

Weber also noted the disadvantages of the bureaucracy. As the modern organizations become more rational, and the results of their systems more predictable, they tend to become less able to make decisions regarding individual cases; the individual becomes subordinate to the efficiency of the bureaucracy. Thus leadership becomes central to a humane bureaucracy.

Weber greatly stressed the charismatic leader, the individual of compelling personality and mystique, who can compel the attention and support of great numbers. In his view social movements can be depicted in terms of the dramatic individual who epitomizes the movement and is able to bring it to fruition. At specific points in history, when traditional or bureaucratic authority is decaying, the charismatic leader emerges, galvanizes support, and assumes power; in turn, his power and appeal become routinized so that his successors can assume control.

Max Weber's theory of power supplemented Marx's theory and complemented the theory of Mills and Hunter (see below). Weber broadened the concept of economic determinism to a wider social determinism by focusing on status and prestige.

C. WRIGHT MILLS (1916–62)

C. Wright Mills's contribution to the idea of a power elite in our country is the concept of total control over social change by a small group. He has characterized the power elite in terms of the military-industrial complex with the addition of governmental representatives. In his view they are men and women whose positions enable them to rise above the ordinary environments of average men and women; they are in positions in which they can make decisions having major consequences.[13] He has further described the elite as "simply those who have the most of what there is to have, which is generally held to include money, power and prestige."[14]

Mills delineated three distinct and general kinds of power: *authority*, or power that is justified by the beliefs of the voluntarily obedient; *manipulation*, or power that is wielded unknown to the powerless; and *coercion*, or power that comes from forcible action.

Mills theorized that the work ethic of the middle class of yesteryear has today been transformed into a "leisure ethic" for that same group. Mills wrote: "Now work itself is judged in terms of leisure values."[15] For the power elite this means providing the society with more and more opportunities for pursuing leisure activities. For the salaried citizen and the wage earner it means working at a job in which he is not interested to take money home to spend on things (which always increase in cost). Thus the impetus is provided for a separation and alienation from work activities, which result in a vicious cycle in which one makes money as fast as (and usually faster than) one can spend it. Mills concluded that modern man views leisure as the time to spend money and work as the way to make it. When the choice is between leisure and work, leisure usually wins, hands down.[16] The leisure sphere consequently attains the higher priority in terms of achievement. To this end the power elite manipulates the whole of society, thereby maintaining its control over the quality of life in that society.

Mills defined several types of Marxists in his book *The Marxists*. He referred to himself as a "plain Marxist," along with such other notable

[13] C. Wright Mills, *The Power Elite*, 5–6.
[14] *Ibid.*, 9.
[15] C. Wright Mills, "Work: The Big Split," in *Approaches to Walden* (ed. by Launat Lane, Jr.), 105.
[16] *Ibid.*, 107.

men as Jean-Paul Sartre and Erich Fromm. Other categories of Marxists he designated as "vulgar" and "sophisticated," the former being unquestioningly dogmatic and the latter being apologetic of flaws in Marxist ideology. According to Mills, the plain Marxists view Marxist thought as being in a state of continual refinement.

In much of his writing and thinking about the concept of a power elite, Mills was influenced greatly by Weber, primarily because Weber, in Mills's view, was perhaps the greatest revisionist of Marx. This opinion can best be illustrated by Mills's Weberian statement that "Marx did not see clearly . . . the nature of capitalism's monopoly form and the political and military manner of its stabilization."[17]

Mills distinguished between the "ruling class" and the "power elite" in that the former encompasses political power and property ownership whereas the latter leaves open the question of economic determinism and the problem of the relative importance of upper economic classes within the higher circles.

Talcott Parsons described Mills as adopting one main version of power as "a zero-sum, or, more precisely, a constant-sum conception. The essential point of Mills is that power is not a facility for the performance of function on behalf of the society as a system, but it is interpreted exclusively as a facility for getting what one group, the holders of power, wants by preventing another group, the 'outs,' from getting what it wants."[18]

According to Mills, there are two consequences of the American industrial society: the rise of an elite of powerful men who are in control of the means of death, production, and political power, and, below those in power, an unorganized mass ruled over and controlled by this elite.

Mills took a strong stand against the monistic view of economic determinism that Marx had proposed. He asserted that economic determinism should be elaborated to include political and military determinism also. He further asserted that men make their own history but that some are freer to do so than others are. He assumed that there is a great difference between the range of action possible for elites and the range of action possible for the masses. Mills's aim was to go beyond the classical theorists Marx and Weber to a "new comparative world society that would seek to understand our time in terms of its historical specificity and by so doing renew the possibility of achieving human freedom."[19]

[17] Irving M. Zeitlin, "The Plain Marxism of C. Wright Mills," in *The Revival of American Socialism: Selected Papers of the Socialist Scholars Conference* (ed. by George Fischer), 242.

[18] Talcott Parsons, *Structure and Process in Modern Societies*, 220.

[19] *Encyclopedia of the Social Sciences*, Vol. 10, 362–64.

The members of the power elite are those who control the great organizations. They are the persons at the head of the great corporations, the armed forces, the state, the communications media. They are the men and women who make the big decisions, and they have the power to make sure that the rest of society accepts their decisions. They represent, in short, the military-industrial complex. According to Mills, a power elite is inevitable in an advanced industrial society.[20] The members of the elite include some from the capitalist class whose wealth and connections have led them to the world of corporate power. Some of them have come up through their own organizations; some have come in from other giant organizations, particularly the military.

According to Mills, the corporate elite can exercise its power in many ways: it can administrate prices as it sees fit; it can fix prices and profits and set salaries; it can decide what kinds of jobs are to be made available and how many of them there are to be; it can decide where to locate plants and offices; it can make investment decisions; and, in the case of this country, it can decide what kind of nation the United States will be.

Mills also stated that the members of the power elite form a unified group with similar outlooks, programs, and values. They have similar interests, first in maintaining themselves in power and then in substantive matters of policy. Their unity is also based on uniformity in the kinds of people who make up the group. As heads of large-scale organizations, they have a great deal of experience in common. They have similar educational and occupational careers. They tend to come from the same religious, ethnic, and occupational backgrounds. Though they are not formally organized, they unite through informal associations and through the interchange of positions.

Below this elite of powerful men and women are the middle levels of power, composed mostly of interest groups. Below the top and middle levels of power is the mass society, those who have little or no power.

The members of the middle level of power are not unified, nor are they independent. Their level of power may be termed the political arena in the "old" sense of politics. Here it must be noted that there is great difference in the kinds of decisions made by members of the middle level of power. As was noted earlier, the concerns of the power elite focus on international issues such as war and peace and poverty. "Middle power," on the other hand, is concerned with holding on to its share of existing resources. Even though middle power may affect and sometimes hamper power-elite policy, Mills saw its members as being

[20] William G. Domhoff and Hoyt B. Ballard, eds., *C. Wright Mills and the Power Elite*, 16.

for the most part irresponsible, perhaps even inconsequential, since they do not usually have an international perspective.

A third level of power is the public. The public is commonly assumed to be a level of power in the justification of a "check and balance" system of government. However, owing to a lack of organization, the masses of people do not compete to affect the decisions which shape the destiny of the nation. Rather, as a group, the people are affected by decisions made without their participation. They have power in the *ideal* of democracy, but not in the existing reality.

Thus, Mills believed, the public has no means of organization to counter the power of the elite and of the middle level. The only group which can effectively oppose the power elite is the "intelligentsia." Mills defined this group as the intellectuals who are concerned with discovering and articulating the meaning and development of societal forces and in relating these forces to the personal problems that people face.[21] The intellectuals offer alternatives for the development of society and thus for the self, and they suggest programs of action for attaining these alternatives.

Mills was in a basic sense a utopian reformer. He thought that knowledge properly used could bring about the good society and that if the good society had not yet been achieved, it was primarily the fault of the men of knowledge. He developed a concept of the "personality market." Because of the shift from the old style of life (the classic pattern of the small business enterprise expanding by competition with other such enterprises) to large, impersonal business complexes, few independent businessmen remain:

This was the economic cradle of the free person—and, given the equality of opportunity and of power that it assumed, the guarantee of political democracy. The new way up is the white collar way: to get a job within a governmental or a business bureaucracy and to rise, according to the rules that prevail, from one pre-arranged step to another.

The great main chance of old becomes a series of small calculations, stretched out over the working lifetime of the individual. And these new middle classes are slowly beginning to give up their independence, in favor of a declaration of collective dependences some 14 per cent of them are now in trade unions.[22]

Mills described the personality market as the "true scene of the new entrepreneur's operation, . . . the top levels of this market may well

---

[21] *Ibid.*

[22] C. Wright Mills, "The Competitive Personality," in *Sociology: A Book of Readings* (ed. by Samuel Koenig), 102.

become an object to be administered rather than a play of free forces driven by crafty wile and unexampled initiative."[23] Businesses are now buying and selling personalities to fit predetermined modes of behavior.

The controller of the personality must manipulate it, make it attractive and salable. It is the only area in which he is "free to act." However, once on the job, the individual usually becomes self-alienated because, in the personality market, the personality itself, along with advertising, becomes the instrument of an alien purpose:

In this market the human expressions are no longer expressions of private aspirations. . . . They are the salaried mask of the individual, available by the week, designed to advance the competitive position of the store with the public.

In due course, this life of alienation sets up its own traits in the personality, selected, constructed, and used as instruments in the competitive struggle of the employees, and between the store and the consuming public. Such is the creative function of the new competition.[24]

But the prospects in the field of the personality market were to Mills even more disquieting: "The really great opportunities for expropriation are in the field of the human personality itself. The fate of competition, and the character it will assume, depends upon the success or failure of the adventures of monopolists in this field."[25]

Mills called upon those caught up in impersonal organizations to seek viable ways to end the abuses of the power elites and, finally, to participate in the use of power.

FLOYD HUNTER (1912–)

Unlike Marx and Mills, Floyd Hunter approaches the study of power from the community level rather than from the national level. He believes that the national power structure is similar to the power structure he found in community situations. In his book *Community Power Structure* he described the processes by which decisions are made and characterized the participants in those decisions. Basically, Hunter's conception of a power elite in a community consists of the "big rich" and the "little rich." The old, established, wealthy families are the big rich, while the newer, not-so-wealthy individuals are the little rich. The little rich usually ascend to relatively authoritative positions within the community power elite by assuming a conservative posture (in the

---

[23] *Ibid.*, 104.
[24] *Ibid.*, 105.
[25] *Ibid.*, 106.

classical sense) to perpetuate the status quo. Some of them act as implementers of the procedures which are established as a result of what the big rich decide to do. Bennis observed that Hunter's small group of decision makers, with their satellite groups of intellectuals, front men, and implementers, is in a real sense a power elite.[26]

Hunter defined power after conducting his study of what he called Regional City: "Power is a word that will be used to describe the acts of men going about the business of moving other men to act in relation to themselves or in relation to organic or inorganic things."[27] He acknowledged that there are other elements within the concept of power which he termed *residual categories* but which he did not deal with in his studies. Those elements are historical reference, motivation, values, and moral and ethical considerations.

Among Hunter's postulates concerning the power structure are the following: (1) power involves relationships between individuals and groups, both leaders and followers, (2) power is a relatively constant factor in social relationships, and (3) power of the individual must be structured into associational, clique, or institutional patterns to be effective. His hypotheses about power structure were: (1) power is exercised as a necessary function in social relationships, (2) the exercise of power is limited and directed by the formulation and extension of social policy within a framework of socially sanctioned authority, and (3) in a given power unit (organization) the number of individuals formulating and extending policy will be smaller than the number of those exercising power. All policymakers are men of power, but not all men of power are, per se, policymakers.[28]

In his study of Regional City, Hunter found a power structure similar to the one Mills had described on the national level. Hunter found that most leaders hold positions as presidents of companies or chairmen of boards or have professional status of some prestige. (Persons of wealth are important as symbolic persons, but they are not important performers in policy matters.)[29]

Businessmen are the community leaders in Regional City, as he believes they are in other cities. Wealth, social prestige, and political machinery are functional to the wielding of power by the business leaders in the community. However, the institutional, associational, and economic groupings do not comprise all of the power scheme in Regional City. Hunter stressed the difference between policymaking and policy execution. Various organizations in the community, he was

[26] Bennis, Benne, and Chin, *op. cit.*, 56.
[27] Floyd Hunter, *Community Power Structure*, 3.
[28] *Ibid.*, 6–7.
[29] Floyd Hunter, *Top Leadership, U.S.A.*, 80.

convinced, may be important in carrying out policy decisions even though they have no real power in policymaking.

In the bulk of the population of Regional City individuals have no voice in policy determination. They make up the "silent group." The voice of the professionals employed in agencies may have something to say about policy, but it usually goes unheeded.

In 1952, while researching the health services of Salem, Massachusetts, Hunter developed a method of determining the power elite in that city. By conducting well-planned surveys, Hunter and his associates were able to select, from an original list of 193 persons, the 10 most influential persons in the town (in terms of community-wide policy and decision making): "The 10 top leaders emerging in the interviewing process belonged predominantly to the industrial and business group of the community. Seven of the top 10 could be so classified. One each from the civic, professional, and religious groups was also among the 10."[30] Factors important in the selection of these persons were social status, economic well-being, political affiliation, and civic-mindedness. This method became known as the "reputational approach" for identifying community leadership.

The initial assertions for Hunter's national power elite study were:

1. At the national level of affairs, as in local community, there is a power structure inside and outside government.

2. Dominant cities containing concentrations of major industries are focal points of power, and they represent a large membership in the "power elite."

3. Power elite individuals idenitfied with dominant urban centers make decisive actions concerning national policy formulation and power execution.

4. National policy-making associations reflect in their decisions matters that have been agreed upon informally by these power elite.

5. Government is of special concern to the rest of the power structure, which seeks to act through and upon government in relation to specific policies.

6. A large portion of the total power structure is not seen in operation because of its diffuse and informal characteristics.[31]

The task of Hunter's national study was twofold: to define community power structures and to discover connections between community power figures and their roles in the development of policy at the national level. It was found that the structure of number-one leaders was small. The number-one men knew the other number-one

---

[30] Hunter, *Community Power Structure*, 27.
[31] Hunter, *Top Leadership, U.S.A.*, 8.

men. They recruited potential leaders into their programs and excluded those who did not fit.

The members of the elite knew and were known by elected and appointed officials, whom they tended to consider inferior to them. They belonged to a few exclusive clubs and associations across the nation. Their operating bases were generally situated in the large urban cities. They included the men of wealth and the military elite of whom Mills spoke. Hunter concluded that the elite were not a single pyramid of influence and authority.

Hunter noted that the major portion of the total national power structure was not seen in operation because of its diffuse and informal characteristics. Members of his power elite occupied prominent positions in business, government, civic associations, and social activities. He found it reasonable to conclude that corporate enterprises were the single most potent forces on the American scene.

Hunter also concluded that the general pattern of action, or the steps in the process of the development of a given national policy, as given by the leaders, was to (1) establish the policy purpose and secure dedication to it, (2) seek an unselfish working together of individuals and groups to achieve what they believe to be a policy direction, (3) recruit successful men to help, (4) widen but restrict the circle of informed men to help, (5) enlist services of an established national organization in the cause, (6) utilize research, (7) use a small, qualified group to give objective criticism, (8) analyze facts and problems by citizen groups, and (9) enlist public opinion.[32]

OTHER THEORISTS

The ideas of several other theorists are contrary to Marx's advocacy of a classless society. They adhere to the elitist theory. The origins of many of the elements of the elitist theory can be found in the writings of Plato, Vilfredo Pareto, Niccolò Machiavelli, Gaeano Mosca, and Robert Michels. They wrote that the concentration of power in a small group of elites is inevitable in society. Each stated, however, that change can occur through the gradual circulation of elites without class conflict and total revolution. Whereas for Marx the subordinate class could organize and overthrow the dominant class, modern-day elitists believe that the masses will always be unorganized and incapable of collective action. Pareto, a contemporary of Weber, took a position somewhat opposed to Marx's basic principle of the progressive development of class systems. It was his belief that the greater part of human actions have their origin not in logical reasoning but in sentiment. Therefore, Pareto felt, the dominance of the power elite was a

[32] *Ibid.*, 189.

natural consequence of the people's attitudes. Innovation and consolidation were the major premises of the power elite. The "rhythm of sentiment" so prevalent in society was, he believed, a major reason for the lack of positive human relations in issues involving the rights and needs of the people.

About the same time that Mills wrote *The Power Elite*, David Riesman wrote *The Lonely Crowd*. Like Mills, Riesman was attempting to describe the structure of power in America; however, he reached an opposite conclusion. Riesman found veto groups, whereas Mills found a power elite.

Harold D. Lasswell, in *Politics: Who Gets What, When and How*, concerned himself with the power authority's relation to the nonelite. He focused on how an elite uses its power to acquire the desirable things in a society and the nature of its challenges from counter-elites. Lasswell argued that every power group seeks to acquire authority or to exercise effective power over authorities.

Saturday Belongs To the Palomía[33]
DANIEL GARZA

Every year, in the month of September, the cotton pickers come up from the Valley, and the braceros come from Mexico itself. They come to the town in Texas where I live, all of them, the whole "palomía" is what we say: it is slang among my people, and I do not know how to translate it exactly. It means . . . the cotton pickers when they come. You call the whole bunch of them the palomía, *but one by one they are cotton pickers,* pizcadores.

Not many of them have traveled so far north before, and for the ones who have not it is a great experience. And it is an opportunity to know other kinds of people, for the young ones. For the older ones it is only a chance to make some money picking cotton. Some years the cotton around my town is not so good, and then the pizcadores *have to go farther north, and we see them less.*

But when they come, they come in full force to my little town that is full of gringos. Only a few of us live there who speak Spanish among ourselves, and whose parents maybe came up like the pizcadores *a long time ago. It is not like the border country where there are many of both kinds of people; it is gringo country mostly, and most of the time we and the gringos live there together without worrying much about such matters.*

In September and October in my town, Saturdays belong to the

33 By Daniel Garza. From *Harper's Magazine*, July, 1962. Reprinted by permission of the author.

pizcadores. *During the week they are in the fields moving up and down the long cotton rows with big sacks and sweating frightfully, but mak-*ing centavitos *to spend on Saturday at the movie, or on clothes, or on food. The gringos come to town during the week to buy their merchandise and groceries, but finally Saturday arrives, and the* pizcadores *climb aboard their trucks on the cotton farms, and the trucks all come to town. It is the day of the* palomía, *and most of the gringos stay home.*

"Ay, que gringos!" *the* pizcadores *say.* "What a people to hide themselves like that. But such is life . . ."

For Saturday the pizcadores *dress themselves in a special and classy style. The girls comb their black hair, put on new bright dresses and low-heeled shoes, and the color they wear on their lips is, the way we say it, enough. The boys dress up in black pants and shoes with taps on the heels and toes. They open their shirts two or three buttons to show their chests and their Saint Christophers; then at the last they put a great deal of grease on their long hair and comb it with care. The old men, the* viejos, *shave and put on clean plain clothes, and the old women put on a tunic and comb their hair and make sure the little ones are clean, and all of them come to town.*

They come early, and they arrive with a frightful hunger. The town, being small, has only a few restaurants. The pizcadores—*the young ones and the ones who have not been up from Mexico before—go into one of the restaurants, and the owner looks at them.*

One who speaks a little English says they want some desayuno, *some breakfast.*

He looks at them still. He says: "Sorry. We don't serve Meskins."

Maybe then one of the pachuco *types with the long hair and the Saint Christopher says something ugly to him in Spanish, maybe not. Anyhow, the others do not, but leave sadly, and outside the old men who did not go in nod among themselves, because they knew already. Then maybe, standing on the sidewalk, they see a gringo go into the restaurant. He needs a shave and is dirty and smells of sweat, and before the door closes they hear the owner say:* "What say, Blacky? What'll it be this morning?"

The little ones who have understood nothing begin to holler about the way their stomachs feel, and the papas *go to market to buy some food there.*

I am in the grocery store, me and a few gringos and many of the palomía. *I have come to buy flour for my mother. I pass a* pizcador, *a father who is busy keeping his little ones from knocking cans down out of the big piles, and he smiles to me and says:* "Que tal, amígo?"

"Pues, así no más," *I answer.*

He looks at me again. He asks in a quick voice, "You are a Chicano?"

"Sí."

"*How is it that you have missed the sun in your face*, muchacho?" *he says.* "*A big hat, maybe?*"

"*No, señor,*" *I answered.* "*I live here.*"

"*You have luck.*"

And I think to myself, yes, I have luck; it is good to live in one place. And all of a sudden the pizcador and I have less to say to each other, and he says adiós and gathers up his flow of little ones and goes out to the square where the boys and girls of the palomía are walking together.

On the square too there is usually a little lady selling hot tamales. She is dressed simply, and her white hair is in a bun, and she has a table with a big can of tamales on it which the palomía buy while they are still hot from the stove at the little lady's home.

"Mamacita, mamacita," the little ones shout at their mothers. "Doña Petra is here. Will you buy me some tamalitos?"

Doña Petra lives there in the town, and the mothers in the palomía are her friends because of her delicious tamales and because they go to her house to talk of the cotton picking, of children, and maybe of the fact that in the north of Texas it takes somebody like Doña Petra to find good masa for tamales and tortillas. Away from home as the pizcadores are, it is good to find persons of the race in a gringo town.

On the street walk three pachucos, seventeen or eighteen years old. They talk pachuco talk. One says: "Listen, chabos, let's go to the good movie."

"O.K.," another one answers. "Let's go flutter the good eyelids."

They go inside a movie house. Inside, on a Saturday there are no gringos, only the palomía. The pachucos find three girls, and sit down with them. The movie is in English, and they do not understand much of it, but they laugh with the girls and make the viegos angry, and anyhow the cartoon—the mono, they call it—is funny by itself, without the need for English.

Other pachucos walk in gangs through the streets of the town, looking for something to do. One of them looks into the window of Mr. Jones' barber shop and tells the others that he thinks he will get a haircut. They laugh, because haircuts are something that pachucos do not get, but one of them dares him. "It will be like the restaurant," he says, "Gringo scissors do not cut Chicano hair."

So he has to go in, and Mr. Jones looks at him as the restaurant man looked at the others in the morning. But he is a nicer man, and what he says is that he has to go to lunch when he has finished with the customers who are waiting. "There is a Mexican barber across the square," he says. "On Walnut Street. You go there."

The pachuco *tells him a very ugly thing to do and then combs his long hair in the mirror and then goes outside again, and on the sidewalk he and his friends say bad things about Mr. Jones for a while until they are tired of it, and move on. The gringo customers in the barber shop rattle the magazines they are holding in their laps, and one of them says a thing about cotton pickers, and later in the day it is something that the town talks about, gringos and* pizcadores *and those of my people who live there, all of them. I hear about it, but forget, because September in my town is full of such things, and in the afternoon I go to the barber shop for a haircut the way I do on Saturdays all year long.*

Mr. Jones is embarrassed when he sees me. "You hear about that?" he says. "That kid this morning?"

I remember then, and I say yes, I heard.

"I'm sorry, Johnny," he says. "Doggone it. You know I'm not ..."

"I know," I say.

"The trouble is, if they start coming, they start bringing the whole damn family, and then your regular customers get mad," he says.

"I know," I say, and I do. There is no use in saying that I don't, because I live in the town for the other ten or eleven months of the year when the palomía *is not here but in Mexico and the Valley. I know the gringos of the town and what they are like, and they are many different ways. So I tell Mr. Jones that I know what he means.*

"Get in the chair," he says. "You want it short or medium this time?"

And I think about the pizcador *in the grocery store and what he said about my having luck, and I think again it is good to live in one place and not to have to travel in trucks to where the cotton is.*

At about six in the afternoon all the families begin to congregate at what they call the campo. *Campo means camp or country, but this* campo *is an area with a big tin shed that the State Unemployment Commission puts up where the farmers who have cotton to be picked can come and find the* pizcadores *who have not yet found a place to work. But on Saturday nights in September the* campo *does not have anything to do with work. The families come, bringing tacos to eat and maybe a little beer if they have it. After it is dark, two or three of the men bring out guitars, and some others have concertinas. They play the fast, twisty* mariachi *music of the places they come from, and someone always sings. The songs are about women and love and sometimes about a town that the song says is a fine town, even if there is no work there for* pizcadores. *All the young people begin to dance, and the old people sit around making certain that the* pachucos *do not get off into the dark with their daughters. They talk, and they eat, and they drink a little beer, and then at twelve o'clock it is all over.*

The end of Saturday has come. The old men gather up their sons and daughters, and the mothers carry the sleeping little ones like small sacks of cotton to the trucks, and the whole palomía *returns to the country to work for another week, and to earn more* centavitos *with which, the Saturday that comes after the week, to go to the movies, and buy groceries, and pay for tamalitos of Doña Petra and maybe a little beer for the dance at the* campo. *And the mothers will visit with Doña Petra, and the* pachucos *will walk the streets, and the other things will happen, all through September and October, each Saturday the same, until finally, early in November, the cotton harvest is over, and the* pizcadores *go back to their homes in the Valley or in Mexico.*

The streets of my town are empty then, on Saturdays. It does not have many people, most of the year. On Saturday mornings you see a few gringo children waiting for the movie to open, and not much else. The streets are empty, and the gringos sit in the restaurant and the barber shop and talk about the money they made or lost on the cotton crop that fall.

SUMMARY

Social power is coming to be recognized as important in such areas as political and social movements, community power systems, decision making, bureaucratic power structures and operations, social stratification and race relations, and political values and attitudes.

Theories of social power can be modified to fit smaller organizations. Some theorists believe that every instance of human interaction and every social relationship growing out of that interaction involves the exercise of power.[34] Power is not a thing possessed but rather a dynamic process that occurs in all areas of social life.

If we think of power in terms of the ability to affect social activities, the concept becomes important in light of all social problems and human activities. Consequently, it seems relevant that the idea of power elites and their control in society is very important to the study of human relations. Particularly important are the ways in which persons who have little power can increase their relative influence and status so that their interests will be better represented.

Most humanistic writers are in agreement with Marx that the economic factor is a determinant of the structure and development of society. However, it is not the sole determinant. To focus only on economics is to oversimplify and distort the complex processes of social change and the nature of social structures. Marx's proposed redistribution of wealth would eliminate the ruling class, which dehumanizes the working class and causes it to be but another product. But does this

[34] See Marvin E. Olsen, ed., *Power in Societies.*

ensure that a new order will not distribute itself again into new classes, which will use another class as the underdogs?

Because Mills recognized the fact that the men in power are more than those who control the economic sphere, he presented a more comprehensive theory of power in an industrialized society. Mills stated that knowledge properly used could bring about the good society and that, if the good society was not yet here, it was primarily the fault of men of knowledge. This is an important concept in planned change and equally important as part of the philosophy underlying the field of human relations.

In Hunter's study of elites on a local level it is easier to see the possibilities for promoting social change, particularly through the political leaders and intellectuals who exercise power. Hunter's studies were methodological, while Mills proposed his ideas from the vantage point of a spectator of history. Some readers might quarrel with Mills's ideas because he was not methodological. Both Hunter and Mills, however, provided valuable insights into community decision making.

The basic idea that these theorists of power elite models have given us is that change can come about through the establishment of countervailing power to offset the existing concentration of power. According to Pareto, the relation between the individual and society is like that of the part to the whole. Any changes in parts of a system affect the whole, and vice versa. This is an important lesson for human relations practitioners. If agents of change can alter small aspects of group life, they will effect changes in the larger network of human relationships.

Chapter 4
SUGGESTED READING

Bendix, Reinhard, and Seymour M. Lipset, eds., *Class, Status and Power: A Reader in Social Stratification.* Glencoe, Ill., The Free Press, 1953.

Bennis, Warren G., Kenneth D. Benne, and Robert Chin, eds. *The Planning of Change.* New York, Holt, Rinehart & Winston, Inc., 1969.

Berger, Peter. *Invitation to Sociology: A Humanistic Perspective.* New York, Doubleday & Co., Inc., 1963.

Bottomore, Thomas B., ed. *Karl Marx.* New York, McGraw-Hill Book Company, 1964.

Cartwright, Dorwin. *Studies in Social Power.* Ann Arbor, University of Michigan Press, 1959.

Domhoff, G. William, and Hoyt B. Ballard, eds. *C. Wright Mills and the Power Elite.* Boston, The Beacon Press, 1968.

Fischer, Ernest. *The Essential Marx.* Translated by Ann Bostock. New York, Herder & Herder, Inc., 1970.

Fischer, George, ed. *The Revival of American Socialism: Selected Papers of the Socialist Scholars Conference*. New York, Oxford University Press, 1971.

French, John R. P., Jr. "A Formal of Social Power," *Psychological Review*, Vol. 63 (1956).

Gerth, Hans, and C. Wright Mills. *Character and Social Structure*. New York, Harcourt, Brace & World, Inc., 1964.

Hegel, Georg W. F. *The Philosophy of Right*. Translated by S. W. Dyne. London, George Bell and Sons, 1896.

Horowitz, Irvin Louis, ed. *Power, Politics and People: The Collected Essays of C. Wright Mills*. New York, Oxford University Press, 1963.

Hunter, Floyd. *Community Power Structure: A Study of Decision Makers*. Chapel Hill, University of North Carolina Press, 1953.

Koenig, Samuel, ed. *Sociology: A Book of Readings*. Englewood Cliffs, N.J., Prentice-Hall, Inc., 1953.

Lane, Launat, Jr., ed. *Approaches to Walden*. San Francisco, Wadsworth Publishing Co., 1964.

Lasswell, Harold D. *Politics: Who Gets What, When, How*. New York, P. Smith, 1936.

Marx, Karl. *The Communist Manifesto*. Translated by Samuel Moore. Chicago, Henry Regnery Co., 1954.

McMullen, Roy. *Art, Affluence and Alienation*. New York, Mentor Books, 1968.

Merton, Robert K. *Social Theory and Social Structure*, rev. ed. Glencoe, Ill., The Free Press, 1952.

Miller, Seymour M. *Max Weber*. New York, Thomas Y. Crowell Co., 1963.

Mills, C. Wright. *The Marxists*. New York, Dell Publishing Co., 1962.

———. *Power, Politics, and People*. New York, Oxford University Press, 1963.

———. *The Power Elite*. London, Oxford University Press, 1956.

Olsen, Marvin E. *Power in Societies*. New York, The Macmillian Co., 1970.

Oswalt, Wendell. *Understanding Our Culture: An Anthropological View*. New York, Holt, Rinehart & Winston, Inc., 1970.

Parsons, Talcott. *Structure and Process in Modern Societies*. New York, The Free Press, 1960.

Revel, Jean-François. *Without Marx or Jesus: The New American Revolution Has Begun*. Translated by Jack Bernard. Garden City, New York, Doubleday & Co., Inc., 1971.

Riesman, David. *The Lonely Crowd: A Study of the Changing American Character*. New Haven, Yale University Press, 1950.

Tucker, Robert C. *The Marxian Revolutionary Idea*. New York, W. W. Norton & Co., Inc., 1969.

Weber, Max. *The Protestant Ethic and the Spirit of Capitalism*. New York, Charles Scribner's Sons, 1958.

———. *The Theory of Social and Economic Organization*. Translated by A. M. Henderson and T. Parsons. New York, Oxford University Press, 1947.

Part Two **STRATEGIES FOR CHANGE**

PRELUDE TO VIOLENCE AND NONVIOLENCE

That hundreds and thousands of white people are living, in effect, no better than the "niggers" is not a fact to be regarded with complacency. The social and moral bankruptcy suggested by this fact is of the bitterest, most terrifying kind.—JAMES BALDWIN

To the casual observer it would appear that violence has now become the rule rather than the exception both in the United States and in other countries. This view overlooks the many instances of nonviolent change. It also tends to become deterministic—prophesying war, terrorism, and murder as inevitable. In order to better understand and cope with the violence of today, we must analyze the historical conditions prompting both the violent and the nonviolent movements in the United States. In looking at violence in the United States, it seems clear that our violence is historical, not traditional. This is not to imply that violence has been infrequent in our past—only that it lacked cohesion:

It is not merely that violence has been mixed with the negative features of our history such as criminal activity, lynch mobs, and family feuds. On the contrary, violence has formed a seamless web with some of the noblest and most constructive chapters of American history: the birth of the nation (Revolutionary violence), the freeing of the slaves and the preservation of the Union (Civil War violence), the occupation of the land (Indian wars), the stabilization of frontier society (vigilante violence), the elevation of the farmer and the laborer (agrarian and labor violence), and the preservation of law and order (police violence). The patriot, the humanitarian, the nationalist, the pioneer, the landholder, the farmer, and the laborer (and the capitalist) have used violence as the means to a higher end.[1]

[1] Richard M. Brown, "Historical Patterns of Violence in America," in *The History of Violence in America* (ed. by Hugh D. Graham and Ted R. Gurr), 75.

117

Another reason why our violence is not synonymous with tradition is that Americans have, for the most part, always liked the "good life." That is, we have tended to forget about the terrible things that happen while clinging tenaciously to those places, people, and things which have been good or favorable to us. Most Americans tend to bury or repress their bad times and reflect on them only under duress. With the exception of the major wars, American historians have also overlooked or somehow circumvented domestic violence in their writings. Even when it is documented, national violence fails to provide the detailed information required to understand fully the reasons for outbreaks of violence: "We must realize that violence has not been the action only of the roughnecks and racists among us but has been the tactic of the most upright and respected of our people. . . . Only then will we begin to solve our social, economic, and political problems."[2]

Because the domestic violence of the past has, for the most part, been that of citizen against citizen, it has become forgettable. If, however, this violence had been consistently aimed at the nation as a whole, it would probably have won historical recognition and would have been recorded for posterity. Conflicts between groups of citizens, no matter how murderous or destructive, have been forgettable, while attacks upon state power, no matter how transient or ineffective, have won historical attention.

OUR VIOLENT PAST

Domestic violence occurs in many forms, but probably the riot is the most commonplace in United States history. Despite assassinations, bombings, and shootouts, riots have more effectively altered intergroup relations than any other form of violence. Although now largely confined to the cities, riots were frequent in rural areas as recently as the early years of the twentieth century. It is important to realize that although the adjectives describing the nature of the riot may change, thereby implying many different types of riots, there are usually only a few underlying reasons for most riots: ethnic consciousness, religion, or racial antagonism. Many so-called election riots erupted from efforts to keep a minority group from voting. Several historic labor riots arose from disputes with strong racial overtones; examples are the Wilmington Riot of 1898 and the Anti-Chinese Riot in Los Angeles in 1871. Many other riots and demonstrations have underscored the fact that America has not become the melting pot it has claimed to be. The truth is that in most communities the people of the melting pot do not melt; or when they do, it is usually because of legal pressure. And as far as nonwhites are concerned, the melting is a myth.

2 *Ibid.*, 76.

The average citizen, reading about a riot or a confrontation between National Guardsmen and students, has become less shocked by the possibility of deaths and destruction of property as aspects of organized and unorganized protest activities. This hardening of our social arteries was a gradual process. When we compare today's violent actions with those of the past, the horror, fear, death, and destruction of the former seem mild. To illustrate, let us now look at just a few of the many acts of violence in America's past. Rather than discuss some of the better-known acts of violence of the past, such as Bacon's Rebellion of 1676, the Stamp Act Riots of 1765, the Boston Massacre of 1770, Shay's Rebellion of 1786, or the Whiskey Rebellion of 1794, let us briefly review other upheavals in American history which have caused one notable commentator to say that violence is "as American as cherry pie."

The Baltimore Election Riot of 1856 was one of the most violent political riots that ever took place. The driving force behind the terrorism that stigmatized this election was the newly formed Know-Nothing party. The riots lasted throughout the last few months of the 1856 election year and into 1857 and 1858. The Know-Nothings were mainly interested in terrorizing immigrants into voting for the Know-Nothing party candidates or, if need be, keeping them from going to the polls to vote for the opposition. The physical violence was left to street groups organized by the Know-Nothings—the Blood-Tubs, the Rough Skins, and the Rip-Raps. The gangs developed several methods of eliminating those voting for the opposition, as well as the opposition itself. The Blood-Tubs, for example, got their name from their methods of intimidation: they took tubs of blood from local butchers, threw their victims into the tubs, then chased them down the street with knives. The sight of the blood-drenched victims was a powerful deterrent to other would-be voters. Such terrorism, coupled with many murderous acts, kept a large number of the immigrants away from the polls and allowed the Know-Nothings to win many local, state, and national offices. Scores of immigrants were killed and hundreds were wounded in the sixty-day period preceding the 1856 elections. Whenever one of the conflicting parties or nationalities retaliated, citywide riots would begin.

An example of economy-related violence from the past is the Railroad Strike of 1877. This strike was the first large-scale strike against the economic conditions growing out of industrialization. Unable to recover from the severe depression of 1873, the railroads were ordered to cut back wages 15 per cent in 1877 and to drastically reduce their work force. At the outset a Baltimore and Ohio Railroad depot in West Virginia was demolished by strikers. The casualties of one day's fighting between railroad workers and the militia called in to clear tracks in Maryland numbered over one hundred. The strike then spread to other states:

Railroads in Pennsylvania, New York, and New Jersey suffered almost complete disruption. The Erie, New York Central, The Delaware Lackawanna Western, and the Canada Southern operating in Ohio, Pennsylvania, and New York were struck on July 24, idling about 100,000 workers. Federal and State troops were used to suppress rioting, and sometimes the State police were themselves the cause of violence. After 13 persons were killed and 43 wounded in a clash between militia and citizens in Reading, Pa., for example, a coroner's jury blamed the troops for an unjustified assault upon peaceful citizens.[3]

The logical query after such a description would center on the success of the strike. Although it had spread from state to state, the strikers did not have the organizations they needed to stabilize and institutionalize their growing position of strength. Several incidents—and deaths later, the strike collapsed.

One who reads about some of the specific acts of violence, torture, and mutilation committed on specific individuals during those early days finds it hard to believe that these acts were perpetrated in the United States during the nineteenth century and not during Attila the Hun's rampage through Europe.

THEORIES OF VIOLENCE

These few examples serve to demonstrate that American history is replete with instances of violence and destruction. The blood-stained list of riots, insurrections, and demonstrations for political, religious, racial, and economic reasons is dreadful. Equally so is their repetitive nature. Records of the use of peaceful techniques to resolve differences are scanty. We have been, in short, a gun-and-knife culture, not a peace culture; we have preferred to maim or kill our opponents rather than to talk with them.

How then have we maintained such a high degree of political stability? One obvious answer is that the federal structure of our society has been largely successful in keeping mass violence from our national political institutions. Another that has been advanced—a weak one—is that America's federal and state institutions have been less important than the federal and state institutions of other countries. In other countries violence has almost always been directed against state or

[3] Philip Taft and Philip Ross, "American Labor Violence: It's Causes, Character, and Outcome," in *The History of Violence in America*, 289.

national political institutions because they have most of the social, political, and economic power. A more plausible explanation is that the American federal government has the tendency to move quickly to crush efforts to mount organized protests. This fact is evidenced in the history of manifestations of frontier, labor, and agrarian discontent.

A second reason why American violence has been diverted from the political arena is that violence in American history has usually taken the form of citizen versus citizen or social group versus social group, and no one citizen or group has been able to collect and organize the resources needed to topple the state or the nation. In America collective violence has proceeded from intergroup tensions; that is, individual frustrations have created racial and ethnic scapegoats: the Know-Nothings and the American Protective Association, the antiabolitionist mobs, the Irish rampage against the blacks in New York in 1863, the lynchings of blacks by whites in the South, the westerners' attacks upon Orientals. Factors contributing to these group-versus-group confrontations have been the size of the country, its racial and ethnic pluralism, and the diffuseness of power under our democratic system of government.

A third reason for America's political stability despite its internal unrest has been the unequal distribution of wealth. The spectrum of the citizenry runs from the opulently well off to the abject poor. It is in those nations characterized by much poverty and little wealth that revolutions are born. Latin American countries, for example, have been plagued with violence, political instability, and domestic turmoil. In contrast, the average well-to-do American who has been insufficiently concerned with public policy to vote on crucial issues is unlikely to attack the government.

The theory of the *uniqueness of the American experience* is often cited to explain or justify the high incidence of violence in the United States. This theory holds that our basic socialization as a nation is grounded in blood and violence, beginning with the conquest of the Indians and then of the frontier. In an idealized version of this theory the frontiersman is a symbol of rugged individualism. As the frontier closed, people rushed to the cities, taking with them the culture of Dodge City shootouts, gunslinging, gangsterism, and vigilantism.

The theory of the uniqueness of the American experience is highly questionable. It appears that the very nature of any nation-state system is based upon the ultimate resort to violence when other forms of diplomacy fail. In this respect there is nothing unique about the American experience. American cities may be no more dangerous today than were the slums of Elizabethan England, but we can argue, as Norman

Mailer did, that our streets are no less safe to walk on than the streets of Paris in 1300 or Naples in 1644.[4] The Australian experience also contradicts the myths of the American experience. The history of Australia fairly well parallels that of the United States. Yet, instead of a high level of violence, Australians have achieved relative tranquillity and a peaceful political life.

A second theory—among the most loudly argued of the theories—is that "outside agitators" are behind every serious act of disruption and violence. The *riffraff theory*, as it is usually called, maintains that spontaneous contagion enables outside agitators to disrupt the status quo. This theory does not adequately account for the process by which some "riffraff" achieve legitimacy and leadership roles in established organizations. Such a view also evades the question why some conflicts are amplified to riotous scales and others are not.

Studies of the participants in the 1967 riots provided further evidence to contradict the riffraff theory. The authors found that (1) a substantial minority of area residents, ranging from 10 to 20 per cent, participated in the riots, (2) one-half to three-quarters of those arrested were employed in semiskilled or skilled occupations (three-fourths of the rioters were employed), and (3) mainly individuals between the ages of fifteen and twenty-four participated in the riots.

While the above theories offer some insight into the conditions that precipitate violence, they do not answer all the questions. There are other theories which deal with contemporary aspects of violence. They have been termed the *deprivation, differential-access,* and *frustration* theories. All three theories are closely related.

The *deprivation theory* focuses on the relative inequity, injustice, and inequality various groups experience. According to this theory, the have-nots look for occasions to attack the haves, and the greater the disparity between them the larger the incentive for high-risk provocation. This view, however, has too narrow a perspective. It neglects the obvious fact that violent outbreaks occur selectively; great deprivation may exist without such outbreaks, and outbreaks may occur without significant deprivation.

The *differential-access theory* holds that the disparities in political influence are a direct cause of violence. The less political access a group has to a remedy for its grievances for a community problem the more violent it tends to become in demanding such access. This theory seeks to forge a link between deprivation and power. Few social practitioners deny the importance of equality of access to the power structure.

[4] Norman Mailer, "Talking of Violence," *20th Century*, Vol. 173 (Winter, 1964–65), 112.

Closely related to the above theories is the *frustration theory*, which holds that the frustrations imposed by external sanctions generate a cumulative internal rage which culminates in violent outbursts. Further, such outbursts frequently result in societal changes, causing some writers to cite our crisis mentality as a nation—we tend to react to frustrations of others instead of acting to prevent or abate such frustrations.

There is no single best theory for explaining patterns of social change. If they are viewed as interrelated, however, all the above theories taken together present a viable explanation of the origins of violent and nonviolent behavior. Inequities, social disorganization, high-stress social conditions, and extreme situations for individuals and groups are quantities in the final equation. The response of those in decision-making positions determines whether progress toward reform will dampen violence or encourage it.

NONVIOLENCE REVISITED

Social problems arise when those involved in the conflict and the established channels for adjustment fail to reflect the democratic process, forcing some groups to resort to violence in an effort to make operative their constitutional rights. At this point it would appear that the use of violence is the paramount pressure which might be employed to bring about social change. While there is no doubt about the efficacy of violence, there are other methods which may be exerted to bring about social change. Nonviolent direct action is one such tactic. The term *nonviolence* means the planned use of propaganda and other measures calculated to influence the opinions, emotions, attitudes, and behavior of hostile, neutral, or friendly groups to support the aggrieved group without resorting to violence.

There are six kinds of nonviolent action. *Nonresistance* is based on the commitment not to fight back. The Mennonites, or Amish, follow this commitment. They hold their beliefs and attitudes so highly that it is very difficult to influence them to fight others to support their values. *Active reconciliation* is the process of seeking social change through the use of friendliness and reconciliation. Nonviolent direct action is ruled out by some members of this group. The Society of Friends (Quakers) has followed this process throughout much of its history. *Moral resistance* is a nonviolent campaign against evil. The major emphasis is placed on education, persuasion, and individual example. The peace societies of New England in the nineteenth century utilized this tactic. *Selective nonviolence* emphasizes a careful choice of violent or nonviolent behavior, depending on the threat. Many young draftees refused to participate in the Vietnam War, but on the other hand some of them resorted to violence to protest the war. *Satyagraha*, or passive resistance, is the theory inaugurated by Gandhi and practiced by him and by his Indian followers in their campaigns against British rule. The follower of *satyagraha* attempts to influence others' opinion through sympathy, patience, truthfulness, and self-suffering. Satyagraha is built on love and refusal to do harm to one's opponent. This practice has parallels with Christian traditions. In the early stages of the civil-rights movement in America, the Reverend Martin Luther King, Jr., practiced *satyagraha*. *Nonviolent revolution* is the peaceful overthrow of oppressive societal conditions. It is achieved when equal rights are assured for all people. Its adherents claim that nonviolent revolution can alter individual and social life.[5]

Whatever their methods, nonviolent strategists depend upon some form of persuasion short of physical aggression. Thus both explicitly and implicitly their major goals are to bring about change in emotions, attitudes, and behavior. The themes which their supporters are expected to rally around must be timely, consistent, and credible. Support and change can be anticipated to the extent that the themes are expressed so that the audience understands their meaning. Gandhi's campaign in 1919 against the Rowlatt acts (which gave the British government extraordinary powers to suppress unrest) was initially a failure because the Indian people failed to comprehend the intended meaning of *satyagraha* and violence broke out. The people did not yet understand the true meaning of Gandhi's philosophy.

It is not completely true to say that man is violent by nature. While there are some historical and social bases for this belief, there is also ample evidence to indicate that we cannot explain aggression as simply being part of our "animal nature." Indeed, animals generally avoid excesses of aggression, especially within their species. A strategy for change which includes nonaggressive behavior must become part of each participant's basic attitude toward change.

An *attitude* is a tendency to respond either positively or negatively to certain objects, persons, or situations. More often than not this response will be consistent with previous responses in similar situations. Attitudes are formed as a result of acting upon stimuli. Attitude formation is similar to a filing system, and each of us has his own unique way of filing his responses. This process, which is an automatic one, is very important; without it the smallest decision would take hours to make. A drawback to conceptualization is that it leads to thinking in terms of stereotypes and to prejudice. We tend to form attitudes that seemingly fit our needs, real or imagined.[6]

[5] Herbert H. Blumberg and Paul Hare, *Nonviolent Direct Actions*, 4.
[6] Richard A. King and Clifford T. Morgan, *Introduction to Psychology*, 594.

Communication plays a very important role in nonviolent action. The nonviolent actor, the communicator, must get his message across to all the groups he intends to influence. This process takes the following course:

1. The communicator devises a message with a particular content.
2. The message is given to a receiver by the use of a medium.
3. The message is somewhat modified (distorted) by the medium.
4. The receiver translates the message into a form which has meaning to him; the message affects him and helps determine what he does about the problem.
5. The original communicator watches for these effects, since they form the feedback to his message, and evaluates this feedback to understand what effect his message actually has had.
6. The communicator gets ideas about how to improve future messages to the same receiver. Thus we decide whether violence or nonviolence is the best way to communicate our feeling about social change.

The message of nonviolence came to the foreground in America in the civil-rights movement and its related protest activities of the 1960's. Civil disobedience is one of the tactics that has been used to challenge the validity of many of our laws. Civil disobedience is functional within the framework of established law because it clarifies the intent and meaning of a law establishing policy. This kind of civil disobedience is not less risky physically than acts of disobedience outside the legal structure. But both forms of disobedience—legal and illegal—challenge the fundamental purpose of the law or policy.[7]

Martin Luther, King, Jr., led the nonviolent southern campaigns through his organization, the Southern Christian Leadership Conference. Other organizations, such as the Student Nonviolent Coordinating Committee and the Conference of Federated Organizations, joined Dr. King in the use of boycotts and sit-ins as the primary civil-rights strategies. Dr. King was skillful in attracting attention to his cause. His protest marches attracted large audiences and provided a model for future minority leaders.

While the nonviolent tactics brought gains for blacks, they did little to put an end to the entrenched racism in the United States. Although there were many instances of violence on the part of the whites during black demonstrations, there were few cases of black violence. During the most oppressive periods, most blacks remained committed to the doctrine of nonviolence. It was not until 1963, when spontaneous violence erupted in the streets in Birmingham, Alabama, Cambridge,

[7] See Ralph Conant, *The Prospects for Revolution*.

125

Maryland, and Nashville, Tennessee, did the calculated use of violence by blacks become a subject of widespread discussion.[8] Even then, most black leaders argued that the riots would block the momentum of civil-rights movements. However, it was not possible for black leaders to control the black masses indefinitely. The despair and the pent-up anger had finally burst into the streets.

DREAMS DEFERRED

Violence has accompanied black-white relations throughout the history of the United States. During the decade of the 1960's there was a change in the mode of violence. Stokely Carmichael and Charles V. Hamilton wrote: "In the fifties a political protest movement was born which had a calming, wait-and-see effect on the attitude of many urban black people. . . . Then, in the spring of 1963, the lull was over."[9] The outbreak of rioting in Birmingham, Alabama, ended the period of passive resistance on the part of the blacks. (Perhaps the American Indian Movement [AIM] occupation of Wounded Knee, South Dakota, will have similar significance for native Americans.)

Until then there had been an extended period of rising expectations but low levels of achievement among black Americans. Retaliatory violence remained a significantly subordinate theme throughout that period. Conversely, white aggression was increasing. When the gap between rising expectations and the realities of the unlikelihood of attaining those aspirations became too great, violence erupted.[10] Violence in America took on a new form. Where before whites had been the aggressors and the blacks had been the targets of aggression, now blacks were the aggressors. Furthermore, the confrontations changed from civilian versus civilian to black civilians versus the police. Beginning in Birmingham and spreading to other cities, the nonviolent demonstrations, mainly led by disciplined and better-educated middle-class blacks, were pushed aside by the newly roused and much more violent black poor.

Morris Janowitz coined the terms *communal riot* and *commodity riot* to differentiate between the riots before the 1960's and those of the 1960's: "Whereas the communal riot involved a confrontation between the white and the black community, the commodity riot, especially as it entered into the third and destructive phase, represents a confrontation

---

[8] Robert F. Williams, "For Effective Self Defense," in *Negro Protest Thought in the Twentieth Century* (ed. by August Meier and Francis L. Broderick), 321–22.

[9] Stokely Carmichael and Charles V. Hamilton, *Black Power: The Politics of Liberation in America*, 154.

[10] August Meier and Elliott Rudwick, "Black Violence in the 20th Century: A Study in Rhetoric and Retaliation," in *The History of Violence in America*, 406–407.

between the black community and law enforcement officials of the larger society."[11]

The communal riots were in part reflections of the environmental struggle between whites and blacks caused by the growth and transformation of the cities. The usual pattern of such riots was an extended period of isolated acts of violence, followed by a small-scale conflict between white and black citizens, which resulted in violence spreading throughout the entire community. The character of the final stage can be perceived by the choice of weapons: knives, clubs, and fists were predominant, with the occasional use of guns. The combat was direct, man-to-man, community-to-community.

What caused the shift from violence between communities to violence between civilians and law-enforcement agencies—the commodity riots? There seem to be three major factors. First, as the United States matured in its view of itself, a climate of support for improvement in race relations evolved. Whites became more sensitive to the needs of blacks and other minorities. Coupled closely with this climate were increasing expectations on the part of the blacks. They could more clearly see their goals of dignity and equality but observed with frustration the slow, seemingly crawling, rate of progress toward their aspirations.

Next, as the migration to the cities continued unabated, the United States Supreme Court outlawed the so-called restrictive covenants by which white property owners agreed not to sell to blacks. This 1948 ruling resulted in an expansion of housing for blacks (though not in a significantly large number of integrated neighborhoods). No more was the black community a clearly distinguished enclave into which white mobs could flow with relative impunity. The third and perhaps in a practical sense the most important cause was better-equipped, organized, and trained law-enforcement agencies, designed, ironically enough, to prevent confrontation between the white and black communities.

Commodity riots may be viewed as having three phases. Initially there is a period of tension in which crowds gather, sometimes committing violent group actions, such as stoning police cars. Then, usually after confrontation with the police, the local social control breaks down —property destruction, such as window breaking, occurs, and looting begins to spread. In the last, most violent, phase social order is usually nonexistent—arson, fire bombing, sniper fire, and countermeasures by law-enforcement agencies increase the level of violence. It is conceivable that the destruction of property and looting, major features of the

[11] Morris Janowitz, "Patterns of Collective Violence," in *The History of Violence in America*, 421.

commodity riot, are forms of striking back at the "symbolic enemy" by the nonwhite community.[12]

The makeup of the participants in the riots of the late 1960's was an indication that they were indeed different from the riots of earlier eras. The earliest and most violent participants were from the lower socio-economic strata of blacks, as was the case in Birmingham. Only after the contagion spread through the larger ghetto area did the usually well-disciplined middle-class blacks participate in the looting. Perhaps the growing acceptance of the legitimacy given to the black struggle led more middle-class blacks to participate in a more violent expression of their frustration.

Why have growing numbers of nonwhite communities resorted to riots in recent history? Three major causes of the riots have been identified: (1) the social and economic conditions of the community, (2) a desire to avenge racism and its accompanying frustrations, and (3) the disintegration of the nonwhite family with its resultant lack of firm personal control. Violence occurs and recurs when an individual or group is denied the opportunity to secure its basic needs. To this list we can add the sense of need for self-defense—both as an individual and as a group.

In the early years of this century visible but token progress was being made by minority-group Americans in their quest for full citizenship. The expectations of minorities matched this progress, and patience was dominant. The attempts of the trade unions to organize the southern blacks in 1946, the integration of the armed forces in the early 1950's, President John F. Kennedy's executive order of 1962 prohibiting discrimination in housing which was financed or which had its mortgage insured by federal funds, and the 1954 and 1964 civil-rights acts were examples of the steady progress being made.[13]

As the expectations and aspirations continued to rise, the visible rate of accomplishments reversed, and a downswing became obvious. Between 1954 and 1958, 530 cases of anti-Negro violence were recorded. In 1957 federal troops were called in to desegregate the public schools in Little Rock, Arkansas. The vast difference between expectations and actual conditions became brutally visible in the Birmingham riot. The curve had gone down too far.

As race relations took a downward path, frustrations over the blockage of progress, coupled with the overt manifestations of racism, began to take a deadly toll of the psyche of nonwhite Americans. What, after

12 *Ibid.*, 418–20.

13 James C. Davies, "The J-Curve of Rising and Declining Satisfactions as a Cause of Some Great Revolutions and a Contained Rebellion," in *The History of Violence in America*, 690–730.

all, is the cause of frustration if it is not the denial of satisfaction of those needs that are basic to all human beings? All persons seek some sense of self, an identity around which they can structure their lives. This need was denied most nonwhites. It became clear that they were in but not part of American society. To add to the oppression, most whites seemed to discount the importance of nonwhites. What greater insult can one individual bestow upon another than to ignore him? Ralph Ellison wrote, "You ache with the need to convince yourself that you do exist in the real world, that you're a part of all the sound and anguish, and you strike out with your fists, you curse and you swear to make them recognize you."[14]

If highly visible nonwhites are social nonentities, then it must follow that for some reason they are also inferior. The result of this plantation logic was that many if not most nonwhite Americans became imbued with self-hatred—a hatred of all manifestations of the differences which made them inferior to whites, a hatred of themselves. Accompanying these attacks on the soul were the physical attacks.

It is important to note that the most serious outbreaks of violence in 1963 and 1964 came from whites determined to block nonwhite demands for full citizenship. In a brief review of those dark years, the level of violence is awesome. Thirty-five southern black homes and churches were bombed, and ten people were killed. On September 15, 1963, four black girls died in the bombing of the Sixteenth Street Baptist Church in Birmingham, Alabama. In 1964 twelve black churches were burned, two civil-rights activists, the Reverend James Reeb and Mrs. Viola Liuzzo, were murdered in Alabama.

DESPERATE PEOPLE USE DESPERATE MEANS

A possible reaction to a continual threat of violence is retaliation. Abandoning integration as a goal, some nonwhites turned to violence against whites. Meeting violence not with passive acquiescence but with an equal or superior amount of violence are concepts desperate people can accept and understand. The right of self-defense has always been one of the accepted, basic rights of members of our society. However, for the nonwhite person in America, his vulnerability, his invisibility, and his self-hatred have caused him to repress this right for generations. It is only in very recent years that black defense against attack has become a major cause of violent racial confrontation.

The concept of self-defense is not new to blacks. The history of new nations illustrates that no people have won liberation without an armed struggle. In 1919, A. Philip Randolph wrote in the *Messenger*: "Anglo-Saxon jurisprudence recognizes the law of self-defense. . . . The black

[14] Ralph Ellison, *Invisible Man*, 7–8.

man has no rights which will be respected unless the black man forces that respect."[15] In 1959 the National Association for the Advancement of Colored People issued a statement supporting this principle. But the NAACP has never condoned mob violence, only the right of blacks individually and collectively to defend their persons, their homes, and their property from attack. This position has gained acceptance and strength in the black community in recent years. It led Stokely Carmichael to say, "Nothing more quickly repels someone bent on destroying you than the unequivocal message: O.K., fool, make your move, and run the same risk I run—of dying."[16]

In defending the right of the Black Panthers to arm themselves, Bobby Seale wrote: "We don't use our guns, we have never used our guns to go into the white community to shoot up white people. We only defend ourselves against anybody, be they black, blue, green, or red, who attacks us unjustly and tries to murder us and kill us for implementing our programs."[17] It is likely that self-defense, whether for actual or imagined attacks, will be a significant factor in future confrontations, especially confrontations involving whites and nonblacks—Indians, Mexican-Americans, and Puerto Ricans.

If a minority community's frustrations and needs are not met, then more violence can be expected. But it is probable that minority-group people will use a different form of violence from that which occurred in the 1960's. The violence of the coming years is likely to be more selectively applied by a cadre of activists who have despaired of the ability of society to change itself. Signs of the coming trend have been seen in recent gun battles with police and the selective shooting of police officers in large cities, such as New York City, Cleveland, Pittsburgh, Detroit, Oakland, and Los Angeles. The essence of this new form of violence is its organization. In the riots of 1964 to 1968 the absence of visible leadership charged with pressing collective demands was prominent. Sniper fire in those years had no organization or singleness of purpose.

The second Battle of Wounded Knee, South Dakota, offers a vivid illustration of how difficult it is for minorities to win violent confrontation with government officials. The 1973 armed seige of Wounded Knee by representatives of the American Indian Movement and their Oglala Sioux supporters resulted in the death of 2 Indians, several people wounded by gunshot, and millions of dollars' worth of property damage. At first glance it seems to be a shallow victory for the dissidents seeking to overthrow the elected Pine Ridge Indian Reservation

---

[15] Quoted in Meier and Rudwick, *op. cit.*, 402.
[16] Carmichael and Hamilton, *op. cit.*, 52.
[17] Bobby Seal, *Seize the Time*, 71.

government. The seventy-day battle ended when federal officials agreed to discuss Indian grievances, including broken treaties and compensation for lost land. At second glance, this was a better ending than the first Battle of Wounded Knee in 1890; the United States Army killed 153 Indians in that confrontation.

If organized violence becomes a means of enacting social change, an entirely new form of racial confrontation will develop. Can this method be successful? Traditionally such conflict succeeds only if it is employed against a political elite which rules the populace by terror. Even then, it is only the first step in a broad political campaign. Conditions in the United States indicate that political violence could even become counterproductive if it is rejected by the minority groups whose interests it is intended to serve. Some writers caution that there is a danger that, in their new-found militancy, blacks, Chicanos, Puerto Ricans, Indians, and women may become the victims of their own rhetoric.

AN INTERNATIONAL LINK

There is a contagion in violence. Americans involved in local and international conflicts learn to be violent. They tend to be most concerned when conflict which takes place in the community or the country has a direct effect upon them. International violence is generally far removed from most Americans and consequently is given less attention. Even so, there is often a close link between local violence and international violence. The link lies in the causes as well as the methods and strategies of conflict. Men fight to be free, to obtain equal opportunity in life's economic struggles, and to protect their families and possessions.

Tactics and techniques are constantly changing. As the methods of conflict become more refined, so too do the urban protests, often expressed in guerrilla warfare. The 1960's witnessed two innovations that may be of long-term significance: the hijacking of airplanes and the kidnapping of important persons. Aerial terrorism has proved to be an effective instrument of violence and means of internationalizing local struggles. This possibility was clearly demonstrated during the 1972 Olympic tragedy, when the games were disrupted by Arab terrorists. The attack ended with the death of eleven Israeli athletes, five Arab terrorists, and one West German policeman. The subsequent hijacking of an airplane led to the release of the three terrorists who survived the incident. Europe appears to be permanently involved in the Arab-Israeli issue; the terrorists (especially Al-Fatah) have access to Arab business offices in Europe, as well as to embassies and consulates that can provide money or a quick change of passports. "So," said one

Palestinian, "even if they were to close all of Al-Fatah's 23 branches in Germany, we'd still get along."[18] Will American terrorists imitate these scenes?

Also in 1972 genocide—the ultimate in violence—occurred in Burundi. The Hutu tribesmen revolted against the Tutsi tribesmen, who controlled the government. At the cost of tens of thousands of Tutsis slain, the revolt was finally put down. In retaliation the Tutsis, who are a one-to-six minority, proceeded to round up and murder virtually every Hutu of wealth, high education, or power. No less than 50,000 and perhaps as many as 100,000 people were slaughtered. According to one United Nations report, Burundi slipped back an entire generation in three terrible weeks.[19]

The United Kingdom, long considered the model for the integrated states of the world, is now facing a serious threat of postimperial fragmentation. The troubles in Northern Ireland are directly attributed to the phenomenon of widening cleavages within the former imperial country following its reduction in stature in world affairs. Of course, social scientists are quick to point out that religion, politics, ghetto living conditions, and income differences also contribute to the strife in Northern Ireland.

Racism is one of the major contributors to new forms of violence in the United States. Nonblack victims of discrimination are slowly resorting to more violent forms of expression. The militant actions of American Indians and Mexican-Americans clearly illustrate the importance of recognizing nonblacks. While much of the current protest in America against the "establishment" appears to be simply a protest against the pecking order of our society, many Americans realize they have been denied rights granted in the Constitution. This list includes nonwhites and women. As the demands for full justice for all people grow ever stronger, so, too, the possibility for violence grows.

In the United States, as in other countries of the world, violence is sometimes condoned and encouraged by citizens who give no serious thought to the consequences—that violence may become our accepted way of life. Those who express concern about the increasing use of violence are frequently dismissed as timid liberals or cowardly pacifists. Some leftist groups advocate violence as an automatically justifiable response to injustice. Interestingly, many right-wing groups advocate violence as a means of controlling the leftists. Most minority-group members have shown remarkable restraint. The same can be said for most majority-group members. Contrary to some writers, violence is not the norm of behavior in America.

18 *Time*, September 25, 1972, 23.
19 *Ibid.*, 33.

The level at which violence is conducted determines our degree of interest in it. Until recently Americans have been able to control violence through compromise and adjustment, although at times they have fallen short of just and equitable solutions. Whether it be tribalism in Africa, racism in America, clandestine struggles, international wars, or other forms of conflict, infringement upon the natural rights of individuals, groups, and nations has a history of resulting in violence. It seems obvious that the restructuring of domestic arrangements and international relations must take this simple fact into account.

Fifth Avenue, Uptown: A Letter From Harlem[20]
JAMES BALDWIN

There is a housing project standing now where the house in which we grew up once stood, and one of those stunted city trees is snarling where our doorway used to be. This is on the rehabilitated side of the avenue. The other side of the avenue—for progress takes time—has not been rehabilitated yet and it looks exactly as it looked in the days when we sat with our noses pressed against the windowpane, longing to be allowed to go "across the street." The grocery store which gave us credit is still there, and there can be no doubt that it is still giving credit. The people in the project certainly need it—far more, indeed, than they ever needed the project. The last time I passed by, the Jewish proprietor was still standing among his shelves, looking sadder and heavier but scarcely any older. Farther down the block stands the shoe-repair store in which our shoes were repaired until reparation became impossible and in which, then, we bought all our "new" ones. The Negro proprietor is still in the window, head down, working at the leather.

These two, I imagine, could tell a long tale if they would (perhaps they would be glad to if they could), having watched so many, for so long, struggling in the fishhooks, the barbed wire, of this avenue.

The avenue is elsewhere the renowned and elegant Fifth. The area I am describing, which, in today's gang parlance, would be called "the turf," is bounded by Lenox Avenue on the west, the Harlem River on the east, 135 Street on the north, and 130th Street on the South. We never lived beyond these boundaries; this is where we grew up. Walking along 145th Street—for example—familiar as it is, and similar, does not have the same impact because I do not know any of the people on the block. But when I turn east on 131st Street and Lenox Avenue, there is first a soda-pop joint, then a shoeshine "parlor," then a grocery store, then a dry cleaners, then the houses. All along the street there are people who watched me grow up along with my brothers and sisters; and, sometimes in my arms, sometimes underfoot, sometimes at my shoulder—or on it—their children, a riot, a forest of children, who include my nieces and nephews.

When we reach the end of this long block, we find ourselves on wide, filthy, hostile Fifth Avenue, facing that project which hangs over the avenue like a monument to the folly, and the cowardice, of good intentions. All along the block, for anyone who knows it, are immense human gaps, like craters. These gaps are not created merely by those who have moved away, inevitably into some other ghetto; or by those who have risen, almost always into greater capacity for self-loathing and self-delusion; or yet by those who, by whatever means—World War II, the Korean war, a policeman's gun or bill, a gang war, a brawl, madness, an overdose of heroin, or, simply, unnatural exhaustion—are dead. I am talking about those who are left, and I am talking principally about the young. What are they doing? Well, some, a minority, are fanatical churchgoers, members of the more extreme of the Holy Roller sects. Many, many more are "moslems," by affiliation or sympathy, that is to say that they are united by nothing more—and nothing less—than a hatred of the white world and all its works. They are present, for example, at every Buy Black street-corner meeting—meetings in which the speaker urger his hearers to cease trading with white men and establish a separate economy. Neither the speaker nor his hearers can possibly do this, of course, since Negroes do not own General Motors or RCA or the A & P, nor, indeed, do they own more than a wholly insufficient fraction of anything else in Harlem (those who do own anything are more interested in their profits than in their fellows). But these meetings nevertheless keep alive in the participators a certain pride of bitterness without which, however futile this bitterness may be, they could scarcely remain alive at all. Many have given up. They stay home and watch the TV screen, living on the earnings of their parents, cousins, brothers, or uncles, and only leave the house to go to the movies or to the nearest bar. "How're you making it?" one may ask, running into them along the block, or in the bar. "Oh, I'm TV-ing it"; with the saddest, sweetest, most shamefaced of smiles, and from a great distance. This distance one is compelled to respect; anyone who has traveled so far will not easily be dragged again into the world. There are further retreats, of course, than the TV screen or the bar. There are those who are simply sitting on their stoops, "stoned," animated for a moment only, and hideously, by the approach of someone who may lend them the money for a "fix." Or by the approach of someone from whom they can purchase it, one of the shrewd ones, on the way to prison or just coming out.

And the others, who have avoided all of these deaths, get up in the morning and go downtown to meet "the man." They work in the white man's world all day and come home in the evening to this fetid block. They struggle to instill in their children some private sense of honor or dignity which will help the child to survive. This means, of course, that they must struggle, stolidly, incessantly, to keep this sense alive in themselves, in spite of the insults, the indifference, and the cruelty they are certain to encounter in their working day. They patiently browbeat the landlord into fixing the heat, the plaster, the plumbing; this demands prodigious patience; nor is patience usually enough. In trying to make their hovels habitable, they are perpetually throwing good money after bad. Such frustration, so long endured, is driving many strong, admirable men and women whose only crime is color to the very gates of paranoia.

One remembers them from another time—playing handball in the playground, going to church, wondering if they were going to be promoted at school. One remembers them going off to war—gladly, to escape this block. One remembers their return. Perhaps one remembers their wedding day. And one sees where the girl is now—vainly looking for salvation from some other embittered, trussed, and struggling boy— and sees the all-but-abandoned children in the streets.

Now I am perfectly aware that there are other slums in which white men are fighting for their lives, and mainly losing. I know that blood is also flowing through those streets and that the human damage there is incalculable. People are continually pointing out to me the wretchedness of white people in order to console me for the wretchedness of blacks. But an itemized account of the American failure does not console me and it should not console anyone else. That hundreds of thousands of white people are living, in effect, no better than the "niggers" is not a fact to be regarded with complacency. The social and moral bankruptcy suggested by this fact is of the bitterest, most terrifying kind.

The people, however, who believe that this democratic anguish has some consoling value are always pointing out that So-and-So, white, and So-and-So, black, rose from the slums into the big time. The existence—the public existence—of, say, Frank Sinatra and Sammy Davis, Jr., proves to them that America is still the land of opportunity and that inequalities vanish before the determined will. It proves nothing of the sort. The determined will is rare—at the moment, in this country, it is unspeakably rare—and the inequalities suffered by the many are in no way justified by the rise of a few. A few have always risen—in every country, every era, and in the teeth of regimes which can by no stretch of the imagination be thought of as free. Not all of these people, it is worth remembering, left the world better than they found it. The determined will is rare, but it is not invariably benevolent. Furthermore, the American equation of success with the big time reveals an awful disrespect for human life and human achievement. This equation has placed our cities among the most dangerous in the world and has placed our youth among the most empty and most bewildered. The situation of our youth is not mysterious. Children have never been very good at listening to their elders, but they have never failed to imitate them. They must, they have no other models. That is exactly what our children are doing. They are imitating our immorality, our disrespect for the pain of others.

All other slum dwellers, when the bank account permits it, can move out of the slum and vanish altogether from the eye of persecution. No Negro in this country has ever made that much money and it will be a long time before any Negro does. The Negroes in Harlem, who have no money, spend what they have on such gimcracks as they are sold. These include "wider" TV screens, more "faithful" hi-fi sets, more "powerful" cars, all of which, of course are obsolete long before they are paid for. Anyone who has ever struggled with poverty knows how extremely expensive it is to be poor; and if one is a member of a captive population, economically speaking, one's feet have simply been placed on the treadmill forever. One is victimized, economically, in a thousand ways —rent, for example, or car insurance. Go shopping one day in Harlem— for anything—and compare Harlem prices and quality with those downtown.

The people who have managed to get off this block have only got as far as a more respectable ghetto. This respectable ghetto does not even have the advantages of the disreputable one—friends, neighbors, a familiar church, and friendly tradesmen; and it is not, moreover, in the nature of any ghetto to remain respectable long. Every Sunday, people who have left the block take the lonely ride back, dragging their increasingly discontented children with them. They spend the day talking, not always with words, about the trouble they've seen and the trouble—one must watch their eyes as they watch their children—they are only too likely to see. For children do not like ghettos. It takes them nearly no time to discover exactly why they are there. . . .

SUMMARY

As has been indicated, violence is the breakdown of law and order. It can be prevented only by the effective functioning of legal, political, and social institutions. To be effective these institutions must recognize and react to forces that may create an atmosphere which leads to violent actions. The social ills which caused the riots in the cities during the early 1960's went unnoticed or were ignored by those institutions which could have taken steps to correct them. A prime example is the city of Cincinnati, Ohio, where, before the disturbances, protest through political and nonviolent channels had become increasingly difficult. In preriot Newark, New Jersey, black and white leaders found themselves on opposite sides of almost every issue.[21]

The Watts riot, which erupted on August 11, 1965, in Los Angeles, California, had its origins in explosive issues set in a stage of poverty and deprivation. The congested Watts ghetto was made up primarily of small prewar rental homes. Living conditions were only slightly better than those of the Harlem dwellers. Thirty per cent of the ghetto's children came from broken homes, and the school dropout rate was more than twice the national average. Most of the persons living in Watts were migrants from the South. Since the majority were unskilled, the unemployment and underemployment rates were more than triple those of surrounding white communities. Twenty per cent of the black families in the area earned less than three thousand dollars each year, and over 50 per cent were on relief.

The hopes of blacks in the Watts area were dying even as the hopes of the blacks in other areas were rising. President Lyndon B. Johnson's antipoverty program had not become active in Los Angeles, partly because of unsympathetic local government administrators. In 1964 a California fair-housing act had been rejected by public referendum. Local observers pointed to Watts as a potential riot area, and the prediction came true. The blacks rioted. The Watts riot lasted for five days and its statistics present a grim picture—34 persons died, 1,032 were reported injured, 3,952 were arrested, and property damage was estimated at forty million dollars. We can only guess how many American Indians, Chicanos, and Puerto Ricans will feel the pressure to riot as their airtight cages of poverty become even more crowded with children who grow impatient with the affluent who encourage them to "be patient."

To prevent riots such as the one in Watts requires rapid change to mend ills. Political, legal, and social institutions must become responsive to the plight of the oppressed. Most responses to the demands of blacks have been more verbal than substantive. Crucial programs, such as rent supplements, aid to education, community-action programs, health-care programs, and pest control must become meaningful projects rather than political rhetoric. Basic programs, such as massive

21 *Report of the National Advisory Commission on Civil Disorders*, 58–60.

public works projects, guaranteed jobs, tax incentives to encourage the private sector to participate in slum problems, and meaningful welfare programs are desperately needed.

One of the keys to ensuring workable programs in these areas is honest communication among all levels of leadership, formal and informal. Nonwhite leaders must be given the opportunity to form and direct programs in their communities. White leaders must become educated to the real needs of minority-group communities. White leaders must be open and responsive to change—even if it means that they surrender some control over nonwhite communities.

The police have crucial roles to play within our communities. They are our first line of defense against violence. There are times, such as during the Watts riot, when the actions of ill-trained persons contribute to violence. Police training should include human relations training.

Violence is a fact of life in all aspects of our society. However, humane institutions can destroy the seeds of violence. In order to have humane institutions, we need programs to develop responsible and humane individuals. Each citizen must be helped to understand the rights and liberties of all others. A common language must be available so that all individuals may communicate one to another and respect the beliefs and rights of others. Our human relationships have a long history of violence, but we are not condemned to perpetuate this style of living—and dying.

Chapter 5
SUGGESTED READING

Abrahamsen, David. *Our Violent Society.* New York, Funk & Wagnalls Co., 1970.

Adelstein, Michael E., and Jean G. Pival, eds. *Women's Liberation.* New York, St. Martin's Press, Inc., 1972.

Baldwin, James. *Nobody Knows My Name.* New York, The Dial Press, 1961.

Bernard, Jessie Shirley. *Women and the Public Interest: An Essay on Policy and Protest.* Chicago, Aldine Publishing Co., 1971.

Bittker, Boris I. *The Case for Black Reparations.* New York, Random House, Inc., 1973.

Blumberg, Herbert H., and Paul Hare. *Nonviolent Direct Actions.* Washington, D.C., Corpus Publications, 1968.

Burma, John H., ed. *Mexican-Americans in the United States: A Reader.* New York, Harper & Row, Publishers, Inc., 1970.

Cahn, Edgar S. *Our Brother's Keeper: The Indian in White America.* Cleveland, The World Publishing Co., 1969.

Campbell, James S., et al. *Law and Order Reconsidered: A Staff Report to the National Commission on the Causes and Prevention of Violence.* New York, Bantam Books, Inc., 1970.

Caplovitz, David. *The Poor Pay More.* New York, The Free Press, 1967.

Carmichael, Stokely, and Charles V. Hamilton. *Black Power: The Politics of Liberation.* New York, Random House, Inc., 1967.

Clark, Kenneth B. *Dark Ghetto: Dilemmas of Social Power.* New York, Harper & Row, Publishers, Inc., 1965.

Cleaver, Eldridge. *Soul on Ice.* New York, McGraw-Hill Book Company, 1968.

Conant, Ralph W. *The Prospects for Revolution: A Study of Riots, Civil Disobedience, and Insurrection in Contemporary America.* New York, Harper & Row, Publishers, Inc., 1971.

Cordasco, Francesco, and Eugene Bucchioni. *Puerto Rican Children in Mainland Schools.* Metuchen, N.J., Scarecrow Press, 1968.

Coser, Lewis A. *The Functions of Social Conflict.* Glencoe, Ill., The Free Press, 1956.

Deloria, Vine, Jr. *Custer Died for Your Sins: An Indian Manifesto.* New York, The Macmillan Co., 1969.

———. *We Talk, You Listen.* New York, The Macmillan Co., 1970.

Douglas, Jack D. *Freedom and Tyranny: Social Problems in a Technological Society.* New York, Alfred A. Knopf, Inc., 1970.

Ellison, Ralph. *Invisible Man.* New York, Signet Books, 1952.

Endleman, Shalom, ed. *Violence in the Streets.* Chicago, Quadrangle Books, Inc., 1968.

Farmer, James. *Freedom—When?* New York, Random House, Inc., 1965.

Gornick, Vivian, and Barbara K. Moran, eds. *Woman in Sexist Society.* New York, Basic Books, Inc., 1971.

Graham, Hugh D., and Ted R. Gurr, eds. *The History of Violence in America.* New York, Bantam Books, Inc., 1969.

Hosokawa, Bill. *Nisei: The Quiet Americans.* New York, W. W. Norton & Co., Inc., 1969.

Howard, John R., ed. *Awakening Minorities: American Indians, Mexican-Americans, Puerto Ricans.* Chicago, Aldine Publishing Co., 1970.

Knowles, Louis L., and Kenneth Prewitt, eds. *Institutional Racism in America.* Englewood Cliffs, N.J., Prentice-Hall, Inc., 1969.

Levine, Stuart, and Nancy O. Lurie, eds. *The American Indian Today.* Baltimore, Md., Penguin Books, Inc., 1968.

Meier, August, and Francis L. Broderick, eds. *Negro Protest Thought in the Twentieth Century.* New York, The Bobbs-Merrill Co., 1965.

Mitchell, Juliet. *Woman's Estate.* New York, Pantheon Books, Inc., 1971.

Moore, Joan. *Mexican-Americans.* Englewood Cliffs, N.J., Prentice-Hall, Inc., 1970.

Morgan, Robin, ed. *Sisterhood is Powerful: An Anthology of Writings from the Women's Liberation Movement.* New York, Random House, Inc., 1970.

Powell, Elwin H. *The Design of Discord.* New York, Oxford University Press, 1971.

Rand, Christopher. *The Puerto Ricans.* New York, Oxford University Press, 1968.

Reische, Diana L., ed. *Women and Society.* New York, H. H. Wilson, 1972.

Report of the National Advisory Commission on Civil Disorder. New York, Bantam Books, Inc., 1968.

Samora, Julian. *La Raza: Forgotten Americans.* South Bend, Ind., University of Notre Dame Press, 1966.

Schrag, Peter. *The Decline of the WASP.* New York, Simon & Schuster, Inc., 1972.

Sexton, Patricia C. *Spanish Harlem: Anatomy of Poverty.* New York, Harper & Row, Publishers, Inc., 1965.

Silberman, Charles E. *Crisis in Black and White.* New York, Random House, Inc., 1964.

Spiegel, Don, and Patricia Keith-Spiegel, eds. *Outsiders U.S.A.: Original Essays on 24 Outgroups in American Society.* San Francisco, Rinehart Press, 1973.

Stambler, Sookie, ed. *Women's Liberation: Blueprint for the Future.* New York, Ace Publishing Corp., 1970.

Steiner, Stan. *The Mexican Americans.* New York, Harper & Row, Publishers, Inc., 1970.

———. *The New Indians.* New York, Dell Publishing Co., 1968.

Steinfield, Melvin. *Cracks in the Melting Pot: Racism and Discrimination in American History.* Beverly Hills, Calif., Glencoe Press, 1970.

Stroud, Drew McCord. *Viewpoints: The Majority Minority.* Minneapolis, Winston Press, 1973.

Stuber, Stanley I. *Human Rights and the Fundamental Freedoms in Your Community.* New York, Association Press, 1968.

Tanner, Leslie B., ed. *Voices from Women's Liberation.* New York, Signet Books, 1970.

United States Commission on Civil Rights. *Racism in America and How to Combat It.* Washington, D.C., Government Printing Office, 1970.

Yette, Samuel F. *The Choice: The Issue of Black Survival in America.* New York, G. P. Putnam's Sons, 1971.

Young, Whitney M., Jr. *To Be Equal.* New York, McGraw-Hill Book Company, 1964.

QUESTION: *What do these Anarchists want with dynamite bombs, anyhow?*
EMMA GOLDMAN: *Why, they want to use them in the great war if the social revolution ever comes.*
QUESTION: *Would you use dynamite?*
EMMA GOLDMAN: *I do not know what I would do. The time may not come when it need be necessary to use it.*—NEW YORK TIMES, October 7, 1893

An analysis of strategies for social change presents the student of human relations with the sobering thought that the logical counter to nonviolence is violence. Without the possibility of violence, nonviolence is but a shallow strategy when used in conflict situations. Generally speaking, people in power positions grant concessions to nonviolent protesters in order to avert violent confrontations. Few changes in power relationships are initiated for purely altruistic reasons.

Most victims of poverty, racism, and sexism, for example, are tempted to resort to violence in order to abate their problems. However, only a small number of alienated persons use violence as a means of gaining their freedom. Frantz Fanon, Malcolm X, Emmeline Pankhurst, and Saul Alinsky have offered tactics for individuals and groups looking for strategies more confrontative than sensitivity training, simulation games, and transactional analysis.

FRANTZ FANON (1925–61)
The writings of Frantz Fanon focused on the harsh realities of racism and oppression. Central to his thought was the belief that conflict—even violent revolution—is the prerequisite for freedom from colonialism. After serving in the French army during World War II, Fanon, a black man from a French colonial state in Africa, entered medical school at Lyons, France. Between 1944 and 1951 he had begun seriously to analyze racism in Europe. In 1951 he received a degree in psychiatry. Slowly he had begun to realize that no matter what his

education or position, most Europeans discriminated against him because of his black color.

In 1960 Fanon went to Ghana as ambassador of the Algerian Provisional Government. He died of leukemia in 1961, on the eve of Algerian independence. During the last year of his life Fanon worked furiously to finish his most renowned work, *The Wretched of the Earth*, which earned him the reputation of being a spokesman for millions of colonized peoples. The book discusses theories and strategies for the violent overthrow of colonial oppression, and it has become a handbook for revolutionaries throughout the world.

The seeds of Fanon's transformation into a theorist of violent revolution were sown in *Black Skin, White Masks*, in which he described in detail the frustration, anger, and alienation of the black man in a white world. There Fanon discussed the effect of colonization on people systematically stripped of their language, culture, and history. Specifically, he described black Algerians who were brainwashed by the French into feeling inferior to justify their oppression. Quoting Aimé Césaire, he said: "I am talking of millions of men who have been skillfully injected with fear, inferiority complexes, trepidation, servility, despair, abasement."

Fanon charged that the racist structure of colonization creates feelings of inferiority in the colonized people. He concluded that the abject conditions of discrimination, derision, and economic oppression cause black people to develop inferiority complexes.[1] Not until they are subjected to propaganda stressing the superiority of the white man and the inferiority of themselves do the people of color suffer for not being white and come to feel alienated: "Because it is a systematic negation of the person and a furious determination to deny the other person all attributes of humanity, colonialism forces the people it dominates to ask themselves the question constantly: 'In reality, who am I?' "[2]

Fanon, a psychiatrist, described in clinical terms the implicit and crucial relationships between psychological health and the socio-economic environment of the oppressed individual. He described the psychological means by which the colonial peoples of the world are divided by the European injection of racism within the society of each colony. It is through successfully internalizing racism among the various minorities, Fanon claimed, that the European succeeds in distributing his own racial guilt. And through the division of the colonized peoples the colonialist maintains his position of power:

The Frenchman does not like the Jew, who does not like the Arab, who

[1] Frantz Fanon, *Black Skin, White Masks*, 98.
[2] Frantz Fanon, *The Wretched of the Earth*, 250.

does not like the Negro. . . . The Arab is told: "If you are poor, it is be-
cause the Jew has bled you and taken everything from you." The Jew
is told: "You are not of the same class as the Arab because you are really
white and because you have Einstein and Bergson." The Negro is told:
"You are the best soldiers in the French Empire; the Arabs think they
are better than you, but they are wrong." But this is not true, the Negro
is told nothing because no one has anything to tell him.[3]

The colonialist further utilizes this strategy to combat insurrection
within the colonies. He sends "men of color" as soldiers to fight the insurrections of other "men of color," effectively using minorities to
oppress each other. To combat this oppression, debasement, and alienation, Fanon called upon the oppressed to rise up to reaffirm their
freedom and equality by seizing it from their oppressors. He wrote
that freedom and equality "given" by one's oppressors mean nothing—
they must be taken:

When it encounters resistance from the other, self-consciousness under-
goes the experience of desire—*the first milestone on the road that leads*
to the dignity of the spirit. Self-consciousness accepts the risk of its life,
and consequently it threatens the other in his physical being. It is solely
by risking life that freedom is obtained; only thus is it tried and proved
that the essential nature of self-consciousness is not bare existence. . . .
   Thus human reality in-itself-for-itself can be achieved only through
conflict and through the risk that conflict implies.[4]

Fanon warned black intellectuals of the danger of losing themselves
in their search for their native history and original cultures. He cautioned that pursuit of history might cause intellectuals to separate
themselves from the masses of their people, who must struggle to
merely sustain their existence. The real struggle, he wrote, lies not in
passively learning history but instead in fighting for the liberation of
the oppressed masses:

In no way should I dedicate myself to the revival of any unjustly
unrecognized Negro civilization. I will not make myself the man of
the past. I do not want to exalt the past at the expense of my present
and of my future. . . . Let us be clearly understood, I am convinced that
it would be of the greatest interest to be able to have contact with a
Negro literature or architecture of the third century before Christ. I
should be very happy to know that a correspondence had flourished
between some Negro philosopher and Plato. But I can absolutely not

[3] Fanon, *Black Skin, White Masks*, 103.
[4] *Ibid.*, 218.

see how this fact would change anything in the lives of the eight-year-old children who labor in the cane fields of Martinique or Guadeloupe.[5]

While the intellectuals should aid in providing the initial ideological leadership for the rest of the population during the prerevolutionary period, all too often they remain more concerned with assimilation into the colonialist society and block the growth of resistance in their appeals to nonviolent reform. They attempt to nullify their black brothers and sisters with their references to white values and ethics and their constant warnings that the people are neither militarily nor politically prepared for decolonization. Thus Fanon wrote: "it is clear that in the colonial countries the peasants alone are revolutionary, for they have nothing to lose and everything to gain. The starving peasant, outside the class system, is the first among the exploited to discover that only violence pays."[6]

While Marxist theory upholds the urban proletariat as the force and leadership behind the revolution, Fanon deviated from his Marxist idols, Marx and Lenin, by focusing almost entirely on the rural populace as the basic force behind the revolution in Africa.[7]

Fanon perceived the goal of the black bourgeoisie as much like that of the white bourgeoisie: to exist in a privileged status above the rural peasantry. In addition he saw the urban black worker as pampered and cultivated by the colonialists, who reap the benefits of the black workers' advanced skills. Thus, black peasants are subjected to the exploitation of the black bourgeoisie and the black proletariat. He believed that an analogy could be drawn between the masses of unemployed and underemployed black people (peasants) and the middle-class and upper-class blacks.

Describing the progression of decolonization, Fanon explained that an early phase of tension within the oppressed society takes the form of *anger turned in upon itself*. The colonized people, responding to their rising frustrations and hostility, unleash their pent-up violence through crime, riots, and killings within their own communities, violating only themselves. Thus, the gulf between thinking about violently attacking one's enemy and actually attacking him is crossed by the ignition of mass consciousness. The transition toward outward revolt, producing first scattered insurrections against the white settlers, begins to instill fear in the hearts of the colonists. The white oppressors, in response to their anxiety, fall into a cycle in which violence is escalated through reprisals, assassinations, and imprisonment, thereby pushing the force behind the native revolt into full swing.

[5] *Ibid.*, 226, 230.
[6] Fanon, *The Wretched of the Earth*, 61.
[7] David Caute, *Frantz Fanon*, 81–83.

144

Fanon warned that the first phase of the revolution, ideological enlightenment, must continue throughout the revolution. A people long oppressed will be easily duped by the psychological maneuvers of the colonialists unless they are persuaded to resist by the black intellectuals. As the colonialists attempt to fall back upon diplomatic strategies of compromise and reconciliation, the masses may be swayed by the new friendly gestures of the white government.

In pointing out the mistakes of earlier revolutionaries in the Third World who did not recognize the strength of the masses or their leaders and did not cultivate their consciousness, Fanon wrote:

They do not go to find the mass of the people. They do not put their theoretical knowledge to the service of the people; they only erect a framework around the people which follows an a priori schedule. . . .

The traditional chiefs are ignored, sometimes even persecuted. . . . The old men, surrounded by respect in all traditional societies and usually invested with unquestioned moral authority, are publicly held up to ridicule.[8]

Revolutionaries not only frequently fail to utilize the resources of the rural communities but also split the united effort of the people and further entrench the antagonisms between the rural and the urban populace. The final effect of their thoughtlessness will emerge, Fanon prophesied, after independence is achieved. The people will remain divided and the progress of the new state will be hampered:

The different strata of the nation never have it out with each other to any advantage; there is no settling of accounts with them. Thus, when independence is achieved, after the repression practiced on the country people, it is no wonder that you find incomprehension to an even greater degree. The country dwellers are slow to take up the structural reforms proposed by the government; and equally slow in following their social reforms, even though they may be very progressive if viewed objectively, precisely because the people now at the head of affairs did not explain to the people as a whole during the colonial period what were the aims of the party, the national trends, or the problems of international politics.[9]

Thus, the strategy proposed by Fanon for the black African revolution follows three basic phases: (1) the consciousness raising and propagandizement of the rural masses, (2) the initiation of violence by the peasantry in the country districts, joined by the support of the urban rebels, and (3) the transfer of the revolt to the urban areas by

[8] Fanon, *The Wretched of the Earth*, 113.
[9] *Ibid.*, 117.

the *lumpenproletariat*, the transient members of the rural communities who left their country homes and tribes to find work in the cities. The *lumpenproletariat* were defined by Fanon as an integral part of the success of the revolution. They are the transitional class between the rural peasant and the urban proletariat; their ranks include both the unemployed and the petty criminals—the pimps and the prostitutes of the urban slums. Through these displaced people who make up the bottom class of the urban social structure, the spirit of the revolution is carried into the cities, and the *lumpenproletariat* becomes the fighting force for the urban phase of the revolution.

Fanon asserted that the result of the national revolution would be a people who were united and transformed by their violent actions, politically aware, and freed from the psychosocial mystifications of colonialism. Through their re-creation in violent revolt, the people would grasp revolutionary truths and be prepared jointly to lead their new nation.[10]

Winning independence, Fanon concluded, would not be enough to maintain freedom. If black Africans are not prepared to counter the greed of their own bourgeoise, as well as the maneuvers of capitalist nations to infiltrate and dominate the new country, the goal of the revolution—freeing of humankind—will be lost. Thus, Fanon called for the new nation to turn its back on capitalistic European society and create a new order of things in the Third World: "We must turn over a new leaf, we must work out new concepts, and try to set afoot a new man."[11]

It is important to note that Fanon's recommendations were for the colonial people in Africa, not the United States, where blacks are recognized as citizens. However, the social and psychological enslavement of black Americans, plus the gap between the lower and middle classes, causes most of Fanon's writings to be relevant to black Americans. Malcolm X injected many of Fanon's concepts about black liberation into his speeches and writings.

MALCOLM X (1925–65)

Born in Omaha, Nebraska, on May 19, 1925, Malcolm Little was the son of the Reverend Earl and Louise Little. Earl Little was a Baptist minister and an organizer for the Universal Negro Improvement Agency, led by Marcus Garvey. Malcolm (who later took the name Malcolm X when he joined the Muslim faith) spent his life in the struggle against racist oppression. His earliest memories were filled with the persecution of his family, mainly because of his father's

[10] *Ibid.*, 147.
[11] *Ibid.*, 96–97.

politico-philosophical beliefs. When he was four years old, Malcolm's family barely escaped death when local whites burned their home. After the fire the Littles moved to the outskirts of East Lansing, Michigan, where Reverend Little was later killed by a white man (five of Earl Little's six brothers were also killed by whites). Malcolm's mother lost her family—and her sanity—during the depression of the 1930's.

Malcolm moved to Boston to live with his older sister, Ella. Although he had risen to the head of his class in a Michigan junior high school, he dropped out of school at the age of fifteen and learned the rudiments of street life in Boston and later in Harlem. A hustler, a pimp, a drug pusher, Malcolm was arrested and convicted of burglary when he was twenty-one. While in prison he learned of the Nation of Islam (the Black Muslims) and was converted to that faith. After returning from prison in 1952, he became actively involved in the Muslim movement, and in 1954 he became Malcolm X, a minister in the Nation of Islam. After being silenced by Elijah Muhammad for making a derogatory comment in 1963 ("the chickens are coming home to roost") about President John F. Kennedy's assassination, Malcolm X left the Muslim movement in March, 1964, and began the work of organizing first the Muslim Mosque, Inc., and soon thereafter the nonsectarian, politically oriented Organization of Afro-American Unity (OAAU), which had been designed as the vanguard for the black revolutionary movement in the United States. On February 21, 1965, soon after returning from his third trip to Africa and the Middle East, he was struck down by an assassin's bullet in New York City.

Malcolm X had risen from the streets of Harlem to become the persuasive teacher and organizer for the Nation of Islam and later had grown into the man who laid the foundation of Afro-American revolt and liberation in America. His strategies evolved from his wealth of experience and from a firm historical base; his tactics were those of unification among the black people of America and with the peoples of the Third World; his goal was the liberation of black people in America and of all humanity oppressed by white colonialism and capitalism. Thus, his policies of enlightenment and mobilization of a united organization of Afro-Americans assisted in creating the first stage toward the modern black revolution. He died before his work was completed, and much was left to be done, but he succeeded in laying a foundation for the liberation of his people; young revolutionaries who choose to follow his message believe the structure is still viable.

Throughout his life Malcolm X stressed that the concept of integration was a myth perpetrated by the white power structure to confuse and placate the unenlightened black people; he further stated that the leaders of the civil-rights movement were merely the puppets of the

147

white government: "The crooked politicians in the government are working with the Negro civil rights leaders, but not to solve the race problem. The greedy politicians . . . give lip-service to the civil rights struggle only to further their own selfish interests. And their main interest as politicians is *to stay in power*."[12]

Before his split with the Nation of Islam, many of Malcolm X's earlier beliefs became noticeably different from the teachings of Islam, especially those concerning social involvement, political revolution, and the characteristics of national unity. On March 8, 1964, he announced his departure from the Nation of Islam and stated that the Black Muslim movement had gone as far as it could because it was too narrowly sectarian and too inhibited.[13] On March 12, 1964, he made a public statement giving his stand. In that statement he explained that he planned to become involved in all phases of the black American movement and that his concern would be not only one of civil rights but particularly one of human rights. He reaffirmed his previous belief in racial separatism but stated that removal to Africa would occur far in the future. He elaborated on this point: before they went home to Africa, black Americans would need immediate action to relieve them from oppression by whites—from unemployment, poor schools, dilapidated housing and unnutritional food. Calling upon the need for unity throughout the black community, he prodded black leaders to forget their organizational differences and antagonisms.[14] He cautioned black leaders:

As leaders, we must stop worrying about the threat that we seem to think we pose to each other's personal prestige, and concentrate our united efforts toward solving the unending hurt that is being done daily. . . . The political philosophy of black nationalism means: we must control the politics and the politicians of our community. They must no longer take orders from outside forces. We will organize, and sweep out of office all Negro politicians who are puppets for the outside forces.[15]

Anticipating the question of white support, he noted that while blacks could accept ideas and financial support from all areas, whites could not join the movement: "There can be no black-white unity until there is first some black unity."[16]

[12] Benjamin Goodman, ed., *The End of White Supremacy: Four Speeches by Malcolm X*, 133. See also Malcolm X and Alex Haley, *The Autobiography of Malcolm X*.
[13] George Breitman, ed., *Malcolm X Speaks*, 18.
[14] *Ibid.*, 20–21.
[15] *Ibid.*, 21.
[16] *Ibid.*

Malcolm X observed that while most blacks are law-abiding, they should not rule out violence in cases of self-defense, particularly when the police or the government are unwilling to provide adequate protection and assistance for black people:

In areas where our people are the constant victims of brutality, and the government seems unable or unwilling to protect them, we should form rifle clubs that can be used to defend our lives and our property in times of emergency. . . . We should be peaceful, law-abiding—but time has come for the American Negro to fight back in self-defense whenever and wherever he is being unjustly and unlawfully attacked.[17]

In a speech on April 3, 1964, which Malcolm X called "The Ballot or the Bullet," he presented several proposals for a new interpretation and expansion of the civil-rights movement through black nationalism and away from traditional strategies of nonviolence. Explaining that for him the ballot only meant enfranchisement, Malcolm X stated that democracy in America had failed its black people and that the civil-rights movement only limited the scope of the black American's resources. He therefore proposed expanding the goals of the movement to include human rights and also allying his people with those of the Third World for a united struggle, focusing on both national and international liberation. Malcolm X admonished blacks to "expand the civil-rights struggle to the level of human rights, take it into the United Nations, where our African brothers can throw their weight on our side, where our Asian brothers can throw their weight on our side, where our Latin-American brothers can throw their weight on our side, and where 800 million Chinamen are sitting there waiting to throw their weight on our side."[18]

In the final period of his life from June, 1964, to February, 1965, Malcolm X was greatly influenced by his trip to Africa and the Middle East. During that period he shifted from the idea of revolution based solely upon racial oppression to one uniting the black American with the Third World in order to fight not only racial oppression but also the capitalistic and colonialistic oppression perpetrated by the American and European powers. From this perspective he saw the human-rights battle as one designed to encompass worldwide human liberation.

Consequently, Malcolm X broadened his definition of brotherhood and specified that even white radicals could join in the revolution, providing that they were truly revolutionary and willing to do whatever was called for in the fight for liberation. But he specified that this time they would follow the leadership of American black people:

[17] *Ibid.*, 22.
[18] *Ibid.*, 35.

149

Now I know it's smarter to say you're going to shoot a man for what he is doing to you than because he is white. If you attack him because he is white, you give him no out. He can't stop being white. We've got to give the man a chance. . . .

I'm not going to be in anybody's straitjacket. I don't care what a person looks like or where they come from. My mind is wide open to anybody who will help get the ape off our back.[19]

The revolutionary strategies proposed by Malcolm X and the Organization of Afro-American Unity were:

1. *Restoration*—the restoration of communications with African countries through the use of personal contact, independent national and international newspapers and publishing ventures, and the enlightenment of the people about their African history and culture.

2. *Reorientation*—the process of reorienting black people away from narrow, selfish perspectives toward broad community and world concerns. Reorientation includes establishing international ties between black America and the other oppressed people of the world. The central task entails teaching people their rights, roles, and responsibilities as members of humankind.

3. *Education*—the creation of innovative educational methods to teach and expand the awareness of black children. Education involves writing black history to enlighten black youth about their heritage. Above all else, this strategy requires blacks to assume control of the educational systems in which their children are taught.

4. *Economic security*—the development of financial means to free black people from economic oppression. This strategy necessitates the formation of a technician pool or bank from which black American technicians can be identified and used to the mutual benefit of black American communities as well as African countries.

5. *Self-defense*—the encouragement of all Afro-Americans to protect themselves and their families against racist attacks, particularly when unassisted by local law-enforcement authorities.

The final phase of the Black Revolution, Malcolm X concluded, consists of moving first from inside America and then into the world arena. Clearly this goal requires the alliance of Afro-Americans and the people of the Third World—those of Africa, Asia, and Latin America. Thus, the strategy shifts from national revolution against racist oppression to international revolution against colonialist oppression throughout the world. Like Fanon, Malcolm X defined the goal of the Black Revolution as the liberation of all humanity. Women's struggle for equality also illustrates viable tactics for social change.

[19] *Ibid.*, 213.

EMMELINE GOULDEN PANKHURST (1858–1928)

Born in Manchester, England, in July, 1858, Emmeline Goulden grew up in a prosperous family in which politics and philosophical ideas were freely expressed and the cause of women's suffrage was openly supported. After attending a finishing school in Paris, Emmeline married Richard Marsden Pankhurst, a man twenty years her senior, who had drafted England's first women's suffrage bill and later formulated the Married Women's Property acts of 1870 and 1882. Two of their five children—Christabel and Sylvia—joined their mother in the struggle for women's rights. After the death of her husband in 1898, Mrs. Pankhurst supported her family by working as the registrar of births and deaths for Manchester. In 1903 she founded the Women's Social and Political Union (WSPU), which was soon to become the revolutionary vanguard of women's suffrage in England. She died in 1928, a month before women were granted full enfranchisement by Parliament.

The revolutionary struggles of Emmeline Pankhurst and the women's suffrage movement that she founded place her in the forefront of revolutionary leaders who have fought for the liberation of humankind. Mrs. Pankhurst and her followers initiated a break with the strategies of the traditional women's suffrage movement, which had typically utilized nonviolent campaigns rather than physical force. Through her enthusiasm and organizational skill she persuaded others to challenge the oppression of the English government.[20]

In the early years of the movement, until 1905, the suffragettes followed the traditional means of appealing to Parliament for the right to vote: they made speeches, lobbied, and wrote articles in defense of women's suffrage. Despite these activities, most members of Parliament remained indifferent to their appeals. In 1905 the members of the WSPU began to abandon their more silent forms of appeal and interrupted governmental meetings with their demands for the vote. When they refused to leave meetings peacefully, WSPU members were arrested and imprisoned. With each trial and prison sentence, Parliament was challenged, and gradually public opinion began to shift in favor of the women's suffrage movement.

The first to begin the trend was Mrs. Pankhurst's daughter Christabel and her friend Annie Kenney. They were imprisoned after they refused to pay fines for "technical assault" of a police officer (Christabel had threatened to spit at her arresting officer). In the following years of struggle the women's suffrage movement used this strategy to publicize its efforts. After each new arrest more women joined the ranks of the WSPU. Women who were imprisoned for their political activities

[20] See Christabel Pankhurst, *Unshackled: The Story of How We Won the Vote.*

began a program of hunger strikes (Gandhi was later to use the same tactic).

There was a brief truce in 1910 when the newly elected Liberal government promised to support an enfranchisement bill. Parliament tabled the bill and added insult to its behavior by passing a bill enfranchising more men. Angered by the deception of their "liberal" supporters in Parliament, Mrs. Pankhurst led WSPU members in a march in which they attempted to force their entry into the House of Parliament. A riot broke out, 150 women were arrested, and hundreds more were brutally assaulted by police during the six hours of confrontation. Following their aborted attempt to enter the House of Parliament, Mrs. Pankhurst and her followers turned to the strategy of guerrilla warfare (it is important to note that the WSPU decided to violate only property, not human life). Following the strategy of destruction and challenge to the government, the members of the movement destroyed private property, burned ticket booths at the race tracks, destroyed the greens of golf courses frequented by members of Parliament, and smashed windows in stores and government buildings. Each time the women were imprisoned, they followed the example set by Emmeline Pankhurst and went on hunger and thirst strikes. During their hunger strikes the militants were often subjected to forced feeding. Once released, they were subject to the infamous Cat and Mouse Act, which permitted hunger-striking prisoners to be rearrested once they had regained their strength. This act turned out to be more embarrassing than effective for the British government.

In her autobiography, *My Own Story*, Mrs. Pankhurst described the organization of the WSPU and the evolution of its revolutionary strategies. While her overall plan for winning the vote shifted with the changing political winds of the period, the basic organizational creed of working only for women's suffrage remained intact:

In the first place, our members are absolutely single-minded; they concentrate all their forces on one object, political equality with men. No member of the W.S.P.U. divides her attention between suffrage and other social reforms. We hold that both reason and justice dictate that women shall have a share in reforming the evils that afflict society, especially those evils bearing on women themselves. Therefore, we demand, before any other legislation whatever, the elementary justice of votes for women.[21]

Mrs. Pankhurst's organization required each member to sign a declaration of loyalty to the suffrage movement. Furthermore, the members pledged to refrain from joining any political party until a women's

[21] Emmeline Pankhurst, *My Own Story*, 57–62, 279–84, 292–99.

suffrage act had been enacted. Members disagreeing with organizational policy were immediately expelled from the ranks. Beyond these requirements the WSPU was not a complex organization. Ms. Pankhurst wrote:

The W.S.P.U. is not hampered by a complexity of rules. We have no constitution and by-laws; nothing to be amended or tinkered with or quarrelled over at an annual meeting. In fact, we have no annual meeting, no business sessions, no elections of officers. The W.S.P.U. is simply a suffrage army in the field. It is purely a volunteer army, and no one is obliged to remain in it. Indeed we don't want anybody to remain in it who does not ardently believe in the policy of the army.[22]

The strategy of the WSPU revolved around the tactics of (1) propagandizement, (2) unification, (3) continued political nonalignment, (4) militant action, and (5) utilization of the press to publicize its activities. The initial phases, propagandizement and unification, began in the early years of the organization and continued throughout the struggle. Soon after its conception the WSPU followed the example of the Salvation Army and carried its message to the people—the members went to the streets, speaking in public squares and urging the general public to join in the struggle for women's political liberation. Concurrently with the attempt to educate the general public to the issues, they also met with other women's groups throughout England and in some of the colonies and provinces, particularly in Canada. Wherever they spoke and in whatever journal they were able to publish articles, they tried to unify women's groups to support the policies of the WSPU. Their audiences included women from every social class— wives of statesmen and of wealthy businessmen, professional women, and working-class women.

While the suffrage movement rested upon little if any revolutionary theory, and while its strategy and tactics were not always unique to history, the struggle of Mrs. Pankhurst and the WSPU stand out in history not only because they represent the first revolutionary organization founded and maintained solely by women but also because their strategies utilized violence as a means toward social-political change, but not the the expense of deliberately taking lives. Not once did a member of the WSPU take a human life. Mrs. Pankhurst stated with pride that the moving spirit of militancy in the suffrage struggle was a deep and abiding reverence for human life. Building on the commitment to preserving human life, Saul Alinsky proposed tactics which took his followers, who were mainly white, one step short of killing their enemies.

[22] *Ibid.*, 149.

SAUL ALINSKY (1909–72)

Saul Alinsky, the only child of Jewish immigrants Benjamin and Sarah Alinsky, was born in a Chicago slum tenement in 1909. His parents were divorced when he was thirteen, and he lived alternately with his mother in Chicago and his father in Los Angeles. In 1926 he graduated from Hollywood, California, High School and entered the University of Chicago to study archaeology. He took some courses in sociology but was not impressed by them because the content was too far removed from reality. In his junior year he made his first major attempt at political intervention when he organized food relief for sriking coal miners in southern Illinois.

Following his graduation from the University of Chicago with a bachelor of philosophy degree, and after an abortive attempt to earn a doctorate, Alinsky became a criminologist for the State Prison Classification Board at the Illinois State Penitentiary in Joliet. While working for the prison system, he became even more aware of the gap between the causes and the treatment of crime and delinquency. During his spare time in the 1930's he worked in several capacities, including serving as an organizer for the CIO and a fund raiser for southern sharecroppers.

In 1938 Alinsky began his career as a "professional radical" by organizing leaders in Chicago's Back-of-the-Yards slum. He gained support of local leaders and proceeded to form a power bloc which pressured meat-packing companies, landlords, businesses, and local politicians to undertake an affirmative action program to transform the area into a model community.[23] In 1940 Marshall Field III gave Alinsky financial support to start the Industrial Areas Foundation (IAF), an agency that contracts to build community organizations.

During World War II Alinsky worked on special assignments for the United States Department of Labor. Following the war he returned to the IAF and organized thousands of oppressed people from New York to California. In 1947 his manifesto, *Reveille for Radicals*, was published by the University of Chicago Press. In that book Alinsky defined the radical as "that person to whom the common good is the greatest social value,"[24] and the liberal was defined as one who "puts his foot down firmly on thin air."[25] Alinsky observed that democracy operates on the basis of pressure groups and power blocs. If the poor are not organized into a self-determining mass, he wrote, they will be effectively excluded from the democratic process. He also asserted that people are not inherently bad, only morally ambivalent and susceptible

[23] Lois Wille, *Chicago Daily News*, January 26, 1968, 1.
[24] Saul Alinsky, *Reveille for Radicals*, 22.
[25] *Ibid.*, 11.

to dehumanizing conditions. The hope for humanity, he concluded, depends on people getting to know each other as human beings.

He continued his activities during the 1950's and made his first move into the black community in 1960, organizing The Woodlawn Organization (TWO), which successfully resisted urban renewal. In 1965 he was invited to Rochester, New York, where he helped organize FIGHT (Freedom, Independence, God, Honor—Today) to combat the discriminatory practices of the Xerox Corporation and Eastman Kodak Company.

In 1968 Alinsky turned his attention to America's white middle class and established an institute for training representatives of the white community to be social revolutionaries. His second book, *Rules for Radicals*, was published in 1971. It showed evidence that Alinsky's love of democracy and belief in self-determination and power had not changed substantially. In *Rules for Radicals* he explained the rationale and tactics of his approach.

His last years were spent teaching others (mainly the "Have-a-Little, Want Mores") to be radicals "who would change the world from what it is to what it could be"[26] and, by organizing the masses of "Have-Nots," to take power away from the "Haves." His central conviction as a radical in a free society was "a belief that if people have the power to act in the long run they will make the right decisions."[27]

As a strategist for the "people's army," Alinsky moved along the entire continuum of change tactics, though stopping short of physical violence. He took a practical approach to the question of ends and means: "ends" meaning what you want and "means" being how to get it. He approached the selection of a tactic in an existential manner, depending on the characteristics of the opposition: "There are certain rules for radicals who want to change the world; there are certain central concepts of action in politics that operate regardless of the scene or the time. To know these is basic to a pragmatic attack on the system."[28]

Alinsky understood the potency of such words as *power, self-interest, compromise, ego, conflict,* and *political legitimacy.* For example, Alinsky explained power in terms of the ability to act. Self-interest was not a noxious term to him but merely a reality of life that could be transcended on specific occasions. If people are to be free, he argued, they must have positive conviction and believe in themselves. He viewed conflict and compromise as integral aspects of social change.

As he trained organizers from every segment and region of society, Alinsky began to identify those qualities which he believed character-

[26] *Ibid.,* xviii.
[27] *Ibid.,* 80.
[28] *Ibid.*

ize a potentially successful organizer: *curiosity*, which has no limits and breaks through accepted patterns; *irreverence* for everything except respect for others and their right for quality of life; *imagination*, which synthesizes and operates as a creative drive; *humor*, used to face the hard realities of life and as a weapon against the opposition; an *organized personality*, which can tolerate the chaos and ambiguity of the job; a *well-integrated political schizoid orientation to change*, which allows comfortable fluctuation of tactics; and a *free and open mind*.

The organizer, as Alinsky characterized him, is an architect and engineer who creates the new from the old. According to Alinsky, the essential difference between a leader and an organizer is that the leader wants power himself, while the organizer's raison d'être lies in securing power for others to use.

Alinsky set the stage for his entrance into a community with various tactics. Where he was unknown, he agitated the opposition and used consciousness-raising maneuvers to make his qualifications as an organizer known to the community. He entered a community only by invitation from a representative segment of the population. He gained support from the community by tempting his opponents into characterizing him as a "dangerous enemy."

Alinsky outlined thirteen rules to be used as weapons against social injustice:

Always remember the first rule of power tactics: Power is not only what you have but what the enemy thinks you have.

The second rule is: Never go outside the experience of your people. *When an action or tactic is outside the experience of the people, the result is confusion, fear, and retreat. It also means collapse of communication, as we have noted.*

The third rule is: Wherever possible go outside of the experience of the enemy. *Here you have to cause confusion, fear, and retreat....*

The fourth rule is: Make the enemy live up to their own book of rules. *You can kill them with this, for they can no more obey their own rules than the Christian church can live up to Christianity.*

The fourth rule carries with it the fifth rule: Ridicule is man's most potent weapon. *It is almost impossible to counterattack ridicule. It also infuriates the opposition, who then react to your advantage.*

The sixth rule is: A good tactic is one that your people enjoy. *If your people are not having a ball doing it, there is something wrong with the tactic.*

The seventh rule is: A tactic that drags on too long becomes a drag....

The eighth rule: Keep the pressure on, *with different tactics and actions, and utilize all events of the period for your purpose.*

The ninth rule: The threat is usually more terrifying than the thing itself.

The tenth rule: The major premise for tactics is the development of operations that will maintain a constant pressure upon the opposition. . . .

The eleventh rule is: If you push a negative hard and deep enough it will break through into its counterside; *this is based on the principle that every positive has its negative. We have already seen the conversion of the negative into the positive, in Mahatma Gandhi's development of the tactic of passive resistance. . . .*

The twelfth rule: The price of a successful attack is a constructive alternative. *You cannot risk being trapped by the enemy in his sudden agreement with your demand and saying "You're right—we don't know what to do about this issue. Now you tell us."*

The thirteenth rule: Pick the target, freeze it, personalize it, and polarize it.[29]

Saul Alinsky lived by his own rules, and his life demonstrated that passion and competence can change communities from what they are to what community residents want them to become.

OTHER DIMENSIONS OF VIOLENCE

Many Americans tend to think of violence only in terms of black-white confrontations. Such a limited view ignores the fact that most violence is not racial in nature. In reality, most of it grows out of efforts of white Americans to destroy each other. The sheer magnitude of intragroup violence on a global scale caused the members of a committee preparing a yearbook focusing on world peace to ponder: "How, we asked each other, could we place the atrocities of Biafra, Bangladesh, Southeast Asia, and Northern Ireland within a framework of rationality? And how could we make our readers sensitively aware of the fact that most human beings live in a world where death and disease are commonplace, education and gainful employment are almost nonexistent, and squalor and stagnation are their environments?"[30]

Much intragroup violence is a counterreaction to structural violence —violence growing out of social structures which impede the equal distribution of rewards for labor in terms of money, power, or social justice. This unequal distribution of rewards exists in families, schools, jobs, and clubs. Children are deprived of their civil rights, women are still treated as second-class citizens, and aged or poor relatives are shunned. Commenting on structural violence, Thornton Monez wrote:

[29] *Ibid.,* 126–30.
[30] George Henderson, ed., *Education for Peace: Focus on Mankind,* xi.

Direct violence is easily recognized because it is volatile, overt, and dramatic, as portrayed in our history books and on our television screens. Structural violence, in contrast, is slower and less readily visible as an agent of destruction. . . . Structural violence expressed in the form of lead-paint poisoning in a slum neighborhood or drastically lowered levels of life expectancy in Latin America is no less violent or life-negating than that which is more directly expressed with napalm or bullets in warfare.[31]

Structural violence in intergroup relationships is not limited to black Americans. Puerto Ricans have the poorest housing, the fewest educational and employment opportunities, and the lowest incomes of all minority groups living in New York City. Although Spanish-speaking people can trace their American heritage back over 450 years, they have yet to achieve the socioeconomic status accorded Anglo-Americans. American Indians have an average life expectancy of forty-four years. Three-fourths of all housing units in San Francisco's Chinatown are substandard. Appalachian whites are generally overlooked in most efforts to improve the quality of life for the poor.

Adolf Hitler's efforts to rid Germany of Jews is a vivid example of how violence can become a national hysteria. Hitler's eugenic creed, which has been adopted by many hate groups, has the following tenets:

1. Men are naturally and innately unequal.

2. These innate differences tend to be hereditary.

3. Innately superior persons tend to rise to the top of the social ladder (thus control of the state belongs to the superior people).

4. Superior stocks of people tend to die out, while inferior stocks tend to increase.[32]

These tenets have generally been refuted by sociological and psychological studies. Historically, the culmination of group hate has been an all-out effort of one group to get rid of another. Hitler used this method when he wrote:

The Jew is the ferment of the decomposition of peoples. This means that the Jew destroys and has to destroy, because he is completely lacking in any concept of work for the common good. . . . He has certain traits which nature has given him and he can never rid himself of these traits. The Jew is harmful to us. Whether he harms us consciously or unconsciously is not the question; we must consciously protect the welfare of our people.[33]

31 Thornton B. Monez, "Working for Peace: Implications for Education," in Henderson, *Education for Peace*, 15.

32 William M. McGovern, *From Luther to Hitler*, 631.

33 Gordon W. Prange, ed., *Hitler's Words*, 7.

At some time most groups have been "Jews" in their own country. The strategies for change proposed by Frantz Fanon, Malcolm X, Emmeline Pankhurst, and Saul Alinsky apply to situations in which intragroup and intergroup exploitation exist. In the final analysis, however, it is clear that no society can exist without order. Violence is the result of the breakdown of social order. Those concerned with abating or preventing violence should remember that social order is maintained by the effective functioning of legal, political, and social institutions.

On Being An Anarchist[34]
NEW YORK TIMES, OCTOBER 7, 1893

The questions were asked by Assistant District Attorney McIntyre.

QUESTION: *You do not believe in the laws of the State?*

ANSWER: *I am an Anarchist, and against all laws. My theory is that the Legislature and the courts are of no use to the mass of the people. The laws passed help the rich and grind the poor.*

QUESTION: *You don't believe in living up to those laws, then!*

ANSWER: *I do not believe in any laws except those of morality.*

QUESTION: *Do you believe in Most and his teachings?*

ANSWER: *Most is an Anarchist and I am an Anarchist, but we do not agree in a great many particulars.*

QUESTION: *Is there any government on earth whose laws you approve?*

ANSWER: *No, Sir; for they are all against the people.*

QUESTION: *Why don't you leave this country if you don't like its laws?*

ANSWER: *Where shall I go? Everywhere on earth the laws are against the poor, and they tell me I cannot go to Heaven, nor do I want to go there.*

QUESTION: *Do you believe in the Constitution of the United States?*

ANSWER: *I think it is excellent in theory but it is not lived up to. It is distorted for the benefit of the rich.*

QUESTION: *You speak of tyrants here! Whom do you mean by that?*

ANSWER: *The Vanderbilts and the Jay Goulds and the representatives of the Government who deprive its working people of food.*

QUESTION: *Why is it that you do not believe in any religion?*

ANSWER: *Because I do not think that any church has ever done a single thing to ameliorate the condition of the poor.*

QUESTION: *Didn't you tell your hearers to take bread by force if they couldn't get it peaceably?*

[34] Excerpted from the *New York Times*, October 7, 1893, report of Emma Goldman's testimony in her trial for inciting a riot.

ANSWER: *No. But I think the time will come, judging by what has happened, when they will be compelled to do so. That is what I told them on the night I spoke.*

QUESTION: *What do these Anarchists want with dynamite bombs, anyhow?*

ANSWER: *Why, they want to use them in the great war if the social revolution ever comes.*

QUESTION: *Would you use dynamite?*

ANSWER: *I do not know what I would do. The time may not come when it need be necessary to use it. . . .*

(On October 16, Emma Goldman, termed a "yellow-haired evangel of disorder by The New York Times's *reporter, was sentenced to one year in the women's penitentiary on Blackwell's Island.)*

Chapter 6
SUGGESTED READING

Abrahamsen, David. *Our Violent Society*. New York, Funk & Wagnalls Co., 1970.

Alinsky, Saul. *Reveille for Radicals*. Chicago, University of Chicago Press, 1947.

———. *Rules for Radicals*. New York, Vintage Books, Inc., 1971.

Aptheker, Herbert. *American Slave Revolts*. New York, International Publishers Co., Inc., 1964.

Arendt, Hannah. *On Violence*. New York, Harcourt Brace Jovanovich, Inc., 1970.

Bienen, Henry. *Violence and Social Change: A Review of Current Literature*. Chicago, University of Chicago Press, 1968.

Bingham, Jonathan B., and Alfred M. Bingham. *Violence and Democracy*. New York, The World Publishing Co., 1970.

Breitman, George. *The Last Year of Malcolm X: The Evolution of a Revolutionary*. New York, Merit Publishers, 1967.

———, ed. *Malcolm X Speaks*. New York, Grove Press, Inc., 1968.

Brinton, Crane. *The Anatomy of Revolution*. New York, Vintage Books, Inc., 1962.

Bullock, Allan. *Hitler: A Study in Tyranny*, rev. ed. New York, Harper & Row, Publishers, Inc., 1962.

Caute, David. *Frantz Fanon*. New York, The Viking Press, Inc., 1970.

Conant, Ralph W. *The Prospects for Revolution: A Study of Riots, Civil Disobedience, and Insurrection in Contemporary America*. New York, Harper's Magazine Press, 1971.

Crankshaw, Edward. *Gestapo: Instrument of Tyranny*. New York, Viking Press, Inc., 1956.

Daniels, David N., Marshall F. Gilula, and Frank M. Ochberg, eds. *Violence and the Struggle for Existence.* Boston, Little, Brown & Co., Inc., 1970.

Delarue, Jacques. *The Gestapo: A History of Horror.* New York, William Morrow & Co., Inc., 1964.

Demaris, Ovid. *America the Violent.* New York, Cowles Book Co., Inc., 1970.

Ellul, Jacques. *Violence: Reflections from a Christian Perspective.* Translated by Cecilia Gaul Kings. New York, Seabury Press, 1969.

Fanon, Frantz. *Black Skin, White Masks.* New York, Grove Press, Inc., 1967.

———. *The Wretched of the Earth.* New York, Grove Press, Inc., 1963.

Feshbach, Seymour, and Robert D. Singer. *Television and Aggression: An Experimental Field Study.* San Francisco, Jossey-Bass, Inc., 1971.

Fogelson, Robert M. *Violence as Protest: A Study of Riots and Ghettos.* Garden City, N.Y., Doubleday & Co., Inc., 1971.

Goldwin, Robert A., ed. *On Civil Disobedience.* Chicago, Rand-McNally & Co., 1969.

Goodman, Benjamin, ed. *The End of White Supremacy: Four Speeches by Malcolm X.* New York, Merlin House, 1971.

Gray, J. Glenn. *On Understanding Violence Philosophically, and Other Essays.* New York, Harper & Row, Publishers, Inc., 1970.

Gurr, Ted R. *Why Men Rebel.* Princeton, N.J., Princeton University Press, 1970.

Henderson, George, ed. *Education for Peace: Focus on Mankind.* 1973 Yearbook. Washington, D.C., Association for Supervision and Curriculum Development, 1973.

Hersey, John. *Algiers Motel Incident.* New York, Alfred A. Knopf, Inc., 1968.

Hitler, Adolph. *Mein Kampf.* New York, Reynal & Hitchcock, 1941.

Hofstadter, Richard, and Michael Wallace, eds. *American Violence: A Documentary History.* New York, Alfred A. Knopf, Inc., 1970.

Irwin, Inez Haynes. *The Story of the Women's Party.* New York, Harcourt, Brace & Co., 1921.

Jackson, George. *Soledad Brother: The Prison Letters of George Jackson.* New York, Bantam Books, Inc., 1970.

Jones, Howard M. *Violence and Reason.* Kingsport, Tenn., Kingsport Press, Inc., 1969.

Kerner, Otto. *Report of the National Advisory Commission on Civil Disorders.* New York, Grosset & Dunlap, Inc., 1968.

Koestler, Arthur. *Reflections on Hanging.* New York, The Macmillan Co., 1967.

Larsen, Otto N., ed. *Violence and the Mass Media.* New York, Harper & Row, Publishers, Inc., 1968.

Leiden, Carl, and Karl M. Schmitt, eds. *The Politics of Violence: Revolution in the Modern World.* Englewood Cliffs, N.J., Prentice-Hall, Inc., 1968.

Lynd, Staughton, ed. *Nonviolence in America: A Documentary History.* Indianapolis, The Bobs-Merrill Co., 1966.

Machiavelli, Niccolo. *The Discourses of Niccolo Machiavelli.* London, Routledge and Kegan Paul, 1950.

————. *The Prince*. New York, E. P. Dutton & Co., Inc., 1948.

Malcolm X and Alex Haley. *The Autobiography of Malcolm X*. New York, Grove Press, Inc., 1965.

McGovern, William M. *From Luther to Hitler*. New York, Houghton-Mifflin Co., 1941.

Megargee, Edwin I., and Jack E. Hokanson, eds. *The Dynamics of Aggression: Individual, Group, and International Analysis*. New York, Harper & Row, Publishers, Inc., 1970.

Menninger, Karl A. *The Crime of Punishment*. New York, Viking Press, Inc., 1968.

Merton, Thomas. *Faith and Violence: Christian Teaching and Christian Practice*. Notre Dame, Ind., University of Notre Dame Press, 1968.

Nieburg, Harold L. *Political Violence: The Behavioral Process*. New York, St. Martin's Press, Inc., 1969.

Oglesby, Carl. *Containment and Change*. New York, The Macmillan Co., 1967.

Pankhurst, Christabel. *Unshackled: The Story of How We Won the Vote*. Ed. by Lord Pethick-Lawrence. London, Hutchinson & Co., 1959.

Pankhurst, Emmeline. *My Own Story*. New York, Hearst's International Library Co., 1914.

The Pentagon Papers as Published by "The New York Times." New York, Bantam Books, Inc., 1971.

Pinkney, Alphonso. *The American Way of Violence*. New York, Random House Inc., 1972.

Prange, Gordon W., ed. *Hitler's Words*. Washington, D.C., American Council on Public Affairs, 1944.

Rossi, Peter H., ed. *Ghetto Revolts*. Chicago, Aldine Publishing Co., 1970.

Rubenstein, Richard E. *Rebels in Eden: Mass Political Violence in the United States*. Boston, Little, Brown & Co., Inc., 1970.

Seal, Bobby. *Seize the Time*. New York, Random House, Inc., 1968.

Stark, Rodney. *Police Riots: Collective Violence and Law Enforcement*. Belmont, Calif., Wadsworth Publishing Co., Inc., 1972.

Suhl, Yuri. *They Fought Back: The Story of Jewish Resistance in Nazi Europe*. New York, Crown Publishers, 1967.

Toch, Hans. *Violent Men: An Inquiry Into the Psychology of Violence*. Chicago, Aldine Publishing Co., 1969.

Usdin, Gene, ed. *Perspectives on Violence*. New York, Brunner/Mazel, Inc., 1972.

Vickers, George, ed. *Dialogue on Violence*. Indianapolis, The Bobbs-Merrill Co., 1968.

Wertham, Frederic. *A Sign for Cain: An Exploration of Human Violence*. New York, The Macmillan, Co., 1966.

Westley, William A. *Violence and the Police: A Sociological Study of Law, Custom, and Morality*. Cambridge, Mass., M.I.T. Press, 1970.

Wilkinson, Doris Y., ed. *Black Revolt: Strategies of Protest*. Berkeley, Calif., McCutchan Publishing Corp., 1969.

Some of the marchers panicked and ran. They couldn't
see where they were going and they ran into cars and
buildings. Those who were too young or too old to move
fast enough got hit the worst. When they got to the
Selma end of the bridge, the possemen and deputies who
had been patiently waiting there attacked them anew
with clubs and whips and chased them through the
streets down toward the Negro quarter.—
WARREN HINCKLE and DAVID WELSH

The term *nonviolence* becomes increasingly relevant to the subject of human relations when it is examined as a method for producing social change. Three prominent proponents of nonviolent social change were Henry David Thoreau, Mohandas K. Gandhi, and the Reverend Martin Luther King, Jr. Two of the three, Gandhi and King, were tragically and ironically killed by the very behavior their lives were dedicated to oppose—senseless acts of violence. Each of the three created his own concept of nonviolence as it relates specifically to facilitating social change. Moreover, it can be documented that Thoreau directly influenced Gandhi, who, in turn, influenced King.

Webster's dictionary defines nonviolence as "abstention on principle from violence." Thus, to be nonviolent is to refrain voluntarily from violence. Thoreau, Gandhi, and King expanded this simple concept into a strategy of planned change by the application of nonviolent coercion and active nonviolent resistance. This concept is in direct contrast to the Marxian theory of raw power. Rather, nonviolent strategies of change involve civil disobedience, conflict confrontation, strikes, sit-downs, and negotiations with the "offender."

HENRY DAVID THOREAU (1817–62)

Henry David Thoreau's contribution to the nonviolent approach to social change was mainly that of a theorist. His outward life, save for a few not-so-drastic events, does not provide an example of the nonviolent activist. Indeed, a case could even be presented that his outward life serves as a primary example of the self-willed isolationist.

163

NONCOERCIVE
    Personal example
    Intercessory prayer
    Conciliatory discussion
    Direct acts of love
    Nonresistance
    Unmerited suffering
    Self-imposed penance
    Arguments and appeals
    Mediation
    Arbitration
    Promises
    Rewards
    Bribes

COERCIVE   *Examples*

NONINJURIOUS

Psychological
- Noncooperation — Active resistance
- Civil Disobedience — Strike, boycott
- Threats / Anger } show of force — "War of nerves"

Physical
- Restraint by manual force
- Bodily obstruction

INJURIOUS

Temporarily incapacitating action — Judo
Disablement with recoverable damage — Broken bone
Pain without permanent harm — Wrestling hold
Damage to personality (psychological) — Neurosis
Permanent physical disablement — Crippling
Permanent damage to personality — Psychosis
Incidental or accidental homicide
Willful murder
Posthumous desecration or mutilation
Torture
Mutilation

Figure 2. Noncoercive and coercive behavior

SOURCE: William R. Miller, *Nonviolence: A Christian Interpretation* (New York, Schocken Books, 1964), 59. Used by permission.

Thoreau's writing, however, does provide us with a nonviolent perspective, or mind-set, for considering social injustice.

Thoreau was read and admired by Leo Tolstoi, Gandhi, and Martin Luther King, Jr. The very term *civil disobedience* derives its currency from Thoreau's essay of that title (although he did not so name it). However, very few of his political ideas were original.

Thoreau can be classified as a literary artist whose medium of expression was his own life. Accordingly, he projected himself into his

work, which is highly personal in tone and style. He was also a trans-
cendentalist who attempted to understand the real world intuitively
rather than by limiting himself to objetcive experience. In *Walden* he
tells of his two years and two months at Walden Pond, where he tried
to create a self-culture and to live a life exemplifying a viable alternative to the prevailing life-style of his time. But he discovered that his
goal of self-culture was not attainable in a posture of isolation from
personal and social relationships. He then returned to New England
society and involved himself in, among other things, the antislavery
movement.

Thoreau held that each man must be attuned to nature and to himself as part of that natural whole. He must be aware of and act upon his
own principles, with an ear to conscience rather than to an external
concept of right or wrong. He further held that man must be free to
discover himself and free to act.

Today, Thoreau is seen as an advocate of man against the state, but
only in a very general sense was that the case. Thoreau's specific concern was with the individual and the kinds of problems which do not
lend themselves to outside solution by any state, whether it be totali-
tarian or democratic. Thoreau much preferred that men rule themselves, and for that reason he was opposed to the state as a governing
body.

Although Thoreau refused to pay taxes for support of churches, he
did pay highway taxes which were to be used for education. His actions
reflected his principles, and he lived *within* a state but not *by* the state.

Thoreau's rebellious notions were derived in large measure from his
friend Ralph Waldo Emerson, whom he idolized. It was through
Emerson's guidance in transcendentalism and Thoreau's own self-
isolation from society that Thoreau was influenced to direct his
thoughts toward nonviolence. He was more than an observer of nature;
he was a participant in it, and in times of trial he preferred to withdraw
from society and society's burdensome laws.

"Civil Disobedience," Thoreau's most famous essay, was his "defense
of the private conscience against majority expediency; . . . it announced
the moral intransigence of later essays such as 'Slavery in Massachusetts' and 'Life Without Principle,' and those essays written in behalf of John Brown, who carried the political faith of the Transcen-
dentalists to the conclusion of bloody action."[1] In "Civil Disobedience"
he also presented an excellent dialectical argument for ignoring or
violating laws that are unjust. It is this aspect of his thinking which
most influenced Gandhi and others, particularly in such passages as
this:

[1] "Henry David Thoreau," *Encyclopedia Britannica*, Vol. 21, 1073.

*Unjust laws exist: shall we be content to obey them, or shall we en-
deavor to amend them, and obey them until we have succeeded, or
shall we transgress them at once? Men generally, under such a government as this, think that they ought to wait until they have persuaded
the majority to alter them. They think that, if hey should resist, the
remedy would be worse than the evil. But it is the fault of the government itself that the remedy is worse than the evil. It makes it worse.*[2]

Throughout his writings Thoreau advocated toleration of social and
cultural differences: "If I devote myself to other pursuits and con-
templations, I must first see, at least, that I do not pursue them sitting
upon another man's shoulders."[3] Among many other persons, Jesus
was influential in Thoreau's arguments about unjust laws and their
remedies. Thoreau used Jesus' confrontation with the moneylenders in
the temple as an illustration, saying that the evil social system worsened
the evil which it attempted to cure.

As has already been pointed out, Thoreau's life experience did not
exemplify methods of nonviolent social change. He did, however,
articulate a nonviolent perspective which was to be fully acted upon
by others. His early tendency to isolate himself from the real world
gave way to his subjective inclination to experience his own human-
ness. This means of coming to know oneself is also a contribution which
Thoreau made to men and women everywhere.

Thoreau was a sharp critic of his society, which emphasized industrial production at the expense of human values. He advocated active
rebellion against the state, including what he called "action from
principle," based on an intuitive perception of what is right.[4] Action
from principle changes things and relations, he maintained. The idea
of passive resistance was based on conscience, not self-interest, and
Thoreau felt that passive resistance should be mounted against the
state when it uses coercion to enforce questionable dictates. This doctrine was expounded to the Concord Lyceum on January 26, 1848, and
again in "Civil Disobedience":

*I heartily accept the motto,—"That government is best which
governs least"; and I should like to see it acted up to more rapidly and
systematically. Carried out, it finally amounts to this, which also I
believe,—"That government is best which governs not at all"; and
when men are prepared for it, that will be the kind of government
which they will have. . . . Government is at best but an expedient; but
most governments are usually and all governments are sometimes, in-*

[2] Henry David Thoreau, *Walden and Other Writings*, 287.
[3] *Ibid.*, 286.
[4] Henry David Thoreau, *The Variorum Civil Disobedience*, 39.

166

expedient.... The government itself, which is only the mode which the people have chosen to execute their will, is equally liable to be abused and perverted before the people can act through it.... For government is an expedient by which men would fain succeed in letting one another alone; and, as has been said, when it is most expedient, the governed are most let alone by it. Governments show thus how successfully men can be imposed on, even impose on themselves, for their own advantage.[5]

The central points of his essay are as follows:

1. The law of conscience is higher than the law of one's land.
2. When one is in conflict between these two laws, it is one's duty to obey the higher law and violate the law of the land.
3. One must be willing to take the full consequences of the action.
4. Going to jail will serve to draw the attention of men of good will to the evil law and help bring about its repeal.

Action which is motivated for good changes things and relations and therefore is essentially revolutionary. Thoreau was interested in better government. He felt that radical social reforms, such as the abolition of slavery (for which he agitated throughout his life), could be changed not through such indirect democratic means as petitions to government representatives but only when individuals take direct action.

A person should conduct himself as an individual, abiding by his own conscience:

I came into this world, not chiefly to make this a good place to live in, but to live in it, be it good or bad. A man has not every thing to do, but something; and because he cannot do every thing, it is not necessary that he should do something wrong.... I think that we should be men first, and subjects afterward. It is not desirable to cultivate a respect for the law so much as for the right.

The mass of men serve the State thus, not as men mainly, but as machines, which are their bodies. They are the standing army, and the militia, jailers, constables, posse comitatus, etc. In most cases there is no free exercise whatever of the judgment or of the moral sense; and wooden men can perhaps be manufactured that will serve the purpose as well.... A wise man will only be useful as a man, and will not submit to be "clay," and "stop a hole to keep the wind away."[6]

Thoreau's doctrine of civil disobedience stemmed from his philosophy of the nature of man. He believed that man should be free and that human society should not crush individual freedom. Therefore, he

[5] Henry David Thoreau, "On the Duty of Civil Disobedience," in *Walden*, 222–23.
[6] *Ibid.*, 223, 224, 229.

believed, when it appeared that the uniqueness of man was threatened, men should resist through civil disobedience: "The only obligation . . . is what I think right."[7]

In Thoreau's mind, any man "more right" than his neighbors constitutes a majority of one.

Thoreau saw injustice in the American system stemming from the concept of majority rule:

After all, the practical reason why, when the power is once in the hands of the people, a majority are permitted, and for a long period continue, to rule, is not because they are most likely to be in the right, nor because they are physically the strongest. But a government in which the majority rule in all cases cannot be based on justice, even as far as men understand it. . . . I quarrel not with far-off foes, but with those who, near at home, co-operate with, and do the bidding of those far away, and without whom the latter would be harmless.[8]

The power of a minority then lies in it capability to take *action*: "A minority is powerless while it conforms to the majority; it is not even a minority then; but it is irresistible when it clogs by its whole weight. . . . This is in fact the definition of a peaceable revolution, if any such is possible. . . . When the subject has refused allegiance, and the officer has resigned his office, then the revolution is accomplished."[9] But what is the ultimate improvement for government?

Is a democracy, such as we know it, the last improvement possible in government? Is it not possible to take a step further towards recognizing and organizing the rights of man?

The authority of government, . . . even such as I am willing to submit to, . . . is still an impure one: to be strictly just, it must have the sanction and consent of the governed. It can have no pure right over my person and property but what I concede to it. The progress from an absolute to a limited monarchy, from a limited monarchy to a democracy, is a progress toward a true respect for the individual.

. . . There will never be a really free and enlightened State, until the State comes to recognize the individual as a higher and independent power, from which all its own power and authority are derived, and treats him accordingly.[10]

And for his own part in such a state: "I please myself with imagining a State at last which can afford to be just to all men, and to treat the individual with respect as a neighbor; which even would not think it

[7] Thoreau, *The Variorum Civil Disobedience*, 33.
[8] Thoreau, *Walden*, 223, 223.
[9] *Ibid.*, 231.
[10] *Ibid.*, 240.

inconsistent with its own repose, if a few were to live aloof from it, not meddling with it, not embraced by it, who fulfilled all the duties of neighbors and fellow-men."[11] Thoreau leaves a clue to the creation of such a state which was later picked up and elaborated by other non-violent theorists: "For eighteen hundred years, though perchance I have no right to say it, the New Testament has been written; yet where is the legislator who has wisdom and practical talent enough to avail himself of the light which it sheds on the science of legislation?"[12]

MOHANDAS K. GANDHI (1869–1948)

Mohandas K. (Mahatma) Gandhi was the first fighter in history who won a war against the oppressors of his country using the weapons of the spirit and nonviolent resistance.

It was while Gandhi was studying for a law degree in Victorian London that he first heard of Thoreau. His teacher was a Professor Henry Salt, a practicing vegetarian and a dedicated scholar. As a result of Professor Salt's influence, Gandhi rejected his earlier ambition "to become an English gentleman" and instead became immersed in the social, political, and economic problems of his native India.

Following graduation, he went to Bombay, the second largest city in India, and, for a time, to South Africa. During this period he read the works of John Ruskin and Leo Tolstoi—but it was the Bhagavad-Gita of his native Hindu religion that ultimately became his greatest source of inspiration. These studies led him to formulate a synthesis of certain ideas found in both Eastern and Western philosophy. When India began its revolt against British rule, Gandhi's implementation of these ideas brought him universal recognition as the "father" of nonviolent protest.

Fundamental to his thought was the assumption that the world is bound in a chain of destruction and that all life in the flesh exists by some violence. Once having recognized the essence of violence, Gandhi proceeded to harness the forces of nonviolence for purposive action, the necessary prerequisites being suffering and self-sacrifice.

Although Gandhi's principle of "constructive conflict" was symbolic in its purpose, he saw that it became fully actualized in practice. Over a period of time Gandhi developed revolutionary techniques of confrontation to bring about change in the social order. The object, of course, was creative resolution of conflict on a massive scale.

Different means of confrontation were used for different purposes. Gandhi used strikes, boycotts, fasts, and other forms of civil disobedience to accomplish his ends. He relied on meditation and asceticism in

[11] *Ibid.*
[12] *Ibid.*

various ashrams to instill in him the "soul force" necessary to sustain him as the leader of resistance to British colonial policies. In 1948 Gandhi was assassinated, and India, as a direct result of his philosophy and strategies, achieved her independence.

Essentially, Gandhi's concept of nonviolence consisted of the strategies he developed to bring about social change and a philosophical construct which he developed to govern his own life.

With regard to the former, two terms identify Gandhi's nonviolent perspective—*satyagraha* ("soul-force") and *passive resistance* (see Chapter 5). Gandhi himself always considered the latter a misnomer, although it became widely accepted as the method by which he achieved his goals. The Mahatma preferred the term *satyagraha* for nonviolent resistance to the social injustices suffered by his people.

With regard to the philosophical construct, three cardinal virtues characterize Gandhi's philosophical understanding of human behavior: (1) truth (*satya*), (2) loving-kindness (*ahimsa*), and (3) inner purity (*brahmacharya*). The first two, truth and love, combine to propel the human soul through the period of temptation and transgression. Inner purity cleanses the soul of sensual passion (this basically is the spiritual orientation which Gandhi integrated into his personal life through such methods as fasting and abstinence from sexual relations).

Just as it did for Thoreau, Jesus' life also provided an example for Gandhi to follow. He stated many times that the New Testament "awakened him to the rightness and value of Passive Resistance."[13] Tolstoi's implied condemnation of war reinforced Gandhi's determination to employ only nonviolent tactics to bring about social change. The dominant theme in Gandhi's life became, "Overcome evil with good," or, stated another way, "Turn the other cheek," or, yet another, "Love your enemy." He came to believe that the use of force was incompatible with the idea of love. As C. F. Andrews, a close friend of Gandhi, put it, "The secret of Gandhi was this: he was the first to organize corporate moral resistance, and to obtain . . . through rigid discipline, a firmly united community ready to go to any lengths of suffering as a body for the sake of conscience."[14]

However, the question has often been raised of Gandhi—as well as of other proponents of nonviolence—that, if he had had might on his side, would he have used it? Assuming that the same conditions could exist (which may be an unreasonable assumption), would Gandhi have abandoned nonviolent methods if suddenly he discovered that his people could employ armed might to achieve their goals much more rapidly than through long suffering and other nonviolent methods?

[13] C. F. Andrews, *Mahatma Gandhi*, 192.
[14] *Ibid.*, 190.

170

Saul Alinsky, a proponent of violent confrontation, pointed out in his *Rules For Radicals* that Gandhi did not speak out against Nehru for using military forces against Pakistan in the struggle for the Kashmir. Alinsky commented that Gandhi may have merely cloaked his goals in a moral cover because it was expedient to do so. After all, in the South African Transvaal the Indians did not have the will to bear arms against their oppressors. Did the Mahatma know that the only method by which he could unite his people was that of passive resistance? It is probable that Gandhi saw the expediency in using violent force in Pakistan, as well as the fact that it would have been suicidal to do so in South Africa.

Gandhi's idea was to apply the formula of love to daily problems. Gandhi believed soul-force to be the most effective way to counter brute force.[15] He said that the battle would be won not by the number of enemies that could be killed but by the numer of enemies in whom the desire to kill could be killed. *Satyagraha* was not predominantly characterized by civil disobedience but was a quiet, and irresistible pursuit of truth. Only on the rarest occasions does it become civil disobedience, and then only after one has made a conscious effort to obey the laws.

The nonviolent—and courageous—nature of *satyagraha* movement is found in the main points that Gandhi laid down as a code for volunteers:

1. Harbor no anger, but suffer the anger of the opponent.
2. Do not submit to any order given in anger.
3. Refrain from insults and swearing.
4. Protect opponents from insult and attack (at risk of life).
5. Do not resist arrest or the attachment of property.
6. Refuse to surrender any property held in trust (at risk of life).
7. If taken prisoner, behave in exemplary manner.
8. Obey the orders of the *satyagraha* unit and leaders.
9. Do not expect guarantees for the maintenance of dependents.

Satyagraha was the quintessence of Gandhism. Therein lies the meaning of his life and his death. This idea and practice were at the center of Gandhi's contribution to the world, and as he explained: "The world rests upon the bedrock of Satya of Truth. Asatya meaning Untruth, also means 'non-existent'; and Satya, or Truth, means 'that which is.' If untruth does not so much as exist, its victory is out of the question. And Truth being 'that which is' can never be destroyed. This is the doctrine of Satyagraha in a nutshell."[16]

15 Erik H. Erikson, *Gandhi's Truth*, 198.
16 E. Stanley Jones, *Mahatma Gandhi: An Interpretation*, 81.

The idea of *satyagraha* slowly evolved and then took possession of Gandhi. He said of it: "Its precepts—return good for evil—became my guiding principle. It became such a passion with me that I began numerous experiments in it."[17] The germ of the idea came from a Gujarati hymn:

> *Thus the words and actions of the wise regard;*
> *Every little service tenfold they reward.*
> *But the truly noble know all men as one,*
> *And return with gladness good for evil done.*[18]

"But it was the New Testament that fixed it in my heart," Gandhi reflected: "The Sermon on the Mount went straight to my heart. The verses, 'But I say unto you, That ye resist not evil: but whosoever shall smite thee on thy right cheek, turn to him the other also. And if any man take away thy coat, let him have thy cloak also,' delighted me beyond measure. . . . That renunciation was the highest form of religion and appealed to me greatly."[19]

Gandhi once said that he was most influenced by (1) the Bible; (2) Tolstoi, with his insistence that the Sermon on the Mount be taken literally and acted on; and (3) John Ruskin's *Unto This Last*, which made him decide on a life of simplicity and service. Gandhi's religion became a serving of God through a serving of his people. Thus, his personal creed was one of nonviolence, simplicity in life style, and dedication to God and humanity.

Satyagraha allows for three stages in the process of winning over an opponent: (1) persuasion through reason; (2) persuasion through suffering, which dramatizes the issues; and (3) nonviolent coercion, characterized by such tools as noncooperation or civil disobedience.[20]

The steps in a *satyagraha* campaign are (1) negotiation and arbitration; (2) preparation of the group for direct action; (3) agitation; (4) issuance of an ultimatum; (5) economic boycott and other forms of strikes; (6) noncooperation; (7) civil disobedience (in this area great care should be exercised in the selection of laws to be contravened); such laws should be either highly symbolic of or central to the grievance; (8) usurpation of the functions of government; and (9) establishment of a parallel government.[21]

Two other influences helped shape Gandhi's ideals and attitudes.

[17] *Ibid.*
[18] *Ibid.*
[19] *Ibid.*, 83.
[20] Joan V. Bondurant, *Conquest of Violence*, 11.
[21] *Ibid.*, 40–41.

Thoreau's essay "Civil Disobedience" expounded upon the belief that a man must obey his own conscience even against the will of his fellow citizens; further, he must, if necessary, submit to imprisonment, remembering that it is only his body, but not his spirit, which is incarcerated. The essay reached Gandhi in South Africa at a critical moment and greatly appealed to him. Concerning it Gandhi said: "When I saw the title of Thoreau's great essay, I began the use of the phrase to explain our struggle to the English readers. But I found that even civil disobedience failed to convey the full meaning of the struggle. I therefore adopted the phrase 'civil resistance.' Nonviolence was always an integral part of our struggle."[22]

Another influence was Gandhi's observation in 1909 of the British suffragettes—especially Emmeline Pankhurst, Christabel Pankhurst, Sylvia Pankhurst, and Flora Drummond—and their use of civil disobedience to achieve their goals.

Gandhi, although not a Christian, decided to take a Christian attitude—the overcoming of evil with good—and there the real revolution began. Gandhi's effort to apply a New Testament principle to public affairs became a revolutionary one. The Sermon on the Mount was revolutionary in the hands of Gandhi; he applied it as a technique and an attitude to public affairs. Gandhi turned resolutions into revolution by the simple method of applying those resolutions.[23]

Another ingredient that went into the making of Gandhi and his revolution was his conception of truth. Perhaps in the end truth may be seen to be the most important element of Gandhi's philosophy. He identified truth as God. He said: "I do not regard God as a Person. Truth for me is God, and God's Law and God are not different things or facts, in the sense that an earthly king and his law are different. Because God is an Idea, Law Himself. He and His Law abide everywhere and govern everything."[24]

Again and again Gandhi said: "I do not say God is Truth; I say, Truth is God." Here he seemed to rule out a personal God and make him identical with an impersonal law. Yet he did use the personification "Law Himself" and later wrote, "It is not possible to *see* God face to face unless you crucify the flesh."[25] Therefore, truth to Gandhi seems to have been identical with this law and also with God. To identify himself with truth was to be identified with God, an identification that had the surety of a law.

Gandhi believed that if one always did the true thing he would have

[22] Jones, *op. cit.*, 83.
[23] *Ibid.*, 85.
[24] *Ibid.*
[25] *Ibid.* Italics added.

the backing of the moral universe. Gandhi believed that the stars in their course should work for one and that they would likewise work against all evil. He further held that men and the universe are made for truth. If truth is the law of our being, then to act according to it is to fulfill ourselves, and to act or think according to untruth is to disrupt ourselves. The thing to do then is to identify ourselves with truth, do the true thing always, and a true result will follow. One should not bother about results. They take care of themselves. The moral universe guarantees them. All that man has to do is to see that he is on the right side of things. The moral universe takes care of the rest. Gandhi asked himself one question in life: In this matter am I on the side of truth? When he decided to adopt truth and nonviolence—one the fact and the other the method of applying the fact—he went forth believing that he had cosmic backing for what he was doing. It gave him an inner steadiness of purpose and a terrific drive—quiet, but terrific. For Gandhi felt himself the agent of cosmic forces working through him: "I will not sacrifice Truth and *ahimsa* even for the deliverance of my country and my religion."[26]

Many writers believe that the greatness of Gandhi consisted in that he would not focus on the end results; he tried to use the right means, hoping that the right result would follow. The means of achieving his ends became the all-important thing to him. He did not want to use a wrong means to get to a right end, for he believed that the means pre-exist in and determine the ends.

Gandhi also taught his followers to combat injustice and oppression through propaganda and constructive work. He held that one must appeal to people's concern for justice and their welfare rather than to their fear, greed, or hatred. In his view propaganda activity was designed not only to arouse and maintain resistance but also to confront opponents with the relative truths on which demands were based. Propaganda was therefore an essential aspect of as well as preparation for *satyagraha*, and it must continue throughout the term of the campaign. Constructive work also had an important role in developing resistance. *Satyagraha* influenced local leaders and invested them with public trust; and some of this confidence was transferred to their methods of action.

Gandhi's life was reflected in his beliefs: (1) that the moral universe is one and that the morals of individuals, groups, and nations must be the same; (2) that the means and the ends must be consistent; (3) that we should hold no ideals which we do not embody or are not in the process of embodying; and (4) that we should demonstrate a willingness to suffer and die for our principles.

[26] *Ibid.*

174

These beliefs combined to propel Gandhi into the twentieth century and enabled him to commence a heroic struggle for the liberation of his people. The epic battle waged by Gandhi made him the greatest revolutionary of his age and, through *satyagraha*, the most gentle and humane.

MARTIN LUTHER KING, JR. (1929–68)

Martin Luther King, Jr., was reared in an environment of racial and anti-Semitic violence. Yet his father's strong belief in and dedication to Christian love were instilled in him at an early age. After much thought, young Martin decided to become a minister. His education provided him with great insight as he read about social action and recognized the pervasive plight of blacks throughout the country. He became interested in the moral influence of contemporary theologians such as Paul Tillich and Reinhold Niebuhr.

King's college experience awakened him to a wide range of philosophical and political alternatives. He was simultaneously drawn to and repelled by Marx. However, it was Thoreau's essay on civil disobedience which stirred him more deeply and permanently than any other educational encounter of the period. It was his conviction that Thoreau's concepts should be coupled with Christian love. He began to see that true pacifism is not unrealistic submission to evil power; rather, it is courageous confrontation of evil by the power of love. Thus came into sharper focus King's belief that it is better to be the recipient of violence than the inflicter of it.

Martin Luther King, Jr., used Gandhian tactics to achieve the goals he desired for his people. He is noted particularly for his nonviolent protest against racial and economic injustice. Although at the time he had not yet been influenced by Gandhi's thinking, when Dr. King was faced with the responsibility of delivering a speech to the mass meeting in Montgomery, Alabama, on December 5, 1955, to organize the bus boycott, he confronted the dilemma which Gandhi had often faced and which had plagued black leaders for many years. As King so cogently stated it, the problem was that of how "to make a speech that would be militant enough to keep my people aroused to positive action and yet moderate enough to keep this fervor within controllable and Christian bounds."[27] He relied upon the strength of his character and his background to face the problem head on and combine two apparently irreconcilable doctrines—militancy and moderation.

As noted earlier, Thoreau's *Civil Disobedience* appears to have been a catalyst in Dr. King's life. He read it in 1944 while at Morehouse College, and he was fascinated by the idea of "refusing to cooperate

[27] C. Eric Lincoln, ed., *Martin Luther King, Jr.: A Profile*, 16.

175

with an evil system." King was initially skeptical of the power of love in the area of social reform. So as his civil-rights movement was beginning in Montgomery, Alabama, he reflected upon Thoreau's warning against lending cooperation to an evil system.

Jesus, Thomas Aquinas, Hegel, Gandhi, Martin Buber, and Paul Tillich are some of the other great men who influenced King. Coupled with his experiences as a young preacher in Montgomery, the ideas of these great men provided him with the resourcefulness to cope with crisis situations for the rest of his too-short life. King differed from Gandhi in that he did not use collective civil disobedience to achieve his goals. His emphasis was upon the individual's right and "personal responsibility to break, ignore, and resist certain local laws—no matter what the personal consequences are—in order to abide by the national law."[28] Of the bus boycott in 1956, King said that "the spirit of the Montgomery movement came from Jesus, the technique from Gandhi."[29] It can easily be seen that individuals who decide to oppose and resist an unjust law as a group act in the same manner as a group acting in a collective fashion. In other words, the distinction between the two kinds of resistance becomes rather academic, since both achieve the same end.

King, like Gandhi, was able to transcend the harshness of reality and in so doing transform the Montgomery movement, and thus the black movement, by giving people a vision of the possibilities of man. Jesus did precisely the same thing. This is the spiritual element which seems to be lacking in more recent social-change movements. King said that the "experience of Montgomery 'did more to clarify my thinking on the question of nonviolence than all the books that I have read.' "[30]

King's "theory," if it can be termed such, was based in his "dream," as he called it. It was his ultimate dream for all mankind, a dream about the nature of truth. In the beginning of his very personal book *The Measure of a Man* he stated his dream: "I believe that unarmed truth and unconditional love will have the final word in reality. That is why right temporarily defeated is stronger than evil triumphant."[31]

His nonviolent tactics are now familiar to most of us—boycotts, sit-ins, stand-ins, swim-ins, pray-ins, mass meetings. Gandhi employed the same tactics in his native India and in South Africa. They are still being used (although not as effectively, partly because of the lack of a charismatic leader). It is unfortunate that nonviolent tactics are employed mainly by minority-group persons. If it were not so easy for

[28] *Ibid.*, 36.
[29] *Ibid.*, 29.
[30] *Ibid.*
[31] Martin Luther King, Jr., *The Measure of a Man*, 11.

176

major powers to use their might, perhaps many lives would be saved and much bloodshed avoided by the employment of the methods set out by Thoreau, Gandhi, and King. Such is the precedent that history gives us. What are the changes that will have to take place before a man of this genius charts a new course for mankind?

The purpose of the nonviolent approach, according to King's thinking, was to create such a crisis and establish such creative tension that those who have refused to negotiate are forced to confront the issue. The point is to dramatize the issue so that it can no longer be ignored. King believed that the tension created by a nonviolent protest was necessary for growth that would lead to understanding:

First, it must be emphasized that nonviolent resistance is not a method for cowards; it does resist. . . . For while the nonviolent resister is passive in the sense that he is not physically aggressive against his opponent, his mind and emotions are always active, constantly seeking to persuade his opponent that he is wrong. The method is passive physically, but strongly active spiritually. It is not passive non-resistance to evil, it is active nonviolent resistance to evil.

A second basic fact that characterizes nonviolence is that it does not seek to defeat or humiliate the opponent but to win his friendship and understanding. . . . The aftermath of nonviolence is to create the beloved community, while the aftermath of violence is tragic bitterness.

A third characteristic is that the attack is directed against the forces of evil rather than against persons who happen to be doing the evil. It is the evil that the nonviolent resister seeks to defeat, not the persons victimized by evil.

A fourth point is a willingness to accept suffering without retaliation, to accept blows from the opponent without striking back. "Rivers of blood may have to flow before we gain our freedom, but it must be our blood," Gandhi said to his countrymen. The nonviolent resister is willing to accept violence if necessary but never to inflict it. He does not seek to dodge jail. If going to jail is necessary, he enters it, "as a bridegroom enters the bride's chamber."

A fifth point is that it avoids not only external physical violence but also internal violence of the spirit. the nonviolent resister not only refuses to shoot his opponent but he also refuses to hate him. At the center of nonviolence stands the principle of love. . . . Love in this connection means understanding, redemptive good will, not a weak passive love but love in action. It is love characterized by the Greek word Agape, *a willingness to sacrifice in the interest of mutuality, a willingness to go to any length to restore community, a recognition of the fact that all life is interrelated, that all men are brothers.*

A sixth basic fact about nonviolent resistance is that it is based on the conviction that the universe is on the side of justice. The nonviolent resister can accept suffering without retaliation for he knows that in his struggle for justice he has cosmic companionship.[32]

The nonviolent campaign not only calls attention to the injustice but also gives self-respect to those who are committed to it. It is significant in that it seeks just ends through just means. King believed that it was wrong to use immoral means to attain moral ends, but he was convinced that it was even more wrong to use moral means to preserve immoral ends.

In addition to his position on nonviolence, King's personal philosophy included a belief in personal idealism, which incorporates a basic tenet of human relations, the positive value placed on all persons. His definition of the "three dimensions of life" and their interrelationships seems very close to a foundation for the study of human relations itself. According to King the first dimension of life is *length*, "not its duration or its longevity, but ... the push of a life forward to achieve its personal ends and ambitions. It is the inward concern for one's own welfare. The *breadth* of life is the outward concern for the welfare of others. The *height* of life is the upward reach for God. Without these three interconnected, working harmoniously together, life is incomplete."[33]

The breadth of life is that dimension of life in which we are concerned about others. An individual has not started living until he can rise above the narrow confines of his personal concerns to the broader concerns of all humanity. Human relations training seeks to remind us that we are interdependent, that we are all somehow caught in an inescapable network of humanity. Therefore, whatever affects one person directly affects all people indirectly.

King employed many of Gandhi's tactics in implementing the concepts of civil disobedience. Like Gandhi, he was imprisoned, beaten, spat upon, and ultimately assassinated. He had a dream which kindled hope for millions. Some believe that if King had a weakness in his philosophy it was his inability to communicate that spirit to the young militants. Somehow his vision and practice were overshadowed by the violent realities of urban rioters and the Ku Klux Klan. His condemnation of the Vietnam War was one of his last desperate efforts to end violence. Though for his efforts he received the Nobel Peace Prize in 1968, and though he achieved important victories for the blacks of America, the discipline to which he subjected himself in preparation for his years of struggle is largely rejected by the militants.

[32] Martin Luther King, Jr., *Stride Toward Freedom: The Montgomery Story*, 83–88.
[33] King, *The Measure of a Man*, 43.

OTHER THEORISTS

The Greek philosopher Socrates practiced a form of nonviolence—civil disobedience. His belief in a single deity was punishable by imprisonment. He refused this punishment, and he also rejected exile, and so he was ultimately faced with the death penalty, which he accepted. Socrates felt that it was his duty to teach the citizens of Athens in hope of changing their beliefs. Socrates was responsible to himself and to his own beliefs and convictions, yet he was also responsible to his government. Thoreau's idea differs somewhat from Socrates' in that Thoreau believed that one should be responsible to himself first, to his country second.

Jesus stressed nonviolent planned change. Saint Paul the Apostle spoke of *agape*—loving others for their own sakes. The Bible speaks of loving one's enemy, whereby one heaps "coals of fire upon his head." The basic Christian philosophy dwells upon unmerited grace and love and speaks of the same persecution and suffering that King and Gandhi referred to.

Throughout history many others have practiced passive resistance, including John Ruskin and Leo Tolstoi. Tolstoi was greatly influenced in his nonviolent viewpoint by Thoreau, Ralph Waldo Emerson, and others. William James introduced a new concern with the psychological roots of nonviolence, emphasizing the need for a positive, constructive expression of the idea. Before the American Revolution, nonviolence was peculiarly identified with the Quakers.

Saul D. Alinsky used the tactics of nonviolence in ways which bordered upon violence. To Alinsky, power tactics meant doing what one could with what one had. He posited thirteen rules for power tactics (see Chapter 6).

The Battle of Selma[34]

WARREN HINCKLE and DAVID WELSH

The legal-size mimeographed forms were deadly complete—name, address, next-of-kin, authorization for representation by counsel. Everyone who marched had to fill one out in case of arrest, injury, or death. But there weren't enough forms to go around Sunday morning when the marchers came in from Boykin and Jones and Marion, from Atlanta, from Chicago, from New York. They came to Brown's Chapel— the red brick church towering over the red brick apartment buildings of the George Washington Carver Homes housing project in the Negro section of Selma.

[34] Condensed from Warren Hinckle and David Welsh, "The Five Battles of Selma," in *Ramparts*, June, 1965. Reprinted by permission of the editors.

Brown's Chapel was the assembly point for the planned march over U.S. Highway 80 through the swamps and hills and white racist strongholds of rural, black belt Alabama to the ornate colonial capitol at Montgomery, where the dual flags of the Confederate States of America and the Sovereign State of Alabama hung together limply in the still air around the capitol dome.

The girl handing out the forms said she needed more. A Negro boy ran down unpaved Sylvan Street, which intersects the federal housing project, and turned right on Alabama Street toward the Student Non-Violent Co-ordinating Committee (SNCC) headquarters located three blocks uptown. He went to the top floor of a three-story, rickety Negro office building with unlighted hallways and atrophied doors set in warped door-jambs. From the Selma City Jail directly across the street, police watched the young Negro go into the dreary building and come out a few minutes later carrying a freshly printed pile of registration forms.

This historic Confederate city on the banks of the muddy Alabama river is a citadel of Southern resistance to integration. Only in the Trailways bus station do Negroes and whites mix. This is why SNCC, in 1963, selected Selma as a prime target for its organizing activities. The Confederate establishment immediately began to skirmish with the civil rights invaders, and when Dr. Martin Luther King and his Southern Christian Leadership Conference (SCLC) joined forces with SNCC in Selma early this year, the Confederate "police action" escalated into a conflict of military proportions not seen in the South since the Battle of Selma nominally ended the Civil War in April of 1865.

Like all wars, this one became deadly serious after the first casualty, Jimmy Lee Jackson, a 26-year-old Negro woodcutter, was gunned down by an Alabama state trooper during a racial demonstration in nearby Marion. When he died eight days later in Selma's Negro Good Samaritan Hospital, he was a war hero. The Montgomery march of Sunday, March 7, was called more to honor Jimmy Jackson than to seriously petition Governor George Wallace for the redress of racial inequities he has sworn to preserve.

As the young Negro left the SNCC offices with a fresh supply of registration forms, his progress was reported to the Confederate Command Post operating in Sheriff Jim Clark's Dallas County Court House offices in downtown Selma. "The nigger's leaving there now . . . he's goin' back down Alabama Street . . . carryin' papers . . . back to the church . . ." A middle-aged woman wearing rimless glasses, a Confederate flag pinned to her white blouse, sat on a stool, her legs crossed, writing everything down A large sign near the doorway of the first floor suite read "Quiet Please, We are Trying to Monitor Three Radios."

One of the command post radios crackled: "There's three more cars of niggers crossing the bridge. Some white bastards riding with them. Heading for Brown's Chapel." The bridge was the Edmund Pettus Bridge, a stumpy concrete edifice stretching between the debris-lined bluffs of the sluggish Alabama River and linking Selma with Highway 80 (the Jefferson Davis Highway), the road to Montgomery. This was the bridge the marchers would have to cross.

It was early afternoon. The State Troopers were preparing to block off traffic on the heavily-traveled thoroughfare. They moved their patrol cars into position on both sides of the divided highway, facing north.

Sheriff Clark's good friend, Colonel Al Lingo, head of the Alabama State Troopers, sat in an unmarked car at the side of the highway, watching his men prepare for battle. Clark and Lingo had worked out battle plans that would not only scatter the Union forces but make their defeat an object lesson. The white citizens of Alabama had grown weary of "moderate" handling of the Selma voter registration demonstrations led by Dr. Martin Luther King. Selma's Public Safety Director, Wilson Baker, had insisted on mass arrests to control the demonstrators. Now the Confederate leadership wanted something more effective. "If the Negroes refuse to disperse, we shall not make mass arrests," Colonel Lingo said. He said it the way a general says his side will take no prisoners.

Filling out a marching form at Brown's Chapel was 16-year-old Viola Jackson of Selma (no relation to the late Jimmy Lee Jackson). Have you ever been arrested? NO. Have you ever been beaten? YES. Do you have any ailments that should be checked before the march? NO. *She handed in the paper and went outside where the marchers were forming.*

The march itself was planned in military style: participants were to line up two abreast, grouped into squads of 25 people, and then into companies of four squads each. The leaders of the march—John Lewis of SNCC and Hosea Williams of SCLC—had originally planned to organize the squads on paper. But the last-minute influx of marchers made that impractical, so everyone was ordered outside to the playground behind Brown's Chapel and told to line up in pairs. Forty-five minutes later, six companies were ready to march.

The Union leadership had, in its own way, prepared for the expected confrontation with the Confederate forces: four ambulances were parked on Sylvan Street; ten doctors and nurses, mostly from New York, had flown to Montgomery and driven to Selma the night before.

They were volunteers of the Medical Committee for Human Rights. When the march started, they followed in the file of ambulances at the end of the line.

Viola Jackson found herself in the second company, first squad. Standing in front of her was a young Negro wearing a sweatshirt. His marching companion was a tall white youth carrying a round knapsack on his back. They introduced themselves. The Negro was Charles Mauldin, an 18-year-old junior at the R. B. Hudson High School, Selma's Negro High, and President of the 1500-member Selma Youth Movement. The white was Jim Benston, an unsalaried member of the SCLC Selma staff.

The march began without heraldry. Viola Jackson and Charles Mauldin and Jim Benston walked together as the three-block-long line moved slowly down Sylvan Street and Water Avenue, through the Negro business district, to the bridge.

The view from the other side of the Pettus Bridge—looking toward Selma—was less than inspiring. The old brick buildings that line the bluffs above the slow-flowing river were gradually falling away. The sloping bluffs were spotted with bricks, discarded building materials and decaying underbrush. Viola Jackson and Charles Mauldin and Jim Benston could look back at the river bluffs and the long line of marchers behind them on the bridge, but they couldn't tell what was happening ahead of them on the highway. All they could see were police cars, State Trooper cars, sheriff's cars—a silent, stationary armada filling all four lanes of the Jefferson Davis Highway. A large, surly crowd of Selma white citizens stood on the trunks of parked cars or jammed the frontage area of roadside businesses, seeking ring-side seats. Newsmen were herded together in front of the Lehman Pontiac building some distance from the marchers and assigned several troopers for "protection."

State Troopers, headed by Major John Cloud, lined the highway three deep. Colonel Lingo watched from his automobile parked near Lehman's Grocery. As the marchers approached, Major Cloud hailed them: "This is an unlawful assembly," he said. "You have two minutes to turn around and go back to your church." The leaders of the march were now within several feet of the phalanx of troopers who held their clubs at the ready. Major Cloud took out his watch and started counting. The silence was total. Exactly one minute and five seconds later Major Cloud ordered, "Troopers forward." The blue-clad troopers leaped ahead, clubs swinging, moving with a sudden force that bowled over line after line of marchers. The first groups of Negroes went to the ground screaming, their knapsacks and bags spilling onto the highway.

The marchers, pushed back by the billy club attack, grouped to-

gether on the grassy, gasoline-soiled dividing strip in the center of the highway. They knelt and began to pray. The troopers rushed in again, banging heads, and then retreated. Viola and two boys knelt together. For two minutes a tense silence was broken only by the sound of the Confederate forces strapping on their gas masks and the buzz-buzz-buzz of the cattle prods.

As the troopers heaved the first tear gas bombs into the praying Negroes, the crowd of several hundred white onlookers broke into prolonged cheering. The first were feeler bombs; the marchers coughed and gagged, but didn't move. Then the troopers let loose with a heavy barrage of gas shells. Several bombs landed near Viola and the two boys, and then they couldn't see each other anymore.

For Charles Mauldin, it was like a quick visit to hell. "The gas was so thick that you could almost reach up and grab it. It seemed to lift me up and fill my lungs and I went down." Some of the marchers panicked and ran. They couldn't see where they were going and they ran into cars and buildings. Those who were too young or too old to move fast enough got hit the most. When they got to the Selma end of the bridge, the possemen and deputies who had been patiently waiting there attacked them anew with clubs and whips and chased them through the streets down toward the Negro quarter.

For Jim Benston, it was worse. After the first tear gas attack, he lay on the ground trying to breathe. He looked up and a trooper was standing in front of him, staring down through the big goggle-eyes of his gas mask. The trooper slowly lifted his tear gas gun and shot it off directly into Benston's face. "I was knocked out for maybe five minutes. When I woke up I was in a cloud. I couldn't breathe and I couldn't see. I was coughing and I was sick. It was like the world had gone away. I laid there on the grass for a few minutes and then I felt around me, trying to see if anybody else was still there. I couldn't feel anybody. They were all gone. I was the only one left." Benston staggered off to his right, through a used car lot, and collapsed in a small field. A dozen or so other marchers lay there, bleeding, coughing, trying to catch their breath. Then Benston heard horses, and shrill rebel battle yells. "They came charging through where we were laying on the grass and tried to hit us with the horses, but the horses had more sense. One posseman tried to get his horse to rear up and land on top of a man near me, but the horse wouldn't do it. Horses have more sense." The marchers got up and ran toward the bridge. The possemen rode in front of them and set off tear gas bombs in their path, forcing them through the new pockets of gas. On the bridge, Benston was clubbed at least 25 times. As he ran down the narrow pedestrian sidewalk, possemen would take turns, galloping by, clubbing him, laughing. He pulled his knapsack up to cover his head and neck. "That knapsack saved my life," he said.

For Viola Jackson, it didn't last long. She was knocked down on the dividing strip and dug her fingernails into the ground. The thick tear gas hung like heavy cigarette smoke between the blades of grass and curled around her fingers. She managed to get up and tried to run, but she couldn't go on. Her breath came shorter. Then she couldn't see, and she fell down onto the ground and didn't get up. More shells fell nearby, and the gas covered her fallen body like a blanket.

The police at first wouldn't let the waiting Union ambulances onto the bridge to pick up the wounded. When they did, finally, the volunteer drivers and doctors and nurses worked frantically, loaded the injured and racing them to the Good Samaritan Hospital.

Sheriff Clark's possemen chased the Negroes down to the housing project, but were stopped by Selma Safety Director Baker. Baker said he had his city police surrounding the project area and saw no need for further force. The Selma Times-Journal quoted Clark as replying to Baker: "I've already waited a month too damn long about moving in."

After the Negroes in the project were forced indoors, Sheriff Clark's posse rode uptown, looking for more Negroes. They yelled at Negroes walking on the streets and beat with their night-sticks on the hoods of cars with Negro drivers. "Get the hell out of town. Go on. We mean it. We want all the niggers off the street."

By dusk, not one Negro could be found on the streets of Selma.

Wednesday afternoon, as the Confederate forces were lining up before the national television cameras for a massive show of force on Sylvan Street, the Sheriff was at his resplendent best. His boots were spit-polished, the crease on the pants of his dark business suit cutting-edge sharp, the alabaster purity of his crash helmet broken only by a painted Confederate flag. In his lapel was a round white button bearing the single word "NEVER." This is Clark's rejoinder to "We Shall Overcome," and it appeared "never" would be the order of the day as the armed forces of the State of Alabama assumed battle formation a half block down from Brown's Chapel. State Troopers, Sheriff's deputies, city policemen, Alabama Soil Conservation officers, even Alabama Beverage Control officers, lined up in two and three squad car rows on Sylvan Street, flanking in reserve to the right and left down Selma Avenue and filling yet another block of Sylvan Street beyond the boundaries of the Negro housing project. The Mayor of Selma had said the Union could not march today and the troops were here to see that they would not.

This huge assemblage of police cars and troopers was good tonic for Sheriff Clark. He moved in between his deputies' cars, playfully snapping the rawhide hanging from his billy club at the Khaki-clad buttocks *of his possemen. He didn't act at all like a soldier who had just been dressed down by his commander-in-chief.*

Governor Wallace had summoned Clark to his capital offices the day before and told him to call off his posse and their whips and horses. Wallace, who seemed concerned about Alabama's image, upbraided Clark for the posse's Attila-the-Hun tactics on Sunday, before the lenses of television cameras. The Governor wasn't really mad about the whips, but he was mad as hell about the television cameras. When Clark left, red-faced and angry, he had instructions to keep his men out of the omniscient television eye. The Sheriff was also told that Wilson Baker would call the shots in Selma and he didn't like that, either.

Wilson Baker is the Director of Public Safety of Selma. For public safety director, read police chief. Mr. Baker is one of the few police officials in Alabama who does not make the title ludicrous by his actions. He thinks like a dedicated cop and not like a storm trooper. He would rather cajole or, at worst, arrest civil rights demonstrators than beat them. This moderate approach has alienated him from Sheriff Clark. "Those two have been at it all month long like two dogs in a pit," a Justice Department observer in Selma said. In the last two months of racial demonstration, Baker's tactics have kept the lid on this troubled and tense town. Massive violence came only once—Sunday at the bridge, when the Clark/Lingo coalition took over.

Baker has been criticized recently by Selma white townspeople— both racists and "moderates." They feel the demonstrations have gone too long and too far. But Baker is the kind of tough cop who does his job without regard to public opinion. This is not to say that Baker isn't a segregationist. He is. But he is a segregationist who seems to have some feeling for the Negro's struggle for human dignity. "If I was a nigger, I'd be doing just what they're doing," he once said.

The Union demonstrators boiled out of Brown's Chapel. They stood in the street, chatting casually, as if they had just come out of a regular Sunday service, then began to form ranks. There were some 500 of them, a good sixty per cent of them white and most of that number ministers and nuns. Baker strode forward to the front echelon of Selma police officers who were lined up across Sylvan Street. Beyond them, the Confederate forces stretched in a flow of color worthy of a Camelot set.

The marchers formed up four abreast and started down Sylvan Street toward the line of police a half block away. When they got within 12 feet, Baker stepped forward and raised his big left hand in a lazy arc, the cigar still between his fingers: "Reverend Anderson, you cannot march today." Standing beside Baker was Joseph T. Smitherman, Selma's young and nervous Mayor. The Rev. L. L. Anderson, a

185

Selma Negro leader who was heading the marchers, made his reply directly to the Mayor:

"We are asking your Honor to permit us to march to the Courthouse. We are not registered voters but we want to be; it is our God-given constitutional right. We shall move like the children of Israel, moving toward the promised land."

The Mayor blinked. The streets were jammed with spectators. People stood on nearby rooftops. The omni-present television cameras were trained directly on him. Newsmen shoved microphones under his nose. He was the Mayor: 35 years old, a former appliance dealer, a close political ally of Governor Wallace. It was his decision to ban any further demonstrations or marches outside of the Brown's Chapel area. He cleared his throat, twice, and folded his slender arms in front of the dark business suit which looked like it belonged on someone a size larger. "You have had opportunity after opportunity to register your people to vote," he said. (The Dallas County Courthouse is open two days a month to register new voters.) "We have enforced the laws impartially ... We expect to see our orders obeyed."

The Mayor stepped back to the sanctuary of the squad cars. The newsmen crowded in around Baker and the Rev. Anderson. "I would like to introduce some people of good will, who have some statements to make," said Anderson. "You can make all the statements you want, but you are not going to march," replied Baker.

The nuns, ministers, priests, rabbis, lay church leaders and the Negro leaders who made up the majority of the marchers, spoke to the press for the next ninety minutes while the youngsters in the housing project played and giggled on the sidewalks.

As the speakers talked on, damning Selma with all the moral fervor at their command, it became evident that only their fellow marchers and the newsmen were listening. The spectators walked idly about the sidewalk; children chased each other in between the rows of brick apartment buildings; the troopers broke ranks, stood in small groups chatting, sipping cokes, slipping their riot helmets back to let the sun on their foreheads. Mayor Smitherman picked up one of the sandwiches and fiddled with the wax paper wrappings for a moment before he opened it. He looked unhappily at the crowd of demonstrators. "I don't understand it," he said. "Martin Luther King can walk into the White House any time he wants for conference with the President. I sent the President a telegram asking for a meeting, but some sort of fifth assistant answered it."

"King? Where is King?" a man asked. "He's in town," said the Mayor. "I don't know why he isn't here."

Martin Luther King wasn't there because he was in trouble in his own movement. His absence explained the absence, also, of the usual throngs of Selma teenagers who gave life and spirit and rhythm to every mass Negro meeting in Selma for two years now. King wasn't there because he was afraid he would be publicly booed by his own people.

Dr. King was at the home of a Selma Negro dentist, Dr. Sullivan Jackson. It was there, early Tuesday morning, that the pajama-clad Nobel Prize winner met with former Florida Governor LeRoy Collins, now head of the Federal Community Relations Service and President Johnson's unofficial Ambassador to the Union forces. Collins had been sent by special jet from Washington to work out a compromise that would avoid repetition of Sunday's bloodshed on Tuesday afternoon, when another attempt at the march to Montgomery (this one led by Dr. King) was scheduled to cross the Edmund Pettus Bridge. A federal judge had issued a temporary restraining order against the march and Dr. King was in a quandry. His organization prided itself on never violating the law—or a court order; yet, he had pledged to lead this march (King was absent Sunday), and civil rights workers and ministers from all over the South were gathering at Brown's Chapel. They all wanted to march. Collins offered a typically Johnson compromise: he had conferred with Colonel Lingo and obtained a pledge that the marchers would be unharmed if they turned back a small distance down Highway 80. Lingo had even drawn a rough map, showing where the Union forces must halt. Collins handed the Confederate map to King: this way, he said, both sides would save face—and King would have a dramatic moment. King hesitated, then took the map. He sent a message to the crowd at Brown's Chapel: "I have decided it is better to die on the highway than to make a butchery of my conscience."

There was, of course, no danger of butchery. The plan worked. The marchers were halted, knelt, said a prayer and turned back. The deal became obvious to SNCC people when Colonel Lingo, in a mild Southern doublecross, pulled his troopers back, leaving the highway to Montgomery open as King rose to lead his followers in retreat to Selma. The move was meant to embarrass King and it did. King later called the second march "the greatest confrontation for freedom" in the South. King was accused of "betraying" the movement and collaborating with the enemy.

King's fall from favor was only momentary. The diverse elements in the Union expeditionary force were united later that week by the death of the Rev. James J. Reeb, a white Unitarian minister from Boston, who died of wounds from a night-time beating at the hands of some Selma white citizens as he left a restaurant in the Negro district. But though

187

momentary, King's disgrace was significant because it illustrated in dramatic fashion a long-standing split in the Union leadership.

It was the same split that divided the Abolitionists in the 1850's and the 1860's over whether to support Lincoln and work within the Republican party for their goals or to continue to take outside, radical social action. It is the old polarity between action and negotiation, between politics and revolution. It is the struggle between those who would work within the Establishment and those who reject the Establishment policies of compromise and consensus, and agitate for more direct solutions. This division is evident in the methodology of the civil rights movement, from the NAACP on the right to SNCC and then the black nationalist groups on the left.

SUMMARY

Humanists tend to exalt the nonviolent movements for their noble and humane tactics. However, a few followers of Gandhi and King acknowledge limitations in applying such strategies to current human relations problems. Theorists and practitioners of human relations prefer to think in terms of nonviolence, and when one recalls Gandhi's victories nonviolence does seem a fitting and successful method for inducing change. Yet the nonviolent method is not always supported by the reality of the situation. For example, it is not always possible to communicate with the opponent, and even if it is possible, communication sometimes begets more resistance to change. Also, casualties resulting from such an approach can be evidenced by continuing police brutality inflicted on protesters and the killing of civil-rights demonstrators and political leaders. One who initiates a nonviolent approach to change must be prepared to meet violence from the opposition.

To implement a successful nonviolent campaign takes time and effort to train the participants. Although it increases the chances of conducting a successful campaign, such effort also has its drawbacks in that it is time-consuming and the momentum of the campaign tends to be slowed. Nonviolent techniques which focus on attitude change are likely to be effective. The modest success of the civil-rights movement is but one example of its potential effectiveness. Coercive techniques such as boycotts and sit-downs produce change in the opponent even though he may not like the fact that circumstances force him to comply. In the final analysis, individuals committed to nonviolence tenaciously cling to the belief that human life is sacred and, therefore, should not be devalued or wasted.

Chapter 7
SUGGESTED READING

Aczell, Tamas, and Tibor Meray. *The Revolt of the Mind: A Case Study of Intellectual Resistance Behind the Iron Curtain.* New York, Frederick A. Praeger, Inc., 1959.

Andrews, C. F. *Mahatma Gandhi.* New York, The Macmillan Co., 1930.

Alinsky, Saul. *Rules for Radicals.* New York, Vintage Books, Inc., 1971.

Bell, Inge P. *CORE and the Strategy of Nonviolence.* New York, Random House, Inc., 1968.

Bondurant, Joan V. *Conquest of Violence: The Gandhian Philosophy of Conflict.* Princeton, N.J., Princeton University Press, 1958.

Brockway, A. Fenner. *Non-cooperation in Other Lands.* Madras, India, Tagore & Co., 1929.

Cadoux, C. J. *Christian Pacifism Re-examined.* Oxford, G. B., Basil Blackwell, 1940.

Case, Clarence M. *Nonviolent Coercion: A Study in Methods of Social Pressure.* New York, The Century Co., 1923.

Dellinger, Dave. *Revolutionary Nonviolence.* Indianapolis, The Bobbs-Merrill Co., 1970.

Deming, Barbara. *Revolution and Equilibrium.* New York, Grossman Publishers, 1971.

Diwakar, Ranganath R. *Stayagraha: The Power of Truth.* Hinsdale, Ill., H. Regnery Co., 1948.

Douglass, James W. *Resistance and Contemplation: The Way of Liberation.* Garden City, N.Y., Doubleday & Co., Inc., 1972.

Erikson, Erik H. *Gandhi's Truth: On the Origins of Militant Non-violence.* New York, W. W. Norton & Co., Inc., 1969.

Finn, James. *Protest: Pacifism and Politics; Some Passionate Views on War and Nonviolence.* New York, Random House, Inc., 1968.

Fisher, Louis. *The Life of Mahatma Gandhi.* New York, Harper Brothers, 1950.

Fry, A. Ruth. *Victories Without Violence.* London, Dennis Dobson, 1952.

Gregg, Richard B. *The Power of Nonviolence,* 2d rev. ed. New York, Schocken Books, Inc., 1966.

Hare, A. Paul, and Herbert H. Blumberg. *Nonviolent Direct Action.* Washington, Corpus Books, 1968.

Haring, Bernhard. *A Theology of Protest.* New York, Farrar, Straus & Giroux, Inc., 1970.

Hiller, E. T. *The Strike: A Study in Collective Action.* Chicago, University of Chicago Press, 1928.

Hirst, Margaret E. *The Quakers in Peace and War.* New York, George H. Doran Co., 1923.

Horsburgh, H. J. N. *Non-Violence and Aggression: A Study of Gandhi's Moral Equivalent of War.* London: Oxford University Press, 1968.

Joner, E. Stanley. *Mahatma Gandhi: An Interpretation.* New York, Abingdon-Cokesbury Press, 1958.

189

King, Martin Luther, Jr. *The Measure of a Man*. Philadelphia, Pilgrim Press, 1968.

——. *Stride Toward Freedom: The Montgomery Story*. New York, Harper & Row, Publishers Inc., 1958.

——. *Where Do We Go From Here: Chaos or Community?* New York, Bantam Books, Inc., 1968.

——. *Why We Can't Wait*. New York, Harper & Row, Publishers, Inc., 1964.

Kuper, Leo. *Passive Resistance in South Africa*. New Haven, Yale University Press, 1957.

Lewis, David L. *King: A Critical Biography*. New York, Praeger Publishers, 1970.

Lincoln, C. Eric, ed. *Martin Luther King, Jr.: A Profile*. New York, Hill and Wang, Inc., 1970.

Lynd, Staughton, ed. *Nonviolence in America: A Documentary History*. Indianapolis, The Bobs-Merrill Co., 1966.

Mabee, Carleton. *Black Freedom: The Nonviolent Abolitionists from 1830 Through the Civil War*. New York, McCall Publishing Co., 1971.

Miller, William A. *Nonviolence: A Christian Interpretation*. New York, Schocken Books, Inc., 1964.

Muse, Benjamin. *The American Negro Revolution: From Nonviolence to Black Power, 1963–1967*. Bloomington, Indiana University Press, 1968.

Oppenheimer, Martin, and George Lakey. *A Manual for Direct Action*. Chicago, Quadrangle Books, Inc., 1965.

Proudfoot, Merrill. *Diary of a Sit-in*. Chapel Hill, University of North Carolina Press, 1962.

Rolland, Romain. *Mahatma Gandhi: The Man Who Became One with the Universal Being*. New York, Century Co., 1924.

Schechter, Betty. *The Peaceable Revolution*. Boston, Houghton Mifflin Co., 1963.

Seifert, Harvey. *Conquest by Suffering: The Process and Prospects of Nonviolent Resistance*. Philadelphia, Westminster Press, 1965.

Sharp, Gene. *The Politics of Nonviolent Action*. Boston, Porter Sargent Publisher, 1973.

Shepherd, Odell. *The Heart of Thoreau's Journals*. New York, Dover Publications, 1927.

Shridharani, Krishnalal. *War Without Violence: A Study of Gandhi's Method and Its Accomplishments*. New York, Harcourt Brace & Co., 1939.

Sibley, Mulford Q., ed. *The Quiet Battle: Writings on the Theory and Practice of Non-violent Resistance*. Garden City, N.Y., Doubleday & Co., Inc., 1963.

Stevick, Daniel B. *Civil Disobedience and the Christian*. New York, The Seabury Press, 1969.

Thoreau, Henry David. *The Variorum Civil Disobedience*. New York, Twayne Publishers, Inc., 1967.

——. *Walden and Other Writings*. Garden City, N.Y., Doubleday & Co., Inc., 1970.

Part Three **PROGRAMS FOR CHANGE**

FROM PSYCHOTHERAPY TO ORGANIZATION CHANGE

The role of behavioral science in organizations has moved from research on the individual, to the group and group interrelationships, to organizational studies on how to effect change affecting interaction, to the present concepts of organizations as systems.—
JACK H. EPSTEIN and ROBERT H. WARREN

Those persons concerned with improving human relationships must be aware of the various approaches to social change. Both individual and group activities are legitimate areas of concern for human relations practitioners:

There are many ways to induce a constructive behavior change in individuals. The practitioner, *or change agent, the man who tries to bring about such change, is not a researcher; he devotes himself to working directly with people on problems of immediate, practical importance. Among the practitioners who devote themselves to treating the mentally ill are the* clinical psychologist *and the* psychotherapist, *who usually have Ph.D. degrees and who use certain techniques of psychological therapy on their patients; the* psychiatrist, *a medical doctor whose specialty is mental illness; and the* psychoanalyst, *usually a psychiatrist who has taken further training in a particular kind of psychological therapy at a psychoanalytic institute. Other practitioners are more interested in attempting to bring about more overt kinds of behavior change related to one's social environment, the* social worker, *for example, or the* human-relations trainer, *who works with psychologically normal persons to help them improve their skills in relating to others. All practitioners share the same general aim of trying to improve the social and psychological performances of the people with whom they are working.*[1]

[1] John Mann, *Changing Human Behavior*, 9.

PSYCHOTHERAPY, PSYCHOANALYSIS, AND GROUP THERAPY

For large numbers of persons psychiatric treatment is needed before they can become fully functioning members of society. The goal of psychotherapy is to relieve the patient of distressing neurotic symptoms or discordant personality characteristics which interfere with his satisfactory adaptation to his social roles. Though this may initially appear to be a very broad goal, the purpose of psychotherapy is quite limited. Psychotherapy—including its most extensive form, psychoanalysis—is nothing more than psychological repair work:

We may describe psychotherapy as the use of psychological investigation of personality, character-pattern, and life problems in the setting of a reliable and good human relationship with the psychotherapist; so that as insight into the causes and nature of his neurotic anxieties and conflicts grow the patient may be able to use the emotional security of the relationship with the therapist to develop a personality increasingly free from internal causes of fear, and therefore increasingly stable and self-assured.[2]

In brief, psychotherapy is a method of treatment which attempts to untangle the patient's personality; the psychotherapist is a guide and observer, and the patient is responsible for the "finished product." Thus psychotherapy is a system of scientific psychology which makes observations of and posits theories about personality in an attempt to predict human behavior and outcomes of human relationships.[3]

Several forms of psychotherapy have evolved in the past few decades. *Existential therapy*, which has developed since World War II, is based on the ideas of the existential philosophers discussed in Chapter 4. It also draws heavily from the writings of Rollo May, Erich Fromm, Carl R. Rogers, and Martin Buber. It deals with the patient and his confrontation with three aspects of the world: his environment, his relationships with other people, and his inner experience.

Gestalt therapy is also based on existential assumptions, but its main focus is on seeing, hearing, touching, and moving. Body movements are significant to Gestalt therapists, who deliberately touch their patients in an attempt to make them more aware of themselves. Both existential and Gestalt therapy stress the here and now—current feelings and occurrences.

Psychotherapy, in comparison with other fields of medicine has suffered from a dearth of research data for two reasons. First, psychotherapy is an extremely complex procedure, involving emotional and cognitive functions, the process of learning, physiological determi-

---

[2] Harry Guntrip, *Healing the Sick Mind*, 1.
[3] Eric Berne, *A Layman's Guide to Psychiatry and Psychoanalysis*, 245.

Table 2. Comparison of Psychoanalysis, Psychotherapy, and Group Therapy

	Psychoanalysis	Psychotherapy	Group therapy
Goals	Extensive relearning, reeducation, and readaptation of the personality	To reduce anxiety in specific areas related to current conflicts and problems	Improve reality testing Socialization Development of psychological aptitude Prepare for later therapy
Method	Rigid; usually couch; concentration on relationship of past experiences to present personality patterns	Less rigid; no couch; concentration on aspects pertinent to present situation	Concentration on group interaction "at moment" between group, therapist, and individual members during group meeting
Relationship	One-to-one; intense; intimate	One-to-one; less intense than psycho-analysis	One-to-group
Interaction	Patient interacts with analyst and outside world	Patient interacts with therapist and outside world	Patient interacts with therapist, a group of people, and outside world
Length	3–5 years	Variable, several months to 1 or 2 years	1–1½ years or longer
Frequency	4–5 times a week	1–3 times a week	Once a week
Depth	Extensive	Less extensive	Superficial
Transference	Very intense; analyzed carefully in terms of past and present	Less intense, related to current situation; may or may not be utilized	Still less intense, related to group situations utilized as group transference
Dreams	Extensively used	Used less; related to current situation	Not used
Free associations	Extensively used	Used less; related to current situation	Not used
Anamnesis (past history)	Extensively used	Partially used	Not extensively used
Interpretations	By analyst	By psychotherapist	By group members, not group therapist

SOURCE: James A. Johnson, Group Therapy: A Practical Approach (New York, McGraw-Hill Book Company, Inc., 1963), 59. Used by permission.

nants of behavior, social attitudes, and ethical values. To plan a well-controlled objective research in such an area seems almost impossible. Consequently, psychotherapy continues to be a subtle art. Some researchers are skeptical that research can be meaningful in psychotherapy. They believe that the intangible elements of psychotherapy must remain if it is to be an effective approach to human change and growth. Second, alternative forms of therapy have emerged in recent years which claim better results, require less time, and are less expensive. The psychotherapist, who ten years ago was considered by many Americans to have most of the answers to their mental anguish, is now being compared with his psychotherapeutic competitors.[4]

Psychotherapy, psychoanalysis, and group therapy have distinctive approaches. Psychotherapy and psychoanalysis employ a one-to-one relationship between therapist and client, whereas group therapy employs a one-to-group relationship. Psychotherapy operates under three handicaps: (1) a long period of time is required to effect basic personality change, (2) the success of the method is dependent on verbal communication, and (3) treatment is expensive. Psychotherapy may require months and sometimes years of treatment, a factor that discourages many potential patients. The patient must be able to describe his thoughts, feelings, and experiences, a factor that limits the usefulness of this technique for basically nonverbal clients. The high cost of psychotherapy makes it prohibitive for persons of low income.[5]

Like psychotherapy, psychoanalysis, sometimes called *depth psychotherapy*, also seeks to effect a change in the basic personality of the patient. In psychoanalysis the patient recalls and restructures past experiences which restrict his emotional growth and maturity. Psychoanalysis has been most successful in treating neurotics of above-average intelligence. Psychoanalysis is even more demanding than psychotherapy of the patient's time and financial resources.

Group therapy was developed partly because of shortage of psychotherapists and psychoanalysts, because it is less expensive and time-consuming, and because some persons respond better to a group situation than to individual therapy. The major technique of group therapy is the use of homogeneous groupings to provide an environment in which patients feel free to discuss their thoughts, feelings, and experiences.

In England the Tavistock Institute of Human Relations pioneered group therapy on a community scale. Founded shortly after World War II, the Tavistock Institute is an organization of psychiatrists and social scientists dedicated to the diagnosis and treatment of community

[4] See Eric Berne, *The Crisis of Psychoanalysis.*
[5] Louis Kaplan, *Foundations of Human Behavior,* 308–12.

problems. Their major premise is that group problems can only be treated by a group. Furthermore, Tavistock is committed to doing things *with* people rather than *to* people. The Tavistock therapists take a neutral role and provide social-science knowledge and techniques for school, industrial, and recreational groups.

Group-therapy methods are not unique to the twentieth century. The Austrian physician Franz Anton Mesmer employed group methods in hypnotic sessions during the latter part of the eighteenth century. Group counseling of patients with alcohol problems, sexual disorders, and stammering difficulties has been practiced in Europe since 1900. However, group therapy did not gain widespread use in the United States until the late 1930's. Presently more than half of the state mental institutions in the United States employ group therapy and group activities in their treatment programs. In addition to mental institutions, child guidance, marital counseling, and drug- and alcohol-abuse programs use group therapy.[6]

THERAPEUTIC RELATIONSHIPS

The therapeutic relationship is firmly anchored in social-science theories of the self. Charles Horton Cooley and George Herbert Mead, two American sociologists, contributed much to our understanding of the origin and development of the *social self*. Cooley's *looking-glass self theory* describes how the awareness of self develops out of social interaction: children gradually acquire the ability to (1) imagine how they appear to other persons, (2) imagine how the other persons judge them, and (3) have a resulting feeling of pride or mortification. Thus, our self-estimates, according to Cooley, depend on interaction with others, and we become socialized by understanding the reactions we produce in others.[7]

Mead pointed out that the social self is a product of our interaction with other persons. According to Mead, the birth of the social self depends on the individual's ability to be an object to himself. As children we learn to imitate other people's responses—to take the roles of others. *Role taking*, Mead noted, is an essential aspect of the development of the social self. In responding to himself, the child (1) develops an awareness of his own responses, (2) learns about the consequences of his responses, and (3) achieves objectivity.[8]

Although psychoanalytic theories tend to place more emphasis on instinctual drives than on self theory, they are also concerned with the nature of the self. Freud believed that people who have a firm grasp on

[6] James A. Johnson, *Group Therapy: A Practical Approach*, 8.
[7] Charles H. Cooley, *Human Nature and the Social Order*, 151–52.
[8] George H. Mead, *Mind, Self and Society.*

197

reality have "ego strength," while those who do not have a strong grasp on reality have "weak egos." Clearly, differences between the self that one believes to be the "real self" and the self that one ought to be can result in psychological imbalance.[9]

Carl R. Rogers cautioned that a large gap between the real self (what we are) and the ideal self (what we would like to be) is an unhealthy condition. Individuals whose behavior continually falls short of what they believe it ideally ought to be are likely to be plagued by self-hate and feelings of inferiority. When this occurs, Rogers concluded, the task of psychotherapy is to help the patient achieve a fuller degree of self-acceptance.[10]

Social class and race are two factors which practitioners frequently overlook when trying to help groups. Social class is the most influential factor in social and cultural behavior patterns. In America, for example, the manner in which persons are born, educated, married, and buried depends upon one overriding criterion—their social class. Race is the second most influential factor. The introduction into a group of persons of a different race from that of the group members is likely to be accompanied by tension and conflict. Even when a group is not burdened with racial and social-class problems, it must deal with emotional anxieties inherent in close relationships:

Whenever any group of people come together for a period of time emotional reactions come to the surface. The closer people are in a group and the more time they spend with each other, the greater will be the emotional interaction among them. Where there is closeness among members of the group there is more anxiety. . . . People avoid closeness because of fear of exposure. If they reveal themselves to others, the self-knowledge of their personal weaknesses, idiosyncrasies, and thoughts generates fears of disapproval and rejection. Fears of exposure encompass such thoughts as badness, worthlessness, helplessness, abandonment, profligacy, inferiority, unlovableness, detection of rage, and sexual inadequacies.[11]

A foremost consideration of human relations practitioners is the minimization of manipulative behavior in groups and the maximization of open, honest, personal-growth-producing behavior:

Manipulation occurs when an individual is caused to do something by another individual in absence of genuine mutuality. The influence may be physical force or skillful exploitation of weakness, as in seduction or deception. Sometimes the influence may be more subtle, as in

[9] See Calvin S. Hall, *A Primer of Freudian Psychology.*
[10] Carl R. Rogers, *Client-Centered Therapy.*
[11] Johnson, *op. cit.,* 26.

advertising or propaganda. Buber would say that such relationships are "I-It" relationships. The other person is viewed as an object to be manipulated rather than a person to encounter. Fromm calls this "the market place orientation," because one person is used for the profit of another.[12]

Recently some practitioners have been accused of manipulating their patients or clients into behaving as they—the practitioners—want them to. From a human relations perspective this practice is hardly conducive to personal growth.

SOCIAL GROUPS

A *social group* exists when the members are united by a feeling of emotional solidarity and common purpose. They have a culture that systematically defines the roles, relationships, and criteria by which members are differentiated from nonmembers. The *small group* may be defined as any group made up of two to thirty persons. Most groups exhibit *ethnocentrism*—the belief that their group is the best and that others are inferior to it.[13]

Merle Ohlsen lists several characteristics of an effective group. The most important characteristic is that the persons assembled must cooperate to fulfill some meaningful purpose. This means that the group (1) knows why it exists, (2) has created an atmosphere in which its work can be done, (3) has developed guidelines for making decisions, (4) has established conditions under which each member can make his unique contributions, (5) has achieved communication among its members, (6) has helped its members learn to give and receive help, (7) has learned to cope with conflict, and (8) has learned to diagnose its processes and improve its functioning. Another important characteristic is that the group provides a safe place in which a member may express his ideas and receive honest reactions from others.[14]

Group membership is a primary source of security (or insecurity) for the individual. Because groups serve as the foremost determiners of self-esteem, feelings of worth depend upon the social status of the groups to which persons belong. It should not be surprising, therefore, that persons who believe that they are members of low-status or underprivileged groups tend toward feelings of self-hatred and worthlessness.

Every group demands of its members some degree of conformity in behavior, attitudes, beliefs, and values. Such demands lead to feelings

[12] Logan J. Fox, *Psychology as Philosophy, Science, and Art*, 59.
[13] George Henderson, *To Live in Freedom: Human Relations Today and Tomorrow*, 49.
[14] Merle M. Ohlsen, *Group Counseling*.

of satisfaction—and also on occasion to frustration. A common source of frustration is a group rule that does not allow for individual initiative. Consequently, many human relations training programs focus on group norms.

SMALL-GROUP RESEARCH

Many studies have examined group size, group composition, rewards, participation, interaction, and group discussion. The conclusions of these studies are summarized below:

1. Group size greatly affects the manner in which group members interact. The smaller the group, the more opportunity each member has to participate and, in theory, the less likely the members are to be frustrated by the interaction. As a group grows in size, problems of maintaining effective leadership and interaction increase.

2. There appears to be significant correlation between the adjustment and ability of group members and their capacity to achieve group goals. The readiness of members to follow or resist authority, to be intimate or to resist intimacy in group situations, also affects the functioning of the group.

3. Groups which offer rewards based on cooperation among members rather than competition are less resistant to change. Intragroup cooperation tends to be more productive than intragroup competition.

4. Participation among group members tends to be unequal, a few individuals doing most of the talking. Furthermore, there is a tendency toward unequal distribution of group rewards.

5. Freedom to participate in group decisions generally results in emotional satisfaction. However, there is little objective evidence to support the belief that group discussion alone produces personality changes.

Charles and Sarah Kiesler have pointed out the following conditions of involvement in groups:

Being aware of others in the same aggregate and defining oneself as a member may still not guarantee that the individual is involved. Everyone knows people who, although nominally members of a group, nevertheless seem completely uninterested in the group. For them to be real members of a group, they would have to feel kinship or identity with the others—to feel they were significant. Social psychologists would say that these people belong to a membership group, *since they belong to the group in name only. A psychological group—called a* reference group—*is defined only when (1) the person is aware of others,*

(2) the person defines himself as a member, or would like to be a member, and (3) the person feels that others are significant to him (emotionally or cognitively). Only in such aggregates will psychological involvement be found.[15]

Using face-to-face communication, small groups pass on the behavior and attitudes of their members. The kind and degree of interpersonal contact, and the goals and functions of the group determine how much the group will influence its members.[16] A review of the literature points out the many gaps in small-group research. From 1900 to 1920 small-group researchers focused on theorizing about man's social nature. During the 1920's they turned their attention to methodology. In the 1930's and 1940's researchers, following Kurt Lewin's lead, studied domestic problems, such as leadership and prejudice. Since the 1940's small-group researchers have scattered their attention over many areas. There has been a proliferation of terms, concepts, and operations, but little replication to substantiate research findings.

In the last three decades at least three thousand small-group studies have been conducted and reported. These studies, varying widely in terms of methodology, range from anecdotal case studies to highly complex experimental studies. Most of the small-group studies have been conducted in the laboratory; few have been carried out in non-laboratory settings.[17] While the laboratory is a good place to gain precision of measurement, control of conditions, and manipulation of variables, studies in laboratories offer the researcher limited ability to generalize to social phenomena in nonlaboratory situations. To qualify as theory, small-group formulations must hypothesize specific outcomes under specific conditions in terms that other researchers can use to test the prediction.

Most small-group research involves little in the way of explicit formulation of theory. Joseph E. McGrath and Irwin Altman cited the following exceptions:

    1. John W. Thibaut's and Harold H. Kelly's theoretical formulations of dyads.[18]

    2. George C. Homans' theory of exchange.[19]

[15] Charles A. Kiesler and Sarah B. Kiesler, *Conformity*, 27.

[16] Leon Festinger, Stanley Schachter, and Kurt Back, *Social Pressures in Informal Groups: A Study of Human Factors in Housing*, 3.

[17] See Joseph E. McGrath and Irwin Altman, *Small Group Research: A Synthesis and Critique of the Field*.

[18] John W. Thibaut and Harold H. Kelly, *The Social Psychology of Groups*.

[19] George C. Homans, "Social Behavior as Exchange," *American Journal of Sociology*, Vol. 63 (1958), 597–607.

3. Leon Festinger's formulations on communication and attraction in groups.[20]

4. John R. P. French, Jr.'s, theory of power.[21]

5. William C. Schutz's theory of interpersonal needs.[22]

I would add Robert F. Bales to McGrath and Altman's list of significant small-group researchers. Influenced by the theories of Talcott Parsons and Edward A. Shils, Bales developed a sociological theory of group interaction and an empirical scoring technique to measure such interaction. Like Parsons and Shils, Bales defines the group as a miniature social system confronted with typical social-system problems—how to adapt to the realities of environmental conditions, how to accomplish group goals, how to satisfy individual members' needs, and how to maintain its existence.

Bales's approach to understanding groups is important since he shifted attention from the group's effect on people and the situation to effects of people and the situation on the group. For example, his research led him to conclude that group members' efforts to adapt to group tasks interfere with their efforts to achieve social integration. Conversely, group members' efforts to achieve social integration tend to interfere with task performance. The dilemma in which the adaptive efforts interfere with social-integration efforts and vice versa is what Bales calls the "equilibrium problems."

While Kurt Lewin is usually credited with turning our attention to the dynamics of small-group interaction, many others also contributed to the study of group dynamics. Sociologists Lester Ward, Emile Durkheim, Georg Simmel, and Charles H. Cooley were pioneers in the study of small-group behavior. Psychologists Norman Triplett, August Mayer, Ernst Newmann, F. H. Allport, and Jacob L. Moreno added still other insights.[23]

Lewin's influence is seen in the works of Martin Deutsch (differential effects of cooperation and competition upon groups), Alex Bavelas (effects of communications networks on group efficiency and satisfaction), and Leon Festinger, Stanley Schachter, and Kurt Back (effects of group cohesion upon pressures to conform to group norms).

BASIC PRINCIPLES OF SMALL-GROUP INTERACTION

Small-group theorists have developed three basic ways of classifying

[20] Leon Festinger, "Informal Communication," *Psychological Review*, Vol. 57 (1950), 271–92. See also Theodore M. Newcomb, *The Acquaintance Process*.

[21] John R. P. French, Jr., "A Formal Theory of Social Power," *Psychological Review*, Vol. 63 (1956), 181–94.

[22] William C. Schutz, *FIRO: A Three-Dimensional Theory of Interpersonal Behavior.*

[23] See Hubert Bonner, *Group Dynamics: Principles and Applications*, ch. 1.

groups: (1) task-oriented groups, such as work groups, (2) socially oriented groups, such as bridge clubs, and (3) combined task and socially oriented groups, such as fraternities and sororities.[24] Human relations are most clearly in evidence in task-oriented groups.

The following forms of behavior aid a group in accomplishing its task:

1. *Initiating*—suggesting new ideas or a changed way of looking at the group problem or goal, proposing new activities.

2. *Information seeking*—asking for relevant facts or authoritative information.

3. *Information giving*—providing pertinent facts or authoritative information or relating personal experience relevant to the group task.

4. *Opinion giving*—stating a pertinent belief or opinion about something the group is considering.

5. *Elaborating*—building on a previous comment, enlarging on it, giving examples.

6. *Coordinating*—showing or clarifying the relationships among various ideas, trying to pull ideas and suggestions together.

7. *Orienting*—defining the progress of the discussion in terms of the group's goals, raising questions about the direction the discussion is taking.

8. *Testing*—checking with the group to see if it is ready to make a decision or to take some action.[25]

Disruptive or nonfunctional forms of behavior which impede group movement toward its goals include the following:

1. *Blocking*—interfering with the progress of the group by going off at a tangent, citing personal experiences unrelated to the group's problem, arguing too much on a point the rest of the group has resolved, rejecting ideas without consideration, preventing a vote.

2. *Aggression*—criticizing or blaming others, showing hostility toward the group or some individual without relation to what has happened in the group, attacking the motives of others, deflating the ego or status of others.

3. *Seeking recognition*—attempting to call attention to one's self by excessive talking, extreme ideas, boasting, boisterousness.

4. *Special pleading*—introducing or supporting ideas related to one's own pet concerns or philosophies beyond reason, attempting to speak for "the grass roots," "the common man," "the underdog."

5. *Withdrawing*—acting indifferent or passive, resorting to excessive formality, doodling, whispering to others.

[24] Thomas W. Madron, *Small Group Methods and the Study of Politics*, 4–5.
[25] Raymond F. Gale, *Discovering Your Unique Self*, 2.

6. *Dominating*—trying to assert authority in manipulating the group or certain members of it by "pulling rank," giving directions authoritatively, interrupting contributions of others.[26]

There are still some serious gaps in small-group research. For example, we know very little about the impact of attitudes toward the task and the work situation on member and group performance or on interpersonal relations in the group. In the area of leadership, studies of authoritarian attitudes have yielded extremely confusing results. Nor do researchers clearly understand why the more task training and experience groups and group members have the better they perform as individuals and groups. There is also very little research on group composition.

Yet despite the incompleteness of small-group research, the conclusions of Dorwin Cartwright's study of behavior change, reported in 1951, still appear valid:

1. In order for the group to act as the medium of change, its members must have a strong sense of belonging.

2. When a process to bring about change is introduced, its success will to a great extent be in proportion to the relation it has to the members' reasons for joining the group.

3. Within the group itself, the greater the prestige of the individual the more he can influence others.

4. If the proposed change will cause group members to deviate from group norms, they will resist the change.

5. Effective change in behavior can most easily be induced by creating a shared perception of the need for the new behavior so that its desirability becomes a group norm.

6. To maximize the probability of successful and lasting change, it is important that the planning and implementation of the change be a group activity.[27]

The Kieslers elaborated upon Cartwright's principles:

1. When an individual *accepts* his group's goal, he will be motivated to work within the group for its attainment. In most cases, group success will necessitate conformity to at least one of the rules and standards of the group....

2. The individual must understand the group goal. A *clear* goal enhances conformity to group standards.

---

[26] *Ibid.*, 2–3.

[27] Dorwin Cartwright, "Achieving Changes in People: Some Applications of Group Dynamics Theory," *Human Relations*, Vol. 4 (1951), 381–93.

3. When group standards are relevant to the group goal, there is greater pressure for conformity.

4. To the extent the group can be successful in attaining its goals, the individual will conform.

5. The individual who contributes to the success of the group will be highly valued. Members who have higher *status* in the group will have greater influence on the others.

6. When cooperation or interdependence will help to reach the group goal, conformity will be greater.[28]

Most of us attempt to live up to the expectations of others in hopes that others will accept and like us, group goals will be successfully attained, and the continuation of the group will be ensured. Clearly, then, feedback from members of our groups allows us to gain information about reality, validate our own opinions and make sure that they are consistent with the opinions of others, and evaluate ourselves and others. These and other principles form the foundation of training groups and encounter groups.

INTRODUCTION TO TRAINING GROUPS AND ENCOUNTER GROUPS

From its beginning the Training group (T-group) program has been based on small-group research; participants in T-groups attempt to gain an objective understanding of the manner in which small groups function (see Chapter 10). T-group participants also attempt to use their knowledge of small-group functions to facilitate individual and group change:

The T-group consists of normal persons who meet for a number of sessions under the guidance and leadership of a professionally trained scientist who, during the meetings, will educate them in the processes that characterize small-group functioning. The T-group is unusual from several points of view. First, it has no assigned task. If the members had one, they would be too busy fulfilling it to observe their own actions and those of others. Second, the members are encouraged to analyze their reactions to themselves and to each other. Third, the trainer refuses to provide positive group leadership by telling the members what to do. Rather, he tends to interpret to them the reason that things are happening as they are. It is generally assumed by most trainers that enhanced understanding of small-group processes will not only increase the diagnostic skills of the group members, but may also lead to new forms of behaviors as members become aware of how others are reacting to them.[29]

[28] Kiesler and Kiesler, *op. cit.*, 31.
[29] Mann, *op. cit.*, 95.

During the time National Training Laboratories (NTL) was developing, Carl Rogers was experimenting with group work at the University of Chicago. One of his foremost purposes in working with groups was to develop theories of interpersonal relationships and communication. In the course of his experiments Rogers learned that intensive group experiences can produce significant learning. By applying the principles of client-centered therapy and phenomenological psychology in his training groups, Rogers was able to help the members achieve personal growth.

NTL and Rogers were foremost in introducing the encounter-group movement. In fact, in the late 1940's and early 1950's NTL was the center of both T-group and encounter-group training. In the mid-1950's there was a shift in emphasis as the encounter-group movement attracted large numbers of clinical psychologists (see Chapter 11). Gradually the clinical approach replaced the social-psychological one, and the study of organizations and community structures was de-emphasized. However, T-groups continued to emphasize the acquisition of behavioral skills by focusing on the personal relationships of trainers and member in the group.

In the late 1950's there was a widening split in the sensitivity-training movement. Few formal organizations were receptive to emphasis on personal development in place of vocational and organizational skill learning. By the early 1960's sensitivity training was focusing on (1) activities concerned with traditional human relations training, which centers on the needs of personnel in industry and (2) activities concerned with self-awareness and personal change growing out of emotional group experience. The encounter aspect of sensitivity training was beginning to take shape.

It is difficult to define the term *encounter*; different persons attach different meanings to it. It is one of the most widely used and least clearly defined terms in sensitivity training. It is also important to note that sensitivity training includes both T-groups and encounter groups. Many writers use the terms *T-group* and *encounter group* interchangeably. Few distinguish encounter groups from the original T-groups, which place greater emphasis on organizational skills and developing effective teamwork. T-groups "differ from encounter groups in that they tend to be less emotional, place more reliance on verbal than on non-verbal communication, and are less concerned with the individual's growth *per se* than with his development within the group."[30]

We should also distinguish group therapy from the encounter group. Traditional group therapy focuses on traumatic events from an indi-

[30] "Human Potential: The Revolution in Feeling," *Time*, Vol. 95 (November 9, 1972), 52.

vidual's past, while the encounter group is limited to current events, the here-and-now. The most significant data in the encounter group are derived from the participants' present behavior. The role of the leader is also different. In group therapy the leader plays a therapeutic role and is a central person, while in encounter groups the leader plays the role of facilitator and the action focuses primarily on the individual group members.

Rogers defines encounter groups as vehicles for providing therapy for normal human beings rather than therapy for the sick: "Group therapy is for the person who is already hurting, who has problems and needs help. Encounter groups are for those who are functioning normally but want to improve their capacity for living within their own sets of relationships."[31] Agreeing with Rogers, Abraham Maslow said, "Although I'm very impressed with groups, I don't think they can help with serious problems—only minor hang-ups. A neurosis just won't fade away at a T-group or a week-end marathon."[32] Jane Howard gave a good summary of the two groups: "Therapy reconstructs, encounter educates; therapy is for the sick, encounter is for the well; therapy relieves discomfort and teaches adjustment, encounter assumes equilibrium and builds to transcendence."[33]

Perhaps it will be easier to understand the differences among the various groups by placing them on a continuum for comparison. The continuum below places T-groups, encounter groups, and therapy groups in a cognitive-affective-behavioral perspective:

T-group	Encounter group	Psychotherapy group
Cognitive	Affective	Behavioral

Unfortunately, distinctions among T-groups, encounter groups, and therapy groups are more theoretical than actual. In practice, the differences are sometimes difficult to distinguish. Methods and techniques initiated in one group are often borrowed by another. The stated purpose of a group may sound like a T-group or encounter-group approach, but the actual functioning of the group will depend more upon the group leader and the participants than upon the group title. Hence, while in theory there are standards for all three kinds of groups, many T-groups and encounter groups tend to be more alike than different. For practical purposes the encounter is thus best defined empirically.

Encounter is often popularly identified with what is called the

[31] "The Group Phenomenon," *Psychology Today*, Vol. 1 (December, 1967), 20.
[32] Robert Buckhout et al., eds., *Toward Social Change: A Handbook for Those Who Will*, 315.
[33] Jane Howard, *Please Touch: A Guided Tour of the Human Potential Movement*, 34.

Table 3. Types of Growth Groups

GROUP TYPE / DIMENSION	TRAINING	ENCOUNTER	MARATHON	THERAPY	COUNSELING
GOALS	To Develop Awareness and Skill-Bldg.	To Develop Awareness and Genuineness	To Break Down Defenses	To Increase Coping	To Develop Effective Planning Skills
TIME ORIENTATION	Here and Now	Here and Now Plus	Here and Now Plus	Past and Present	Present and Future
SETTING	Education, Business	All over	All over	Clinical	Educational
ROLE OF FACILITATOR	Model and Scan	Model and Confront	Confront Aggressively	Treat	Facilitate group helpfulness
CLIENTELE	"Normals"	Anyone	Anyone	Persons deficient in coping	"Normals"

SOURCE: J. William Pfeiffer and John E. Jones, eds., *Handbook for Group Facilitators* (Iowa City, Iowa, University Associates Press, 1972), 146. Used by permission.

"attack approach"—an intense, aggressive confrontation between group members. However, because an encounter group can take many forms, this description is too narrow. John Mann offers a comprehensive definition: "An encounter group consists of a group of people who want to encounter—themselves, each other, those aspects of their potentials which they have overlooked, avoided, ignored. It is not a substitute for life; it is a place to learn how to live more fully."[34]

By focusing on the relationships and the crises that develop in the group, encounter is a method of self-exploration and self-discovery. It is also a means to overcome the superficial ways in which people interact in everyday life. Group members are encouraged to relate openly and honestly in order to develop closer and more communicative relationships with one another. In many aspects, the encounter group is an experience of emotional reeducation; the emphasis is on personal and interpersonal growth and development. By expanding self-awareness and exploring both subjective feelings and interpersonal behaviors, encounter groups try to make the experience of life more rewarding.

An encounter group is also an "energy system." Energy is a key to human potential. Defenses, emotional tension, and resistances drain a person of energy. Encounter groups attempt to remove blockages in persons; unblocking energy releases potential. The group member realizes that he is capable of being more of a person than he thought he could be.

People join encounter groups for many different reasons. Some seek

[34] John Mann, *Encounter: A Weekend With a Stranger*, viii–ix.

208

a quick emotional high; others join encounter groups to meet members of the opposite sex or as an inexpensive substitute for psychotherapy. Some regard encounter groups as an opportunity to go berserk or run wild. All these motives are counter to one of the basic tenets of the human-potential movement—responsibility. In both encounter groups and T-groups members are encouraged to take responsibility for themselves—for their actions, feelings, and behavior.

Most participants are committed to the task of becoming "more human"—that is, growing and developing their potential to become *fully functioning*, a term coined by Carl Rogers to describe a mentally healthy person. Growth is learning new ways of relating; it is "an emergence and fulfillment of an unguessed inner potential . . . a process of fulfilling, realizing, emerging and becoming."[35] Group members are encouraged to achieve a more honest expression of themselves. In doing so, they will become more meaningful individuals, capable of coping more effectively with their environment.

The proliferation in the past few years of training groups, encounter groups, and therapy groups is an indicator that people are seeking something that is not being met in conventional social settings. The sociocultural climate of contemporary America is peculiarly suited to the theory and technique which underlie encounter therapies: "It is a fascinating fact that with almost no support from universities, little recognition from academic people and no support from government grants 'basic encounter groups' have become the most rapidly growing psychological trend in our culture."[36]

TOWARD ORGANIZATION DEVELOPMENT

Managers in formal organizations have been among the first to use T-groups and encounter groups to achieve group unity and to maximize productivity. They have also been quick to realize that some group members have deep-seated psychological problems which require psychoanalysis, psychotherapy, or group therapy. Independently, the various approaches to individual, group, and organizational change are grossly inadequate. Collectively, they provide viable means for growth.

Most managers now realize that if their organizations are to be effective they must satisfy the psychological needs of their members. The concern for improving organizational effectiveness has resulted in many programs of training, which are referred to as programs of or-

[35] Quoted in Herbert A. Otto and John Mann, eds., *Ways of Growth: Approaches to Expanding Awareness*, 101.

[36] Robert W. Siroka, Ellen K. Siroka, and Gilbert A. Schloss, *Sensitivity Training and Group Encounter*, 200.

ganization development (OD) (see Chapter 12). Organization development utilizes T-groups, encounter groups, and—in a few cases— therapy.

The following eight principles summarize organizational cohesion, solidarity, and productivity:

1. A group tends to be attractive to an individual and to command his loyalty to the extent that it:
   a. Satisfies his needs and helps him to achieve goals that are compelling to him.
   b. Provides him with a feeling of acceptance and security.

2. Each person tends to feel committed to a decision or goal to the extent that he has participated in determining it.

3. A group is an effective instrument for change and growth in individuals to the extent that:
   a. Those who are to be changed and those who are to exert influence for change have a strong sense of belonging to the same group.
   b. The attraction of the group is greater than the discomfort of the change.
   c. The members of the group share the perception that change is needed.
   d. The group provides an opportunity for the individual to practice changed behavior without threat or punishment. . . .

4. Every force tends to induce an equal and opposite counterforce. The preferred strategy for change, other things being equal, is the weakening of forces resisting change rather than the addition of new positive forces toward change.

5. Every group is able to improve its ability to operate as a group to the extent that it consciously examines its processes and experiments with improved processes. (In the literature this phenomenon is referred to as the "feedback mechanism.")

6. The better an individual understands the forces influencing his own behavior and that of the group, the better he will be able to contribute constructively to the group and at the same time to preserve his own integrity against subtle pressures toward conformity and alienation.

7. The strength of pressure to conform is determined by the following factors:
   a. The strength of the attraction a group has for the individual.
   b. The importance to the individual of the issue on which conformity is being requested.

    c. The degree of unanimity of the group toward requiring conformity.

8. The determinants of group effectiveness include the extent or degree to which:

    a. A clear goal is present.

    b. The group goal mobilizes energies of group members behind group activities.

    c. There is agreement or conflict among members concerning which one of several possible goals should control the activities of the group.

    d. There is agreement or conflict among the members concerning means that the group should use to reach its goal.

    e. The group is organized appropriately for its tasks.[37]

Like individual change, organizational change tends to be met with much resistance. Therefore change agents must demonstrate not only enthusiasm but also considerable skill in human relations training techniques.

The Role of Behavioral Science In Organizations[38]
JACK H. EPSTEIN and ROBERT H. WARREN

This article concentrates on the role (functions, activities, direction) of behavioral science in organizations in which people earn a livelihood. Organizations per se are inanimate and meaningless unless we become concerned with the people in them. This concern, for our purposes, will take the route of individual and group motivation and its immediate periphery (e.g., needs, leadership, goals, communications, perception, expectations) with respect to organizational growth and effectiveness. The strong threads of behavioral science which will stand out in this pattern are psychology, social-psychology, intra and inter group dynamics, and, perhaps, some of the newer areas of manageship and "organizationology."

The final portion of this article will include some prognoses about the future role of behavioral science in organizations. These observations are based upon subjective determinations which are, in turn, based on such objective facts as the increasing number of Want Ads for industrial psychologists and behavioral scientists, the increasing number of college students enrolled in behavioral science research. These predictions (in the sense of prior to knowledge rather than fore-

[37] Gale, *op. cit.*, 7–8.

[38] By Jack H. Epstein and Robert H. Warren. Reprinted from *Personnel Journal*, October, 1968, by permission of the editor.

telling) will, hopefully, result in a myriad of questions, problems, and possibilities, the answers and solutions to which will be neither easy to come by nor obvious.

DEFINITIONS

It seems appropriate to begin with some definitions of terms. Webster defines behavior as: "A mode of conducting oneself. The way in which an organism, organ acts, especially in response to a stimulus."

Behavioral science is the study of human behavior in a "scientific" manner. It is interested in studying behavior, specifically human behavior in response to various stimuli—internal and mental, or external and physical. Behavioral science connotes all of the factors that go into man's fundamental personality: his needs, his emotions, his thinking, and his ability to relate his thoughts and feelings. It believes that man's actions are a result and a composite of all of these factors.

Behavioral science studies human behavior to "establish generalizations that are supported by empirical evidence collected in an impersonal and objective way. The evidence must be capable of verification by other interested scholars and the procedures must be completely open to review and replication."[39]

Like any discipline, the behavioral sciences strive to conduct research that is systematic and cumulative and offers the how and why of its findings.

For the purposes of this paper we will discuss the role of the behavioral sciences within organizations. Organizations take many forms, but for the scope of this study we shall deal only with organizations in which people earn a living. Our concept of organization is:

The rational coordination of the activities of a number of people for the achievement of some common explicit purpose or goal, through the division of labor and function, and through a hierarchy of authority and responsibility.[40]

Role can be defined as the functions, activities, behavior of individuals with respect to a field, occupation, discipline, or profession in daily life.

We shall conclude our definitions of terms by defining the behavioral scientists. The behavioral scientist centers on three of the social sciences: anthropology, psychology, and sociology. He can also represent political science, psychiatry, geography, biology, physiology, economics, education, and business administration.

Whatever his profession, the behavioral scientist works within the

[39] Bernard Berelson, *The Behavioral Sciences Today.*
[40] Edgar H. Schein, *Organizational Psychology.*

framework of the scientific method. He applies tests of statistical and clinical validity to the evidence he collects. He does basic research by measuring and counting and by observing existing phenomena. He conducts experimental work based on a given hypothesis related to a theory, constructs, or concepts, and postulates generalizations or "laws" based on the evidence he gleans.

History rarely furnishes us with dates that mark the absolute beginning of cultural developments. To adopt a date as the beginning of the behavioral sciences is an impossibility. It suffices that the behavioral sciences are a distinct phenomenon of our times, in that some 90 to 95 per cent of all behavioral scientists are still living.

BACKGROUND

By the early 1950's, the behavioral sciences were a field in the full bloom of expansion. Business leaders had become vitally interested in the motivational factors behind consumer purchases. Labor and industry were fascinated with what made men work and how productivity could be increased. Due to a growing abundance of jobs, workers enjoyed a greater degree of choice as to how much they would produce and how well they would perform on the job. Therefore, industry began thinking in terms of providing an environment conducive to positive self-motivation.

Also underlining the rising prominence of the behavioral sciences in organizations in the fifties was the growing affluence of the American public. More income was remaining for the average American family after the purchase of the basic necessities. The consumption of option type commodities grew rapidly in this decade. Therefore, persuasion and resultant behavior became a matter of considerable business concern. Further, the source string of labor was shortening on both ends. Our population group in ages 25–34 was shrinking and the more elderly were retiring earlier.

These developments, among others, caused organizational leadership to look hopefully to the disciplines of human psychology, sociology, social-psychology and the semi-science of education for insights into human behavior. It was hoped that professionals in these fields would help to predict people's choices, satisfactions, attitudes, and behavior. It was also during this period that Rensis Likert began his research, the results of which now appear in its New Patterns of Management. Likert determined that work groups were most effective in meeting individual and organizational goals when supervisors/managers were perceived to be facilitative, supportive, and permissive in their style of managing. Further, he found that formal group leaders were "linking pins" correcting general organizational elements. For example, a leader/manager of one group was a member of the group leaders above him. Therefore, another aspect of effectiveness of organizations is the extent to which leaders are perceived by their subordinates as influential in dealing with problems which affect them and their well being.

Basic to the application of behavioral studies to organizations were the determinations made in regard to groups. Group studies indicated that individuals are not primarily rational beings but are basically social and purposive. Persons belong to all sorts of groups; families, work units, and communities. It is from these that individuals obtain many of their habits, values, ideas and motivational stimuli.

A basic property of groups is that they tend to generate and enforce the shared feelings of their members. Also, the individuals within groups play a significant role in shaping the attitudes and goals of the group to which they belong. These characteristics make possible the identifying and transforming of group needs and aspirations to a position somewhat tandem to organizational needs and goals.

With the consolidation of organized labor, growing competition from abroad, increasing pressures of automation and increasing need for managerial talent, American organizational leadership began to realize that its primary advantage was in the optimum use of its human resources.

AN EMERGING FIELD

This growing realization helped to trigger the intensified inquiry into the how and why of behavior as it manifested itself at work in specific situations under observable, measurable, and discriminating conditions. The prime effort was placed on manipulating the environment in which the rank and file individual worked. From here the field moved on to the supervisory, manager and executive levels as the core group which was responsible for effecting practices leading to organizational improvement. Supervisor and manager development was the vehicle for affecting change. It was during the mid and late fifties that the human relations era made a big impact. Recognizing the permanence of change, together with the need for a qualitative work force, organizational leaders selected human development and improvement programs as a way of making the organization more effective. Due to the factors of power, authority, responsibility, and complexity, the managerial hierarchy was prepared for growth opportunities which, hopefully, would lead to organizational change for "the better." In other words, individuals were sent to training and development programs from different parts of the total organization. It was expected that, upon return, these managers would, through changed behavior, in-fluence subordinates, colleagues and bosses to change. Further, the behavior of the "trained" manager in working within his group would have a tremendous impact on that group's effectiveness. The emphasis was on changing individuals by increasing their knowledge and skill and providing opportunity for review of attitudes and values systems as both the lever and the fulcrum for organizational improvement.

Once again, we need to mention Likert's findings pertaining to managerial permissiveness, facilitativeness and support as keys to or-ganizational effectiveness. McGregor's "Theory Y" is in the same demo-cratic vein. Maslow's hierarchy of needs has been related to positive motivation efforts for improving organizations. Herzberg's theory of motivation as applied at Texas Instrument Co.[41] has established a kind of reverse causality scheme for organizational effectiveness. There, apparently, individual needs become primary and organizational needs secondary. Put another way, "what is good for the individual is good for the company."

Concurrently, with the emphasis on individual manager improve-ment we find a subtle shifting to considering groups as the core of change in organizations. Kurt Lewin's findings came to the fore, as did the role of the informal organization with respect to organizational well being. Intra and inter-group dynamics and effectiveness, along with studies of leadership patterns in these groups, cropped up. Alex Bavelas' communication networks experiments in work organizations are an example of the role of behavioral science during this period.

Another example is the conference leadership training that was and is being conducted as a means of improving organizational effective-ness through increasing individual expertise about group dynamics. T-group or Sensitivity Training goes into this area in greater depth and breadth, attempting to develop "intrinsic" insights into intra and inter-personal relationships and, through this awareness, to proceed on to planned change. This sort of laboratory approach gets into both "basic" and "applied" research.

Blake's approach via the Managerial Grid departs further from indi-vidual development and treats organizational segments as entities. Through this approach, organizations proceed in a work-laboratory setting. This certical training and development over a long-run seems to be aiming at the achievement of "Theory Y" in an organization.

The Gestalt Psychology approach has been translated into a way of viewing organizations as a total system made up of subsystems. Some

[41] M. Scott Meyers, "Who Are Your Motivated Workers?" *Harvard Business Review*, January–February, 1964.

authorities believe that organizations are open systems affecting and being affected by the environment. Others believe that organizations are social systems within themselves.

In summary, we find that the role of behavioral science in organizations has moved from research on the individual, to the group and group interrelationships, to organizational studies on how to effect change affecting interaction, to the present concepts of organizations as systems with the behavioral sciences concentrating on systems effectiveness.[42]

Let us now consider more specifically some of the areas of emphasis of behavioral science in organizations.

BEHAVIORAL SCIENCE EMPHASIS IN ORGANIZATION

The following aspects of organizational life have received concentrated attention by behavioral scientists. These are presented to make the point that the field is both deep and wide. The following quote should provide a common frame of reference for reviewing these aspects:

In no area of social inquiry has a body of general law been established, comparable with outstanding theories in the natural sciences in scope of explanatory power or in capacity to yield precise and reliable predictions. . . . It is also generally acknowledged that in the social sciences there is nothing quite like the almost complete unanimity commonly found among competent workers in the natural sciences as to what are matters of established fact, what are the reasonably satisfactory explanations (if any) for the assumed facts, and what are some of the valid procedures in sound inquiry. . . . The social sciences are a battleground for interminably warring schools of thought, and that even subject matter which has been under intensive and prolonged study remains at the unsettled periphery of research.[43]

This is not to imply that we have a pessimistic point of view. On the contrary, we are optimistic because of the strides already made in the behavioral sciences due in great measure to improve research methods.

Motivation. *It is generally accepted that the key to performance is motivation. This elusive potential has been defined as a drive within the individual which, dependent upon his expectations of the level of*

---

[42] W. F. Whyte's studies in restaurants resulted in keeping people apart by introducing mechanical things—the spindle or order keeper on which the waitresses placed orders for the chiefs to fill—to reduce conflict and friction.

[43] Bernard Berelson and Gary A. Steiner, *Human Behavior: An Inventory of Scientific Findings.*

satisfaction he can achieve, incites him to action. The relationship between motivation and group or individual productivity and effectiveness has produced a considerable number of assumptions, concepts, research, (mostly on nonadults) and theories. Maslow, Fromm, Herzberg and now McClelland have contributed in this area. Some factors that seem to affect motivation are the needs, perceptions and goals of an individual and group and how these needs and goals can be realized. The study of human motivation is a key factor for managerial consideration with respect to such things as providing a work climate conducive to individual self-generation and positive motivation for meeting with individual and organization needs.

Decision Making. *This aspect of organizational life has had considerable treatment by behavioral scientists. This includes a realm of elements affecting the making of decisions by individuals and groups. Some of these considerations include power and authority, attitudes and value systems, and creativity, as an organization strives to make rational rather than intuitive decisions at its various levels of operations. This rationality includes weighing of alternatives and both immediate and long range forces and after effects which can ensue from the implementation of a decision.*

Conflict. *This deals with the how and why of friction that exists or arises in an organization, its manifestation in interpersonal and intra and interdepartmental relaionships, and its optimum resolution. The effect of conflict on motivation, goal establishment and achievement, a group's ability to function under stress, and the knowledge and skill necessary to face up to and cope with conflict are some of the insightful cognitions valuable to people at work.*

Leadership. *It is generally conceded that leadership is determined by the existential nature of the situation. The development of leadership is of prime importance to organizational growth, perpetuation and effectiveness. Leadership is something that is shared from time to time, situation to situation, by boss and subordinate. The relative effectiveness of democratic, laissez-faire, or autocratic leadership in different types of organizations of various sizes are some of the results of studies in this area.*

Power and Authority. *This deals with the sources and limitations of power: the behavioral relationship between responsibiilty and authority roles played by peers, superiors, and subordinate relationships. Problems of ethics and delegation fall into this category.*

Organizational Theory. *In addition to the study of individuals and groups, the behavioral sciences have contributed considerably to the study of organizations. The transformation of the United States from a rural to a technologically urban society and culture has changed our way of life from one of autonomy and independence to a life characterized by proximity and interdependence.*

Traditionally, organizations have been viewed as a means of accomplishing (its) goals and objectives as determined and defined by management. Little thought has been given to the inner workings and internal purposes of the human organization and how these factors might offset and undermine human collaboration pulling and pushing together toward "organizational" goals. The behavioral sciences have helped to define and describe "theories" (some are yet untested, but nevertheless valuable) of organization. They have helped to develop new frameworks for structuring organizations which would have a better chance than previously, considering today's rapid changes, of stimulating and obtaining the optimum output of potential inherent in the humans who are the organization.

In addition, productivity, managerial style and control, status, job design, communications, appraisals, reward and punishment systems, and climate are among the myriad items relating to organizational theory and effectiveness.

To understand modern man, it has been said that it is necessary to know him in formal organizations. Behavioral science made a great contribution to the theory of organizations. Organizations have been defined by size, by form, by tolerance for internal variation, by number and kind of transactions with their environments. Organizations have been theorized as social, closed and open systems. Systems can vary as to whether they have one goal or more than one. They can vary as to whether their goals relate to internal relationships or with the relations of the system to its environment or both. Systems can vary as to their flexibility in modifying an existent or in acquiring new goals.

Organizational studies consist of many diverse approaches and methodologies. Two authorities define organizational theory as:

. . . both the end product and the starting point of scientific research. On the one hand, the objective of all scientific endeavor is to develop a body of substantive theory, that is, a set of interrelated verifiable generalizations that account for and predict the empirical phenomena that can be observed. On the other hand, scientific research must be guided by a theoretical framework, that is, a system of interrelated concepts that suggest theoretically fruitful lines of empirical investigations.[44]

Organizational theory began concentrating upon the anatomy of formal groups. Concepts of organizations have been built around, individually or in concert, these four concerns:

[44] Peter M. Blau and W. R. Scott, *Formal Organizations: A Comparative Approach.*

(a) The division of labor; (b) the scalar and functional processes which refer to the growth of the chain of command, the delegation of authority and responsibility, unity of command, and the obligations to report, (c) the structure, and (d) the span of control.

The concentration on organizational theory has resulted in new concepts of management. Thus management has become less authoritarian, less preoccupied with administrative efficiency, and less concerned with hierarchal structures. The emphasis instead has shifted to a managerial concern with the many influences and environments within society that the organization has to deal with in its on-going life.

As indicated earlier, the study of organizational theory has resulted recently in a series of "systems" concepts as to how organizations function. The basic notion of a system is that it is a set of interrelated parts, the totality of which is greater than the sum of the parts. One significance of this is that organizations do not, therefore, exist in themselves. They are intimately connected with a wider variety of other units which cannot be ignored. A corporation, for example, can be a social system or a system of financial flowing. When an organization is defined from a systems point of view, no single group is dominant. The task of self definition and effectiveness is really a never ending one for most organizations because of the need for designing and coping with the entire realm of organizational theory and effectiveness.

Planned change. *This is perhaps the greatest challenge and role for behavioral sciences in organizations today. Here, efforts and studies deal with effecting technological, managerial, and organizational change within an organization through participation and/or nonparticipatory methods. The implementing of change, when indicated, and the consolidation of the effect of this change on organizational efficiency, morale and effectiveness, fall into this category.*

Planned change is one of the more recent applications of the behavioral sciences to organizational life. Warren Bennis is one of the definitive authors of this concept. Planned change is thought of as the best possible alternative between a laissez-faire and a radical Marxist approach to the changing organization. Planned change has been defined as:

a conscious, deliberate and collaborative effort to improve the operations of a system whether it be a self-system, social system or a cultural system, through the utilization of scientific knowledge.[45]

The primary functions of the behavioral scientist in planning change according to Bennis, Benne and Chin, is to serve to bridge the com-

[45] Warren G. Bennis, Kenneth D. Benne, and Robert Chin, eds., *The Planning of Change.*

munications gap between the findings of the research experts and their applied meaning for the organization.

Planned change does not come about within a vacuum. Some of the factors which indicate the necessity for determining the need for implementing planned change are:

Technological change, in which the human consequences are not always adequately anticipated, thus bringing about social disruptions.

The collapse of automatic adjustment, in which changes occur too fast and their implications are too wide to be left to "nature."

The collapse of community, in which society has become more individualistic and mobile, so that the community is no longer the basis of joint decision and action.

The fragmentation of the service professions, each with separate training and different orientation, few with cross-professional communication, yet all trying to serve the same organization.

Schein[46] lists the following six stages as the process of planned change an organization can use. Schein calls this the adaptive-coping cycle:

—Sensing a change in the internal or external environment.

—Importing the relevant information about the change into those parts of the organization which can act upon it.

—Changing production or conversion processes inside the organizations according to the information obtained.

—Stabilizing internal changes which reduce the managing of undesired by-products (undesired changes in related systems which have resulted from the desired changes).

—Exporting new products, services, and so on, which are more in line with the originally perceived changes in the environment.

—Obtaining feedback on the success of the change through further sensing of the state of the external environment and the degree of integration of the internal environment.

Resistance to change or being in love with the "status quo"—the causes rather than the symptoms—appears to be the concern of behavioral scientists. It seems that this route will lead to findings which can be operationally applied by practitioners in moving toward more healthy organizations. It is generally agreed that a change agent is quite helpful in implementing a planned change process. Outside consultants and in-house managers of training and development have individually and in consonance performed this role.

[46] Schein, *op. cit.*

Chapter 8
SUGGESTED READING

Bales, Robert F. *Interaction Process Analysis: A Method for the Study of Small Groups.* Reading, Mass., Addison-Wesley Publishing Co., Inc., 1969.
Bennis, Warren G., Kenneth D. Benne, and Robert Chin, eds. *The Planning of Change.* New York, Holt, Rinehart & Winston, Inc., 1969.
Berelson, Bernard. *The Behavioral Sciences Today.* New York, Harper & Row, Publishers, Inc., 1963.
———, and Gary A. Steines. *Human Behavior: An Inventory of Scientific Findings.* New York, Harcourt, Brace & World, Inc., 1964.
Berne, Eric. *The Crisis of Psychoanalysis.* New York, Holt, Rinehart & Winston, Inc., 1970.
———. *A Layman's Guide to Psychiatry and Psychoanalysis.* New York, Simon & Schuster, Inc., 1968.
Blau, Peter M., and W. R. Scott. *Formal Organizations: A Comparative Approach.* San Francisco, Chandler Publishing Company, 1962.
Bonner, Herbert. *Group Dynamics: Principles and Applications.* New York, The Ronald Press Co., 1959.
Buckhout, Robert, et al., eds. *Toward Social Change: A Handbook for Those Who Will.* New York, Harper & Row, Publishers, Inc., 1971.
Cartwright, Dorwin. "Achieving Changes in Peoples: Some Applications of Group Dynamics Theory," *Human Relations,* Vol. 4 (1951).
———, and Alvin Zander, eds. *Group Dynamics: Research and Theory.* Evanston, Ill., Row, Peterson & Co., 1960.
Cooley, Charles H. *Human Nature and the Social Order.* New York, Charles Scribner's Sons, 1902.
———. *Social Organization.* New York, Scribner's Sons, 1927.
Etzioni, Amitai, and Eva Etzioni, eds. *Social Change: Source, Patterns, and Consequences.* New York, Basic Books, Inc., 1964.
Festinger, Leon. "Informal Communication," *Psychological Review,* Vol. 57 (1950).
———. *A Theory of Cognitive Dissonance.* Stanford, Stanford University Press, 1957.
———, Stanley Schachter, and Kurt Back. *Social Pressures in Informal Groups: A Study of Human Factors in Housing.* Stanford, Stanford University Press, 1950.
Fiedler, Fred E. *Leader Attitudes and Group Effectiveness.* Urbana, University of Illinois Press, 1958.
Fox, Logan J. *Psychology as Philosophy, Science, and Art.* Pacific Palisades, Calif., Goodyear Publishing Co., 1972.
Gale, Raymond F. *Discovering Your Unique Self.* Dubuque, Iowa, Kendall/Hunt Publishing Co., 1969.
Goffman, Ervin. *Interaction Ritual.* New York, Doubleday & Co., Inc., 1967.
Guntrip, Harry, *Healing the Sick Minds.* New York, Appleton-Century Crofts, Inc., 1964.

Hall, Calvin S. *A Primer of Freudian Psychology.* New York, New American Library, Inc., 1954.

Hare, A. Paul. *Handbook of Small Group Research.* New York, The Free Press, 1962.

———, et al. *Small Groups: Studies In Social Interaction.* New York, Alfred A. Knopf, Inc., 1955.

Henderson, George. *To Live in Freedom: Human Relations Today and Tomorrow.* Norman, University of Oklahoma Press, 1972.

Homans, George C. *The Human Group.* New York, Harcourt, Brace & World, Inc., 1950.

———. "Social Behavior as Exchange," *American Journal of Sociology,* Vol. 63 (1958).

Howard, Jane. *Please Touch: A Guided Tour of the Human Potential Movement.* New York, McGraw-Hill Book Co., 1970.

Johnson, James A. *Group Therapy: A Practical Approach.* New York, McGraw-Hill Book Co., 1963.

Kaplan, Louis. *Foundations of Human Behavior.* New York, Harper & Row, Publishers, Inc., 1965.

Kiesler, Charles A., and Sarah B. Kiesler. *Conformity.* Reading, Mass., Addison-Wesley Publishing Co., 1970.

Knowles, Malcolm, and Hulda Knowles. *Introduction to Group Dynamics.* New York, Association Press, 1959.

Lewin, Kurt. *Field Theory in Social Science.* New York, Harper & Row, Publishers, Inc., 1951.

Luft, Joseph. *Of Human Interaction.* Palo Alto, Calif., National Press Books, 1969.

Madron, Thomas W. *Small Group Methods and the Study of Politics.* Evanston, Ill., Northwestern University Press, 1969.

Mann, John. *Changing Human Behavior.* New York, Charles Scribner's Sons, 1965.

———. *Encounter: A Weekend with Intimate Strangers.* New York, Pocket Books, Inc., 1970.

Martin, David G. *Learning-Based Client-Centered Therapy.* Monterey, Calif., Brooks/Cole Pub. Co., 1972.

McGrath, Joseph E., and Irwin Altman. *Small Group Research: A Synthesis and Critique of the Field.* New York, Holt, Rinehart & Winston, Inc., 1966.

Mead, George H. *Mind, Self, and Society.* Chicago, University of Chicago Press, 1934.

Mills, Theodore M. *Group Transformation.* Englewood Cliffs, N.J., Prentice-Hall, Inc., 1965.

———. *The Sociology of Small Groups.* Englewood Cliffs, N.J., Prentice-Hall, Inc., 1967.

Neel, Ann F. *Theories of Psychology: A Handbook.* Cambridge, Mass., Schenckman Publishing Co., 1970.

Newcomb, Theodore M. *The Acquaintance Process.* New York, Holt, Rinehart & Winston, Inc., 1961.

Ohlsen, Merle M. *Group Counseling.* New York, Holt, Rinehart & Winston, Inc., 1970.

Otto, Herbert A., and John Mann, eds. *Ways of Growth: Approaches to Expanding Awareness.* New York, Grossman Publishers, Inc., 1968.

Roby, Thornton B. *Small Group Performance.* Chicago, Rand-McNally & Co., 1968.

Rogers, Carl R. *Client-Centered Therapy.* Boston, Houghton Mifflin Co., 1951.

Sayle, Leonard, and George Strauss. *Human Behavior in Organizations.* Englewood Cliffs, N.J., Prentice-Hall, Inc., 1966.

Schein, Edgar. *Organizational Psychology.* Englewood Cliffs, N.J., Prentice-Hall, Inc., 1965.

Schutz, William C. *FIRO: A Three Dimensional Theory of Interpersonal Behavior.* New York, Holt, Rinehart & Winston, Inc., 1958.

Shepherd, Clovis R. *Small Groups: Some Sociological Perspectives.* Scranton, Pa., Chandler Publishing Co., 1964.

Sherif, Muzafer, and Carolyn Sherif. *Reference Groups.* New York, Harper & Row, Publishers, Inc., 1964.

Simmel, Georg. *Conflict and the Web of Group Affiliations.* Translated by K. A. Wolff. Glencoe, Ill., The Free Press, 1955.

Siroka, Robert W., Ellen K. Siroka, and Gilbert A. Schloss. *Sensitivity Training and Group Encounter.* New York, Grosset and Dunlap, Inc., 1971.

Skinner, B. F. *Beyond Freedom and Dignity.* New York, Bantam Books, Inc., 1971.

Southhard, Samuel. *People Need People.* Philadelphia, The Westminister Press, 1970.

Taylor, Howard F. *Balance in Small Groups.* New York, Van Nostrand Reinhold Co., 1970.

Thelen, Herbert A. *Dynamics of Groups at Work.* Chicago, University of Chicago Press, 1954.

Thibaut, John W., and Harold H. Kelly. *The Social Psychology of Groups.* New York, John Wiley & Sons, Inc., 1959.

Warters, Jane. *Group Guidance.* New York, McGraw-Hill Book Company, 1960.

*The implicit model of psychiatric thinking has been
predominantly one according to which a disease process,
organic or psychological, afflicts a person and then,
secondarily, affects other persons. The emphasis is on
passivity and process. The model demands a patient,
someone who undergoes the process of pathological
change, who submits to treatment, who wants to be cured.
It is only in the last few years that some workers have
begun seriously to question whether this invalid is in
fact invalid or invalidated.*—DAVID COOPER

Psychotherapy has been defined as a "verbal or otherwise symbolic
interaction of a therapist with a patient guided by an orderly and integrated series of concepts and directed toward beneficial change in a
patient."[1] Thus the term *psychotherapy* embraces a wide variety of
techniques whose goal is to help the emotionally disturbed individual
modify his behavior so that he can make a more satisfactory adjustment to his environment.

On the whole, modification of behavior is dependent upon the
patient's understanding of his unconscious motives and conflicts. Some
psychotherapists believe that patients can learn more adaptive ways
of coping with their problems without exploring factors in the past that
have led to the development of the problem. The one common feature
of all forms of psychotherapy is communication between the patient
and the therapist, in which the patient is encouraged to express freely
his fears, emotions, and experiences without being condemned or
judged by the therapist. The therapist, while being sympathetic and
understanding, seeks to remain emotionally uninvolved but to project
detached objectivity, which supposedly will enable him to view the
patient's difficulties more clearly.[2]

Although some therapists have reported success with psychotics, the
techniques of psychotherapy have been used most successfully with
the milder forms of mental disorder, the neuroses. The neurotic is
usually aware that he has problems, is eager for help, and is able to

[1] Ernest R. Hilgard and Richard C. Atkinson, *Introduction to Psychology*, 551.
[2] *Ibid.*

communicate with the therapist. The psychotic, on the other hand, is frequently so involved in his fantasy world and so unaware of reality that it is extremely difficult to communicate with him. The process of establishing contact with the psychotic must be undertaken before psychotherapy can begin. This, of course, is much easier said than done.

Many persons have made significant contributions in the theory and practice of psychotherapy. Among them are Sigmund Freud, Carl R. Rogers, Sidney M. Jourard, Abraham H. Maslow, Jacob L. Moreno, and Frederick S. Perls.

SIGMUND FREUD (1856–1939)

Sigmund Freud was the founder of psychoanalysis, and his theories on the psychic makeup of the individual have given rise to the methods currently employed in psychotherapy. Erich Fromm said of him, "Freud's aim was to found a movement for the ethical liberation of man, a new secular and scientific religion for an elite which was to guide mankind."[3] From a human relations perspective it is clear that Freud was a highly significant and important agent for social change. His search for truth and his personal courage enabled him to endure the vilifications of the Victorian critics of his era. They considered him "unmedical" and unscientific, as well as fanatical in his emphasis upon the sexual rather than the physiological roots of human disorders.

One of Freud's most controversial concepts was the belief that man's behavior is dominated by hidden or unconscious motives and emotions; in other words, people have little conscious understanding of themselves and, consequently, little control over their behavior. Freud also introduced the theory that the basis of the adult personality is first determined by the experiences one undergoes while still an infant. In his clinical experience Freud observed that the adult who has not matured is especially bothered by infantile urges of a sexual and/or aggressive nature.

Freud explored the unconscious determination of behavior. He identified the primary subdivisions of the mind as the conscious, preconscious (readily accessible to consciousness), and unconscious realms, of which the unconscious is the most important determinant of behavior. He likened these subdivisions to an iceberg of which only a small surface (the conscious) shows above the water, with the largest portion (the unconscious) below the surface.

A central theme of Freud's personality theory was that of maximizing instinctual gratification while minimizing punishment and guilt,

[3] Erich Fromm, *Sigmund Freud's Mission: An Analysis of His Personality and Influence.*

which he termed the "pleasure principle." He postulated that the personality is made up of the id, the ego, and the superego. The id consists of the instincts (life, death, sexual libido). The ego in its executive capacity selects which instinctual drives or impulses to gratify—but only after contending with the superego, which reflects the traditional values and taboos of society and tries to repress the ego. Freud also proposed that one passed through certain stages of psychosexual development, which he defined as oral, anal, phallic, and genital. The danger is that one can become fixated or suffer from arrested development as a result of psychological trauma. In adulthood this condition is manifested by character types which correspond with behavior appropriate to an earlier stage of development. Certain defensive patterns become ingrained. For instance, the major defense of the phallic character is repression—the active process of pushing instinctual wishes from consciousness.[4]

Freud was the first scientist to develop a comprehensive theory of personality. As noted earlier, his original assumption was that emotional illness grows out of traumatic, or shocking, experiences which often occur early in childhood and frequently involve sexual experiences. These experiences are filled with shame for the child, and so they are pushed out of consciousness into relatively inaccessible parts of the personality, which Freud called the unconscious. To support his fundamental assumption, Freud spent most of his life formulating theories of motivation, conflict and frustration, psychosexual development, guilt and anxiety, and personality defenses.[5]

Psychoanalysis allows the patient, with the help of his analyst, to become aware of memories and motives of which he has not been conscious. Various methods are used to bare the unconscious, the most common being free association. The patient is instructed to say aloud everything that he thinks of without any attempt to guide it. Through analysis of information produced by means of free association, the therapist begins to gain clues to the possible underlying causes of the personality disorder.

The analysis of dreams is another technique used in Freudian psychoanalysis. The therapist encourages his patient to keep a record of his dreams and to bring them to the therapy session for discussion and analysis. Transference, the process by which the patient responds unconsciously, and usually emotionally, to the analyst—as he does to other important people in his life—is of vital importance. The interpretation of behavior resulting from transference is the core of the psychoanalytic process. It enables the patient to see how his present

[4] Salvatore R. Maddi, *Personality Theories: A Camparative Analysis*, 483.
[5] George W. Kisker, *The Disorganized Personality*, 65.

226

behavior has emerged from his early experiences, many of which he has repressed.[6]

Psychoanalytic theory was the forerunner of a new view of man which stresses man's relationship to others, nature, and himself. Unlike the Freudian image of man as isolated and dependent upon innate drives for energy, this view emphasizes relationship as the variable governing the energy inherent in the passionate strivings of man.

CARL R. ROGERS (1902–)

Whereas Freud focused on the perception of the analyst as being of therapeutic significance, Carl R. Rogers emphasizes the patient's view of himself as critical to the process of treatment. Rogers also differs from Freud in that his is an actualization theory which assumes a certain psychological equilibrium, while Freud's theories were oriented to the psychopathological and inner conflicts of the patient.[7]

Rogers' client-centered therapy makes use of the concept of "self" in regaining normal behavior patterns. Included in Rogers' therapy is his definition of the "helping relationship," in which at least one of the parties has the intent of promoting the growth, development, maturity, functioning, and "coping with life" of the other.

According to Rogers, the therapist tries to bring about changes by creating an atmosphere in which the client feels his own worth and significance. To have therapeutic value, the change in the client must be a change in feeling, a change in attitude—not merely a change in understanding.

Rogers' approach to understanding personality, psychotherapy, and interpersonal relationships provides an interesting contrast to that of Freud. Technique is minimized, and the necessary and sufficient conditions for inducing psychotherapeutic personality change exist when:

1. The client and the therapist are in contact.

2. The client is in a state of imbalance—there is a discrepancy between his perceived self and his actual self.

3. The therapist's perceptions of this relationship are accurate symbolizations of the actual experience.

4. The therapist experiences unconditional favorable (that is, positive) feelings toward his client.

5. The therapist experiences an empathic understanding of the client's internal frame of reference.

6. The client perceives the unconditionally favorable regard of the therapist for him, as well as the empathic understanding of the therapist.

[6] *Ibid.*, 536.
[7] Carl R. Rogers, *On Becoming a Person: A Therapist's View of Psychotherapy.*

Everything is couched in terms of the experiences of the client and the therapist. Nonetheless, most responses of client-centered therapists are reflections of feelings based on their perception of the internal frame of reference of the client. Rogers has described the acceptance and support of anything the patient says without evaluation as the most important strategy of the therapist.

Rogers has also incorporated group processes into his therapy. His theories of group therapy focus upon one-to-one relationships within the group, as well as on the responsibility of the therapist in intervening at timely and appropriate times. He has outlined several tendencies of participants in group psychotherapy: (1) milling around in an unstructured situation, (2) resisting personal expression and exploration, (3) describing past feelings, (4) expressing negative feelings, (5) trusting enough to express personally meaningful information, (6) expressing immediate feelings about others in the group, (7) developing a group consensus of appropriate ways to aid individual members, (8) displaying authentic self-acceptance and initiation of change, (9) removing façadelike behavior patterns, (10) giving feedback to one another, (11) confronting others at an emotional and reactionary level, (12) extending a helpful relationship outside the group, (13) providing the opportunity for a basic encounter among group members, (14) expressing positive feelings toward another member of the group, (15) showing evidence of actual behavioral changes by group members.

Rogers concluded that personality change (the changing relationship between the self and the self-ideal) can be facilitated psychotherapeutically in client-consultant situations and/or group-therapy circumstances. To test his theories, Rogers developed a nondirective, client-centered approach to psychotherapy in which psychotherapy provides an opportunity for the patient to grow and truly become a person by realizing his inner potentialities. The client-centered approach is based on the theory that human nature is fundamentally sound and that individuals have a capacity for self-actualizzation and healthy adjustment.[8] This capacity may be blocked by emotional conflicts, distorted ideas, or a faulty self-image. In such cases the individual is regarded not as a sick person who needs a doctor (hence Rogers used the term "client" rather than "patient") but as an individual who has rejected or lost touch with his true and unique self. In spite of this rejection his capacity for self-realization remains, and the objective of therapy is to bring it to the fore so that he may resolve his own conflicts, correct his self-image, and reorganize his personality and approach to life.

[8] *Ibid.*

In the words of Rogers, successful client-centered therapy conducted under optimal conditions

*would mean that the therapist has been able to enter into an intensely
personal and subjective relationship with his client—relating not as a
scientist to an object of study, not as a physician expecting to diagnose
and cure, but as a person to a person. It would mean that the therapist
feels this client to be a person of unconditional self-worth; of value no
matter what his condition, his behavior or his feelings. It would mean
that the therapist is genuine, not hiding behind a defensive façade, but
meeting the client with the feelings the therapist is experiencing. It
would mean that the therapist is able to let himself go in understanding this client; that no inner barriers keep him from sensing what it
feels like to be the client at each moment of the relationship; and that
he can convey something of his empathetic understanding to the client.
It means that the therapist has been comfortable in entering this relationship fully, without knowing cognitively where it will lead, satisfied
with providing a climate which will permit the client the utmost freedom to be himself.*

*For the client, this optimal therapy would mean an exploration of
increasingly strange and unknown and dangerous feelings in himself,
the exploration proving possible only because he is gradually realizing
that he is accepted unconditionally. Thus he becomes acquainted with
elements of his experience which have in the past been denied to
awareness as too threatening, too damaging to the structure of the self.
He finds himself experiencing these feelings fully, completely, in the
relationship, so that for the moment he is his fear, or his anger, or his
tenderness, or his strength. And as he lives these widely varied feelings,
in all their degrees of intensity, he discovers that he has experienced
himself, that he is all these feelings. He finds his behavior changing in
constructive fashion in accordance with his newly experienced self. He
approaches the realization that he no longer needs to fear what experience may hold, but can welcome it freely as a part of his changing
and developing self.*[9]

Rogers' development of client-centered therapy resulted from his
conviction that personal growth occurs in a situation where a "helping relationship" is provided. Change in the client appears to come
about through meaningful experience in the relationship: "I can state
the overall hypothesis in one sentence, as follows. If I can provide a
certain type of relationship, the other person will discover within himself the capacity to use that relationship for growth, and change and
personal development will occur."[10]

[9] *Ibid.*, 284–85.   [10] *Ibid.*, 33.

The function of the therapist is to create a situation in which this process of self-correction and personality growth can occur. Rogers believes that several elements are essential for establishing such a helping relationship. The therapist must be a warm person who feels what Rogers has called an "unconditional positive regard" for his client, prizing him as a person regardless of his particular attitudes and behavior. In addition, the therapist must be able to experience an empathic understanding of his client's life. Moreover, he must be able to communicate that understanding to the client through two processes, reflection and clarification. In the process of reflection he merely repeats what the client has said—or part of what he has said—in a tone that conveys understanding but neither approval nor disapproval. In clarification he restates the kernel of what the client has tried to say. The effect is to hold up a mirror to the client so that he will be able to see himself more clearly and recognize his feelings and attitudes for what they are.

In client-centered therapy the therapist explains that the client himself will lead the way throughout the entire process, for thus he can find an answer to his problems. The therapist explains that only by this procedure can therapy be accomplished, since the client's problems are unique to himself, and they can be solved only in the light of his own personality and not on anyone else's terms.

Rogers views the therapeutic process as one dependent on interpersonal relationships and communications. This view has led him to formulate a general theory of interpersonal relationship:

Assuming (a) a minimal willingness on the part of two people to be in contact; (b) an ability and minimal willingness on the part of each to receive communication from the other; and (c) assuming the contact to continue over a period of time; then the following relationship is hypothesized to hold true.

The greater the congruence of experience, awareness and communication on the part of one individual, the more the ensuing relationship will involve: a tendency toward reciprocal communication with a quality of increasing congruence; a tendency toward more mutually accurate understanding of the communications; improved psychological adjustment and functioning in both parties; mutual satisfaction in the relationship.[11]

It should be noted that only one of the persons in the relationship needs to feel congruence for changes to occur in the other person. Congruence refers to acceptance and awareness of experiences.

The therapist tries to establish a permissive atmosphere by encour-

[11] *Ibid.*, 344.

aging his client to feel free to discuss any topic and say anything he likes. Initially, most clients express negative feelings toward themselves. The therapist responds by echoing and clarifying the client's comments in hopes of stimulating the client to explore his attitudes further. In the course of this process the client gradually reveals that he has positive as well as negative feelings toward himself. The therapist subtly encourages him to express positive feelings in the same way that he has elaborated on his negative feelings. By adopting an accepting attitude toward both sets of feelings, the therapist helps his client accept himself as he is, contradictions and all. Rogers has summed up the relationship for the client as the "process of becoming a person":

Each individual appears to be asking a double question: "Who am I?" and "How may I become myself?" I have stated that in a favorable psychological climate a process of becoming takes place, that here the individual drops one after another the defensive masks with which he has faced life; that he experiences fully the hidden aspects of himself; that he discovers in these experiences the stranger who has been living behind these masks, the stranger who is himself. I have tried to give my picture of the characteristic attributes of the person who emerges; a person who is more open to all of the elements of his organic experience; a person who is developing a trust in his own organism as an instrument of sensitive living; a person who accepts the locus of evaluation as residing within himself; a person who is learning to live in his life as a participant in a fluid, ongoing process, in which he is continually discovering new aspects of himself in the flow of his experience. These are some of the elements which seem to me to be involved in becoming a person.[12]

When the process succeeds, the client experiences congruence. If the client achieves complete congruence, he is then a "fully functioning person."

Rogers has described the aim or goal of life in terms similar to those of the Danish philosopher Sören Kierkegaard:

. . . away from self-concealment, away from being the expectations of others, . . . toward friendly openness to what is going on within him, . . . he moves toward acceptance of the "is-ness" of himself, he accepts others, . . . he trusts and values the complex inner processes of himself, . . . he is creatively realistic and realistically creative, . . . taking continual steps toward being, in awareness and in expression, that which is congruent with one's total organismic reactions. To use Kierke-

[12] *Ibid.*, 123–24.

gaard's more aesthetically satisfying terms, it means "to be that self which one truly is." It is a continuing way of life.[13]

Ideally, as the therapy process continues, the client drops his defenses and his faulty assumptions about himself. Self-condemnation and self-approval both recede, and a more objective evaluation takes their place. He begins to see himself, his situation, and his relationship to others in better perspective. Moreover, as he releases his emotions and gains better insight, his tensions subside and he realizes that he is becoming a real person. This realization gives him the courage to accept aspects of his personality that he has formerly repressed or disowned. Finally, he begins to set up achievable goals and to consider the steps that he must take to reach them. He then makes tentative moves in a positive direction, and when these efforts bring increased feelings of adequacy and satisfaction, his need for help decreases. The decision to terminate the sessions, like all other phases of the therapy, comes from the client and represents a final step toward independence.

Rogers has identified seven stages of the process of change. In the first stage the individual is not in touch with his feelings, with his "self." He may be unwilling to change, seeing no need for change and believing that there is danger in the act of changing. Following a period when he experiences and receives himself, he moves to stage two, where problems are not acknowledged except in terms of the past. In stage three he sees himself and related matters as objects. In stage four there is a willingness to discuss the "here-and-now," but there is usually little acceptance of those feelings. In stage five feelings and experiences are recognized, and the client becomes willing to accept responsibility for his behavior. In stage six the client moves to immediacy; feelings and experience are not inhibited by the newness of the process; the self ceases to be an object. In stage seven there is a blend of the therapeutic process with that of the whole life experience. These stages can be described as those in which the therapist and the client become involved in the "process of becoming." Stage seven, defined again in terms of becoming, can be seen as the point in which an individual is integrated, or unified within himself from surface level to the level of depth.

SIDNEY M. JOURARD (1926–)

Jourard's classic work, *The Transparent Self: Self-Disclosure and Well-Being*, sets forth his basic theories of man's personality as well as of psychotherapy. Jourard's theories rest on the assumption that when a man really wants to be known by others and to know himself, he can do so through the process of "self-disclosure"—talking about himself

[13] *Ibid.*, 181.

to another person. Jourard has focused on the social roles people attempt to play: "Healthy personalities are people who play their roles satisfactorily and at the same time derive personal satisfaction from role enactment; more, they keep growing and they maintain high-level physical wellness."[14] He has pointed out that counselors, guidance workers, and psychotherapists have to treat persons who, though they have successfully adapted to their roles, in the process of adaptation have developed personality disorders.

Jourard credits Freud with the realization that, by allowing patients to "be," by letting them disclose their innermost feelings and thoughts, they can overcome many of their frustrations, anxieties, and neuroses. Jourard distinguishes between role relationships and interpersonal relationships and notes that underneath the role is the person who is playing the role. In many cases roles replace the real self until a person becomes the image of his self-image rather than his own real self. In other terms this is known as self-alienation. In such cases self-disclosure can be very threatening to a person: "If there is any skill to be learned in the art of counseling and psychotherapy, it is the art of coping with the terrors which attend self-disclosure and the art of decoding the language, verbal and nonverbal, in which a person speaks about his inner experience."[15]

Jourard believes that too many therapists strive to construct a psychological model when interviewing a client, rather than facilitating the client's efforts at self-disclosure by love and understanding. In this respect Jourard is of the same school of thought as Martin Buber and Erich Fromm. He emphasizes the affirmation of being human as a primary means of arriving at an understanding of the client. In defining therapy, Jourard redefines Karen Horney's term *real self*:

By real self, first of all, we are refering to subjective experience which only the person himself can observe directly, since he is the one who is experiencing it. The immediate subjective experience which the term real self refers to comprises feeling (affection, anger, anxiety, guilt, and so on) and cognitive content (memories, perceptions, or, more generally, thoughts). Wants and wishes, as these are consciously experienced, are also an integral component of the real self: a wish to hurt somebody, a longing to disagree with someone, or a desire to eat, sleep, make love, and so on.

The real self refers to the subjective, or private, aspect of a person's behavioral repertoire. . . . Nobody, without the co-operation of the person himself, can discover what a person is thinking, feeling, or

[14] Quoted in Warren G. Bennis et al., eds., *Interpersonal Dynamics: Essays and Readings on Human Interaction*, 721.
[15] *Ibid.*, 279.

wanting. The person himself must be willing to translate his thoughts, feelings, and wishes into words and/or actions before the other indi- vidual (in an interpersonal relationship) can have an accurate idea of the person's real self.[16]

Therapy, according to Jourard, seeks to achieve basic changes in the patient's modes of relating to his real self and to his social environ- ment: "If we regard the patient's presymptomatic personality struc- ture as *symptom-producing*, it becomes apparent that simply removing symptoms will not be a causal treatment. The optimum aim should be to so change the personality that the individual will no longer react to life situations in ways which encourage the development of symptoms."[17]

In these terms psychotherapy is not so much a science or technique as a way of "being" with another person. Jourard is explicit in his state- ment that there are many reasons and ways to "be" with a person. In psychotherapy the client should experience his freedom, should be allowed to become himself. To be one's real self is essential to healthy personality, and it is therefore necessary to know how one goes about *being* his real self:

One indication of degree of real-self being is found in the nature of a person's self-disclosure. Humans have the capacity to fake, to dissem- ble, to seem to be what they are not, and they also have the capacity to reveal their true feelings and thoughts and true information about themselves. True disclosure of self in "dialogue" with one's fellow man seems to be the most direct indicator of real-self being. When a person lets others know what he genuinely thinks and feels, and when he an- swers their questions about him truthfully and without reserve, he is said to be engaged in real-self being.[18]

Jourard has thus set forth an essential ingredient in the therapeutic relationship—feedback: "Full self-disclosure between the participants in an interpersonal relationship promotes growth, then by creating impasses and conflicts in the relationship. It is in the resolution of the impasses that growth of personality occurs, but without communica- tion, there would never be sharply defined impasses."[19]

Finally, Jourard has defined impasses in interpersonal relationships as opportunities for growth of the individual when handled correctly. Thus, growth in personality occurs by meeting conflicts and impasses

[16] Sidney M. Jourard, *Personal Adjustment: An Approach Through the Study of Healthy Personality*, 350–51.
[17] *Ibid.*, 437.
[18] *Ibid.*, 160–61.
[19] *Ibid.*, 346–47.

head-on and reconciilng them. Recognizing and accepting conflict is therefore the necessary condition for its resolution.

According to Jourard, the goal of psychotherapy is not what people generally refer to as "adjustment" but should facilitate a growing personality. Jourard prefers the term "personality therapy" rather than "psychotherapy" because he believes that the therapist should be concerned with personality, not with symptoms. When the therapist treats symptoms, he cautions, he treats the by-product of the personality. The conditions responsible for the symptoms persevere as long as the personality structure remains unaltered.

Jourard has described the patient as one whose psychological or emotional growth has slowed or stopped. He believes that the task of the therapist is to engage in those activities which will serve to release the patient's adaptive capacities and remove the barriers to further growth toward mental health. Among those activities that the therapist can engage in to help the patient achieve that growth are the following: listening, reflecting, and interpreting; rewarding healthy behavior; directly or symbolically satisfying many of the patient's needs; respecting the patient, not "using" him; encouraging and permitting free emotional expression; trying to understand the patient and to promote self-understanding in the patient; and inspiring faith and hope in the patient.

In a healthy interpersonal relationship an individual is willing and able to communicate *all* of his real self to the other person when it is appropriate to do so. Jourard developed an instrument known as the "self-disclosure scale," which ranks items on a continuum from "easy to disclose" to "difficult to disclose." As a general rule, only selected aspects of the real self can be communicated to another person with comfort—those aspects which are consistent with (1) the self-concept, (2) the conscience, (3) the social mores, (4) the public self that has been constructed apropos the other person, and (5) the other person's actual concept of the discloser.

There are elements of Transcendentalism—or, if you will, mysticism —in Jourard's definition of a healthy personality. There is also in his concepts something of Rogers and—as we shall see in the next section— Abraham H. Maslow. While Rogers focused on experience, Maslow spoke about personal needs; Jourard incorporated both of these aspects of the personality within his theoretical formulation.

In Jourard's view the psychotherapeutic relationship between therapist and client is one of "invitation." The therapist's faith in a growing personality leads him to invite the client to grow with a fellow seeker. It is a mutual process of decision making, of experiencing, of honesty, and of trust.

ABRAHAM H. MASLOW (1908–70)

Abraham H. Maslow's approach to psychotherapy has been to study people whom he believed to be "self-actualizing." Maslow used the term to describe persons who have achieved a high degree of self-fulfillment and personal satisfaction. Maslow estimated that only a small percentage of any population becomes fully self-actualized. Psychotherapy was viewed by Maslow as a method by which people can be educated about themselves so that their lives will become qualitatively richer and deeper in meaning. Moreover, Maslow believed that only those persons who are aware of the here-and-now can be self-actualizers: "I have tried to express this . . . as a contrast between living fully and preparing to live fully, between growing up and being grown."[20]

Rogers and Maslow are much alike in their concepts of actualization, but Maslow differs from Rogers in that he postulates not one but two forces within the person. These two forces are the *actualization tendency* and the *survival tendency*, the former leading to a meaningful existence (and therefore the superior force of the two) and the latter concerned with the maintenance of life. Maslow concluded that the two tendencies do not conflict.

Maslow's hypothesis of the hierarchy of needs is one of his most important contributions to personality theory. This hierarchy, arranged from lower to higher levels, includes the fulfillment of (1) physiological needs, such as hunger and thirst; (2) safety needs, such as security, stability, and order; (3) belongingness and love needs, such as needs for affection, affiliation, and identification; (4) esteem needs, such as needs for prestige, success, and self-respect; and (5) the need for self-actualization.

The order of listing is significant in two ways. It is the order in which such needs tend to appear in the normal development of the individual, and it is also the order in which they need to be satisfied. If the individual's earlier needs are not satisfied, he never gets around to doing much about the later needs. Each need becomes important after the preceding one is satisfied. The first four are related to the survival tendency. Obviously, the fifth has to do with the actualization tendency. Maslow also described what he called the "Jonah complex," the fear of one's own greatness. Most persons value their own "peak experiences"—glimpses of their greatness. However, peak experiences cannot be endured for any great length of time, for they give the individual feelings of euphoria which frequently distort reality. Fortunately, by their very nature, peak experiences are transitory. In addition, Maslow believed that most persons fear greatness in others and yet

[20] Abraham H. Maslow, *Toward a Psychology of Being*, 30.

236

Figure 3. A hierarchy of needs

Source: J. William Pfeiffer and John E. Jones, eds., *Handbook for Group Facilitators* (Iowa City, Iowa, University Associates Press, 1972). Used by permission.

concurrently respect and admire that greatness. He called this fear-admiration "countervaluing." There are many reasons for this fear, including resentment of the threat of our own averageness.

Maslow also discussed the fear of "sinful pride" or, in Greek terms, "the fear of hubris." This fear is related to man's suspicion of his great aspirations. Like Jourard, Maslow incorporated in his theories the idea that "being" is an end in and of itself. Thus he sought to refute the Freudian belief that understanding must always be self-motivated. Furthermore, Maslow concluded that in the perception of self-actualizing persons and in the peak experiences of average persons cognition is not ego-centered but object-centered: "The perceptual experience can be organized around the object as a centering point rather than being based upon the ego."[21] This conclusion has important implications in psychotherapy: a client can overcome his neuroses through a process of accepting himself rather than through some process of molding himself into what he wants to become.

Maslow's position falls within the province of humanistic psychology, which he has characterized as the "third force" in American psychology, the other two being behaviorism and psychoanalysis. Whereas many psychologists, and particularly psychotherapists, study man from the perspective of his weaknesses and limitations, Rogers,

[21] *Ibid.*, 74.

237

Jourard, and Maslow have studied man from a positive perspective. Of the psychotherapeutic method itself, Maslow has said:

Psychotherapy takes place in seven main ways: (1) by expression (act completion, release, catharsis) . . . ; (2) by basic need-gratification (giving support, reassurance, protection, love, respect); (3) by removing threat (protection, good social, political and economic conditions; (4) by improved insight, knowledge, and understanding; (5) by suggestion or authority; (6) by direct attack on the symptoms, as in the various behavior therapies; and (7) by positive self-actualization, individuation, or growth. For the more general purposes of personality theory, this also constitutes a list of the ways in which personality changes in culturally and psychiatrically approved directions.

We can now describe at least three ways in which patients and therapists can relate to each other, the authoritarian, the democratic, the laissez-faire, each having its special usefulness at various times. But precisely these three types of relationships are found in the social atmosphere of boys' clubs and in styles of hypnosis ,in types of political theory, in mother-child relationships and in kinds of social organization found in infrahuman primates. . . .

It will be seen that gratification of the basic needs is an all important (perhaps the most *important) step along the path to the ultimate, positive goal of all therapy, namely self-actualization.*

It will also be pointed out that these basic needs are mostly satisfiable only by other human beings, and that therefore therapy must take place mostly on an interpersonal basis. The sets of basic needs whose gratifications constitute the basic therapeutic medications, e.g., safety, belongingness, love, and respect, can be obtained only from other people.[22]

Maslow defined man's nature in terms of needs, capacities, and tendencies that are genetically based. He also defined these needs as being either good or neutral rather than evil. From this perspective, full and desirable development consists of actualizing man's nature and fulfilling his potentialities. For Maslow, psychopathology results from the denial, twisting, or frustration of man's essential nature. Consequently, he believed that anything is good which is conducive to the development of man's nature in the direction of self-actualization. Anything that frustrates or blocks man's development of his inner nature is bad or abnormal. Pathology results from the disturbing of the course of self-actualization in man; therefore, according to Maslow, psychotherapy—indeed, therapy of any kind—is useful insofar as it helps re-

[22] Abraham H. Maslow, *Motivation and Personality*, 242.

store the person to the path of self-actualization and development along the lines his inner nature dictates.

Self-actualizzation is an intrinsic need for health. But, in Maslow's theory, in a sense it is different from the basic needs. Thus, he refers to the motivations of self-actualization as "meta-needs." When man's meta-needs are not fulfilled, he may become sick. Examples of the resulting pathologies are alienation, anguish, apathy, and cynicism.

Maslow concluded that psychotherapy and personal growth center on need gratification by means of interpersonal relations, the ultimate goal being self-actualization. Since most of man's basic needs can be satisfied only by other human beings, therapy must take place primarily on an interpersonal basis. Therapeutic results may occur to some degree independently of theory, or even with no theory at all. For example, friendship or marriage may satisfy a man's needs through the interpersonal relationship thus formed and may thereby be therapeutic in its effect through the gratification of some of his needs. For these reasons Maslow believed that psychotherapy is not a unique relationship, since its fundamental qualities can be found in other good interpersonal human relationships:

Any ultimate analysis of human, interpersonal relationships, e.g., friendship, marriage, etc., will show (1) that basic needs can be satisfied only interpersonally, and (2) that the satisfactions of these needs are precisely those [which are] the basic therapeutic medicines, namely, the giving of safety, love, belongingness, feeling of worth, and self-esteem.

We should inevitably in the course of an analysis of human relations find ourselves confronted with the necessity, as well as the possibility, of differentiating good from poor relationships. Such a differentiation can very fruitfully be made on the basis of the degree of satisfaction of the basic needs brought about by the relationship. A relationship—friendship, marriage, parent-child relation—would then be defined (in a limited fashion) as psychologically good to the extent that it supported or improved belongingness, security, and self-esteem (and ultimately self-actualization) and bad to the extent that it did not.

These cannot be satisfied by trees, mountains, or even dogs. Only from another human being can we get fully satisfying respect and protection and love, and it is only to other human beings that we can give these in the fullest measure. But these are precisely what we find good friends, good sweethearts, good parents and children, good teachers and students giving to each other. These are the very satisfactions that we seek from good human relationships of any kind. And it is precisely these need gratifications that are the sine qua non *preconditions for the production of good human beings, which in turn is the ultimate (if not immediate) goal of all psychotherapy.*[23]

Maslow believed that, if the relationship between the therapist and the patient is to be the medium through which the patient is to obtain his necessary therapeutic medicines, the therapist ought to be as conscious as possible of the relationship he forms with the patient:

To sum up, even though forming a satisfactory human relationship may not be an end in itself but rather a means to an end, it must still be regarded as a necessary or highly desirable precondition for psychotherapy, since it is usually the best medium for dispensation of the ultimate psychological medicines that all human beings need.

[Psychotherapy] ought then to be looked upon as a healthy desirable relation, even to some extent and in some respects as one of the ideal relationships between human beings. By theory, it ought to be looked forward to, eagerly entered upon. This is what should follow from previous considerations. In actuality, however, we know that this is not the case very often.[24]

Maslow expressed the hope that a patient, as a consequence of forming a good human relationship with his therapist, could, by transfer of training, form deeply solid friendships with others. From this point of view therapy can be defined as preparing the patient to achieve on his own good human relationships. Maslow envisioned a society which is healthy, just as the individual is healthy—a society which is motivated to self-actualization, just as the individual is motivated to self-actualization. The realization of such a society, of course, entails education and training.

Maslow's influence on psychotherapy has been significant. Eric Berne, Everett Shostrom, and Thomas A. Harris are but a few of the contemporary psychotherapists who have been influenced by his theories and concepts.

JACOB L. MORENO (1892-   )

Psychodrama has long been a term in the human relations practitioner's vocabulary. Jacob L. Moreno pioneered psychodrama, a technique involving spontaneous role playing. Many psychiatrists use this method of therapy to facilitate change in their clients. In this procedure group members reconstruct a situation and play the persons involved in the events, which oftentimes are taken from their own personal lives. The

[23] *Ibid.*, 248–49.
[24] *Ibid.*, 252.

technique has pitfalls: Moreno cautioned that when a psychodrama is enacted by inexperienced persons unaware of the complexities intrinsic to the method, role playing can confuse and even harm the persons involved.

Psychodrama is an outgrowth of the Theater of Spontaneity, which Moreno founded in Vienna in 1921. In his early experiments he found that playing unrehearsed parts was not only excellent training for actors but frequently had a salutary effect on their interpersonal relationships.[25] He wrote: "Psychodrama began with my rejection of the couch and the free association technique, and their replacement by an open, multidimensional space (the stage or any other open field) and the psychodramatic techniques."[26]

Moreno defined psychodrama as "the science which explores the 'truth' by dramatic methods."[27] He developed the technique as a therapeutic tool to offer an alternative to purely verbal approaches, which operate wholly on a symbolic level. In contrast to the usual psychotherapy techniques, psychodrama is based on a personal encounter among individuals involved in a situation. Even though the situation is simulated, it comes alive and elicits genuine emotions, generates new insights, and can help establish new behavior patterns.

In the years since Moreno introduced the psychodrama, it has undergone many modifications and variations. In the basic method an actual stage setting is employed, the therapist serving as "director," the patients as "protagonists," and a group of trained individuals, called "auxiliary egos," playing different roles in the drama. The audience serves as a reaction panel and a reservoir of additional auxiliary egos. The action may take two general forms: the protagonist-centered drama revolves around a personal problem of the patient; the group-centered drama deals with a problem, either symbolic or real, involving all the participants. An example of the group approach is "family psychodrama," in which members of a family group act out their difficulties in the presence of a therapist.

In setting up a psychodrama, the therapist asks the patient to choose a situation and indicate what kinds of auxiliary egos are needed. If the patient is uncooperative, the director-therapist himself sets up the situation. In either case a problem situation is dramatized. In the course of the drama the auxiliary egos pick up clues from the behavior of the protagonist and shape their roles to suit the situation. The auxiliary egos project themselves as fully as possible into the action and "live" their parts, not merely go through the motions:

[25] Jacob L. Moreno, *Who Shall Survive?*, 36.
[26] Jacob L. Moreno, *Sociometry, Experimental Method and the Science of Society*, 108.
[27] *Ibid.*, 102.

The patient is now an actor on the stage, acting before a smaller or larger audience of other patients. The physician-patient relation has become subsidiary. Again, we are in the midst of an overhauling of theory. With the new operation, new concepts and theories are emerging. It consists of two procedures: (a) treatment of the audience (group psychotherapy); (b) representatives of the group portray on the stage the problem from which the audience ails (action therapy). The group is facing the mirror of itself (in many versions) on the stage. It looks into this mirror and sees itself. The responses coming from the shock to the audio egos (members of the audience) and to the auxiliary egos (actors on the stage) are systematically followed up.[28]

The psychodramatic method generally employs five instruments: (1) the stage, (2) the subject, or patient, (3) the director, (4) the staff of therapeutic aides or auxiliary egos, and (5) the audience.

The first instrument, the stage, provides the patient with a living space which is multidimensional and flexible to the maximum, in contrast to the living space of reality, which is often narrow and restraining and in which he may easily lose his equilibrium. The stage space becomes an extension of life beyond the reality of life itself.

The second instrument, the subject, or patient, is asked to be himself on the stage, to portray his own private world. He is told to be himself, not an actor. He must act freely as things rise up in his mind; that is why he must be allowed freedom of expression, spontaneity. Next in importance to spontaneity comes the process of enactment. The verbal level is both included and transcended in this process. There are several forms of enactment: pretending to be in a role, reenacting or acting out a past scene, living out a problem presently pressing, creating life on the stage, and testing oneself for the future.

The third instrument, the director, has three functions: producer, therapist, and analyst. As producer he must be on the alert to turn every clue the subject offers into dramatic action, to make the line of production one with the life line of the subject, and never to let the production lose rapport with the audience. As therapist he attacks and shocks the subject, as well as laughing and joking with him. At times he may become indirect and passive; at such times the session seems to be run by the patient. As analyst he may complement his own interpretation by responses elicited from informants in the audience, from spouse, parents, children, friends, or neighbors.

The fourth instrument, the auxiliary egos or therapeutic actors, are extensions of the director, exploratory and therapeutic, but they are also extensions of the patient, portraying the actual or imagined per-

[28] *Ibid.*, 108.

sonae of the life drama. The function of the auxiliary egos is threefold: the function of actors, portraying roles in the patient's world; the function of therapeutic agents, guiding the subject; and the function of the social investigator.

The fifth instrument, the audience, has a dual purpose. It may serve to help the patient, or, being itself helped by the subject on the stage, may become the patient.

Perhaps the most unique dimension in which psychodrama takes place is based on Moreno's concept of "surplus reality"—reality which is not an exact repetition of life experiences. For example, the protagonist may choose to be a car or chair and talk about how he feels as a car or chair. In fact, he can choose to be any age, sex, nationality, or profession. According to Moreno, these acts of extended involvement make the protagonist the creator of his world rather than its artifact.

As a result of his experiments Moreno concluded that no matter what kind of psychotherapy is practiced, there are certain common denominators in all the methods. Mutual commitment, on the part of both the client and the therapist, is essential. This commitment leads to a willingness to share emotions and become directly involved.

FREDERICK S. PERLS (1893–1970)

Frederick S. Perls, Ralph Hefferline, and Paul Goodman laid the foundation for Gestalt therapy as a means toward psychological growth. Through his work Perls illustrated the therapeutic value of Gestalt theory in human relations training. Perls's theories were extensions of the earlier works of Max Wertheimer, Wolfgang Köhler, Kurt Koffka, and Kurt Lewin.

Unlike traditional psychology, which in effect fragments the human personality and considers the individual as merely a sum of his or her basic parts, the Gestalt approach focuses on the whole person as greater than his parts. Gestalt therapists believe that the organism (that is, the individual), rather than being a *summation* of its elements, is a subtle *coordination* of its various parts.[29] Thus Gestalt therapy concerns itself with the multirelationships between the person and his environment.

Perls underscored the significant therapeutic value of enhancing one's awareness of the here-and-now. He believed that the psychological properties implicit in the formation of a good Gestalt—one that presents the brightness, unity, and clarity of the experienced figure— reveal the reality and the depth of an experience. An incomplete Gestalt, or resisted experience, would be present if the figure lacked clarity, sharpness, or completeness; thus an "incomplete situation" would exist, and the individual's blocking of or resistance to the ex-

[29] Frederick S. Perls, *Gestalt Therapy Verbatim*, 5.

perience would become evident. Even if the individual is remembering the past or planning for the future, he is doing so in the here-and-now. According to Perls, when an individual continuously loses himself in the past or the future, he loses the present moment: "People who live futuristically never catch up with the events for which they have prepared and do not reap the fruits of their sowing. They rehearse for even the most unimportant interview and then they have no ability to act spontaneously when it arrives. Situations for which they have failed to prepare catch them utterly at a loss."[30]

In *Ego, Hunger and Aggression: The Beginning of Gestalt Therapy*, Perls presented the theory that the dominant need of the present moment emerges as the figure and will not fade into the background of experience until that need is either dealt with or satisfied.[31] Until the person becomes fully aware of that figure and how he reacts to it, it will continue to re-emerge in dominance, blocking the flow of other experiences or activities and fragmenting his energies. Often this resistance is hidden in the individual's habitual behavior or routines; consequently he blocks experience without even being aware that he is doing so.

Perls defined the role of the Gestalt therapist as that of a catalyst in helping the client become aware of the process involved in contacting or resisting the figure-ground relationship of his experience:

The therapy, then, consists in analyzing the internal structure of the actual experience, with whatever degree of contact it has: not so much what is being experienced, remembered, done, said, etc., as how what is being remembered is remembered, or how what is said is said, with what facial expression, what tone of voice, what syntax, what posture, what affect, what omission, what regard or disregard of the other person, etc. By working on the unity and disunity of this structure of the experience here and now, it is possible to remake the dynamic relations of the figure and ground until the contact is heightened, the awareness brightened and the behavior energized. Most important of all, the achievement of a strong gestalt is itself the cure, for the figure of contact is not a sign of, but is itself the creative integration of experience.[32]

As a catalyst, the therapist, whether in a group setting or in a one-to-one relationship, helps create the impetus for the individual to begin the process of heightened awareness. Perls described his goal as that of helping a client develop skills to deal with his emergent problems, so

[30] Frederick S. Perls, Ralph K. Hefferline, and Paul Goodman, *Gestalt Therapy: Excitement and Growth in the Human Personality*, 39.

[31] Frederick S. Perls, *Ego, Hunger and Aggression: The Beginning of Gestalt Therapy*, xi.

[32] *Ibid.*, 232.

that once an awareness of the process has begun it will continue to flow. Thus Perls defined the role of the therapist as one of facilitation, of helping the client learn how he functions as a whole. Consequently, the role of the therapist is not to teach the client something about himself but to provide the opportunity for him to begin to learn about himself from his own experience. Perls was convinced that the responsibility for behavior, change, learning, and growth lies with the individual. He captured the importance of personal growth, "owning" one's behavior or feelings through his "Gestalt Prayer":

> *I do my thing and you do your thing.*
> *I am not in this world to live up to your expectations.*
> *And you are not in this world to live up to mine.*
> *You are you, and I am I,*
> *And if by chance, we find each other, it's beautiful.*
> *If not, it can't be helped.*[33]

The Anti-Hospital: An Experiment In Psychiatry[34]
DAVID COOPER

Psychiatrists set out to cure people. Somehow or other a bad (ill, mad) state of affairs arises in someone and somehow or other this has to be transformed into a good (well, sane) state of affairs. The implicit model of psychiatric thinking has been predominantly one according to which a disease process, organic or psychological, afflicts a person and then, secondarily, affects other persons. The emphasis is on passivity and process. The model demands a patient, someone who undergoes the process of pathological change, who submits to treatment, who waits to be cured. It is only in the last few years that some workers have begun seriously to question whether this is in fact invalid or invalidated.

Nowhere does this distinction become more crucially relevant and nowhere is it more smothered in ambiguity than in the field of schizophrenia. Schizophrenics occupy about two thirds of the beds in most mental hospitals, and mental hospital beds are nearly half the total hospital beds in the country. In most European countries about 1 per cent of the population go to the hospital at least once in their lifetime with the diagnosis schizophrenia and the Swiss psychiatrist E. Bleuler estimated that for every one schizophrenic in the hospital there are about ten "at large" in the community. If one takes note of recent research into the familial origin of schizophrenia and its conclusion, that

---

[33] Perls, *Gestalt Therapy Verbatim*, i.

[34] By David Cooper. This article first appeared in *New Society* (March 11, 1965), the weekly review of the social sciences, 128 Long Acre, London WC2, England. Reprinted by permission.

schizophrenia is not a disease in one person but rather a crazy way in which whole families function, then one realises the massive social problem presented by this disease or perhaps pseudo-disease. For the emerging view is that acute schizophrenia is not a disease process with as yet undetermined somatic or psychological causes, but rather that it is a microsocial crisis situation in which one member of a group, usually a family group, is elected by a process which is often violent and arbitrary to become the patient.

The implication for the psychiatric ward is that we must understand very clearly the nature of this sort of violence. We must understand how the patient-to-be becomes mystified by others and then progressively invalidated as an autonomous person. The invalidation must not be continued in the ward, and staff must begin to refuse to enter into the traditional covert collusion with the patient's family. In the past this collusion has often meant that staff become implicated in a progressive violence that is perpetrated, in the name of treatment, against the labelled patient.

STAFF SELECTION

If the conventional psychiatric ward and hospital are in many ways opposite to those indicated by the nature of the schizophrenia problem, why not explore this contradiction by setting up in the heart of a mental hospital an experimental unit which ideologically would be in some sense an anti-hospital? It was agreed that we should do this at our hospital—a large mental hospital of 2,300 patients just northwest of London.

To carry this out in a wholly responsible way entailed taking certain precautions. One had to be quite sure that the patients in the anti-hospital stood to gain significantly more than they would in a conventional ward (although in practice this would not be likely to prove difficult). One would have to be on the lookout for disintegrative effects on the rest of the hospital that might harm the other patients. Finally, one had fully to realise that extremely difficult problems would arise for the anti-hospital staff and that some might not stay the course: careful initial selection and adequate help subsequently were clearly necessary.

After a year during which staff were selected and emotionally prepared, we commenced the unit in January 1962 with 19 male patients in what, until that time, had been the insulin coma ward. About two thirds of the patients had been diagnosed as schizophrenic and they were adolescent or young adult men. In the second year the unit expanded into a 30 bed ward. Both wards were close to the geographical centre of the hospital. The original programme was highly structured. It began every morning with a community meeting of all the patients and staff, followed after a staff meeting by three subgroups each meeting with a doctor therapist, and then, in the afternoon and evening, occupational therapy and recreational groups. In addition to the patient and staff group transactions there were family meetings consisting of the patient, his nuclear family and a therapist. No "physical treatments" were used, apart from occasionally tranquillisers. It took the staff about a year to become disenchanted with this way of functioning and to be prepared to tolerate a progressive destructuring of the programme in a way that was felt might be liberating and creative for the patients and which might also ultimately have similar results for the staff.

We had one central conviction, founded on repeated unhappy experiences in conventional psychiatric admission wards, that before we have any chance of understanding what goes on in the patients the staff have to have at least some elementary awareness about what goes on in themselves. We therefore aimed to explore in our day to day work the whole range of preconceptions, prejudices and fantasies that staff have about each other and about the patients.

This is undoubtedly a major task. The psychiatric institution throughout its history has found it necessary to defend itself against the madness which it is supposed to contain—disturbance, disintegration, violence, contamination. The staff defences, insofar as they are erected against illusory rather than real dangers, may be collectively termed institutional irrationality: What, then, is the reality of madness in the mental hospital and what is illusion? What are the defining limits of institutional irrationality?

It has long been recognised that a great deal of violent behaviour in mental patients is a direct reaction to physical restraint. If any member of the public were to be seized by several burly men and thrust into a straitjacket for reasons which were obscure to him, and if his attempts to find an explanation were without avail, his natural reaction would be to struggle. We are no longer in the era of straitjackets, and padded rooms are on the way out, but it is not so long ago that the writer saw a patient, kicking and screaming in a straitjacket, carried by several policemen into the observation ward: one had only to dismiss the policemen and remove the straitjacket to end the patient's violent reactions.

Today psychiatrists resort to "chemcial restraint"—sedatives and tranquillisers—and to electroshock and bedrest. The effect of these less drastic measures, however, is much the same if they are used, as they often are, without any reasonable explanation. The expectation set up when a patient is given a large dose of tranquilliser is that there is danger in him which must be controlled. Patients who are very

247

*sensitive to such expectations often oblige by providing the violence—
at least until they are subdued by a larger dose of the same "treatment."
This is not to say that disturbed patients should not be given tranquillisers but simply that there should be clarity in the mind of the
doctor and of the patient about what is being done.*

*There rarely is. The meaning of this situation is only too often lost in
the quasi-medical mystique of "illness" and "treatment." Why should
one not, for instance, tell the patient: "I'm giving you this stuff called
Largactil to quieten you down a bit so that we can get on with the rest
of our job without feeling too anxious about what you are going to get
up to next!"*

*Let us look at some of the ways in which we have tried to put our
philosophy into action.*

REBELLING IN BED

*One of the commonest staff fantasies in mental hospitals is that if
patients are not coerced verbally or physically into getting out of bed
at a certain hour in the morning they will stay in bed until they rot
away. Behind this is staff anxiety over non-conformism with the time
regulation and general control in their own lives. The patient is that
frightening aspect of themselves that sometimes does not want to get
out of bed in the morning and come to work. It is obviously true that if
they succumbed to this temptation they would lose their jobs. It is also
true that young schizophrenic patients will eventually leave hospital
and take jobs which they will have to attend punctually. But all this
ignores the life historical significance of the "staying in bed problem."
In the past the patient has probably depended entirely on his mother
to get him up in the morning. Shortly prior to his admission he has
often rebelled against this enforced dependence by what, for various
reasons, is the only course available to him, namely staying in bed
despite his mother's efforts to get him up. This "withdrawal" is often
one of the "presenting symptoms" of schizophrenia.*

*In the hospital one can repeat the family pattern, that is to say gratify
the patient's dependent needs by getting him up; this is really getting
up for him. Or one can take the "risk" of leaving the decision to him in
the hope that he will one day get up himself. In fact, after many heated
discussions of this issue in the unit and a great deal of policy difference
between the nursing shifts it was found that if the usual vigorous rous-
ing procedures were abandoned and patients left to get up themselves
they invariably did rise, even if in some cases they would spend most
of the day in bed for several weeks. No one rotted away after all and the
gain in personal autonomy seemed worthwhile.*

Staff at first and then patients would comment in the community meetings on the getting up problem in terms of dependent need but the point was also brought home in more active ways. At one time all the occupants of a six bed dormitory rebelled against the community meeting by staying in bed until after eleven o'clock. One of the charge nurses went upstairs to see what was going on. One of the patients left to go to the toilet and the nurse seized the opportunity to take off his white coat (worn not as uniform but as protective clothing for certain messy jobs like washing up) and climb into the vacant bed. The patient, on his return, appreciating the irony of the situation, had little option but to take the vacated "staff role," put on the white coat and get the others out of bed.

Another fantasy prevalent in the mental hospital concerns patient work. It is held implicitly, and sometimes stated, that if patients are not fully occupied in domestic ward jobs and the various occupational therapy projects, or helping in hospital maintenance departments, they will become "withdrawn," "institutionalised," "chronic patients." The bitter truth is that if they submissively carry out all these required tasks they become what is implied by these labels anyhow. If one wishes to encounter the ultimate in withdrawn chronic institutionalisation one has only to visit one of the more "active" and productive "factories in a hospital" or "industrial occupational therapy departments." There is, relatively speaking, something remarkably healthy about the chronic schizophrenic, preoccupied with his inner world, spending the day hunched over the central heating fitting in a decrepit back ward. If he does not have the solution to the riddle of life at least he has fewer illusions.

WHAT SHOULD PATIENTS DO?

In the unit we had some desperate confrontations on this matter. Patients resisted conventional occupational therapy projects. We had begun to question the ancient myth that tells us that Satan makes work (destructiveness, masturbation, promiscuity) for idle hands, but were not certain about where we went from there. Work projects would at least form a group, make a happy ward family. But perhaps people had come to the hospital to get away from "happy families." Or rather they had been sent to hospital to keep the family happy. We worked through a number of virile destructive jobs, knocking down an air raid shelter, breaking up an aero engine: these jobs it was felt would provide a "safe outlet" for "dangerous aggressive impulses." The jobs were done without enthusiasm and the staff soon began to realise their irrelevance to the real problems of anger. People had real reasons to be angry with real other people at home and in hospital (this was not entirely reducible to projection). The aero engine was an innocent party.

Our anxieties led us to put forward, consider, and then reject a number of other typical hospital projects of a trivial nature, such as putting together the manufactured elements in (ironically) toy doctor's sets. Patients reacted contemptuously to these tasks and we came to share their feelings. Most of them were young men of at least average intelligence, well able to acknowledge the incongruity of the projects offered them.

It was only after the first year of the unit's life that the staff group, including the young female occupational therapist, were able to tolerate a situation in which no organised work project was presented to the community. Whatever project had been offered disintegrated after some weeks when patients "skived off" to private activities elsewhere within and outside the hospital. Sanctions in the form of reduction of pocket money (up to 22s 6d per week allowance for patients who work in the hospital) did not affect the issue at all. What were we getting so anxious about and what were we trying to do anyhow?

The occupational therapist who had already abandoned her green uniform found herself gravitating towards a role that seemed nearer to the nursing role. She even considered resigning and joining the staff as an assistant nurse. It was at this time that we became particularly aware of the fact of role diffusion, the breakdown of role boundaries which was a necessary stage on the way to staff and patients defining themselves and their relationships with each other not on the basis of an imposed abstract labelling system, based on a few technical or quasi-technical functions, but in terms of the personal reality of each member of the community.

There was a progressive blurring of role between nurses, doctor, occupational therapist and patients which brought into focus a number of disturbing and apparently paradoxical questions: for example, can patients "treat" other patients and can they even treat staff? Can staff realise quite frankly and acknowledge in the community their own areas of incapacity and "illness" and their need for "treatment"? If they did what would happen next and who would control it?

It was at this point that the most radical departure from conventional psychiatric work was initiated. If the staff rejected prescribed ideas about their function and if they did not quite know what to do next, why do anything? Why not withdraw from the whole field of hospital staff and patient expectation in terms of organising patients into activity, supervising the ward domestic work and generally "treating patients." The staff group decided to limit their function to controlling the drug cupboard as was legally required (some of the more "overactive and impulsive" patients were on the tranquilliser Lar-

gactil) and to dealing with ward administrative issues involving other hospital departments over the telephone.

A necessary prelude to this major policy change was explanation to the nursing office and other hospital departments. The kitchen staff for instance were informed that if the aluminum food containers were returned unwashed they should leave them until they were cleaned. If people wanted to eat they would have to clean the containers. These decisions were made quite clear to everyone in the community meetings.

Despite these explanations and superficial acceptance of them, subsequent events were dramatic. In the first phase dirt accumulated higher and higher in the corridors. Dining room tables were covered with the previous day's unwashed plates. Signs of horror were evoked in visiting staff, in particular nursing officers on their twice daily rounds. Patients decided their own leave periods, getting out of bed, attendance at meetings. Staff were anxious throughout but particularly since no patients showed signs of organising themselves to attend to these matters.

External administrative pressure on the ward staff rapidly mounted. The patients were divided in their response. A few began to demand more nurse attention. Those less urgently dependent expressed some dissatisfaction but at the same time made it clear that they appreciated the more authentic elements in the policy change.

BREAKING DOWN AUTHORITY

Subsequent events must be seen in relation to the problem of doctor centredness in mental hospital ward administration. In conventional wards all but the most trivial decisions have to be either made by or blessed by the doctor. The doctor is invested and sometimes invests himself with magical powers of understanding and curing. Whether the formal training of psychiatrists includes qualifications in magical omnipotence is perhaps uncertain, but the image is reinforced and perpetuated in many ways. The same person who is supposed to have a psychotherapeutic relationship with patients assumes a general practitioner role in relation to their bodily ailments. Not only that but psychiatrists attend the staff sick bay and medically care for nurses with whom they work. The resulting confusion of controlled frustration and wholesale gratification can well be imagined.

If the white coat and stethoscope is one means by which the psychiatrist defends himself from patients, that is to say from his own projected disturbance, the printed form is another. Doctors have accepted, only too readily in many cases, a mass of legal and administra-

tive responsibilities which keep them from getting near their patients but which, to a far greater extent than is commonly admitted, could be left to efficient, suitably trained non-medical administrators. As things stand, however, the doctor visiting the ward included a pile of official forms and certificates in his (often unwanted) armamentarium and these forms structure his relationships with staff and patients before anything else he does or they do can have any effect.

In addition to this medical, legal and administrative prestructuring of the psychiatrist's role there are occasionally more realistic factors which lead to his assumption of the central position in the ward, namely training and experience in psychotherapeutic skills and small group sociology, although these skills are by no means universal among psychiatrists.

In the staff groups the level of dependency on the doctor is not much different from that in the staff-patient groups. The problem for nurses is to change their position from one in which they mediate the doctor-for-the-patient and the patient-for-thedoctor to one in which they involve themselves in relationships without the mediating or mediated "third." This shift of position is fantastically difficult. After two years of work centred largely on this issue we have barely shifted at all in the unit—but we have shifted a little.

It was during the "experimental" phase of staff withdrawal that the staff group was able to make some advance. The author was away on holiday for a month. Official pressure on the unit to introduce conventional controls was at its peak. Anxiety among the staff was considerable and there was an added factor of conflict between the two shifts (7 A.M. to 2 P.M. and 2 P.M. to 9 P.M.) of nurses. Much of the latter conflict was based on the mistaken attribution of certain intentions to the doctor The suggestion that staff should withdraw from their supervisory, directive role, informing the patients how this would happen, was in fact generated by one shift of nurses. This had been gently confirmed by the doctor (the author) and was accepted with only a few, unimportant reservations by the whole staff group. Because of earlier happenings in the unit which led to the idea among hospital staff that the unit doctor had new, ultra-permissive ideas, the staff decision was regarded as the "doctor's policy"—it might be pretty crazy but if it originated in the mind of a senior doctor it had unquestionably to be carried out.

The advance made by the staff group was frankly to recognise their anxiety as intolerable and, in the doctor's absence, to arrive at a group decision to reimpose some staff controls on what went on in the ward. It was decided to supervise eating and cleaning arrangements and to assist on attendance at community meetings and adherence to the rule that weekend leave was only granted from Saturday morning (after the community meeting) to Sunday night. It was decided that persistent offenders against these rules would have to choose between conforming to them or discharge from the unit. On my return I lent my confirmation to these decisions and in fact two patients who had blatantly broken the rules were shortly discharged (and in both cases this confrontation with a group reality led to consequences which were favourable).

This leads us on to the central problem of the psychiatric hospital of distinguishing between authentic and inauthentic authority. The "official" practice of psychiatry in this country, whatever progressive mantle it may don, aims only too often at enforcing conformism to the rigid, stereotyped dictates and needs of authority persons who refract on to the patient massified and alienated social expectations and hidden injunctions as to who and what he may be. The authority of the authority person is granted him by arbitrary social definition rather than on the basis of any real expertise he may possess. If staff have the courage to shift themselves from this false position they may discover real sources of authority in themselves. They may also discover such sources of authority in "the others" who are defined as their patients.

This begins to get disturbing—particularly when the patients sometimes happen to be those who are clinically the most psychotic in the ward. One of the most memorable group meetings in the unit was dominated by an extremely fragmented patient who was just beginning a lengthy project of reintegration: all the staff and patients were lulled into a fascinated somnolence by his account of a "bizzarre," imaginary world tour. We became a sort of collective infant at the breast of the mother-narrator. I made a formal comment in these terms but interpretation was not necessary. At a certain point indicated by the narrator everyone snapped themselves out of the fantasy awareness to find themselves on a more integrated level of group reality. And there was no doubt about who had led them there.

SUMMARY

Freud's theory of personality development does not adequately recognize the role that culture plays in shaping the personality. Freud almost completely ignored social factors, and he relied too heavily on sex as a cause of emotional difficulty. Psychoanalysis is limited in its applicability to human relations problems in these respects: it is often an interminable process, the high cost of private treatment limits its availability to patients who can afford it, and it devotes too much time to the patient's past behavior and life rather than focusing on the here-and-now.

Feminists criticize Freudian psychology because of its alleged sexist orientation, for example its use of such concepts as "penis envy." From the feminist perspective the psychotherapeutic encounter is designed to help women adjust to both an inferior sex role and male domination. Furthermore, the feminist argument continues, most male therapists are incapable of sexually liberating their female clients because they (the male therapists) subscribe to the superior male and inferior female sex-role concept.

Another criticism leveled at psychotherapy is that most psychotherapists are trained to only understand behavior patterns within the Western nuclear family, which is not universal. Consequently, such therapists are likely to encourage clients who live in other family arrangements to adopt Western nuclear family behavior and norms.

On the other hand, there are many good things that can be said for Freud's contribution to the field of human relations. First, it can be argued that since it takes many years to acquire the faulty attitudes and distorted feelings that make therapy necessary, and since the human being is so complex, the long process of psychotherapy is valuable and probably inevitable. Second, by recognizing the power of the unconscious and the preconscious upon man's attitudes and behavior, Freud made us aware that these variables are important when attempting planned change. Moreover, Freud discovered ways in which the therapeutic relationship can be a means toward re-educating the patient toward more awareness, understanding, and control. In short, Freud's concepts have applicability in any field of human endeavor into which the nonrational elements of human behavior may enter.

Similarly, there are many's helpful insights to be gained from Moreno's psychodrama. The method enables the individual to release his emotions by acting them out in a setting that is emotionally safe and relatively controlled; it may also drain off some of his tension. It gives him new insight into his attitudes and behavior by showing him how other individuals react to him. By encouraging spontaneity, it helps him meet real situations of life more spontaneously and effectively. In this respect Moreno's methods fit well into Perls's Gestalt therapy.

Much more could be said about Rogers' client-centered therapy. The theory is a constantly developing one, changing with experience and research. It is one of the most detailed, best integrated, and most consistent psychotherapeutic methods currently employed. Some writers take issue with Rogers' idea that the client must perceive the therapist's empathic understanding before constructive personality change will occur. Even so, concepts taken from Rogers' approach to psychotherapy have been applied in the fields of education, social work, business and industrial administration, and religious activities.

One of the important elements of Jourard's contributions is his conviction that the therapist should value the client over any commitment to a therapeutic technique. Jourard's idea of a healthy personality as one which is growing was a positive step beyond the traditional idea of health in terms of particular standards.

Maslow stands out in the area of psychotherapy with his positive approach to mental health. His theories about needs and how the psychotherapeutic relationship meets those needs have been widely accepted and applied in other helping professions.

Chapter 9
SUGGESTED READING

Agel, Jerome, ed. *The Radical Therapist.* New York, Ballantine Books, Inc., 1971.

Bennis, Warren G. et al., eds. *Interpersonal Dynamics: Essays and Readings on Human Interaction.* Homewood, Ill., Dorsey Press, 1968.

Brammer, Lawrence M. *Therapeutic Psychology: Fundamentals of Counseling and Psychotherapy.* Englewood Cliffs, N.J., Prentice-Hall, Inc., 1968.

Carkhuff, Robert R. *Helping and Human Relations: A Primer for Lay and Professional Helpers.* New York, Holt, Rinehart & Winston, Inc., 1969.

———. *The Development of Human Resources: Education, Psychology and Social Change.* New York, Holt, Rinehart & Winston, Inc., 1971.

———, and Bernard G. Berenson. *Beyond Counseling and Therapy.* New York, Holt, Rinehart & Winston, Inc., 1967.

———, and Charles B. Traux. *Toward Counseling and Psychotherapy.* Chicago, Aldine Publishing Company, 1967.

Chruder, Herbert J., and Arthur W. Sherman. *Personal Adjustment,* 2d ed. Cincinnati, South-Western Publishing Company, 1963.

Corsini, Raymond J. *Methods of Group Psychotherapy.* New York, McGraw-Hill Book Company, 1957.

Culbert, Samuel A. *The Interpersonal Process of Self-Disclosure: It Takes Two to See One.* Washington, D.C., National Education Association, 1968.

Curran, Charles A. *Counseling and Psychotherapy.* New York, Steed and Ward, Publishers, 1968.

Detre, Thomas P. *Modern Psychiatric Treatment.* Philadelphia, J. B. Lippencott Company, 1971.

Erikson, Erik. *Childhood and Society.* New York, W. W. Norton & Co., Inc., 1964.

Fagan, Joel, and Irma Lee Shepherd, eds. *Gestalt Theory Now.* Palo Alto, Calif., Science and Behavior Books, 1970.

Frankl, Victor. *Man's Search for Meaning.* New York, Simon & Schuster, Inc., 1970.

Freud, Sigmund. *Basic Writings of Sigmund Freud.* New York, Modern Library, Inc., 1938.

———. *A General Introduction to Psychoanalysis.* Garden City, N.Y., Garden City Publishing Company, 1920.

Fromm, Erich. *Sigmund Freud's Mission: An Analysis of His Personality and Influence.* New York, Grove Press, Inc., 1959.

Ginott, Haim G. *Group Psychotherapy with Children.* New York, McGraw-Hill Book Company, 1961.

Glasser, William. *Reality Therapy: A New Approach to Psychiatry.* New York, Harper & Row, Publishers, Inc., 1965.

Goble, Frank. *The Third Force: The Psychology of Abraham Maslow.* New York, Pocket Books, Inc., 1970.

Goffman, Ervin. *The Presentation of Self in Everyday Life.* New York, Doubleday & Company, Inc., 1959.

Grier, William H., and Price M. Cobbs. *Black Rage.* New York, Bantam Books, Inc., 1968.

Hall, Calvin S., and Lindsey Gardner. *Theories of Personality.* New York, John Wiley and Sons, Inc., 1970.

Heider, Fritz. *The Psychology of Interpersonal Relations.* New York, Ernest R., and Richard C. Atkinson. *Introduction to Psychology,* 4th ed. New York, Harcourt, Brace & World, Inc., 1967.

Horney, Karen. *Our Inner Conflicts: A Constructive Theory of Neurosis.* New York, W. W. Norton & Co., Inc., 1945.

Jaspers, Karl. *The Nature of Psychotherapy: A Critical Apprailsal.* Chicago, University of Chicago Press, 1964.

Jourard, Sidney M. *Disclosing Man to Himself.* Princeton, N.J., D. Van Nostrand Company, 1968.

———. *Personal Adjustment: An Approach through the Study of Healthy Personality.* New York, The Macmillan Company, 1958.

———. *The Transparent Self: Self-Disclosure and Well-Being.* Princeton, N.J., D. Van Nostrand Company, 1964.

Jung, Carl G. *Memories, Dreams, Reflections.* New York, Random House, Inc., 1963.

———. *The Undisclosed Self.* Boston, Little, Brown & Company, Inc., 1958.

Kisker, George W., *The Disorganized Personality.* New York, McGraw-Hill Book Company, 1964.

Lazarus, Richard S. *Adjustment and Personality.* New York, McGraw-Hill Book Company, 1961.

Maddi, Salvatore R. *Personality Theories: A Comparative Analysis.* Homewood, Ill., Dorsy Press, 1968.

Maslow, Abraham H. *Motivation and Personality.* New York, Harper & Row, Publishers, Inc., 1954.

———. *Self-Actualizing People: A Study of Psychological Health.* New York, Brooklyn College, 1951.

———. *Toward a Psychology of Being.* Princeton, N.J., D. Van Nostrand Company, 1968.

Masserman, Jules H., and Jacob L. Moreno, eds. *Progress in Psychotherapy: Techniques of Psychotherapy.* New York, Grune and Stratton, Inc., 1958.

May, Rollo, et al. *Existence: A New Dimension in Psychiatry and Psychology.* New York, Basic Books, Inc., 1958.

———, ed. *Existential Psychology.* New York, Random House, Inc., 1961.

Moreno, Jacob L. *Group Psychotherapy.* Beacon, N.Y., Beacon House, Inc., 1945.

———. *Sociometry, Experimental Method and the Science of Society.* Beacon, N.Y., Beacon House, Inc., 1951.

———. *The Theatre of Spontaneity: An Introduction to Psychodrama.* Beacon, N.Y., Beacon House, Inc., 1947.

———. *Who Shall Survive?* Washington, D.C., Nervous and Mental Disease Publishing Company, 1934.

———. "The Viennese Origins of the Encounter Movement, Paving the Way for Existentialism, Group Psychotherapy, and Psychodrama," *Group Psychotherapy,* Vol. 22 (1969).

Moreno, Zerka T. "Beyond Aristotle, Breuer & Freud: Moreno's Contribution to the Concept of Catharsis," *Group Psychotherapy and Psychodrama,* Vol. 24 (1971).

Patterson, C. H. *Theories of Counseling and Psychotherapy.* New York, Harper & Row, Publishers, Inc., 1966.

Perls, Frederick S. *Ego, Hunger and Aggression: The Beginning of Gestalt Therapy.* New York, Random House, Inc., 1969.

———. *Gestalt Therapy Verbatim.* Walnut Creek, Calif., Real People Press, 1969.

———, Ralph K. Hefferline, and Paul Goodman. *Gestalt Therapy: Excitement and Growth in the Human Personality.* New York, Dell Publishing Company, Inc., 1951.

Polster, Erving, and Miriam Polster. *Gestalt Therapy Integrated: Contours of Theory and Practice.* New York, Brunner/Mazel Publishers, 1973.

Pope, Benjamin. *Psychological Diagnosis in Clinical Practice.* New York, Oxford University Press, 1967.

Rank, Otto. *Will Therapy and Truth and Reality.* New York, Alfred A. Knopf, Inc., 1945.

Reich, Wilhelm. *Murder of Christ: Emotional Plague of Mankind.* New York, Ferrar, Straus and Giroux, 1953.

Reik, Theodore. *Search Within: The Inner Experiences of a Psychoanalyst.* London, Regenery, 1962.

Ruitenbeek, Henrik, ed. *Psychoanalysis and Existential Philosophy.* New York, E. P. Dutton & Co., Inc., 1962.

Rogers, Carl R. *Counseling and Psychotherapy: Newer Concepts in Practice.* Boston, Houghton Mifflin Company, 1942.

———. *On Becoming a Person: A Therapist's View of Psychotherapy.* Boston, Houghton Mifflin Company, 1961.

———. *Psychotherapy and Personality Change.* Chicago, University of Chicago Press, 1954.

Rokeach, Milton. *The Open and Closed Mind.* New York, Basic Books, Inc., 1960.

Rosenbaum, Max, and Milton Berger, eds. *Group Psychotherapy and Group Function.* New York, Harper & Row, Publishers, Inc., 1953.

Sanger, Clifford J., and Helen S. Kaplan. *Progress in Group and Family Therapy.* New York, Brunner/Mazel Publishers, 1972.

Stollak, Gary E., Bernard G. Guerney, Jr., and Meyer Rothberg, eds. *Psychotherapy Research.* Chicago, Rand-McNally & Company, 1966.

Sullivan, Harry Stack. *Conceptions of Modern Psychiatry.* New York, W. W. Norton & Co., Inc., 1953.

Thomas, Alexander, and Samuel Sillen. *Racism and Psychiatry.* New York, Brunner/Mazel, Inc., 1972.

Whitaker, Dorothy S., and Morton A. Lieberman. *Psychotherapy Through Group Process.* New York, Atherton Press, 1967.

Wittels, Fritz. *Freud and his Time.* New York, Liverright Publishing Corp., 1931.

Wolf, Alexander, and Emanuel K. Schwartz. *Psychoanalysis in Groups.* New York, Grune and Stratton, Inc., 1962.

Yalom, Irving. *The Theory and Practice of Group Psychotherapy.* New York, Basic Books, Inc., 1970.

*From the beginning, Don, an intense, eager, apparently
anxious member, had rushed in with suggestions for
group action. . . . As the sessions continued, his interventions had decreased in relevancy to what was happening in the group. . . . One member of the group asked
Don directly why he always brought up something of
his own just when the group was beginning to discuss a
group problem. Don hotly denied that he had deliberately done so.*—LELAND P. BRADFORD

T-group training (laboratory training in groups) is defined as any
group process whose major learning activity is the exploration and
analysis by group members of their own experiences. Participants are
encouraged to tune in, turn on, and talk up about how they are feeling
at the moment. The group is the medium through which the learning
occurs. T-groups place the major emphasis on analyzing the *process* of
interaction within the group, particularly as it applies to organizational
development.

T-group training utilizes the experience and interpersonal relations
which occur in a temporary, laboratory-created group to help the participants develop insights into group processes, to develop insights into
the way they themselves function in groups, and, finally, to gain skills
in participation in groups.[1] Herbert A. Thelen stated that the aim of
training in the laboratory method is to help people learn to behave in
groups in such a way that the groups solve the problems for which they
were assembled and to ensure that the individuals within the group
have meaningful, rewarding, and need-meeting experiences.[2]

Roy M. Whitman described the T-group as "a collection of hetero-
geneous individuals who gather for the purpose of examining the interpersonal relations and group dynamics that they themselves generate
by their interaction. . . . This training sensitizes the individual to the
group process affecting him, the influence of other individuals upon

[1] Warren G. Bennis, Kenneth D. Benne, and Robert Chin, eds., *The Planning of
Change,* 718.
[2] Herbert A. Thelen, *Dynamics of Groups at Work,* 131.

him, and his own role in causing the group and individuals to respond to him in a certain way."[3] The primary goal of the T-group is not to produce change per se but rather to provide feedback and support for testing whether change will help the individual improve in his interpersonal and intergroup relationships.

In describing the T-group, Robert T. Golembiewski and Arthur Blumberg emphasized the importance of the creation of a learning laboratory in which (1) a miniature society is created, (2) the orientation is toward working with processes for the purpose of emphasizing inquiry, exploration, and experimentation with behavior, (3) the orientation is toward facilitation of learning, (4) the atmosphere is psychologically safe for learning, and (5) what is to be learned is determined by the members even though a professional trainer is usually available to provide guidance.[4]

Golembiewski and Blumberg noted that T-groups also focus on the concepts "learning how to learn" and "the here-and-now." The inductive orientation of the T-group teaches members that the only real answers are provided by themselves and not by an authority figure. In addition, they must learn to develop a high tolerance for a lack of structure, since the training situation is especially loose in the early stages. Consequently, openness to experience is a desirable characteristic for T-group members.

According to the National Training Laboratories for Group Development (NTL), whose activities are described later in this chapter, the purposes of human relations training are to help each member to realize fully his individual growth and to improve his ability to work effectively with others in similar situations.[5] In the training laboratory an effort is made to create a climate which encourages learning, understanding, insight, and skills in the areas of self, group, and organization awareness. In broad terms NTL objectives include (1) self-insight, (2) better understanding of other persons and awareness of one's impact on them, (3) better understanding of group processes and increased skill in achieving group effectiveness, (4) increased recognition of the characteristics of larger social systems, and (5) greater awareness of the dynamics of change.

Although the foregoing definitions and descriptions of the T-group process vary in some respects, each emphasizes three goals: analysis of

[3] Roy M. Whitman, "Psychodynamic Principles Underlying T-Group Process," in Leland P. Bradford, ack R. Gibb, and Kenneth D. Benne, eds., T-Group Theory and Laboratory Method, 310.

[4] Robert T. Golembiewski and Arthur Blumberg, eds., Sensitivity Training and the Laboratory Approach, 5.

[5] National Training Laboratories for Group Development, Reading Book: Nineteenth Annual Summer Laboratories in Human Relations, 2.

Table 4. An Overview of Sensitivity Training

Basic Approach of Laboratory Training	Kinds of Target Data	Kinds of Learning
"Sensitivity training attempts to accomplish the end of behavioral change through a philosophy and technique of training which is best described as a concern with 'how' — how a trainee appraises himself, how a group behaves, how another would react in a given situation. In short sensitivity training has as its purpose the development of an executive's awareness of himself, of others, of group processes, and of group culture." * The basic learning vehicle in any laboratory program is the T-Group. The T-Group is intended to help people:† 1. Explore the impact of their behaviors and values on others; 2. Determine whether they want to change their behaviors and values; 3. Test new behaviors and values, if individuals consider them desirable; and 4. Develop awareness of how groups can both stimulate and inhibit personal growth and decision making.	The focus is on the public, "here-and-now" data available only to T-Group members. These here-and-now data include: 1. The specific *structures* developed, such as the leadership rank-order; 2. The *processes* of group life, with especial attention to getting a group started, keeping it going, and then experiencing its inevitable "death"; 3. The specific *emotional reactions* of members to one another's behavior and to their experiences; and 4. The varying and diverse *styles* or *modes* of individual and group behavior, as in "fighting" the trainer or in "fleeing" some issue that has overwhelmed group members.	Interaction in T-Groups generates three basic kinds of learning by participants, to varying degrees in individual cases: 1. Learning that is largely cognitive and oriented toward techniques, as for effective committee functioning; 2. Learning that highlights deep emotional needs of which the participant was variously aware, and that shows how such needs can be satisfied; and 3. Learning that demonstrates the significance of "unfinished business," and that illustrates how and with what effects the press against the consciousness of such matters may be relieved.

*From William G. Scott, Organization Theory (Homewood, Ill., Richard D. Irwin, Inc., 1967), 332.

†Based on Chris Argyris, *Interpersonal Competence and Organizational Effectiveness* (Homewood, Ill., Dorsey Press, 1962), 156.

SOURCE: Robert T. Golembiewski, "Theory in Public Administration: Defining One 'Vital Center' for the Field," Florida State Unversity *Lecture Series*, Nov. 17, 1967. Used by permission.

Table 4. Continued

Levels of Learning	Basic Goals for Outcomes
Laboratory programs typically try to touch on three loci at which learning can be applied; but the first level receives most attention: 1. *Personal learning*, when the person learns about himself-in-interaction in the T-Group; 2. *Transfer learning* when personal learning is extended to "external" contexts (e.g., a worksite) to increase understanding or to improve functioning; and 3. *Environmental learning*, when the concern is to restructure some external context (e.g., an organization) so as to make it more personally satisfying and rewarding while also enhancing the effectiveness of those involved.	Laboratory programs enhance authenticity in human relations by seeking to increase: 1. Individual awareness about self and others; 2. Acceptance of others; and 3. Acceptance of self. Laboratory programs seek to free individuals to be more effective while they are more themselves, both as persons and as members of organizations, by seeking to enhance the development of: 1. Sensitivity to self and others; 2. Ability to diagnose complex social situations and to conceptualize experience in behavioral science terms; and 3. Action skills and attitudes required to capitalize on increased sensitivity and enhanced diagnostic skills.

group process, particularly as it applies to organizational development; recognition by each member of the influence of other members upon him; and recognition of how his behavior influences group members.

IN THE BEGINNING

Kurt Lewin, a social psychologist, came to the United States from Nazi Germany intent on testing theories pertaining to techniques that groups might learn to avoid the totalitarianism he had barely escaped. Basically, Lewin's theories were concerned with the social restraints imposed on groups by technology, economics, law, and politics. He considered the small group the obvious link between individual and social dynamics.

Lewin is best known for his theory of *force-field analysis*, which holds that events are determined by immediate forces rather than by distant ones. He reasoned that behavior could be changed if people could identify the forces that restrained them from desirable action and the ones that drove them toward it. Lewin was instrumental in organizing the Research Center for Group Dynamics at the Massachusetts Institute of Technology.

In 1946, in collaboration with Kenneth Benne, Leland P. Bradford, and Ronald Lippitt, Lewin sought to assist the state of Connecticut in resolving racial conflict. During one of the staff planned meetings, participants were invited to observe the staff in operation and to feed back to the staff their observations about what had transpired, both on an individual and on the group level. According to Golembiewski, the results were stimulating and exciting, and out of this experience some members of the staff began to develop theoretical reasons for what had happened. They decided to plan similar learning situations that could be enlarged for more groups.[6] Out of the 1946 community leadership training program came the establishment of the NTL, which sponsored the first formal program in sensitivity training, held in Bethel, Maine, during the summer of 1947.

One feature of the first NTL workshop was a small, continuing group called the Basic Skills Training Group (BST), in which designated participants shared their perceptions of group interaction. These perceptions formed the basis for discussion and analysis by the group. The BST group was designed to become the nucleus for teaching change-agent skills and concepts and also for training others to understand and to help with group development. The BST group was not successful because it incorporated too many objectives, but out of this effort came the inception of the T-group. In 1950, NTL became a part of the Adult Education Division of the National Education Association, and in 1962 it was made an independent division.

Since 1947, NTL and the T-group concept have continued to grow. Interest on the part of persons engaged in many occupational fields has led NTL to develop special training programs for management, church workers, community leaders, school administrators, national organizations, and industries. T-groups are being used in programs of management development for in-service education to help resolve the difficulties of the individual within a bureaucratic structure. Most groups focus on difficulties of communication, interpersonal relations, feelings of belonging, and loneliness.

The original NTL summer session has now grown into a full program of training, consultation, research, and publication. Similar programs have developed over the United States and in foreign countries. Regional training and research centers have been set up at various locations, usually in affiliation with universities—for example, the Western Training Laboratory in California and the Intermountain Laboratory in Group Development in Utah. Many private concerns have been established across the country. Staff members for the growing number of laboratories are constantly being trained with the assistance of the National Institute of Mental Health and other interested agencies which finance training programs.[7]

According to Jane Howard, NTL officials have plans for establishing the world's first university devoted entirely to behavioral sciences.

[6] Golembiewski and Blumberg, *op. cit.*, 4.
[7] Kenneth D. Benne, "History of the T-Group in the Laboratory Setting," in Bradford, Gibb, and Benne, *op. cit.*, 83.

Postdoctoral, doctoral, and master's degree programs in applied behavioral science and in humanistic psychology will be offered. It is also planned that the new university will offer experimental curricula and a "think tank" where resident and visiting social scientists can try to bridge the gaps that separate behavioral-science knowledge from action.[8]

THE LABORATORY APPROACH

The process within the T-group can be discussed from the standpoint of what Robert R. Blake and Jane S. Mouton called "keys to understanding" the laboratory approach.[9] The keys represent a way of looking at T-groups in order to focus on group activity and understand the process taking place. These keys are (1) the laboratory as a replica of the human side of an actual organization, (2) the strategy for acquiring knowledge, and (3) the feedback for reflective behavior.

When the laboratory becomes a replica of the human side of an organization, there are participants from various ranks within the organization. The participants attempt to mix and to work together, realizing that there are inherent status problems. Those with lesser rank tend to feel the same desires for understanding and appreciation as do those with higher rank. In a model training group all participants make an effort to express themselves in an open and trusting manner so that other members will not only know their frustration but also understand what makes them tick and the talents they have to offer.

When the participants are able to put aside their status in the laboratory setting, problems of participation and communication are minimized, and they can begin to become effective group participants. Likewise, when those with high rank in "real" life are encouraged to forget prerogatives, privilege, and prestige, they too join up to get the job done, thereby becoming more effective leaders.

The *leveling process*—expressing true feelings—is an integral part of T-group strategy. With inhibitions removed, participants are able to see how they tend to disregard, misuse, distrust, and violate each others' feelings, thoughts, and values. When participants attempt to work together under laboratory conditions, human problems in an organization are reproduced in action. Learning how to work with others in setting realistic goals and then looking back to determine how their performance is leading toward those goals, and also looking at the process involved in achieving the goals, are part of the total experience. The participants learn much about themselves and about others. In-

[8] Jane Howard, *Please Touch: A Guided Tour of the Human Potential Movement*, 222.

[9] Robert R. Blake and ane S. Mouton, *Group Dynamics: Key to Decision-Making*, 10.

sights emerge that frequently were believed impossible before the T-group experience. These same insights can then be applied to the "real" situation.

The T-group is usually composed of ten to fifteen members. Each group creates its own pattern of interaction. Initially, authority, power structure, processes, goals, procedures, and norms are missing or ambiguous. In a successful T-group the members practice the processes of inquiry, exploration, and experimentation, pulling themselves from a state of near chaos to a state of integration. Their efforts in this process provide basic curricula for their learning as they write and read and often rewrite their own "textbook" of group interaction:

As the T-group struggles with the problem of formation, of goal clarification, of individual difficulties in working out patterns of membership adequate for both the individual and the group, the learning emphasis can be focused on the development of cultural norms in the group, on the process of social relationships, on individual perceptual and motivational systems, or on individual group and value systems.[10]

A trainer or leader is present, not as an authoritarian leader but rather as an agent of balance whose job it is to diagnose interaction, to prevent group members from being hurt, and to bring about the leveling process which indeed may be a confrontation between members. When the group is first formed, the trainer creates a vacuum by refusing to carry out the usual expectations of a "leader's" role. He does not intervene through leadership, agenda, or setting of procedures. He thereby forces group members to assume responsibility for their own learning.

There are several distinct roles in a training program of three days' duration or longer. As an *initiator of diagnostic training concepts*, the trainer must help the group realize that its own processes and problems must provide much of the "curriculum." The trainer may be non-directive, as described above, or, in a short training session, he may spell out his responsibility. A major function of the trainer is to make diagnostic observations at such times as he feels that the group is able to learn and internalize from these experiences.

Occasionally the trainer becomes an *innovator of learning experiences*. In this role he initiates various techniques and methods to stimulate a maximum learning experience. The trainer may provide tasks if he perceives that the group needs a task for specific learning. An example might be a role play illustrating nonverbal behavior that blocks communication.

Another function of the trainer is to act as a *standards protector*. After a group has set up its own standards, the trainer may have to

10 National Training Laboratories, *op. cit.*, 11.

remind it of those standards. For example, he may need to remind the members that they are straying from the goal of the "here-and-now." It may also be necessary at times to insist on "looking at the behavior" of persons rather than "looking at their motivation."

In situations where an individual may be verbally or physically attacked and hurt by the group, the trainer may find it necessary to intervene and set up standards to control or prevent personal attacks. He must be aware of the psychological makeup of individuals so that he will know when to intervene. On the other hand, the group may occasionally be severely punished by one individual, in which case the trainer should also intervene.

There is considerable debate concerning the extent to which a trainer should become a group member. Certainly the trainer does not perform the typical group function, but when the group matures to the point that it is able to take over the diagnostic function and begins to realize the contributions of the various members, it is in a sense accepting the trainer as a group member.

Another key to understanding the group process is based on feedback. For example, when a member says, without a chance for clarification, "I've been with the company for ten years," one does not know whether the person has had ten years' experience in learning or whether he has had five years of a learning experience two times. That is, we must understand the message being communicated. This statement could only be clarified through feedback, which means "trying some behavior and getting back signals on how others react to it. Feedback is a social mirror—it tells how others react to your behavior. The distinctive feature about training feedback is that people tell one another what they would ordinarily avoid saying."[11]

In essence, *feedback* is the process of "leveling" and letting another person know how one feels. It may be either positive or negative. Effective feedback is possible within a T-group because of the psychologically safe atmosphere that is the group norm. It is a continuous checking and rechecking process which permits a person to measure how his own behavior is seen by another, to determine whether or not he accurately understands the actions and motivations of others, to decide whether his judgments of events are congruent with those of another person, and to determine whether or not he understands the dynamics that make for group effectiveness. Feedback can be compared to a guided missile system in that it helps an individual keep his behavior "on target" in the process of achieving his goals. Without feedback there can be no definite indication whether one is making clear progress toward that target.

[11] Blake and Mouton, *op. cit.*, 14.

Warren Bennis, Jack Gibb, and Robert Tannenbaum are three important theorists in training-group concepts. Summaries of their theories and concepts which relate specifically to the field of human relations, as well as relevant concepts of others in the field, will be presented in the following pages.

WARREN G. BENNIS (1925–)

Warren G. Bennis is a graduate of the Massachusetts Institute of Technology and president of the University of Cincinnati. He has written many articles and books on the subject of human relations.

Bennis noted a general agreement about the goals of laboratory education and T-group experiences. He outlined four objectives for such education: (1) self-awareness, (2) understanding of the conditions that affect group experiences, (3) understanding of group dynamics, and (4) training for persons who desire to increase their skills in interpersonal and group settings.[12] (Many of Bennis' concepts of T-groups were developed in collaboration with Herbert A. Shepard.)

In addition to these general goals Bennis outlined certain "meta-goals," or values which are common to T-group experiences and which shape and direct the learning to be derived in the laboratory method. He suggested that four meta-goals should be included in human relations theory and training: (1) an expanded consciousness and recognition of choice, (2) the spirit of inquiry, (3) authenticity in interpersonal relations, and (4) a collaborative conception of the authority relationship.

An expanded consciousness and recognition of choice refers to the process of placing oneself within a broader environmental perspective. This requires a willingness to look at ourselves and possible new ways of behaving.

The spirit of inquiry is based on the willingness to experiment within the group—to try on new roles and behavior. Bennis observed that in laboratory training all experienced behavior is a subject for questioning and analysis, limited only by the participants' threshold of tolerance to truth and new ideas.

Authenticity in interpersonal relations has to do with a ground rule (or at least the tendency to accept the rule) of expressing feelings in order to create valid lines of interpersonal and intergroup communication. Authentic behavior is analogous to being our real selves in a role-playing situation. This meta-goal involves "leveling."

A collaborative conception of the authority relationship focuses on the interdependence between trainers and participants and the extent to which each assumes the responsibility for producing group growth.

12 Bennis, Benne, and Chin, *op. cit.*, 681.

Table 5. Phases of Group Development
Phase I. Dependence-Power Relations*

	Subphase 1 Dependence–Submission	Subphase 2 Counterdependence	Subphase 3 Resolution
1. Emotional Modality	Dependence — Flight	Counterdependence — Fight: Off-target fighting among members. Distrust of staff member. Ambivalence.	Pairing. Intense involvement in group task.
2. Content Themes	Discussion of interpersonal problems external to training groups.	Discussion of group organization; i.e., what degree of structuring devices is needed for "effective" group behavior?	Discussion and definition of trainer role.
3. Dominant Roles (Central Persons)	Assertive, aggressive members with rich previous organizational or social science experience.	Most assertive counterdependent and dependent members. Withdrawal of less assertive independents and dependents.	Assertive independents.
4. Group Structure	Organized mainly into multi-subgroups based on members' past experiences.	Two tight subcliques consisting of leaders and members, of counterdependents and dependents.	Group unifies in pursuit of goal and develops internal authority system.
5. Group Activity	Self-oriented behavior reminiscent of most new social gatherings.	Search for consensus mechanism: Voting, setting up chairmen, search for "valid" content subjects.	Group members take over leadership roles formerly perceived as held by trainer.
6. Group movement facilitated by:	Staff member abnegation of traditional role of structuring situation, setting up rules of fair play, regulation of participation.	Disenthrallment with staff member coupled with absorption of uncertainty by most assertive counterdependent and dependent individuals. Subgroups form to ward off anxiety.	Revolt by assertive independents (catalysts) who fuse subgroups into unity by initiating and engineering trainer exit (barometric event).
7. Main Defenses	Projection Denigration of authority.		Group moves into Phase II

* Course terminates at the end of 17 weeks. It is not uncommon for groups to remain throughout the course in this phase.

Source: Robert T. Golembiewski, "Theory in Public Administration: Defining One 'Vital Center' for the Field," Florida State University Lecture Series, Nov. 17, 1967. Used by permission.

Table 5. Continued

Phase II. Interdependence-Personal Relations

	Subphase 4 — Enchantment	Subphase 5 — Disenchantment	Subphase 6 — Consensual Validation
Emotional Modality	Pairing-Flight. Group becomes a respected icon beyond further analysis.	Fight-Flight. Anxiety reactions. Distrust and suspicion of various group members.	Pairing, understanding, acceptance.
Content Themes	Discussion of "group history," and generally salutary aspects of course, group, and membership.	Revival of content themes used in Subphase I: What is a group? What are we doing here? What are the goals of the group? What do I have to give up — personally — to belong to this group? (How much intimacy and affection is required?) Invasion of privacy vs. "group giving". Setting up proper codes of social behavior.	Course grading system. Discussion and assessment of member roles.
Dominant Roles (Central Persons)	General distribution of participation for first time. Overpersonals have salience.	Most assertive counterpersonal and overpersonal individuals, with counterpersonals especially salient.	Assertive independents.
Group Structure	Solidarity, fusion. High degree of camaraderie and suggestibility. Le Bon's description of "group mind" would apply here.	Restructuring of membership into two competing predominant subgroups made up of individuals who share similar attitudes concerning degree of intimacy required in social interaction, i.e., the counterpersonal and overpersonal groups. The personal individuals remain uncommitted but act according to needs of situation.	Diminishing of ties based on personal orientation. Group structure now presumably appropriate to needs of situation based on predominantly substantive rather than emotional orientation. Consensus significantly easier on important issues.

Table 5. Continued

Group Activity	Laughter, joking, humor. Planning out-of-class activities such as parties. The institutionalization of happiness to be accomplished by "fun" activities. High rate of interaction and participation.	Disparagement of group in a variety of ways: high rate of absenteeism, tardiness, balkiness in initiating total group interaction, frequent statements concerning worthlessness of group, denial of importance of group. Occasional member asking for individual help finally rejected by the group.	Communication to others of self-system of interpersonal relations; i.e., making conscious to self, and others aware of, conceptual system one uses to predict consequences of personal behavior. Acceptance of groups on reality terms.
Group movement facilitated by:	Independent and achievement attained by trainer-rejection and its concomitant, deriving consensually some effective means for authority and control. (Subphase 3 rebellion bridges gap between Subphases 2 and 4.)	Disenchantment of group as a result of *fantasied expectations of group life.* The perceived threat of self-esteem that further group involvement signifies creates schism of group according to amount of affection and intimacy desired. The counterpersonal and overpersonal assertive individuals alleviate source of anxiety by disparaging or abnegating further group involvement. Subgroups form to ward off anxiety.	The external realities, group termination and the prescribed need for a course grading system, comprise the barometric event. Led by the personal individuals, the group tests reality and reduces autistic convictions concerning group involvement.
Main Defenses	Denial, isolation, intellectualization, and alienation.		

Bennis summed up his theory of meta-goals by stating that he cared "far more about developing choice and recognition of choice points than I do about change."[13] Bennis pointed out that T-groups more or less deroutinize everyday processes for participants and thereby slow down the pace so that it can be analyzed. Attitudinal changes follow the Lewinian model of *unfreezing, new information,* and *refreezing.* The T-group gives rise to unfreezing and, consequently, an expanded awareness of how one is behaving. At the same time the T-group allows participants to make a conscious choice of behavior patterns. Bennis attributed this freedom to the absence of the control mechanisms that are part of all institutions. Such control mechanisms, he concluded, tend to regulate behavior such as group mission, authority patterns, norms for intimacy and control, decision apparatus, communication, traditions, and precedents.

According to Bennis, T-group theory is based on two important areas that the group must deal with: (1) the T-group is concerned with the individual group member's orientation toward authority, and (2) the T-group members are concerned with their interactions with one another. Bennis called these two areas authority relations and personal relations. Within each of these two phases of group development are three subphases.[14]

Phase I of group development is the *dependence phase.* Subphase 1 is called *dependence-flight.* The first days of group life are filled with behavior whose remote, as well as immediate, aim is to ward off anxiety. Bids for leadership fail because no one is willing to share leadership functions. Subphase 2 is *counterdependence.* The trainer refuses to satisfy the needs of the group, and counterdependency replaces the overdependence phase. Subphase 3 is *resolution.* During this period the group unifies in pursuit of a goal and develops an internal authority system.

Phase II is the *interdependence phase.* The concern for affection occupies the group. The problems center around attitudes toward interdependence and sharing intimacy and friendship, cohesiveness, and cooperation. Subphase 4 is called *enchantment-flight.* This subphase is marked by a high rate of interaction and participation. Subphase 5 is called *disenchantment.* There is a disenchantment of members with the group as shown by a high rate of absenteeism and frequent statements about the worthlessness of the group. Subphase 6 is the *consensual validation.* This aspect of group life shows acceptance of the group on reality terms. Consensus is significantly easier on important issues.

[13] *Ibid.,* 686.
[14] Quoted in Golembiewski and Blumberg, *op. cit.,* 92.

In his conclusions Bennis relied upon other professionals in the field of human relations. For example, when discussing techniques for applying behavioral science to planned organizational change through T-groups, Bennis cited Chris Argyris, Leland Bradford, Jack Gibb, Kenneth Benne, and Edgar Schein.

JACK R. GIBB (1914–)

One of Jack R. Gibb's most significant contributions to T-group theory is found in an article entitled "Role Freedom in a TORI Group," in which he and his wife, Lorraine, described the climate for trust formation.[15] TORI (Trust-Openness-Realization-Interdependence) theory holds that the major barriers to growth are fears and distrust and invalid life views that rationalize these fears and distrust. In each aspect of growth Gibb illustrates that distrust is movement away from other persons and trust is movement toward others. According to Gibb, the critical aspects of group growth are *acceptance* (membership), *data flow* (decision making), *goal formation* (productivity), and *control* (organization).

Acceptance is the concern of individuals in a group. This stage of group development is characterized by a high degree of fear and distrust, which can be evidenced through persistent self-defense, attempts at changing others' attitudes, avoidance of feeling, and other similar defensive concerns. Resolution of this stage of development occurs when the group begins to show signs of acceptance and trust.

Data flow is the second group concern. Through socialization we learn to be defensive about both data output and data input. Denial, flattery, and artificial politeness are characteristic of this stage of group development. Training and growth can enable the group to improve listening skills, increase spontaneity and expression, and move the group to the third developmental stage.

Goal formation is the third concern of the group. This concern manifests itself in the group's efforts to define its purpose and meaning as a group. Gibb cautioned that premature goal formulation beyond trust and data boundaries leads to unrealistic or overaspirational goals. The pursuit or lack of pursuit of such goals leads to apathy or various forms of resistance. When a group has failed to achieve acceptance among its members, the "persuasive" model of action comes into play.

Control is the most mature stage of group development. At this stage individual members are concerned with the influence they can exert in the group. Advice giving and power struggles are characteristic of this stage of development. These manifestations show that the group has unresolved control problems. The control problems disappear when

[15] In Arthur Burton, ed., *Encounter*, 44.

data-collection and interpersonal-acceptance problems are solved.[16]

Group formation is a continuing set of resolutions to the problems deriving from the four focal concerns of acceptance, data, goal, and control. A T-group trainer may use either of two kinds of leadership to facilitate group maturity: *persuasive leadership or participative leadership.* Participative leadership leads to healthy group functioning, whereas persuasive leadership produces unhealthy group functioning. Gibb therefore proposed that the trainer should try to employ participative methods as much as possible. The trainer should be trusting, open, permissive, and interdependent. In fact, Gibb observed that groups can have maximum participation when there is no trainer. Trainerless groups are optimally effective when group activities become the concern of all members, who alternately assume leader and follower roles. However, Gibb readily acknowledged that trainerless groups are found in few settings. Therefore, in most instances the trainer is needed to facilitate group growth by focusing on a series of work cycles, each cycle consisting of the following sequences: planning, acting-observing, process analysis, and generalizing for future situations.

Gibb concluded that the T-group is an ideal situation for trust formation and the establishment of the supportive climate needed for good human relations. However, if the trainers in a group do all of the work in setting the climate, trust will more than likely not be forthcoming.

Another significant contribution Gibb has made to T-group theory lies in the area of communication. His lectures on defensive communication outline the categories of behavior characteristics of defensive climates in small groups. He listed six categories of defensive climates: evaluation, control, strategy, neutrality, superiority, and certainty. Gibb stated that persons become defensive when they perceive threat. Threat can be reduced by a supportive climate in which (1) description rather than evaluation is utilized, (2) the orientation is problematic rather than based on control, (3) the atmosphere is spontaneous rather than strategic, (4) persons feel empathetic rather than neutral, (5) all are equal rather than stratified, and (6) persons are not taken for granted.

Among Gibb's contemporaries in the study of the T-group are Bennis, whose work has been summarized above; Kenneth D. Benne, who concentrates on the formation and management of polarization; Leland P. Bradford, who studies the problem of membership attainment; Robert R. Blake and Jane S. Mouton, who have written extensively about the member-trainer relationship; Murray Horwitz, who

[16] Bradford, Gibb, and Benne, *op. cit.*, 287.

focuses on the process of legitimation within groups; Herbert A. Shepard, who examines the effects of influence in the training milieu; and Roy M. Whitman, who focuses upon the dynamics of trainer entry into the T-group.

ROBERT TANNENBAUM (1915–)

Robert Tannenbaum was the first director of the Human Relations Research Group (HRRG) of the Graduate School of Business Administration and Institute of Industrial Relations at the University of California, Los Angeles. HRRG's primary interest in human relations centers on businesses and the effectiveness with which they implement their personnel policies. As a result, HRRG and Tannenbaum have long been active in the development of sensitivity-training programs for businesses.

In 1958 Tannenbaum observed that qualities in the followers may influence the choice of leadership. The more authoritarian members may demand strong direction by one person, while the more equalitarian members are apt to value leaders who are responsive to individual and group feelings.[17]

Tannenbaum pointed out that the social sciences gave rise to the concept of group dynamics, which significantly altered the image of the successful executive. Research efforts increasingly noted the importance of seeking information from subordinates and employees in working out problems and making decisions. In a 1958 article Tannenbaum brought the significance of emerging concepts of T-group experiences to the attention of the business world. He wrote, "The net result of the research findings and of the human relations training based upon them has been to call into question the stereotype of an effective leader."[18]

Tannenbaum identified the learning results of the T-group in his sensitivity training. According to Tannenbaum, in sensitivity training more attention is given to personal and interpersonal awareness than in the T-group. However, in common usage sensitivity groups may be T-groups or encounter groups. Tannenbaum believes that sensitivity training represents one means for assisting the personal growth of persons who, while "normal" by most cultural standards, may indeed be driven to abnormal behaviors by these very standards.[19]

Basically, sensitivity training is an approach to human relations training which is aimed at getting people to feel and to behave dif-

---

[17] Joseph Luft, *Group Processes: An Introduction to Group Dynamics*, 44.

[18] Robert Tannenbaum and William H. Schmidt, "How to Choose a Leadership Pattern," *Harvard Business Review*, March–April, 1958, 96.

[19] Bradford, Gibb, and Benne, *op. cit.*, 125.

ferently and not merely to think differently about the day-to-day handling of human problems. Sensitivity training is based on the following premises:

1. Much work is done through personal contacts with others, either as individuals or as members of groups.

2. Effectiveness in dealing with others is often handicapped by lack of specific kinds of interpersonal understanding and skills.

3. People who have such understanding and skills seem more effective in their interpersonal relations.

4. There is evidence that people can learn to improve their interpersonal understanding and skills.

HRRG's sensitivity-training program was greatly influenced by NTL's methods of applied group dynamics. In collaboration with Irving Weschler and Fred Massarik, Tannenbaum emphasized the usefulness of the small-group experience, which allowed a high level of participation, involvement, and free communication.[20] Tannenbaum's major contribution to T-group theory lies in the area of leadership theory. He believes that a comprehensive theory of leadership must include the following variables: (1) the leader and his psychological attributes, (2) the follower with his problems, attitudes and needs, and (3) the group situation, in which followers and leaders relate with one another.[21]

Leadership, as defined by Tannenbaum, is an interpersonal influence, exercised in a given situation and directed, through the communication process, toward the attainment of one or more specified goals. In a T-group situation the trainer has options about what kind and how much leadership to exert within the group. The amount and nature of leadership should vary according to the needs of the group.

Tannenbaum classified the functions of the trainer in five main categories:[22]

1. *Creating situations conducive to learning.* The trainer may utilize his influence to guide the group through educational situations. Because the trainer initially represents an authority figure, he may aid in setting up situations between trainees in which insights and group discussion may develop.

2. *Establishing a model for behavior.* By his own behavior the trainer helps establish the atmosphere within the group. By his activity in the group, his acceptance of critiicsm, his nonevaluative comments,

[20] Robert Tannenbaum, Irving R. Weschler, and Fred Massarik, eds., *Leadership and Organization: A Behavioral Science Approach,* 133.

[21] *Ibid.,* 24.

[22] *Ibid.,* 139.

his willingness to deviate from planned programs, and his ability to raise questions and to express his own feelings, he helps establish an atmosphere of acceptance and freedom of expression in which the group may face up to interpersonal problems rather than avoid them.

3. *Introducing new values.* By his behavior, both implicitly and explicitly, the trainer introduces values into the group.

4. *Facilitating the flow of communication.* The trainer acts in ways to facilitate communication by identifying barriers, raising questions, clarifying issues, encouraging full participation, and identifying sources of difficulty which may be above the group's level of awareness.

5. *Participating as an expert.* Trainers are often called upon for knowledge and guidance, but Tannenbaum believes that the group members should be made responsible for setting their own goals and deciding their own methods in the group experience.

Tannenbaum observed that there are four components of leadership. One component is the *interpersonal influence*, the leader's efforts to affect the behavior of his followers through communication. The second is the *situation*, which Tannenbaum defined as including only those aspects of the objective context which have attitudinal or behavioral impact on the individuals in the influence relationship. The third component is the *definition*, which includes interpersonal influence by means of the communication process. The fourth component is the *goal*, either a single or a complex of goals, which fall in the following four categories: organizational goals, group goals, personal goals of the follower, and personal goals of the leader.[23]

Tannenbaum concluded that social sensitivity, or empathy, is not enough. Behavioral flexibility, or action flexibility—the abiilty to behave appropriately—is also necessary. Broadly speaking, sensitivity training seeks to develop both social sensitivity and behavioral flexibility. Thus, the training method seeks to produce both *attitudinal* and *behavioral changes.* These changes are not to be made in a specific direction pointed out by the trainer; instead, each trainee is encouraged to get a better look at himself and to experiment with new and perhaps personally more appropriate behavior.

Deficiency in social sensitivity and behavioral flexibility is often related to unresolved personality conflicts. Tannenbaum believes that the starting point of sensitivity training is to help the trainee gain better insight into himself. The training situation enables trainees to receive feedback on their behavior. An important aspect of understanding ourselves is learning to recognize the defenses we use to ward off real or

[23] *Ibid.,* 25–29.

imagined threats to our personal security. During the later stages of the training the trainee begins to recognize these blind spots.

Another important tool for understanding others is *insight*. Insight involves awareness of the group process, recognition of the culture of the group, and development of specific and identifiable behavioral skills. All interpersonal relations involve communication. Personnel policies, leadership styles, organizational values, and countless other variables create the organization's total personality, or the culture in which the organization's members operate.

Finally, Tannenbaum noted that sensitivity training is designed to enable the trainee to behave appropriately in light of both his past behavior and his newly developed understanding. As the participants put into practice their understanding of themselves and others, they learn how to effectively communicate, listen, inform, and evaluate within group settings.

OTHER THEORISTS

William C. Schutz has postulated two dimensions central to his theory of *group compatibility* which are similar to Bennis' two major concerns: authority relations and interdependence relations.[24] According to Schutz, group compatibility rests on orientations toward authority and orientations toward personal intimacy.

Wilfred R. Bion is another theorist whose ideas are complementary to Bennis' group-development theory.[25] Bion's concepts of *dependency* and *pairing modalities* correspond to Bennis' dependence and interdependence areas. Bion also acknowledged the dependence-flight modality, but he defined it in terms of modes of behavior, whereas Bennis used it to characterize the means used by the group for maintaining its orientation during a given subphase.

Kurt Back studied the development of T-groups from the point of view of the participation pattern ("who spoke to whom") and kind of interaction (work-oriented, positive-meaning, or negative-meaning).[26] Back concluded that the status struggles of the members and the influence of the trainer are important in the dynamics of group growth and development.

Margaret E. Barron and Gilbert K. Krulee observed that group growth seemed to follow a definite pattern from initially resisting the acceptance of responsibility and the mode of operation to gradually

[24] William C. Schutz, *FIRO: A Three-Dimensional Theory of Interpersonal Behavior.*

[25] Wilfred R. Bion, *Experiences in Groups, and Other Papers.*

[26] Kurt W. Back et al., *Social Pressures in Informal Groups: A Study of Human Factors in Housing.*

understanding and accepting the method of operation and, finally, to a period of well-organized and productive meetings. The period of resistance helps to focus the attention of the members on their behavior as it contributes to or hinders the functioning of the group.[27]

Leland P. Bradford defined group growth in a T-group as a cyclic process in which learning recurs.[28] The T-group approaches and re-approaches the same basic problems of relationships to authority, of social distance and interpersonal relationships, of goal formation, of decision making, of norm setting, and of communication. According to Bradford, growth lies not in ultimate solutions but in the readiness to face up to basic problems and in the improvement of methods by which the group approaches those problems. Bradford also wrote about authority problems and control problems which are important to group development.

Contradictory to Tannenbaum's theories about leadership, Robert R. Blake and Jane S. Mouton developed an "instrumented" T-group in which there is no trainer; the group steers and evaluates itself with the help of feedback from daily administered T-group scales.[29]

Saul Alinsky developed a model for building a community organization.[30] It corresponds almost exactly to the four modal concerns in group development identified by Jack Gibb. Whereas Gibb proposed acceptance, data flow, goal formation, and social control, Alinsky proposed entry, data collection, goal setting, and organizing.

Business organizations currently use several forms of T-groups in their training programs, including the following:

1. *Stranger labs*, which consist of executives from different companies and professions.

2. *Cousin labs*, which consist of individuals holding similar organizational rank.

3. *Diagonal slices labs*, which consist of members from the same company but of different ranks and departments.

4. *Family labs*, which consist of an entire work unit within an organization, for example, a supervisor and his subordinates.

Trainer-Intervention: Case Episodes[31]

LELAND P. BRADFORD

Group Cleavages. *Most T Groups, within three or four sessions, face a*

[27] See Bradford, Gibb, and Benne, *op. cit.*, 398.
[28] *Ibid.*, 1–2.
[29] Robert R. Blake and Jane S. Mouton, *The Managerial Grid: Key Orientations for Achieving Production through People*.
[30] Saul D. Alinsky, *Rules for Radicals*.
[31] By Leland P. Bradford. From Leland P. Bradford, Jack R. Gibb, and Kenneth E.

sharp cleavage. On one side are those members who have come to realize that group problems of communication, standard setting, and decision making will be solved, and that individuals will learn, only as the problems are squarely faced and action in the group is adequately explored and studied. On the other side are those individuals who, for a variety of reasons, are bothered or threatened by efforts to understand group action or individual behavior. This cleavage grows slowly, usually comes to a crisis, and is resolved sufficiently for the group to move ahead—although it is never solved for all members. Sometimes one or more members continue for days to try to keep the group on "safe" topics dealing with issues far away from the present experience of the group. The cleavage is seldom clear-cut, because so many different struggles and anxieties are part of it; and the crisis may occur and recur as different events help to shape the direction of the group.

In one T Group, composed entirely of industrial managers from a number of companies, the purposes and anxieties of three separate individuals—all differently motivated—combined after the second session both to highlight and to further complicate a cleavage in the group. The second session had witnessed more realistic discussion than had the opening session. Specific interpersonal problems emerged in the group, and some members showed evidence of wanting to dig into them. As a result, there were brief efforts to look at group process, interspersed with discussions on generalized topics.

The third session opened with comments by a few members who noted that they felt clearer about the purpose of the T Group. They had just listened to a theory session concerned with emotional patterns and group behavior, and they now felt that the task was to bring out on the table and discuss some of the emotional feelings of various group members so that the group could better understand its problem.

From the beginning, Don, an intense, eager, apparently anxious member, had rushed in with suggestions for group action. He had been the first to move on the opening day with a suggestion leading toward introductions. However, as the sessions continued, his interventions had decreased in relevancy to what was happening in the group. Most of his contributions were lengthy, and all of them dealt with some topic that was far from the group and usually rooted in some personal situation he faced in his work back home. His interventions came at times when the group was moving toward a decision—usually toward a decision to discuss behavior within the group. One member of the group asked Don directly why he always brought up something of his own

Benne, eds., *T-Group Theory and Laboratory Method: Innovation in Re-Education.* Copyright © 1964 by Leland P. Bradford, Jack R. Gibb, and Kenneth E. Benne. Reprinted by permission of John Wiley & Sons, Inc.

279

just when the group was beginning to discuss a group problem. Don hotly denied that he had deliberately done so. He said he had been sitting there, thinking both about the group and his own problems, and it seemed to him the questions he had in his own situation were ones that would interest and help the group. After all, he added, his company was sending him here to get something out of the program.

At this point, another member asked, "If you spend all the time bringing your problem in, how will the rest of us get any help on ours? It seems to me that we will get the most help as we figure out what we are doing here and how we can improve the situation."

A third member rushed in, however, to defend Don. "Everybody," he said, "must have the right to speak. If Don has something to say to the group, no matter what it is, we should all litsen to it. I, for one, think that Don's problems are very serious problems, and I would like to hear him talk about them at greater length."

Don took this as sanction to continue describing a particular back-home situation. His description continued for nearly five minutes. Attention in the group continued to fade, and restlessness became apparent.

After Don had finished his statement, one trainer commented on the growing lack of attention when individual back-home problems were discussed, as compared with the greater attention when present group problems were being discussed. At the same time, he added, a number of group members specifically stated that they did not wish to work on present group problems. The trainer indicated that this seemed to present a dilemma to the group.

At this point Bill re-entered the discussion. Bill had pushed for a designated leader from the beginning of the first session. He had said flatly that every group had to have a leader, that it was impossible to proceed without a leader, and that this group particularly needed one. He had then offered his services as leader. The fact that he so openly offered his own services shocked and somewhat embarrassed the group, and, while there was some movement to accept, his open bid died for lack of support.

Bill now said, in response to the trainer's intervention, that clearly the reason for all of the difficulty was the lack of an established agenda and a leader. There was no one to discipline group members and keep them from wandering from point to point.

A considerable number of voices rose in Bill's support, seemingly because the group was uncertain as to what to do about Don and was fearful of conflict. Bill urged that a leader be selected to choose a topic and to insist on everyone's following it. He again offered himself as leader.

At first there were a few statements, from those least fearful of exploring the causes of group difficulty, to the effect that they did not really feel the need for a leader. Movement of the group, however, toward naming a leader became apparent, and those who were unhappy about this merely stated that they had nothing against having a leader. They just wanted to get a few things (unspecified) clarified before they decided upon a leader.

Bill, sensing movement to his side, loudly demanded a vote. A few rapidly—others slowly—raised their hands, until eleven out of the twelve group members (not including the trainers) had voted. One individual did not vote. Bill immediately declared that a consensus had been reached and that he was the leader.

The member who had not voted said, "I didn't vote, and therefore there is no consensus. You're trying to railroad us." There was a sigh of relief from one member. It was as if the group, which had almost made a decision having many consequences, marched down the hill again.

There was expressed criticism of Bill for trying to override the group; there was also expressed criticism of the individual who had not voted. There was prolonged discussion as to wether such abstention was a vote against, and whether, in fact, Bill did not have consensus. This argument gradually faded.

One member accused the abstainer of blocking the group's will. One trainer asked whether the group had a will. Was this merely an assumption? How could the group tell whether it had a will? This precipitated a discussion which centered for a time on group decision making, on consensus, on conformity pressures, on tendencies for individuals not to say what they really felt.

Gradually the discussion turned back to the present issue and the abstainer was asked why he had abstained. He responded by saying that while he was not really against a leader, he felt the group had not thoroughly thought through what the leader would do, and he was uncertain whether the leader should select the topic for the group or, in fact, whether the group should have a topic at all. He said that he personally was enjoying the discussion, did not consider it a random one, and felt that the group was getting somewhere, particularly when it tried to understand feelings and when it felt able to talk openly about what various members of the group had done. He said, for example, that he felt that Don was using the group for his own purposes, irrespective of what other members wanted. Group members were letting him get away with it because they were afraid to tackle the situation. They did not know exactly what to do.

It was at this point that Harry came into the discussion. By far the biggest man in the group and with the loudest voice, Harry had not participated much during the preceding sessions. When he did participate, his blooming voice and aggressive body action stopped the group in its tracks. Already two or three members were agreeing with Harry even when their agreement reversed previous statements they had made. They seemed to be traumatized by Harry's overpowering masculinity.

In this instance, Harry said he was astonished and shocked by what was happening. This was worse than brainwashing. It clearly was an invasion of privacy. People had no right to speak to other people in the way that they had spoken to Don. He, for one, was not going to permit this kind of behavior. Definite lines should be established in the group as to what should be discussed, and these should certainly exclude any discussion of individuals or what they did.

A number of people agreed, including some who had been most interested in discussing the here-and-now feelings and behavior of the group.

One of the trainers raised the question as to whether Harry was setting standards for the group and whether the group sanctioned it. Some members of the group said it was all right for Harry to set these boundaries for the group because it was good for them. Others were less certain. They seemed to be on the horns of a dilema. On the one hand, as one of them put it, he did not come here just to talk about somebody else's work situation. He was interested in exploring what was actually happening in the group. On the other hand, he did not want to see anyone hurt. (The assumption seemed to be building that Don had been deeply hurt.) So, perhaps Harry was right.

The issues became more clearly joined. What should be the area of discussion of the group? Should topics suggested by various members be discussed? Someone suggested that each member contribute a topic on a piece of paper, that they elect Bill chairman, and that he arrange the topics in the order to be discussed.

Another person suggested that Harry be appointed leader. Harry said he preferred to sit back for a while.

Even against the rather devastating force of Harry's behavior, a couple of members kept alive the desirability of trying to understand the struggles they were having. When was it right to talk about the group? How could they talk about the group without talking about members in the group? Was this really brainwashing?

Thus the cleavage between those who wanted assigned topics and those who were interested in exploring behavior deepened and widned. The cleavage was further complicated by a variety of issues of personal concern. It was at this point that the group session came to an indecisive and frustrating conclusion.

Trainer Analysis. *In the clinic meeting of the two trainers there was much to be discussed. What were the forces operating in the group? It was clear that the group was slowly—and with much back-tracking—working toward facing some of its major problems. Could the group, as a group, tolerate sufficient ambiguity and lack of structure to tackle fundamental problms of group building? Or would the anxiety and need for clear structure among some members keep the group in flight to safe discussions of generalized topics or vaguely described situations back home? If the group moved, would it find ways of moving effectively? Here, the trainers saw the need for carefully timed modeling on their part to aid the group in moving. Could they find the right time to point up a group-process problem which the group was studiously ignoring, describe the group behavior symptomatic of the problem, and discuss calmly some of the emotional content of the issues?*

A second major problem facing the group was that of membership. How could the group help various individuals to decide to take out membership in the group? Again, the trainers wondered whether, if they identified the problem of developing open pathways to membership, the group would be able to use these pathways on its own. The trainers saw these basic problems further complicated by the actions and anxieties of three individuals—Don, Bill, and Harry. They discussed each along the following lines.

Don seemed anxious about his place and influence in the group, but more worried about his typical relations to people and fearful that the group discussion might reach his own actions. As a consequence, he seemed to alternate between periods of withdrawal and periods of monopolizing the group's time in an effort to keep it from focusing on an individual or group problem. His anxiety was communicated to the group and left members uncertain as to how to relate to him and to his contradictory behavior. On the one hand, he invoked a standard of fairness in letting a person talk when he had something to say. On the other, he admitted trying to induce the group to do what he wanted it to do and to pay attention to him. The group members were caught between concern for his anxiety and hostility because of his manipulation.

Bill presented a different problem. On the surface he showed none of Don's anxieties. Although he seemed concerned for the group, he seemed rigid in his belief that the group needed a designated leader and a set agenda and that he could provide the leadership. Was Bill fearful of a discussion of emotional, interpersonal, and intragroup problems, or was he merely uncomfortable with lack of structure, or did he wish to control the group? Was he reacting to past patterns of behavior, or was there a deeper anxiety? The trainers were inclined to

283

believe the latter. At all events, his calmness, assurance, and seeming stability actually served to keep the group uncertain about its own direction.

Harry presented a third force. While he was the most masculine and aggressive member of the group in outward behavior and dominated it with his physical proportions and his tone of voice, his behavior indicated to the trainers his own very definite anxieties about discussing personal feelings, even though he took the position of protecting weaker members in the group. His protective efforts actually created more anxiety and a greater tendency on their part to submit to his edicts. The trainers discussed what they could and should do to help Harry become able to bring out on the surface and talk about his anxieties about closeness or intimacy, about others' perceptions of himself and particularly about his own feelings of inadequacy. At the same time, the trainers discussed what they could do to help the group gain strength, both as individuals and as a group, to withstand Harry's efforts to control them. Tackling Harry immediately themselves would polarize the group, create fears in the group as to the outcome, increase dependency. At the same time, the situation would have to be faced if not by the group alone, then by the trainers. The trainers agreed that their first efforts should be to keep the issue on the table. The group might free itself from undue influence by Harry, but still invite Harry into membership. Later, if they were to tackle Harry directly, as was very probable, it should be in terms of later reacting as a group member, with the intention of helping Harry be aware of what he was doing to the group. Before proceeding further, they examined in some detail three interventions they had made.

The first came after Don's long monologue. At this point, one trainer referred to the dilemma evidenced by the lack of attention to there-and-then discussions but, at the same time, the expressed desire to keep away from the here-and-now. The trainer had tried to couch the intervention in such a way as to draw attention to the behavior in the group, and not only to Don. He had also tried to focus group attention on the decision as to whether to discuss back-home situations or here-and-now behavior.

The trainers felt that the intervention did open the issue, but that Bill had tried to close it again. They realized that in some eyes, especially Harry's, the intervention struck too close to Don and, by implication, to him. They expected this intervention to be referred to a number of times, particularly as a horrible example of how someone could be hurt. They discussed other interventions that might have been made. One less direct intervention might have been to ask whether the group wished to analyze what had happened to the group and within members over the incident.

The second intervention was made toward the end of the discussion on leadership and after the vote had been taken. One of the trainers had asked the group to what extent a leader, if they had selected one, would have been able to solve all of the group's problems. Was a leader a crutch upon which the group could lean? Did they need a crutch?

This intervention had aroused some discussion within the group. Those who did not particularly want a leader had been encouraged to speak up. Those who did became defensive. The trainers understood that the intervention appeared to place them on the side of some people and against others, even though the intervention was directed toward a group problem. They knew, however, that interventions will frequently be interpreted as supporting one faction or another, but that issues change as well as adherents. They held firmly to the realization of their responsibility to help create a learning group and to aid individual learning. Therefore, they should continuously stress the desirability of questioning the behavior in the group.

The third intervention raised the question as to whether Harry was setting standards for the group and where his sanction had come from. This seemed, to the trainers, a crucial point. Standards imposed by one strong person can immobilize the group. Whether or not the group would be able to face the important issue of how standards are set, it seemed important that the question be raised. The intervention produced no immediate effect, but the trainers felt that it would be picked up later in the group.

The trainers then considered the dilemmas facing the group and the movements which should occur if the group were to grow and if individual learning were to take place.

Certainly it would be a loss to the group and a prevention of learning if Harry succeeded in building strong boundaries around the group and kept it from analyzing its own process. While the group could ultimately accept leadership which was sensitive to the group's needs, Bill's present assumption as to how the leader should behave would prevent the group from moving into an analysis of its own problems. It seemed necessary to have Bill examine with the group why he sought leadership so strongly. The trainers talked about appropriate timing and ways of opening up the issue with Bill.

Don's anxieties about himself and his tendencies to manipulate the group might well block the group if members did not learn how to help Don become a more effective member. This would not be easy to do. Efforts to help Don to look at his anxieties would be very threatening to him. Don would need much tolerance and patience, but not sanction to block the group. The trainers felt that Don needed emotional support to join the group, but not sanction to manipulate the group.

Harry presented still a third problem. Until the group members could gain courage to face Harry, he could not be helped. The trainers faced a difficult task.

Clearly, the issue of there-and-then and here-and-now discussion had to be seen by the group and some of the confusions surrounding it removed. The group needed to see that discussing the process of the group itself was not brainwashing or too great an invasion of privacy. Only as the group did analyze its own process and the behavior of its members, including the trainers (public property, because the behavior was present for everybody to see), could the group develop and much learning take place.

The trainers felt that forces in the group would move toward facing this problem. They were prepared, however, to intervene where necessary, to keep the issue clarified in the group and open for group solution.

SUMMARY

Learning occurs in a T-group when from an initial vacuum there develops a functioning group which then begins actively to explore interpersonal relations and group issues. Thus the question of how a T-group develops and functions is of great practical and theoretical interest in understanding its potential for improving human relations. Gibb's and Bennis' theories of group development are significant in aiding one's understanding of T-group functioning. Equally important is Tannenbaum's assessment of the role of the T-group leader.

The T-group has great potential for initiating planned change, but it also has drawbacks. Important in the concept of T-group training is the opportunity it affords individuals to experiment with ways of behaving. A T-group situation allows individuals to try out forms of behavior in a situation which is purely experimental. Not only can one learn about his own motives, feelings, and strategies in dealing with other persons, but also he may learn of the reactions he produces in others as he interacts with them.

The T-group is advantageous because the most significant learning comes from peer members rather than from a teacher. The method affords each individual the opportunity to learn about groups, their processes, and leadership and membership skills, as well as means for changing and improving social situations. It is hoped that participants will be able to transfer behavior and actions beyond the T-group setting.

Despite evidence to the contrary, some critics of the T-group charge that the learned behavior in the T-group setting does not transfer to the outer cultural milieu. And since T-group trainers are in short supply, the entire human-potential movement has been criticized for this shortage.

W. Cleon Skousen and others denounce T-groups under the assumption that such groups exist for the purposes of understanding and manipulating behavior in such a way they fail to consider the concept of free will. Skousen contends that since T-groups act on the premise that all behavior is determined by inheritance and environment that such groups are anti-Christian in nature: ". . . so much of sensitivity training is devoted to challenging and discrediting the Judaic-Christian value-system of any who may participate in a T-Group. At the base of this sensitivity training technique lies an ideological war against the entire warp and woof of American culture."[32]

Perhaps the most damaging criticism leveled at T-groups is that frequently they fail to provide learning that is transferable from the group to the "real" world. Opponents charge that training programs make an attempt to increase egalitarian democracy in business without regard for the realities of business life. John E. Drotning cautioned:

Laboratory training may be a tremendous behavioral tool, but it may also be totally inappropriate for many of its present applications. Does it make sense to think that a large firm can be turned into one "big happy family" by means of laboratory training? Managers must manage; they must hand out both rewards and punishments, and the possibility of handing out punishment is a strong barrier to open, frank, and trusting interaction between superiors and subordinates.[33]

He added that sensitivity implies open and democratic management which is involved with self-actualization, when in reality only those people who want to get ahead are concerned with becoming self-actualized—and they are in the minority.

Another concern is that participants in the T-groups are stripped of their "back-home" titles and roles so that they can deal with the prejudices attached to their roles, social system, and occupations. Some writers suggest that ignoring back-home situations is not the way to deal with them and further suggest: "If one desires to use the assigned names exercise, why not do it for a few days, return to real names, and see whether group members revert to previously held prejudices?"

[32] W. Cleon Skousen, "Chief, Watch Out for those T-Group Promoters!" in Golembiewski and Blumberg, *op. cit.*, 256.

[33] John E. Drotning, "Sensitivity Training: Some Critical Questions," *Personnel Journal*, Vol. 45 (November, 1966), 604.

Other critics comment on the need for further research and the scant evidence that sensitivity training changes behavior back on the job. Still others believe that in the absence of research evidence which demonstrates that sensitivity training changes behavior, one is left with nothing but anecdotal evidence and examples drawn from experience, and certainly any number of people qualify as judges in this sense.[34]

Max Birnbaum, a colleague of Bennis, acknowledged faults in T-group training but, instead of disavowing the effective characteristics of T-groups, suggested only that in certain situations laboratory training would be a waste of time and money.[35] For example, when morale is poor in a school system because decisions are handled in an authoritarian manner, effort would be better invested in ridding the system of the superintendent instead of subjecting the entire staff to training. Birnbaum stated that large-scale training of teachers under a superintendent's sponsorship would create intolerable pressures on a principal who is fearful and unsure of his position and who has always run a "tight ship." Birnbaum further commented that T-group training has tremendous validity for school people as long as it takes place in a setting in which individuals can be relatively anonymous. But trouble comes when it takes place in a school system where participants are co-workers. In this case resistance is heightened and the revelation of highly charged intimate personal information makes continuing work relationships extremely difficult.

Another criticism of T-groups concerns tension or pressures within the groups and the resulting consequences. The groups are often accused of invasion of privacy. Odiorne, writing about extremely sensitive individuals, described the T-group as a "great psychological nudist camp in which he bares his pale sensitive soul to the hard-nosed autocratic ruffians where he gets roundly clobbered. He goes away with his sense of inferiority indelibly reinforced."[36] T-group members are encouraged to be open about their feelings of hostility, anxiety, sadness, happiness, and so on. Although this may be freeing and exhilarating for some, others are not able to stand the pressures that encourage this exposure of self. Trainers must not let their groups become therapy groups, Odiorne cautions.

Still another criticism of T-group sessions is that they are in essence group-therapy sessions guided by unqualified persons. Of course, the difference between the training group and the therapy group is one of

---

[34] See George S. Odiorne, "The Trouble with Sensitivity Training," in Golembiewski and Blumberg, *op. cit.*, 277.

[35] Max Birnbaum, "Sense and Nonsense About Sensitivity Training," *Saturday Review*, Vol. 52 (November 15, 1969), 82–83.

[36] Odiorne, *op. cit.*, 282.

emphasis. In Skousen's view group therapy emphasizes the strengthening of convictions and attitudes, while sensitivity training serves the purpose of manipulating, altering, or destroying attitudes.[37] Many critics believe that T-group leaders are usurping the role of psychiatrists. When conducted by well-trained leaders, this does not happen.

Lack of screening of group members is another area of criticism. In many instances the only qualification for membership is an individual's connection with or employment by a company or system. Seldom is there a selection process other than self-selection, which results in an occasional psychotic break after exposure to the intense group pressure. Odiorne commented that the ability to pay the registration fee is the prime requisite for membership and that too many participants are emotionally unprepared for sensitivity training. Psychiatrists Steven L. Joffe and Donald J. Scherl described several cases of acute psychosis which were precipitated by T-group experiences. They were convinced that none of these individuals should have been admitted to T-groups.[38]

Another charge often heard is that "anyone can be a trainer." Louis A. Gottschalk became a member of a two-week T-group session in the Human Relations Laboratory at Bethel, Maine, and wrote about his experiences as a psychiatrist would view them.[39] He found the trainers in his group inconsistent in their ideas and haphazard in their actions. He felt that they were neither professionally nor emotionally equipped to handle the psychological dynamics that arose in their groups. He was convinced that they did not have sufficient professional training to allow them to separate their own anxieties and projections from the feelings and reactions of the participants.

Two kinds of sensitivity training are particularly susceptible today to exploitation by the enthusiastic amateur or the enterprising entrepreneur. They are conducted in the areas of sexual experience and sexual identity. Although each requires a minimum of knowledge to stimulate a response by members, in each case a knowledgeable professional is needed to induce a positive educational outcome. Some critics sarcastically conclude that anyone can become a trainer by collecting a small bag of easily learned exercises and buying several records.

A final criticism is that too many trainers achieve their "qualifications" by participating in groups until they feel that they have acquired enough information and skills to act as leaders.

[37] Skousen, *op. cit.*, 254.
[38] Steven L. Joffe and Donald J. Scherl, "Acute Psychosis Precipitated by T-Group Experiences," *Archives of General Psychiatry*, Vol. 21 (1969), 443.
[39] Louis A. Gotschalk, "Psychoanalytic Notes on T-Groups at the Human Relations Laboratory, Bethel, Maine," *Comprehensive Psychiatry*, Vol. 7 (December, 1966), 472–87.

The charges by the critics are both just and unjust. When one considers that T-groups possess potentials as both vehicles for growth and weapons for destruction, surely some guidelines are in order. Joffe and Scherl offer the following suggestions:

1. Participation should be completely and truly voluntary.
2. Participation should be based on informed consent with respect to purposes and goals.
3. Participants should be screened at least by questionnaire and preferably by interview.
4. Participants should understand what types of behavior are permissible during the T-group.
5. Follow-up for all participants should be available to help deal with group termination.[40]

All trainers should undergo thorough professional training, including a supervised internship, and should meet certain standards. NTL and other groups are presently considering standards for certification. There is little doubt that more professionalization is needed in human relations so that the public will recognize T-groups and other methods of training as reliable and profitable experiences.

Several factors affect the trainer's roles and also some of the multiple roles of the trainees. The purposes and design of the training program will determine the way a trainer carries out his role. This, of course, affects the over-all purposes of the training program, of which the laboratory method may be only a part. Next, the length of a training program is important. A two- or three-day program means that the trainer has to provide more structure than he does for a two- to three-week program. Group composition will also determine how the trainer should behave in a group. Sex distribution, age, occupations, and race are but a few of the characteristics that should be considered in designing a program.

If the group is knowledgeable about certain aspects of the training sessions, repetition might be counterproductive. Knowing the expectations of the participants would avoid many failures encountered when participants expect much more than the trainers are prepared to facilitate. Too, the expectations of the trainers should be considered. If too much is expected, or too little, anxiety on the part of both the trainer and the trainees is likely to result.

Despite the flaws in the methods, T-groups offer much assistance to persons trying to resolve conditions of alienation. Essential in applying T-group methods to current problems in human relations is the fact that since they focus on feelings, values, attitudes, perceptions, and

[40] Joffe and Scherl, *loc. cit.*

skills within the individual, they offer great possibilities for improving interpersonal relations.

Chapter 10
SUGGESTED READING

Alinsky, Saul D. *Rules for Radicals.* New York, Random House, Inc., 1971.
Back, Kurt W. *Beyond Words: The Story of Sensitivity Training and the Encounter Movement.* New York, Russell Sage Foundation, 1972.
Back, Kurt W., et al. *Social Pressures in Informal Groups: A Study of Human Factors in Housing.* New York, Harper & Row, Publishers, Inc., 1950.
Bennis, Warren G., Kenneth D. Benne, and Robert Chin, eds. *The Planning of Change.* New York, Holt, Rinehart & Winston, Inc., 1969.
Bion, Wilfred R. *Experiences in Groups, and Other Papers.* New York, Basic Books, Inc., 1961.
Birnbaum, Max. "Sense and Non Sense About Sensitivity Training," *Saturday Review,* Vol. 52 (November 15, 1969).
Blake, Robert R., and Jane S. Mouton. *Group Dynamics: Key to Decision Making.* Houston, Gulf Publishing Company, 1961.
Bradford, Leland P., Jack R. Gibb, and Kenneth D. Benne, eds. *T-Group Theory and Laboratory Method: Innovation in Re-Education.* New York, John Wiley & Sons, Inc., 1967.
Burton, Arthur, ed. *Encounter: Theory and Practice of Encounter Groups.* San Francisco, Jossey-Bass, Inc., 1969.
Cooper, Cary L., and I. L. Mangham. *T-Groups: A Survey of Research.* New York, John Wiley & Sons, Inc., Interscience Press, 1971.
Drotning, John E. "Sensitivity Training: Some Critical Questions," *Personnel Journal,* Vol. 45 (November, 1966).
Golembiewski, and Arthur Blumberg, eds. *Sensitivity Training and the Laboratory Approach.* Itasca, Ill., F. E. Peacock Publishers, Inc., 1970.
Gordon, T. *Group-Centered Leadership.* Boston, Houghton Mifflin Company, 1955.
Gorman, A. H. *The Leader in the Group.* New York, Teachers College Press, Columbia University, 1963.
Gottschalk, Louis A. "Psychoanalytic Notes on T-Groups at the Human Relations Laboratory, Bethel, Maine," *Comprehensive Psychiatry,* Vol. 7 (December, 1966).
Harrison, Roger. "Group Composition Models for Laboratory Design," *Journal of Applied Behavioral Science,* Vol. 1 (1965).
Horwitz, Leonard. "Transference in Training Groups and Therapy Groups," *The International Journal of Group Psychotherapy,* Vol. 14 (1964).
Howard, Jane. *Please Touch: A Guided Tour of the Human Potential Movement.* New York, McGraw-Hill Book Company, 1970.
Joffe, Steven L., and Donald J. Scherl. "Acute Psychosis Precipitated by T-Group Experiences," *Archives of General Psychiatry,* Vol. 21 (1969).

Lewin, Kurt. *Field Theory in Social Science*. New York, Harper & Row, Publishers, Inc., 1961.

———. *Principles of Topological Psychology*. New York, McGraw-Hill Book Company, 1936.

———. *Resolving Social Conflict*. New York, Harper & Row, Publishers, Inc., 1948.

Lifton, Walter M. *Working with Groups: Group Process and Individual Growth*. New York, John Wiley & Sons, Inc., 1962.

Luft, Joseph. *Group Processes: An Introduction to Group Dynamics*, 2d ed. Palo Alto, National Press Books, 1970.

Mann, Richard D. *Interpersonal Styles and Group Development*. New York, John Wiley & Sons, Inc., 1967.

Mill, Cyril R., ed. *Selections from Human Relations Training News*. Washington, D.C., National Training Laboratories Institute for Applied Behavioral Sciences, 1969.

Pfeiffer, J. William, and John E. Jones. *Handbook of Structured Experiences for Human Relations Training*, Vols. I, II, III. Iowa City, Iowa, University Associates Press, 1969, 1970, 1971.

——— and ———, eds. *The 1972 Annual Handbook for Group Facilitators*. Iowa City, Iowa, University Associates Press, 1972.

——— and ———, eds. *The 1973 Annual Handbook for Group Facilitators*. Iowa City, Iowa, University Associates Press, 1973.

Schutz, William C. *FIRO: A Three-Dimensional Theory of Interpersonal Behavior*. New York, Holt, Rinehart & Winston, Inc., 1958.

Tannenbaum, Robert, Irving R. Weschler, and Fred Massarik, eds. *Leadership and Organization: A Behavioral Science Approach*. New York, McGraw-Hill Book Company, 1961.

Thelen, Herbert A. *Dynamics of Groups at Work*. Chicago, The University of Chicago Press, 1967.

Weschler, Irving R., and Jerome Reisel. *Inside a Sensitivity Training Group*. Los Angeles, University of California Institute of Industrial Relations, 1960.

Curiously enough, the first expression of genuinely significant "here and now" feeling is apt to come out in negative attitudes toward other group members or the group leader.—CARL R. ROGERS

The year 1962 signaled the turning point in the development of the encounter-group movement. In that year Michael Murphy, a thirty-year-old graduate in psychology from Stanford University, and his brother inherited 150 acres of land in the Big Sur region of California. Murphy had visited India and the Far East in order to study Eastern religions and forms of meditation in the hope of finding viable approaches to personal growth. In 1962, with the assistance of his Stanford roommate, Richard Price, Murphy founded the Esalen Institute— "a forum to bring together a wide variety of approaches toward the enhancement of the human potential."[1] Murphy has described Esalen in the following manner: "Our primary concern is the affective domain —the senses and feelings, although we certainly are interested in the cognitive. . . . We hope to educate people . . . in what Aldous Huxley called the 'non-verbal humanities'—long neglected in our culture because of the heavy emphasis which is placed on the verbal-rational aspect of man."[2]

The Esalen Institute was founded on the principles of humanism— that is, a way of life centering on the dignity and worth of human beings and their capacity for self-realization. Since no particular dogma is espoused other than that of individuality, Esalen has been able to attract participants from every field, including behavioral psychologists, psychotherapists, historians, Zen scholars, Hindu mystics, and teachers of many backgrounds and in many areas.

[1] *Esalen Newsletter*, 1968, 1.
[2] Michael Murphy, "Esalen: Where It's At," *Psychology Today*, Vol. 1 (December, 1967), 35.

293

Esalen is a personal-growth center where participants can experiment with new behavior and where they can encounter and experience themselves and others. Esalen is not a training institute like NTL but an educational institute which focuses on the human side of the individual. Thus, primary focus of Esalen's encounter groups is on feelings rather than on thoughts and on the interpersonal relationships that can form the basis for action and dialogue as well as learning.

As a lecturer at Esalen, Frederick Perls was instrumental in popularizing the encounter movement. Perls, the founder of Gestalt therapy, was convinced that people are out of touch with their feelings because of societal pressure to develop their intellect. Only a balanced person, Gestalt therapists conclude, has the capacity to experience life intellectually, emotionally, and sensorially.

By expanding their awareness in the "here-and-now," Perls helped his clients assume responsibility for themselves and accept themselves more fully. Encounter groups have adopted many Gestalt methods. Partly because of Perls's charisma and partly because of his techniques, Gestalt therapy is now an integral part of encounter-group activities.

Virginia Satir has also helped shape the goals of Esalen. Her major emphases have been on the goals of heightened individual self-esteem, improved communication, interpersonal understanding, and methods of developing potentials for new growth in any relationship. Nonverbal communications, role playing, and expression in art are but a few of the techniques she has utilized.

In the following pages are discussed the contributions of Michael Murphy, William C. Schutz, Carl R. Rogers, Martin Buber, Sidney M. Jourard, Erich Fromm, and Ronald D. Laing to the development of encounter-group theories and practices. Their humanistic philosophy of valuing individual growth is a basic tenet of all encounter groups.

MICHAEL MURPHY (1930–)

Michael Murphy's contribution to the encounter-group movement can be described not as a theory but as a collection of philosophies. While he cannot be tied to a particular philosophy or dogma, his influence was instrumental in developing the humanistic concept that is unique to the Esalen Institute.

Murphy has stated that Esalen will always be "willing to explore any approach which will extend the abilities of man. Esalen refuses to subscribe to any dogma—in philosophy, in psychology, or in religion—and for our seminars and encounter groups we bring in leaders from every field to contribute their own approach to the precarious conditions of being human."[3] This is a very important concept, for Murphy

[3] *Ibid.*, p. 34.

adheres to the philosophy that man transcends conceptualized ideas of existence.

Murphy recognizes the risks inherent in establishing an organization such as Esalen. Today Esalen is controversial; members from some disciplines call it an institute for fakery, while others call it the most important educational institute in the world. Because such individuals as Perls, William C. Schutz (a pioneer in the field of expanding of human awareness, discussed below), and Bernard Gunther (founder of the technique of "sensory awakening") have been associated with Esalen, it is frequently called the center of the human-potential movement.

Murphy and Price are to be credited with great foresight and vision in establishing an institute where creative efforts can be brought to bear in developing new methods of personal and interpersonal relations. The Esalen Institute has given rise to scores of other institutes with similar objectives. It has also done much to synthesize the thinking of social scientists throughout the world by developing programs in conjunction with human-potential institutes in other countries, among them Tavistock Clinic in London and Shalal in Vancouver, British Columbia.

WILLIAM C. SCHUTZ (1925–   )

William C. Schutz is primarily concerned with the potential that he believes we all have to become self-fulfilling human beings. Schutz's Fundamental Interpersonal Relations Orientation (FIRO) theory defines the ways in which people need other people. According to Schutz, every individual has three interpersonal or social needs: inclusion, control, and affection:

Inclusion *refers to the need to be with people and to be alone. The effort in inclusion is to have enough contact to avoid loneliness and enjoy people; enough aloneness to avoid enmeshment and enjoy solitude. The fully realized man can feel comfortable and joyful both with and without people, and knows with how much of each—and when— he functions best.*

In the area of control *the effort is to achieve enough influence so that a man can determine his future to the degree that he finds most comfortable, and to relinquish enough control so that he is able to lean on others to teach, guide, support, and at times to take some responsibility from him. The fully realized man is capable of either leading or following as appropriate, and of knowing where he personally feels most comfortable.*

In affection *the effort is to avoid being engulfed in emotional en-*

295

tanglement (not being free to relate without a deep involvement), but also to avoid having too little affection and a bleak, sterile life without love, warmth, tenderness, and someone to confide in. The fully realized man is aware of his needs, and functions effectively not only in close, emotionally involving situations, but also in those of lesser intensity. As in the other two areas, he is able to give and take, comfortably and joyfully. This approach to the human potential shall be called Interpersonal Relations.[4]

Schutz believes that the underlying philosophy of the human-potential thrust encompasses *openness* and *honesty*. In this respect he complements Sidney Jourard's theory of self-disclosure. Schutz has also emphasized that in order to maintain healthy minds people should develop and maintain healthy bodies, for, if a body is healthy, it can be directed toward full personal functioning. Society and culture must support and enhance each individual's attempts to become fully self-realized:

Fulfillment brings to an individual the feeling that he can cope with his environment; the sense of confidence in himself as a significant, competent, lovable person who is capable of handling situations as they arise, able to use fully his own capacities, and free to express his feelings. Joy requires a vital, alive body, self-contentment, productive and satisfying relations with others and a successful relation to society.[5]

Schutz called the attempts of various investigators to arrive at theories and methods for developing personal growth the *human-potential movement*:

The underlying philosophy behind the human-potential thrust is that of openness and honesty. A man must be willing to let himself be known to himself and to others. He must express and explore his feelings and open up areas long dormant and possibly painful, with the faith that in the long run the pain will give way to a release of vast potential for creativity and joy. This is an exhilarating and frightening prospect, one which is often accompanied by agony, but which usually leads to ecstasy.[6]

In summary, the fully realized person will acquire a finely tuned body and mind, both developed to their full potential. The fully realized person will be able to relate positively to others and thereby achieve joy.

[4] William C. Schutz, *Joy: Expanding Human Awareness*, 19.

[5] *Ibid.*, 15.

[6] *Ibid.*, 16–17.

CARL R. ROGERS (1902–)

Rogers drew heavily upon his experiences with thousands of clients. In his speech to the Student Union Forum Committee in Wisconsin in 1960 he provided a summary of what he learned from his relationships with his clients. The speech, entitled "This is Me," can be found in Rogers' *On Becoming a Person: A Therapist's View of Psychotherapy.* In this book Rogers shares some personal learnings which focus upon his own lifelong attempt to understand himself and others. His search for self is the common denominator of all the humanists.

Rogers believes that a humanist would find it of enormous value to permit himself to understand another person. This comment points up the fact that we tend to evaluate other persons rather than to understand them. With great joy he wrote: "I have found it highly rewarding when I can accept another person."[7] Accepting another person means taking what you do not like along with what you do like—taking him as he is. In another passage Rogers observed: "In my relationships with persons I have found that it does not help, in the long run, to act as though I were something that I am not."[8] In other words, if, in interaction, one person does not relate his real feelings and thoughts to another person, the relationship is limited in direct proportion to the extent that a façade is maintained.

In the foreword to *Person to Person: The Problems of Being Human,* Rogers wrote, "The assumption is that the subjective human being has an importance and a value which is basic: that no matter how he may be labeled or evaluated he is a human person first of all, and most deeply."[9]

Rogers' philosophy stresses an existential orientation in which man chooses his fate. In all his writings Rogers stresses the value of the individual. This internal process of valuing is dynamic, not static, and it recognizes that the worth of living is in the process of living, not in some static goal to be reached. Like other existential psychologists, Rogers believes that the basis for a healthy personality is healthy interpersonal relations. To facilitate the personal-growth process, Rogers lists three prerequisites for a meaningful relationship: (1) *genuineness*—being aware of one's own feelings, or being that which one truly is, (2) *acceptance of others*, including unconditional positive regard of them, and (3) *understanding others*—being empathetic.

Rogers describes seven stages in the positive process of "becoming," ranging from an unwillingness to communicate with oneself to a com-

[7] Carl R. Rogers, *On Becoming a Person: A Therapist's View of Psychotherapy,* 20.

[8] *Ibid.,* 16.

[9] Carl R. Rogers and Barry Stevens, *Person to Person: The Problem of Being Human; A New Trend in Psychology,* 2.

plete self-trust and awareness of one's own feelings. Becoming is a direction, not a goal; it is an autonomous, self-directed movement: "The way to do is to be."[10]

It must be noted that the central theme of Rogers' philosophy is individualism. Each person is challenged to question his purpose in life and his identity. He is also challenged to seek answers to such questions so that he can fulfill his purpose and identity, as he defines them.

Rogers' client-centered therapy and/or helping relationship has at its base the theory that the purpose is to facilitate the client's ability to define himself ("get in touch with himself") and to act in accordance with that definition. The major goal of psychotherapy was summed up by Rogers in a quotation attributed to Sören Kierkegaard: "To be that self which one truly is."[11] If this goal is to be achieved, the client must be allowed to function freely; thus attainment of self-identity enables one to live in satisfaction with himself.

Rogers suggested that the following changes should occur in therapy as the person moves toward what he is: he (1) moves away from façades, (2) moves away from "oughts," (3) moves away from expectations, that is, expectations of others, (4) moves away from pleasing others, (5) moves toward autonomy, or self-direction, (6) moves toward being a "process"—that is, a flowing (growing) being, (7) moves toward complexity, or being all of what he is in each moment, (8) moves to an openness to, and even welcoming of, experience, (9) moves toward accepting others, and (10) trusts himself. The obvious repetition of the word "moves" emphasizes the point that the direction—the process of growth—is as much valued by Rogers as the goal itself.[12]

According to Rogers, the end of therapy is awareness. The person adds to common experience the full and undistorted awareness of his experiencing—of his neural and psychological reactions. In awareness he ceases, or at least minimizes, the distortions of experience:

In this sense he becomes for the first time the full potential of the human organism, with the enriching element of awareness freely added to the basic aspect of sensory and visceral reaction. The person comes to be what he is, as clients so frequently say in therapy. What this seems to mean is that the individual comes to be—in awareness— what he is—in experience. He is, in other words, a complete and fully functioning human organism.[13]

[10] Rogers, *On Becoming a Person*, 164.
[11] *Ibid.*, 166.
[12] *Ibid.*, 167–76.
[13] *Ibid.*, 104.

MARTIN BUBER (1878–1965)

Many writers have speculated that the principal reason for Buber's commitment to humanism is the fact that he escaped the Nazi regime in Germany. He studied philosophy and art history at the universities of Vienna, Leipzig, Berlin, and Zurich. No doubt this is another of the reasons for Buber's espousal of humanism, but it is also important to note that Buber was a Zionist and a religious Hasidic; these influences caused him to seek a oneness with his environment and with God. Technically, he was an existential philosopher who espoused humanistic values that have great importance for encounter-group behavior.

Buber's primary concern was with the human being. He looked for an understanding of human beings in and through the limitations of everyday existence. What appears to make Buber unique as a humanist is that he tried to live his philosophy. His life gave meaning to his understanding of the nature of human existence and its relationship to God. In fact, in all his works Buber stressed commitment to God—the eternal Thou.[14]

In his book *I and Thou* Buber focused on the area of relationship—man to man and man to aspects of his world. For Buber human existence is both personal and impersonal in nature. The personal is embedded in the I-Thou reality, which in turn enables one to experience unity with all of creation. The I-It reality is exploiting—with the result that one becomes alienated from others.[15]

The I-Thou relationship involves risk taking, since no part of the self is withheld. The I-Thou relationship also involves true listening. The Thou cannot be addressed in a limited fashion but must be encountered in all its dimensions.

In the I-It relationship one person relates to another with only part of himself, basing the relationship on objective knowledge and not allowing for personal spontaneity; the part of himself that remains outside the relationship cannot be injured by the other person because the other person cannot reach it—the relationship lacks mutuality. This is the way most people learn to relate to one another, and as a result they become programmed to act in the I-It mode.

In Buber's view man becomes human and life is made important only through the I-Thou relationship. However, the I-Thou relationship must evolve freely and cannot be attained through "trying." It must be spontaneous, otherwise it will not truly be an I-Thou relationship. This philosophy emphasizes the importance of confirmation—acceptance of the potentiality of the other. The keystone of Buber's

---

[14] Martin Buber, *I and Thou*, 11.

[15] See Will Herberg, ed., *The Writings of Martin Buber*.

philosophy is that real living is an encounter and that there is significance in every encounter:

*Man's threefold living relation is, first, his relation to the world and
to things, second, his relation to men—both to individuals and to the
many—third, his relation to the mystery of being—which is dimly apparent through all this but infinitely transcends it—which the philosopher calls the Absolute and the believer calls God, and which cannot in
fact be eliminated from the situation even by a man who rejects both
designations.*[16]

Buber concluded that man's dialogue brings him into the "between
man and man" relationship, as well as into the "between man and God"
relationship. In the latter meeting man becomes and transcends himself; human life touches upon absoluteness and acquires absolute
meaning that surpasses its own conditioned nature.

Warning against the "thingification" of men and the world involved
in I-It, Buber stated that there should be self-giving love, which does
not require the suppression of the self:

*Love is between I and Thou. . . . Love ranges in its effect through the
whole world. In the eyes of him who takes his stand in love, and gazes
out of it, men are cut free from their entanglement in bustling activity.
Good people and evil, wise and foolish, beautiful and ugly, become
successively real to him; that is, set free they step forth in their singleness and confront him as Thou. In a wonderful way, from time to time,
exclusiveness arises—and so he can be effective, helping, healing, educating, raising up, saving. Love is responsibility of an I for a Thou.*[17]

Buber concluded that freedom is found in the creative fulfillment of
man's destiny—that is, his openness to the encounter with the eternal
Thou. Freedom has no part in the world of It, which is governed by
the laws of causality. The mark of man's freedom is his ability to decide,
to respond, to *be* one with another.

Everyone must somehow justify himself and others in terms of these
realities. The I-I relationship is the basic, and the most crucial, relationship whereby a man may know himself and accept himself as he
truly is. Man relating to objects, or even treating other people as
objects, is seen as an I-It relationship. In objective, more distant terms,
there are It-It, We-We, and Us-Them ("good guys versus bad guys")
relationships. But it is the I-Thou relationship that remains the most
meaningful—and the most difficult to achieve.

[16] Martin Buber, "Between Man and Man," in *The Search for Meaningful Existence:
A Humanistic Approach to Modern Man's Religious and Moral Values* (ed. by Charles
B. Ketcham), 82.
[17] *Ibid.*, 89.

SIDNEY M. JOURARD (1926–)

Jourard's classic *The Transparent Self: Self-Disclosure and Well-Being* offers the hypothesis that human beings can achieve health and fuller functioning only insofar as they have courage to be themselves among others and correspondingly when they find goals and objectives that have value and meaning for them. This hypothesis was also Jourard's declaration of his commitment to humanism and his intention to show others how to discover their own potentialities for self-realization and optimum functioning as human beings through encounter.

Jourard agrees with Buber's I-Thou concept of man to the extent that he too defines fulfillment in terms of others. Jourard maintains that one cannot come to a complete understanding of himself except through disclosing his innermost private thoughts and feelings to another, significant human being. He explains his theory of *self-disclosure* by relating it to intrapersonal and interpersonal problems, such as the problem of the male role in society and openness in marriage.

Like Buber, Jourard also focuses on the spiritual nature of man, man's concept of God, and man's understanding of himself. Using such terms as "inspiration" and "dispiration," Jourard says that "when a man finds hope, meaning, purpose, and value in his existence, he may be said to be 'inspirited.' "[18] It is obvious then, that "dispiration" implies the lack or the loss of hope, meaning, purpose, and value.

Jourard emphasizes the need for existential behavior which fully expresses what one is at the moment. Predicated upon "freedom to become," being "real" permits growth and learning to occur. In other words, being "real" is saying what we think, expressing what we feel, and accepting responsibiilty for this behavior.

Jourard believes that psychology has thus far treated only half of the human being's potentialities for being—the half he shares with animals, objects in nature, and man-made things. The other half—the more important half—of his being, the capacity for freedom, tends to be ignored. He describes what he considers to be the factors involved in psychologically freeing behavior: "letting be," openness (disclosing one's experience to another person), focusing on oneself and others, commitment to values, self-confidence, and a concept of self as transcending symbols.

ERICH FROMM (1900–)

Erich Fromm is a major exponent of humanistic ethics, wherein "man himself is both the norm giver and the subject of the norms, their formal source or regulative agency and their subject matter."[19] He received a

---

[18] Sidney M. Jourard, *The Transparent Self: Self-Disclosure and Well-Being*, 53.
[19] Erich Fromm, *Man for Himself: An Inquiry into the Psychology of Ethics*, 19.

doctorate in psychology, philosophy, and sociology at the University of Heidelberg in 1922. He also completed additional study at the University of Munich and the Berlin Psychoanalytic Institute. Fromm came to the United States as a refugee from Nazi persecution. He later established a home in Mexico.

Fromm believes that the first "duty" of an organism is to be alive, but to be alive is a dynamic, not a static, concept. He postulates that organisms have an inherent tendency to actualize their specific potentialities:

The aim of man's life . . . is to be understood as the unfolding of his powers according to the laws of his nature.

To sum up, good in humanistic ethics is the affirmation of life, the unfolding of man's powers. Virtue is responsibility toward his own existence. Evil constitutes the crippling of man's powers; vice is irresponsibility toward himself."[20]

An individual, while sharing the core of human qualities with all the other members of his species, is always an individual, a unique entity, with his own potentialities. According to Fromm, we can affirm our human potentialities only by realizing our individuality. The duty to be alive is the same as the duty to become oneself, to develop into the individual we potentially are.

Fromm formulated character types on the basis of *productive* and *nonproductive* orientation. The nonproductive orientations are defined by their principal orientation characteristics: the receptive orientation, the exploitative orientation, the hoarding orientation, and the marketing orientation, which is a specific concomitant of modern life. As a result of the societal focus on organizational roles the individual's self-esteem suffers, and he becomes alienated from his psychological and physical being. Concomitantly he begins to experience others as commodities, not as themselves but as their salable parts; thus individuality is useless ballast; *equality* becomes *interchangeability*; human relationships are superficial.

As opposed to these nonproductive orientations, Fromm characterizes the productive orientation of personality as

a mode of relatedness in all realms of human experience. It covers mental, emotional, and sensory responses to others, to oneself, and to things. Productiveness is man's ability to use his powers and to realize the potentialities inherent in him. If we say he must use his powers we imply that he must be free and not dependent on someone who controls his powers. We imply, further, that he is guided by reason, since he can make use of his powers only if he knows what they are, how to use

[20] *Ibid.*, 29.

them, and what to use them for. Productiveness means that he ex-
periences himself as the embodiment of his powers and as the "actor";
that he feels himself one with his powers and at the same time that
they are not masked and alienated from him. . . . Productiveness is
associated with creativeness.[21]

The concept of love is essential to an understanding of Fromm's
humanism: "Genuine love is rooted in productiveness and may properly be called 'productive love.' . . . Although the objects of love differ
and consequently the intensity and quality of love itself differ, certain
basic elements may be said to be characteristic of all forms of productive love. These are *care, responsibility, respect,* and *knowledge.*" According to Fromm, to love a person means "to be related to his human
core, to him as representing mankind. Love for one individual, insofar
as it is divorced from love for man, can refer only to the superficial and
to the accidental; of necessity it remains shallow."[22]

RONALD D. LAING (1927–)

The works of Ronald D. Laing, a noted British psychiatrist and a
pioneer in nontraditional therapy, present the student of human relations with a wide range of individual and social concerns and insights.
In his many books and articles Laing focuses on the individual, particularly the schizophrenic and the nuclear family. In addition to his
writings and his private practice in London, Laing's professional activities further reveal the timeliness and relevance of his work to the
field of human relations.

An existential thread is woven through Laing's writings, as evidenced by his concern for both individual and group alienation. His
main conclusion is that, whether or not an individual in our society is
considered "normal" or "abnormal," "sane" or "mad," he is likely to
have split himself off from the whole of his experience. In the following
poem in *Knots*, Laing describes how alienation is subjectively experienced:

> *One is inside*
> *then outside what one has been inside*
> *One feels empty*
> *because there is nothing inside oneself*
> *One tries to get inside oneself*
> *   that inside of the outside*
> *   that one was once inside*
> *   once one tries to get oneself inside what*

[21] *Ibid.*, 91–92.
[22] *Ibid.*, 105.

one is outside:
to eat and to be eaten
to have the outside inside and to be
    inside the outside
But this is not enough. One is trying to get
the inside of what one is outside inside, and to
get inside the outside. But one does not get
inside the outside by getting the outside inside
for;
although one is full inside of the inside of the outside
one is on the outside of one's inside
and by getting inside the outside
one remains empty because
while one is on the inside
even the inside of the outside is outside
and inside oneself there is still nothing
There has never been anything else
and there never will be[23]

For Laing, the individual is defined first in terms of experience, the interpretation of one's environment being a function of the self (the center of personal orientation) and second in terms of the action generated by the self. Action, he explains, is the transformation of experience into the objective world. Through the language of social phenomenology, Laing describes the self as separate but related to others through the realm of *interexperience.* Thus one can experience the *experiencing* of the other in relation to oneself. One can never experience the other's experience, but through inference one can experience the other as he experiences himself:

I see your behavior. You see my behavior. But I do not and never have and never will see your experience of me. Just as you cannot "see" my experience of you. My experience of you is not "inside" me. It is simply you, as I experience you. And I do not experience you as inside me. Similarly, I take it that you do not experience me as inside you.

"My experience of you" is just another form of words for "you-as-I-experience-you," and "your experience of me" equals "me-as-you-experience-me...."

I do not experience your experience, which is invisible to me (and nontastable, nontouchable, nonsmellable, and inaudible), yet I experience you as experiencing. . . . *I experience myself as experienced by me....*

[23] Ronald D. Laing, *Knots,* 83.

The study of the experience of others is based on inferences I make, from my experience of you experiencing me, about how you are experiencing me experiencing you experiencing me.[24]

Laing believes that traditional psychiatry and psychology have added to man's alienation from society. Psychology, he believes, has replaced the study of the person with the study of the person as an object or an organism; through the traditional jargon of psychology and the medical models of psychiatry the study of the individual has become even further fragmented, splitting the individual further from his experience, environment, and relationships with self and others.

If the psychiatrist defines his patient as an organism, conceptualizing his behavior within a framework of completely presupposed categories and characteristics, Laing continues, then the psychiatrist will relate to the patient in a fragmenting and depersonalizing manner. In all his works Laing emphasizes the importance of treating psychotics as persons (rather than as mere conglomerates of schizophrenic characteristics) with individual modes and means of dealing with their worlds as they perceive them. He emphasizes the need for empathy and human concern within the relationship of therapist and patient:

Psychotherapy must remain an obstinate attempt of two people to recover the wholeness of being human through the relationship between them.

Any technique concerned with the other without the self, with behavior to the exclusion of experience, with the relationship to the neglect of the persons in relation, with the individuals to the exclusion of their relationship, and most of all, with an object-to-be-changed rather than a person-to-be accepted, simply perpetuates the disease it purports to cure.[25]

Looked at within Laing's framework of the whole, individual madness and social alienation become all the more understandable and frightening. Most people are socialized to forget that they are whole beings, who are, in turn, a part of a whole world system. According to Laing, not only have they forgotten but they have been taught to forget that they have forgotten. Laing warns against the well-intentioned but deluded psychiatrist or psychosurgeon who kills the soul of the patient to "save" the patient. He also deplores teaching children to kill (and to be proud of being reared to kill) their fellows. Why, he asks, have "normal" persons killed roughly one hundred million other persons in the last fifty years?

[24] Ronald D. Laing, *The Politics of Experience*, 18–19.
[25] *Ibid.*, 53.

The Process of the Encounter Group[26]

CARL R. ROGERS

Description of Past Feelings. *In spite of ambivalence about the trust-worthiness of the group, and the risk of exposing oneself, expression of feelings does begin to assume a larger proportion of the discussion. The executive tells how frustrated he feels by certain situations in his industry; the housewife relates problems she has with her children. A tape-recorded exchange involving a Roman Catholic nun occurs early in a one-week workshop, when talk has turned to a rather intellectualized discussion of anger:*

BILL: *What happens when you get mad, Sister, or don't you?*

SISTER: *Yes, I do—yes I do. And I find when I get mad, I, I almost get, well, the kind of person that antagonizes me is the person who seems so unfeeling toward people—now I take our dean as a person in point because she is a very aggressive woman and has certain ideas about what the various rules in a college should be; and this woman can just send me into high "G"; in an angry mood. I mean this. But then I find, I. . . .*

FACIL[27]: *But what, what do you do?*

SISTER: *I find that when I'm in a situation like this, I strike out in a very sharp tone, or else I refuse to respond—"all right, this happens to be her way"—I don't think I've ever gone into a tantrum.*

JOE: *You just withdraw—no use to fight it.*

FACIL: *You say you use a sharp tone. To* her, *or to other people you're dealing with?*

SISTER: *Oh no! To* her.

This is a typical example of a description *of feelings which in a sense are obviously current in her but which she is placing in the past and describes as being outside the group in time and place. It is an example of feelings existing "there and then."*

Expression of Negative Feelings. *Curiously enough, the first expression of genuinely significant "here and now" feelings is apt to come out in negative attitudes toward other group members or the group leader. In one group in which members introduced themselves at some length, one woman refused, saying that she preferred to be known for what she was in the group and not in terms of her status outside. Very shortly after, a man in the group attacked her vigorously and angrily*

[26] From Carl R. Rogers, *Carl Rogers on Encounter Groups,* 17–19. Copyright © 1970 by Carl R. Rogers. Reprinted by permission of Harper & Row, Publishers, Inc.

[27] Sometimes referred to as leader or trainer, for this person the term facilitator is most used in this book.

for this stand, accusing her of failing to cooperate, of keeping herself aloof from the group, of being unreasonable. It was the first current personal feeling brought into the open in that group.

Frequently the leader is attacked for his failure to give proper guidance. One vivid example of this comes from a recorded account of an early session with a group of delinquents, where one member shouts at the leader, "You'll be licked if you don't control us right at the start. You have to keep order here because you are older than us. That's what a teacher is supposed to do. If he doesn't do it we'll make a lot of trouble and won't get anything done. (Then, referring to two boys in the group who were scuffling, he continues) Throw'em out, throw'em out! You've just got to make us behave!"[28]

An adult expresses his disgust at people who talk too much, but points his irritation at the leader. "It's just that I don't understand why someone doesn't shut them up. I would have taken Gerald and shoved him out the window. I'm an authoritarian. I would have told him he was talking too much and he had to leave the room. I think the group discussion ought to be led by a person who simply will not recognize these people after they've interrupted about eight times."[29]

Why are negatively toned expressions the first current feelings to be expressed? Some speculative answers might be the following. This is one of the best ways to test the freedom and trustworthiness of the group. Is it really a place where I can be and express myself, positively and negatively? Is this really a safe place, or will I be punished? Another quite different reason is that deeply positive feelings are much more difficult and dangerous to express than negative ones. If I say I love you, I am vulnerable and open to the most awful rejection. If I say I hate you, I am at best liable to attack, against which I can defend. Whatever the reasons, such negatively toned feelings tend to be the first "here and now" material to appear.

Expression and Exploration of Personally Meaningful Material. *It may seem puzzling that, following such negative experiences as the initial confusion, the resistance to personal expression, the focus on outside events, and the voicing of critical or angry feelings, the event most likely to occur next is for some individual to reveal himself to the group in a significant way. The reason for this no doubt is that the individual member has come to realize that this is in part his group. He can help to make of it what he wishes. He has also experienced the fact that negative feelings have been expressed and accepted or assimilated without catastrophic results. He realizes there is a freedom here, albeit*

[28] T. Gordon, *Group-Centered Leadership,* 214.
[29] *Ibid.,* 210.

a risky freedom. A climate of trust is beginning to develop. So he be-
gins to take the chance and the gamble of letting the group know some
deeper facet of himself. One man tells of the trap in which he finds
himself, feeling that communication between himself and his wife is
hopeless. A priest tells of the anger he has bottled up because of un-
reasonable treatment of one of his superiors. What should he have
done? What might he do now? A scientist at the head of a large re-
search department finds the courage to speak of his painful isolation,
to tell the group that he has never had a single friend in his life. By the
time he finishes, he is letting loose some of the tears of sorrow for him-
self which I am sure he has held in for many years. A psychiatrist tells
of the guilt he feels because of the suicide of one of his patients. A man
of forty tells of his absolute inability to free himself from the grip of
his controlling mother. A process which one workshop member has
called "a journey to the center of self," often a very painful process, has
begun....
..A recorded example of such exploration is found in a statement by
Sam, member of a one-week workshop. Someone had spoken of his
strength.

SAM: *Perhaps I'm not aware of or experiencing it that way, as strength.*
(Pause) I think, when I was talking with, I think it was the first
day, I was talking to you, Tom, when in the course of that, I ex-
pressed the genuine *surprise I had, the first time I realized that I*
could frighten someone—It really, it was a discovery that I had to
just kind of look at and feel and get to know, you know, it was
such a new *experience for me. I was so used to the feeling of*
being frightened by others that it had never occurred to me that
anyone could be—I guess it never had—that anyone could be
frightened of me. And I guess maybe it has something to do with
how I feel about myself.

Such exploration is not always an easy process, nor is the whole group
receptive to such self-revelation. In a group of institutionalized adoles-
cents, all of whom have been in difficulty of one sort or another, one
boy reveals an important aspect of himself and is immediately met by
both acceptance and sharp nonacceptance from other members.

GEORGE: *This is the thing. I've got too many problems at home—um,*
I think some of you know why I'm here, what I was charged
with.
MARY: *I don't.*
FACIL: *Do you want to tell us?*
GEORGE: *Well—uh—it's sort of embarassing.*

CAROL: *Come on, it won't be so bad.*

GEORGE: *Well, I raped my sister. That's the only problem I have at home and I've overcome that, I think. (Rather long pause.)*

FREDA: *Oooh, that's weird!*

MARY: *People have problems, Freda, I mean ya know. . . .*

FREDA: *Yeah, I know, but yeOUW!!!*

FACIL: [To Freda] You know about these problems, but they still are weird to you.

GEORGE: *You see what I mean; it's embarassing to talk about it.*

MARY: *Yeah, but it's OK.*

GEORGE: *It* hurts *to talk about it, but I know I've got to so I won't be guilt-ridden for the rest of my life.*

Clearly Freda is completely shutting him out psychologically, while Mary in particular is showing a deep acceptance. George is definitely willing to take the risk.

The Expression of Immediate Interpersonal Feelings in the Group. *Entering into the process, sometimes earlier, sometimes later, is the explicit bringing into the open of feelings experienced in the immediate moment by one member toward another. These are sometimes positive, sometimes negative. Examples would be: "I feel threatened by your silence." "You remind me of my mother, with whom I had a tough time." I took an instant dislike to you the first moment I saw you." "To me you're like a breath of fresh air in the group." "I like your warmth and your smile." "I dislike you more every time you speak up." Each of these attitudes can be, and usually is, explored in the increasing climate of trust.*

The Development of a Healing Capacity in the Group. *One of the most fascinating aspects of any intensive group experience is to observe the manner in which a number of the group members show a natural and spontaneous capacity for dealing in a helpful, facilitating, and therapeutic fashion with the pain and suffering of others. As one rather extreme example of this I think of a man in charge of maintenance in a large plant who was one of the low-status members of an industrial executive group. As he informed us, he had "not been contaminated by education." In the initial phases the group tended to look down on him. As members delved more deeply into themselves and began to express their own attitudes more fully, this man came forth as without doubt the most sensitive member of the group. He knew intuitively how to be understanding and accepting. He was alert to things which had not yet been expressed but were just below the surface. While the rest of us were paying attention to a member who was speaking, he would frequently spot another individual who was suffer-*

ing silently and in need of help. He had a deeply perceptive and facili-
tating attitude. This kind of ability shows up so commonly in groups
that it has led me to feel that the ability to be healing or therapeutic is
far more common in human life than we suppose. Often it needs only
the permission granted—or freedom made possible—by the climate of
a free-flowing group experience to become evident.

Here is a characteristic instance of the leader and several group
members trying to help Joe, who has been telling of the almost com-
plete lack of communication between himself and his wife. A lengthy
excerpt from the recorded session seems justified, since it shows in what
varied ways members endeavor to give help. John keeps putting before
him the feelings his wife is almost certainly experiencing. The facili-
tator keeps challenging his facade of carefulness. Marie tries to help
him discover what he is feeling at the moment. Fred shows him the
choice he has of alternative behaviors. All this is clearly done in a spirit
of caring, as is even more evident in the recording itself. No miracles
are achieved, but toward the end Joe does come to realize that the
only thing that might help would be to express his real feelings *to his*
wife.

JOE: *I've got to be real careful when I go somewhere if I know a lot of*
people and do things, so that my wife just doesn't feel that she's
left out; and of course, I—things have changed so in the last year
that I have hope, but for a while I didn't. I don't know whether
we can break through it or not. [Pause]

JOHN: *It comes to me over and over again that she wants very much to*
get inside—inside you.

JOE: *She does.*

JOHN: *I, I didn't mean in a hurting way, I mean. . . .*

JOE: *No. [Pause] But it's how to do it. And gosh, I've gotta let her in;*
but gosh, I've also gotta be so careful *and the chances don't come*
very often. . . .

FACIL: *Do you feel you got somewhere in this group by being careful?*
[Pause]

JOE: *Well, I've been pretty hard the other way here. In other words I*
think we haven't been careful here at all.

FACIL: *I don't either. I think you've taken a lot of risks.*

JOE: *What I meant by being careful is, I've gotta be careful about how*
I say anything or it's twisted on me.

FACIL: *If—well, I guess I'll be more blunt. If you think she can't tell*
when you're being very careful, you're nuts.

JOE: *Yeah, I agree.*

FACIL: *And if somebody approaches me—and I feel they're moving*

310

very gingerly and carefully, then I wonder, what's he trying to put over on me?

JOE: Well, I've tried it the other way—the worst thing is—maybe, to begin with I was too blunt. That's when we got into our arguments.

FACIL: Yeah, but it sounds—I really appreciate the risk you're taking, or the trust you're putting in us to tell us about this kind of situation. Yet you start talking about the elements outside of yourself.

JOHN: I keep wanting to ask if you can feel *her feelings?*

JOE: Well, uh, now—feelings, I, yes I'm getting so I can feel her feelings much more and—uh—I—uh—the things that bothered me was I remembered some feelings that she wanted to come in, and at that time I turned her down. Now that's where I got turned off. And—but I can feel right away when she's upset and so then I—well I don't know—you see then I. . . .

FACIL: What does that do to your feelings? Suppose you come home and you find that she's quiet, because you've been away and she's wondering about what has been going on and she's quite upset. What's that going to make you feel?

JOE: Uh—a tendency to withdraw.

MARIE: What would you be feeling—withdrawal? Or would you be feeling upset, or maybe even anger?

JOE: I did before—not now so much—I can get that pretty much. I've watched that pretty carefully.

MARIE: Yes, but that isn't my question, Joe.

JOE: All right.

MARIE: I'm not asking if you can control it or push it away. What will the *feeling* be there?

JOE: Uh—I'm pretty much at the place now where it's just sort of withdrawal and wait; and I know if I can get by that evening, it'll be different tomorrow morning.

FRED: Do you feel it might be defensive, and do you express this defense in withdrawing because. . . .

JOE: Well, she doesn't like it.

FRED: But you like it less this way than getting involved in an argument or disagreement?

JOE: Yeah—because the only thing that might work is—is if I just expressed the feelings. And I hope that'll make a difference—that "I resented what you just said" or something like that, because before I would answer her, and boy, it was off! That just didn't work, *and then she would always say I started it—but* with my

311

being so conscious now of when she's upset—I mean—I've got that real clear, and I just haven't known how to handle it.

Clearly each of these several individuals is trying in his own way to help, to heal, to form a helping relationship with Joe so as to enable him to deal with his wife in a more constructive, more real way.

SUMMARY

Critics of the encounter movement claim that it is overly concerned with persons who are basically well adjusted. The encounter group, they say, is not for the impoverished or for the working class; it is a middle-class phenomenon (a criticism, it should be noted, also leveled at psychotherapy, T-groups, and organization development). Everett Shostrom said, "It speaks usually to those who are not sick, but rather normal—normally depressed, normally dissatisfied with the quality of their lives."[30] Even so, encounter groups are at least partly serving in the function of preventive mental health. They are also instruments of institutional change. An individual becomes aware of his feelings about change, learns to adapt more easily to change, and makes change a constructive possibility. Several writers suggest that the encounter group has profound implications for our fast-moving society. As Rogers wrote, "Man's greatest problem, at this point in our swiftly changing technological progress, concerns our ability to assimilate change."[31]

Another major criticism of encounter groups is that there is no theoretical frame of reference. People often feel that the movement is carefree and irresponsible, one in which people act without meaning and one which lacks theory to guide or interpret experiences. Arthur Burton has observed: "Encounter groups have been so busy being expressive that they have had little time to look to their theories. But history demonstrates that a technique without a rationale eventually falls into disuse."[32]

Without the support of research findings, the growth of encounter groups indicates that America has moved headlong into the human-potential movement. Psychology and philosophy form the foundation upon which encounter-group humanism is built. The primary objective is a successful relationship with oneself and others. Contemporary psychologists have stated that, to achieve a successful interpersonal relationship, one needs to become self-actualized. Or, more appropriately

[30] Everett Shostrom, "Group Therapy: Let the Buyer Beware," *Psychology Today*, Vol. 2 (May, 1969), 39. For an excellent critique of encounter groups, see Morton A. Lieberman, Irvin D. Yalom, and Matthew B. Miles, *Encounter Groups: First Facts*.

[31] Carl R. Rogers, "Interpersonal Relationships: USA 2000," *Journal of Applied Behavioral Science*, Vol. 4 (July–September, 1968), 265.

[32] Arthur Burton, ed., *Encounter*, ix.

stated, one should be continually in the process of *becoming* self-actualized. The fully self-actualized person is only an ideal—a positive movement from psychological "incongruence" to "congruence."

Client-centered therapeutic technique has now been extended beyond the realm of psychotherapy. Applications of client-centered principles have been applied to government, industry, and education. For example, Rogers believes that one cannot *teach* someone else to teach. In the field of education, learning must emanate from the students themselves. Furthermore, learning is continuous, and there should be no final evaluation (hence no grades, no degrees). Education, like personal growth, should be a process of becoming. Rogers believes that this approach to education will produce not only healthy personalities but also more creative personalities.

Humanistic principles of encounter place major emphasis on the concepts of *identity* and *responsibility*. Each person must be responsible for and responsive to his true self, his inner needs. With their emphasis on inner-directedness, some psychologists and philosophers claim that many forms of behavior which clinicians label "mental illness" are really adaptive manifestations of a sick society. With Laing, Fromm believes that what we call "normal" or "well-adjusted" is merely conformity to a societal norm based on "false needs." As the debate continues, thousands of persons are attending encounter groups in hopes of finding ways to restructure themselves and society.

Chapter 11
SUGGESTED READING

Blank, Leonard, Gloria Gottsegen, and Monroe G. Gottsegen, eds. *Confrontation: Encounters in Self and Interpersonal Awareness.* New York, The Macmillan Co., 1971.

Buber, Martin. *I and Thou.* Translated by Walter Kaufmann. New York, Charles Scribner's Sons, 1970.

Bugental, J. F. T., ed. *Challenges of Humanistic Psychology.* New York, McGraw-Hill Book Company, 1967.

Burton, Arthur, ed. *Encounter: Theory and Practice of Encounter Groups.* San Francisco, Jossey-Bass, Inc., 1969.

Chapman, A. H. *Put-offs and Come-ons.* New York, G. P. Putnam's Sons, 1968.

Diamond, Malcolm L. *Martin Buber: Jewish Existentialist.* New York, Oxford University Press, 1960.

Dow, Robert A. *Learning Through Encounter.* Valley Forge, Pa., Judson Press, 1971.

Egan, Gerard. *Encounter: Group Processes for Interpersonal Growth,* Monterey, Calif., Brooks/Cole Pub. Co., 1970.

Fast, Julius. *Body Language*. New York, M. Evans Co., Inc., 1970.

Fromm, Erich. *Man For Himself: An Inquiry into the Psychology of Ethics*. Greenwich, Conn., Fawcett Publications, Inc., 1968.

Goldberg, Carl. *Encounter: Group-Sensitivity Training Experience*. New York, Science House, 1970.

Gordon, T. *Group-Centered Leadership*. Boston, Houghton Mifflin & Co., 1955.

Gunter, Bernard. *Sense Relaxation: Blow Your Mind*. New York, Collier Books, 1968.

Gustaitis, Ross. *Turning On*. New York, The Macmillan Co., 1969.

Hall, Edward T. *The Silent Language*. Greenwich, Conn., Fawcett Publications, Inc., 1959.

Herberg, Will, ed. *The Writings of Martin Buber*. New York, Meridan Books, 1958.

Hodes, Aubrey. *Martin Buber: An Intimate Portrait*. New York, The Viking Press, Inc., 1971.

Janov, Arthur. *The Primal Scream: A Revolutionary Cure for Neurosis*. New York, G. P. Putnam's Sons, 1970.

Jourard, Sidney M. *The Transparent Self: Self-Disclosure and Well-Being*. Princeton, N.J., D. Van Nostrand Co., 1964.

Ketcham, Charles B. *The Search for Meaningful Existence*. New York, Weybright & Talley, 1968.

Laing, Ronald D. *Knots*. New York, Random House Inc., 1970.

———. *The Politics of Experience*. New York, Ballantine Books, Inc., 1967.

Lewis, Howard R., and Harold S. Streitfeld. *Growth Games: How to Tune in Yourself, Your Family, Your Friends*. New York, Harcourt Brace Jovanovich, 1970.

Lieberman, Morton A., Irvin D. Yalom, and Matthew B. Miles. *Encounter Groups: First Facts*. New York, Basic Books, Inc., 1973.

Maliver, Bruce L. *The Encounter Game*. New York, Stein and Day, 1973.

Mann, John. *Encounter: A Weekend with Intimate Strangers*. New York, Pocket Books, Inc., 1970.

May, Rollo. *Man's Search for Himself*. New York, W. W. Norton & Co., Inc., 1953.

Mintz, Elizabeth. *Marathon Groups: Reality and Symbol*. New York, Appleton-Century-Crofts, Inc., 1971.

Moustakas, Clark E. *Individuality and Encounter: A Brief Journey into Loneliness and Sensitivity Groups*. Cambridge, Mass., H. A. Doyle Publishing Co., 1968.

———. *The Self: Exploration in Personal Growth*. New York, Harper & Row, Publishers, Inc., 1956.

Mowrer, O. Hobart. *The New Group Therapy*. New York, Van Nostrand Reinhold Co., 1964.

Murphy, Michael. "Esalen: Where It's At," *Psychology Today*, Vol. 1 (December, 1967).

Otto, Herbert A. *Group Methods to Actualize Human Potential: A Handbook*. Beverly Hills, Calif., Holistic Press, 1970.

314

———, and John Mann. *Ways of Growth: Approaches to Expanding Awareness.* New York, Grossman Publishers, Inc., 1968.

Perls, Frederick S. *In and Out of the Garbage Pail.* Lafayette, Calif., Real People Press, 1969.

Peterson, Severin. *A Catalog of the Ways People Grow.* New York, Ballantine Books, Inc., 1971.

Rogers, Carl R. "Interpersonal Relationships: U.S.A. 2000," *Journal of Applied Behavior Science,* Vol. 4 (July–September, 1968).

———. *On Becoming a Person: A Therapist's View of Psychotherapy.* Boston, Houghton Mifflin Co., 1961.

———. *Sensitivity Training and Group Encounter, An Introduction.* New York, Grossett and Dunlap, Inc., 1971.

———, and Barry Stevens. *Person to Person: The Problem of Being.* Lafayette, Calif., Real People Press, 1967.

Schutz, William C. *FIRO: A Three-Dimensional Theory of Interpersonal Behavior.* New York, Holt, Rinehart & Winston, Inc., 1958.

———. *Here Comes Everybody.* New York, Harper & Row, Publishers, Inc., 1971.

———. *Joy: Expanding Human Awareness.* New York, Grove Press, 1967.

Severin, Frank T. *Humanistic Viewpoints in Psychology.* New York, McGraw-Hill Book Company, 1965.

Shepard, Martin, and Marjorie Lee. *Marathon 16.* New York, G. P. Putnam's Sons, 1970.

Shostrom, Everett. "Group Therapy: Let the Buyer Beware," *Psychology Today,* Vol. 2 (May, 1969).

Sohl, Jerry. *The Lemon Eaters.* New York, Dell Publishing Co., 1967.

Solomon, Lawrence N., and Betty Berzon, eds., *New Perspectives on Encounter Groups.* San Francisco, Jossey-Bass, Inc., 1972.

Stevens, John D. *Awareness: Exploring, Experimenting, Experiencing.* Moab, Utah, Real People Press, 1971.

Strauss, Anselm. *Mirrors and Masks: The Search for Identity.* Glencoe, Ill., The Free Press, 1959.

CHAPTER 12 **ORGANIZATION DEVELOPMENT**

---

*In the first conference the general theme was diagnosing
the relationships between the parts of the system and
trying to find some way of giving and accepting feedback. . . . The theme of the second conference was learning
to solve problems better.*—RICHARD BECKHARD

An organization is made up of people engaged in a variety of interrelated activities. Ever since the Hawthorne experiments the major
task confronting an organization has been how to coordinate individual
effort so as to achieve production goals.[1] Robert R. Blake and Jane S.
Mouton noted the following factors affecting formal organizations:

    1. They have an explicit reason for their existence.

    2. They are made up of people and, therefore, take on cultural
aspects, which serve as a basis for order and regularity.

    3. They exist in a world where change is the norm.[2]

Organizational development programs have come about as the result of a need for changing managerial strategy, adapting the organization to cope with the new demands placed upon it by both individuals
and the environment at large, improving the organizational climate
and intergroup relations, motivating the work force, planning more
effectively, and, recently, solving the problems associated with
mergers.

OBJECTIVES OF OD

Organization development (OD) is an educational process by which
human resources are identified, allocated, and expanded in ways that

---

[1] See Paul R. Lawrence and Jay W. Lorsch, *Developing Organizations: Diagnosis
and Action,* 30.

[2] Robert R. Blake and Jane S. Mouton, *Building a Dynamic Corporation Through
Grid Organization Development,* 5–7.

make them more readily available to the organization.[3] Successful OD allows an organization to improve its problem-solving capabilities. Another basic objective of organization development is to create self-renewing, self-correcting systems of persons who learn to organize themselves in various ways according to the nature of their tasks.

According to Richard Beckhard, "Organization development is an effort (1) *planned*, (2) *organization-wide*, and (3) *managed* from the *top*, to (4) increase *organization effectiveness and health* through (5) *planned interventions* in the organization's 'processes,' using *behavioral-science* knowledge."[4]

Building on Beckhard's observations, Jack K. Fordyce and Raymond Weil concluded that an OD undertaking requires one basic condition: the persons involved must be willing to work jointly, at least to the point of engaging honestly with one another and not for an ulterior purpose.[5] Basing their efforts on the foregoing assumptions, successful change agents perform the following tasks:

1. Work with the people to be affected by the changes.

2. Create linkage with all those individuals who can influence the outcome.

3. Form a tentative general goal, which will result eventually in a specific group goal.

4. Change the quality of relationships from destructive competition toward collaboration and healthy competition by encouraging direct and open communication.

5. Build active feedback loops among all knowledgeable sources to assess the situation as realistically as possible and to monitor the organization's progress.[6]

Some managers use OD as a long-range effort to introduce planned change based on a diagnosis which is shared by the members of an organization. Such an OD program must involve an entire organization or a coherent "system" or part thereof. Its goal is to increase organizational effectiveness and enhance organizational choices and self-renewal. The major strategy of OD is to intervene in the ongoing activities of the organization to facilitate learning and to make choices among alternative ways of proceeding.

Although the specific objectives of an OD effort vary according to organizational problems, common objectives typically emerge. These

[3] Warren G. Bennis, *Organization Development: Its Nature, Origins, and Prospects,* 28–32.

[4] Richard Beckhard, *Organization Development: Strategies and Models,* 100.

[5] Jack K. Fordyce and Raymond Weil, *Managing With People: A Manager's Handbook of Organization Development Methods,* 18.

[6] *Ibid.*

objectives reflect problems which are common to most organizations and prevent the creative release of human potential within organizations. Most organizations have one or more of the following needs:

1. To build trust among members throughout the organization.

2. To create throughout the organization an open, problem-solving climate in which problems are confronted and differences are clarified, both within groups and between groups.

3. To assign decision-making and problem-solving responsibilities.

4. To increase the sense of sharing in organizational goals and objectives.

5. To move toward more collaboration between interdependent persons and groups within the organization.

6. To increase each individual's awareness of group "process" and its consequences for performance.[7]

Clearly, then, the objectives of OD efforts have a better chance of being achieved through planned interventions based on the research findings and hypotheses of the behavioral sciences. Behavioral scientists have successfully helped organizations, first, to examine their procedures, norms, and values; second, to generate alternatives in these areas; and, finally, to make an evaluation. Using knowledge and techniques from the behavioral sciences, organization development attempts to integrate organizational goals with individual needs for growth.

Some of the basic assumptions underlying organization development are the following:

1. The attitudes most members of organizations hold toward work and their resultant work habits tend to reflect their work environment and how they are treated by the organization. Therefore, efforts to change attitudes toward the organization should often be directed at changing the way the person is treated rather than at attempting to change the person.

2. Work which is organized to meet individual worker needs, as well as to achieve organizational requirements, tends to produce the highest productivity and quality of work.

3. Most members of organizations are not motivated to achieve organization goals through tight controls and threats of punishment. Rather, most individuals seek challenging work and desire responsibility for accomplishing organizational objectives to which they are committed.

[7] Bennis, *op. cit.*, 100.

4. The basic building blocks of any organization are its people, and the basic units of change are groups, not individuals.

5. The culture of most organizations tends to suppress the open expression of feelings which people have about each other and about their organization. Suppression of feelings adversely affects problem solving, personal growth, and satisfaction in one's work. The expression of feelings is an important part of becoming committed to a decision or a task.

6. Groups which learn to work in a constructively open way by providing feedback to each other become better able to profit from their own experiences and also to utilize more fully their own resources in the task. Furthermore, the growth of individual members is facilitated by relationships which are open, supportive, and trusting.

7. People are committed to and care about what they help to create. When change is introduced, it will be most effectively implemented if the groups and indiivduals involved have a sense of ownership in the process. Commitment is most likely to be attained where there is active participation in the planning and conduct of the change.

8. The basic value underlying all OD theory and practice is that of "choice." Through the collection and feedback of relevant data—made available by trust, openness, and risk—more choice becomes available to the work force and the organization.

OD STRATEGIES

OD efforts should be directed toward making the human resources within an organization optimally responsive and available. Outside consultants may initially share the responsibility for this process, but ultimately an organization must rely on its informal capacity for understanding itself and for future growth. In contrast to *management development*, which is oriented toward the individual manager, OD focuses on groups and changing relations among persons. The system, whether it is a unit of the organization or the entire organization, is the target of OD effort.

A frequent strategy in OD programs is the use of an *action-research model* of intervention. There are three processes in an action-research approach, all of which involve extensive collaboration between a consultant and the organization: (1) data gathering from individuals and groups, (2) feedback to key clients or client groups in the organization, and (3) joint action planning based on the feedback. Action research is designed to collect data from the entire system and then to use that information to plan the future of the system.

Some building blocks of an OD program are the following:

Table 6. A Comparison of Traditional Training and Organization Development

Dimension	Traditional Training	Organization Development
Unit of focus	The individual	Groups—teams or work units
Content of training	Technical and administrative skills	Interpersonal and group membership competence
Target Subjects	Primarily first line employees and supervisors, Managers trained outside organization	All levels, frequent initial intervention with upper management in-house
Conception of learning process	Cognitive and rational	Cognitive, rational, and emotional-motivational
Teaching style	Subject matter and teacher centered	Participant, immediate experience, and subject matter centered
Learning goals	Rationality and efficiency	Awareness and adaptation
View of Organization	Discrete functional skill units	Social system

SOURCE: William B. Eddy et al., eds., *Behavioral Science and the Manager's Role* (Washington, D.C., National Training Laboratories Institute for Applied Behavioral Science, 1969), 255. Used by permission.

1. *Team building*—a focus on early identification and solution of the group's problems, particularly interpersonal and organizational roadblocks which stand in the way of the team's collaborative, cooperative, and creative functioning. Work procedures can be made more effective by using different approaches and by viewing leadership as a shared function to be performed by various members of the group. The interpersonal relationships within a team can be improved by working on communication skills—skills leading to openness and expression of what one thinks and feels, understanding and acceptance among team members, trust and respect, and—when it occurs—conflict management.

2. *Intergroup problem solving*—a focus on bringing groups together for the purpose of reducing destructive competitiveness and resolving intergroup conflicts over such matters as overlapping responsibilities or confused lines of authority.

3. *Confrontation meeting*—a focus on specific problem-solving mechanisms when problems are known to exist. Frequently an action-research format is employed. The entire management group of an organization is brought together, problems and attitudes are identified and shared, priorities are established, and task forces are assigned.

4. *Goal-setting and planning*—a focus on supervisor-subordinate pairs and teams throughout the organization. The goal is systematic

performance improvement and target setting with mutual commitment and review.

5. *Third-party facilitation*—a focus on using skilled third parties to help in the diagnosis, understanding, and resolution of difficult human problems.

6. *Consulting pairs*—a focus on a manager and a consultant from either within or without the organization.

In an effective OD effort each member of the organization begins to see himself as a resource to others and becomes willing to provide help to others when asked to do so. Such a helping relationship becomes an organizational norm. Once such a norm is established, each member of the organization becomes a potential consultant to the others, and the organization becomes less dependent on outside resources.

A major feature of organization development is its heavy reliance on laboratory training methods. These methods, with their emphasis on experience-based learning in skill development, are especially appropriate when the goal is to develop interpersonal competence to include communications skills and ability to manage conflict and to provide insight into oneself and the work group of which one is a member. Thus OD is not merely sensitivity training but also an all-encompassing means to upgrade both the efficiency and the morale of an organization.

PHASES IN THE OD PROCESS

Goodwin Watson outlined seven phases in the OD process: (1) felt dissatisfaction, (2) diagnosis, (3) creative design, (4) strategy for bringing about change, (5) leadership activity for change, (6) adaptation, evaluation, and revision, and (7) commitment to a continuing process of improvement.[8]

Significant learning begins with a genuine desire for change. Little can be accomplished toward changing any social system until something occurs to interrupt its even flow. As long as people in power positions believe that a change is not needed, not much will happen.

Watson has recommended that certain critical factors and questions should be kept in mind when analyzing a situation: (1) The history of the difficulty—when was it noticed? (2) What have been the past attempts to deal with it? (3) Where and when does it appear? (4) Is the problem found in other social systems? (5) What is the attitude of the people involved? Herbert A. Thelen has provided additional insight:

To me, the most important conditions to understand are those that I

[8] Goodwin Watson, "Model for Chaging a Social System through Introducing Innovations," in *Basic Reader in Human Relations Training: Part VI* (ed. by Goodwin Watson), 82–83.

can control, and they include: my own behavior, the topic or task, and the organization (individual, self-selected small group, committee, large group, society, and so on) which provides the milieu for individual effort.[9]

Proposed remedies or changes can emerge from proper diagnosis. An objective, realistic, and comprehensive analysis will likely mean congruent, adaptable, and achievable revisions. The best designs for change evolve from creative individual and team effort from within the system and also from the outside. As an example of working from within, Charles C. Jung stated that one role of the consultant may be to provide linkage across gaps between the individuals comprising a group and various kinds of resources that can help them do their jobs more effectively.[10]

The two phases of plotting a change strategy are (1) analyzing the situational forces which either resist change or are most likely to do so and (2) reducing the resistance factor when it occurs. As he relates to other individuals within the system, the change agent is likely to cast himself in one of three roles:

1. *The cynic*, who operates on the basis that the situation is naturally conflictual or competitive. He plays the win-lose (zero-sum) game in which some of the participants must lose. He expects to succeed at the expense of others.

2. *The guileless one*, who assumes that all he needs is "a little help from his friends." Naturally, everyone is his friend. He plays the win-win game in which all participants will win. That is, he does not try to succeed at the expense of others.

3. *The pragmatist*, who considers the reality of a situation. He learns how to play the win-lose game and the win-win game simultaneously—although he prefers the latter.[11]

Both the formal and the informal structures of an organization must be considered as potential sources of resistance. According to Kenneth D. Benne, "Informal groupings often exert such strong restraining influences on institutional changes initiated by formal authority that, unless their power can be harnessed in support of a change, no enduring change is likely to occur."[12]

[9] Herbert A. Thelen, "Concepts for Collaborative Action-Inquiry," in *Concepts for Social Change* (ed. by Goodwin Watson), 44–45.
[10] Charles C. Jung, "The Trainer Change-Agent Role Within a School System," in *Change in School Systems* (ed. by Goodwin Watson), 90.
[11] "The Significance of Human Conflict," in Watson, *Basic Reader in Human Relations Training*, 36–43.
[12] Kenneth D. Benne, "Maintaining Change in the Client-System and Terminating the Helper-Client Relationship," in Watson, *Basic Reader in Human Relations Training*, 59.

One way to reduce resistance is to elicit and include all points of view when one is either diagnosing the difficulty or designing the change. As Thelen stated:

the actors in the situation are not mere tabulae rasae *to be coerced into new performance. Rather, they are: human energy systems which provide the motive power as well as the specific behaviors of change. . . . Explicitly consider the conditions that must be set up in order to facilitate the proposed action; who must be involved, how, in what kinds of groupings. In short, define the roles of each person to be involved and decide on who is going to communicate what to whom and when.*[13]

An OD program is not likely to get off the ground without solid support from the leader. In the preceding section were mentioned the restraining forces which come into play when changes are introduced. It is foolhardy to plan a succession of events without gaining the support of the people in power, and as Richard Beckhard soberly reminds us: "Organization development is an effort (1) *planned*, (2) *organization-wide*, and (3) *managed* from the *top*. . . ."[14]

However, when the leaders themselves decide to initiate an OD program, progress is not necessarily assured. The success of their efforts will depend upon their understanding of human motivation and their basic managerial attitudes toward people. Another consideration is the willingness of the managers to assume their share of the responsibility for existing problems and for proposed revisions. Finally, the success of an OD program will depend upon the way in which the organization is structured. Managers have the power not only to influence what goes on in their imediate interpersonal surroundings but also to set up organizational structures and reward systems which will determine such matters as who communicates with whom, who will cooperate and who will compete, how motivated subordinates will be, and so on.[15] Blake and Mouton summed it up: "The character of a company, whether dynamic, forceful, initiating, and risk-taking, or mechanical, repetitive, conservative, dull, aimless, or backward-looking, is established at the top."[16]

Structures must be devised to provide opportunities for continual feedback and evaluation in the change process. Without open channels of communication a change agent cannot know the outcome of his efforts: he is neither confronted with failure nor rewarded for success. In this regard Edgar Schein has suggested that criteria which measure

[13] Thelen, *op. cit.*, 44–46.
[14] Beckhard, *op. cit.*, 7.
[15] Edgar H. Schein, *Process Consultation: Its Role in Organization Development*, 64.
[16] Blake and Mouton, *op. cit.*, 35.

the *values* and *interpersonal skills* of the people who make up a system should serve as the basis for critique.[17] Interpersonal skills are the client's ability to diagnose and work on his own problems in the interpersonal, group, and organizational areas.

When a social system successfully undergoes a series of alterations through the innovative process, adaptation to change can become the norm—a way of life. One key source of norms resides in the "critical incidents" and how they are handled. These incidents usually occur within the context of conflict episodes. What happens immediately following the event can become a determinant of future norms. Richard Walton devotes a major portion of his book *Interpersonal Peacemaking: Confrontations and Third-Party Consultation* to an examination of the dynamics involved when individuals engage in conflict.

Today OD is considered a continuing process that involves deliberate change efforts and uses behavioral-science technology. The forward approach is reflected in the observation by Matthew B. Miles and his coauthors that "technologies for planned change are designed to increase the accuracy of internal communication, increase upward influence of subordinates, aid the problem-solving adequacy of administrative teams. . . ."[18] An OD focus thus encompasses an entire organization and all its constituent parts. Members of the organization participate in this process by determining how their organization should operate. Change agents (also referred to as consultants, development specialists, and facilitators) work with members of the organization in this process of organizational self-renewal.

Five persons who have contributed much to the theories of organization development are Warren G. Bennis, Richard Beckhard, Edgar Schein, Paul Lawrence, and Jay W. Lorsch.

WARREN G. BENNIS (1925–)

Warren Bennis believes that "OD is a response to change, a complex educational strategy intended to change the beliefs, attitudes, values and structure of organizations so that they can better adapt to new technologies, markets and the dizzying rate of change itself."[19]

Some illustrations of OD strategies are (1) team development, (2) intergroup conflict, (3) confrontation meeting, and (4) data feedback. Exercises in *team development* provide each member of a group

---

[17] Schein, *op. cit.*, 123–24.

[18] Mathew B. Miles et al., "The Consequences of Survey Feedback: Theory and Evaluation," in *The Planning of Change* (ed. by Warren G. Bennis, Kenneth D. Benne, and Robert Chin), 457–58.

[19] Bennis, *op. cit.*, 10–15.

with useful feedback concerning individual behavior and group effectiveness. Communication, trust, and the handling of conflict are the main issues in team development. Exercises in *intergroup conflict* are similar to those of team development, except that groups provide feedback to one another. Identifying fundamental conflicts and attempting a resolution are the means which lead to the larger goals of personal health and greater productivity. The *confrontation meeting* is a strategy and forum where problems can be defined and strategies designed to bring about a solution. This approach requires a total organization effort, and both large and small groups are utilized in the process. *Data feedback*, which utilizes the data taken from surveys and questionnaires, is an excellent method for clarifying goals and lines of communication. The information comprising data feedback is usually concerned with organizational policies, jobs, and interpersonal relations.

When one's role in OD is that of a change agent, Bennis advises that the strategy and program be designed with the following considerations in mind: (1) it is an educational strategy adopted to bring about a planned change, (2) the changes sought depend on the organization, (3) it involves educational strategy which emphasizes experienced behavior, (4) change agents are usually external to the client system, (5) it involves a collaborative relationship between the change agent and the client system, (6) the change agents share a social philosophy, and (7) change agents share a set of normative goals based on their philosophy.[20]

Bennis, a disciple of Douglas McGregor, advocates the democratic system with its emphasis on ideals and free choice. For Bennis, democracy in action is primarily evidenced by collaboration and the use of rational means or, more specifically, the problem-solving approach with regard to conflict resolution.

The basic value system underlying effective organizational theory and practice centers upon democratic assumptions. In turn, the normative goals of change agents are derived from a democratic paradigm. When translated into organizational goals, the list would include

improving interpersonal competence of managers; effecting change in values so that human factors and feelings come to be considered legitimate; developing increased understanding among and within working groups to reduce tensions; developing "team-management"; developing better methods of "conflict resolution" than suppression, denial and the use of unprincipled power; viewing the organizations as an organic system of relationships marked by mutual trust, inter-

[20] *Ibid.*, 69.

dependence, multi-group membership, shared responsibility, and conflict resolution through training or problem solving.[21]

Bennis has also outlined three kinds of programs for implementing planned change within an organization: training, consulting, and applied research. In addition, he has outlined six dimensions of the organization which are affected by planned change: legal, political, economic, technological, social, and personal.

Bennis noted that organizations are primarily complex, goal-seeking units. In order to survive, they must also accomplish a secondary task of (1) maintaining the internal system and coordinating "the human side of enterprise" and (2) learning to adapt to the changing external environment.

There is a growing belief that the effectiveness of bureaucracy should be evaluated by human as well as economic criteria. According to this approach, social satisfaction and personal growth of employees must be considered as well as the productivity and profit of the organization. Bennis stated that, although various proponents of "good" human relations have been fighting bureaucracy on humanistic grounds, large organizations seem most likely to fail because of their inability to adapt to rapid change in the environment.

Bennis listed six problem areas confronting most organizations:

1. The first problem is *integration* of individual needs and organizational goals. Bennis observed that twentieth-century organizations are being forced to bring about a better fit between individual needs and organizational goals.

2. *Social influence* as a concept of power and how it is distributed is a second organizational problem. The rise of trade unions and improved general education have blunted the effects of authoritarian rule.

3. Effective *collaboration* for the utilization of resources is a requisite for lasting control of conflict. The increased specialization of skills has resulted in a greater need for effective interdependence. Moreover, in large organizations the leadership function is too complex for one person.

4. The problem of *adaptation* or an appropriate response to changes induced by the environment plagues most organizations. It is compounded by the fact that in highly industrialized societies the social environment is more turbulent and consequently less predictable. Human beings must adapt to technological change taking place at an unprecedented rate.

5. The problem of *identity*—commitment to organizational goals

21 Beckhard, *op. cit.*, 62.

—is particularly troublesome in large organizations. Twentieth-century conditions make it difficult for an individual to identify with a large organization. Cybernation and mechanization have produced role conflict and ambiguity.

6. *Revitalization,* the problem of dealing with growth and decay, is the sixth problem area. Bennis uses the term to embrace all the social mechanisms that have a regenerative capacity. The elements of revitalization are an ability to learn from experience and to codify, to store, and to retrieve the relevant knowledge; an ability to learn how to learn; an ability to acquire and use feedback mechanisms which are self-analytical; and an ability to direct one's own destiny.

To summarize Bennis underscores the fact that OD is an educative *strategy* to bring about planned change. In turn, change is directly correlated to the demands felt by the organization. OD also relies on strategy which emphasizes *experienced behavior*—for example, feedback and sensitivity training. The change agents for OD are usually *external* to the client system. However, the change agent and the client enter into a *collaborative relationship.* Whatever change is to be initiated should be based upon a *value-oriented social philosophy.* Finally, a set of *shared normative goals* between change agent and client further characterizes OD.

Bennis concluded that there are some quantifiable conditions which dictate organizational life-style: environment, population characteristics, work values, tasks and goals, and the motivation of the people within the organization. New modes of relating within work groups are essential to prevent or abate alienation between individual and organizational goals.

RICHARD BECKHARD (1918–)

Richard Beckhard designed his strategies and models of OD in conjunction with a study of contemporary organizational systems. He formulated a diagnostic approach which consists of examining the various *subsystems* that comprise the total organization and then inquiring into *organizational process.* By *subsystems* Beckhard means such functional work groups as top management or the production or research departments. By *organizational process* he means such specifics as how decisions are made, how goals are set, and how conflict is managed—what methods are employed in planning, what communication patterns and styles are in effect, and what relationships exist between interacting groups.

Beckhard offers several hypotheses about the nature and functioning of organizations:

1. The basic foundation of an organization is its people, and the basic unit of change is its people.

2. A necessary change goal is the reduction of inappropriate competition among parts of the organization and the development of cooperation.

3. Decision making in a healthy organization is delegated to the sources of information rather than being made a function of a set role or level of hierarchy.

4. The subunits of an organization tend to manage their affairs in terms of predetermined goals. Controls are set in terms of production measurements, not human relations strategy.

5. One goal of a healthy organization is to develop open communication, mutual trust, and confidence.

6. People support what they help create. Individuals to be affected by a change should be given an opportunity to participate in the planning and implementation of that change.

Beckhard suggests several important requirements in planning a strategy for change: (1) determining appropriate goals, (2) selecting appropriate leverage points, (3) determining the appropriate helping role, and (4) planning for continuous data collection. He differentiates between "means goals" and "ends goals," and notes that change goals can be either. Means goals deal with process, while ends goals pertain to organization structure or particular responsibilities of groups or individuals.

The leverage point is the strategy devised by the change agent to help the client achieve his objective. To be effective, this strategy must be based on a careful analysis of all the relevant factors affecting both the organization and its individual members.

Beckhard asks the question, "What way shall the change agent relate to the problem?" In other words, what is the right helping role for the change agent to assume? He discussed several approaches to this aspect of organizational change. The change agent may decide to suggest changes through management, through subunits of the system, or through teams of people from all levels within the organization, or he may suggest a self-study approach to allow the organization to come up with its own analysis and solutions.

Beckhard recommended the implementation of a continuous data-collection capability within the organization. By this means the organization can perpetually renew itself. However, this is one of the most difficult goals to achieve in an OD process. The flexibility required in such a data-collection process is frequently too threatening for managers who must work under constant evaluation.

Beckhard lists the following characteristics of a successful OD process: (1) it is a planned program involving the whole system, (2) it is a long-term effort, (3) the top management of the organization is aware of and committed to the program and to its implementation, (4) the change is related to the organization's mission, (5) it focuses on changing attitudes and behavior, (6) it usually relies on some form of experience-based learning activities, and (7) responsibility for the work efforts rests primarily with groups.[22]

OD involves both the diagnosis of the various subsystems and the diagnosis of the processes occurring in these subsytems. From the diagnoses a strategy for change emerges. The strategy usually involves team development; intergroup relationships among subsystems, planning, and goal-setting processes; and educational activities for upgrading the knowledge, skills, and abilities of key personnel.

Beckhard devised the confrontation meeting, a technique designed to allow a top-management team to assess its state of health in a very short amount of time. The assessment includes the development of plans for improvement. The confrontation meeting includes (1) climate setting, (2) information collecting, (3) information sharing, (4) priority setting and group action planning, (5) organization action planning, and (6) immediate follow-up by the top-management team.[23]

According to Beckhard, most organization-wide planned change efforts cite the implementation of ways to improve team effectiveness as a goal. Several activities have been devised to help teams become more effective. It is not uncommon for team members to spend an inordinate amount of time trying to become technically competent and to be task-oriented leaders. But Beckhard would suggest that in the beginning team members take a short period of time to examine how they will work together, what their methods will be, and what their priorities are.

Beckhard describes four methods that have proved successful in team building. One method uses the *interview feedback* and *action-planning* processes. A consultant interviews each team member before the team meets. He asks questions which focus on the effectiveness of the team and the organization's operations. The responses are recorded and categorized. The team meeting begins with the consultant feeding back the information collected from the team members. After the data have been shared, the team members work through the data. They are encouraged to make action plans for dealing with those procedures or issues which need to be improved. Ideally, they will develop sugges-

[22] *Ibid.*, 27.
[23] *Ibid.*, 38–39.

tions for handling matters that will later be forwarded to other parts of the organization. The focus of the entire meeting is on action planning based on the information produced before and during the meetings.

Another form of team building has *education* as its goal. A work team attends a program in which the members learn concepts and means of using various instruments designed to help them analyze their own team effectiveness and managerial styles. They also gain proficiency in organization diagnosis and goal setting. Following the training the team members turn their attention to improving their own effectiveness. This stage is specifically concerned with analyzing the team members' relationships with each other and with other groups with which they interact and diagnosing the current state of their organization.

The third form of team building discussed by Beckhard is the *unstructured group*. In this method a team usually leaves the site to attend a workshop or training laboratory. The laboratory method of inducing behavior, examining it, generalizing from it, and trying to apply it to actual work settings is the major technique used. This method focuses on interpersonal relationships and some team processes, such as decision making and communication. It gives secondary emphasis to action planning and task performance. In the workshop method the participants are encouraged to gain skills and take them back to the job and thereby develop a cohesive work unit.

A fourth form of team building is the *functional team meeting*. In such a meeting people from different locations but with similar functions come together to share information and to develop standards and a strong sense of membership in their profession or work.

Beckhard believes that intergroup relationships are a major part of any organization. He warns that if one subgroup's goals or methods of achieving those goals frustrate another group, then destructive competition follows and the entire organization suffers. He advises that in such an event the parties should get together and, if necessary, compromise.

As noted earlier, Beckhard is particularly interested in the areas of goal setting and planning. He believes that a healthy organization tends to set goals at all levels and that the organization as a whole engages in systematic goal-setting activities. A consultant must be concerned with three forms of goal setting: (1) individual goal setting, (2) team goal setting, and (3) organization-wide goal setting.

In summation, Beckhard characterizes the societal environment as capable of causing conflict between the individual and his culture. This conflict may become particularly acute within a system in which people work to meet their social and personal needs. Ideally, planned change within a system will convince the individual that he is fulfilling his human potential as well as meeting his organization's needs. The result will be increased motivationed production as the individual becomes a human ingredient rather than an extension of the production line.

EDGAR SCHEIN (1928–)

Edgar Shein's theory of organizational development incorporates the Lewinian concepts of "unfreezing," "changing," and "refreezing."[24] In this way Schein has attempted to show how individuals and organizations undergo change, which he defines as the "process": the seeking out, processing, and utilization of information for the purpose of achieving new perceptions, attitudes, and behaviors."[25] Schein states that any form of change must follow these steps: (1) *unfreezing*—creating motivation to change; (2) *changing*—developing new responses based on new information; and (3) *refreezing*—stabilizing and integrating the changes.

Schein also theorized that the principles and strategies in the use of laboratory training can be effective in facilitating change in social systems, such as businesses, universities, and hospitals. Much of his work is an extension of concepts of other professionals in the field of organization development, especially those of Rensis Likert, Douglas McGregor, Gordon Allport, and Chris Argyris. Schein collaborated with Warren Bennis in much of the work in OD, and, for that reason, his theories and concepts complement and supplement those of Bennis.

Schein proposed what he calls *process consultation* as a means to aiding OD. Process consultation is defined as a set of activities on the part of the consultant which helps the client perceive, understand, and act upon events which occur in the client's environment.[26] Process consultation, unlike other forms of consultation, does not necessarily demand a "clear mission" or "clear need." In Schein's consultation design there is an underlying assumption that most organizations could be more effective than they are if they could identify the job-related processes (for example, work flow, interpersonal relations, communications, and intergroup relations) that need improvement.

One of the characteristics of process consultation is that it is a joint operation between the consultant and the organization. The consultant teaches diagnostic and problem-solving skills, but he does not work on the actual problem. Rather, the client must solve the problem himself.

Schein sees process consultation as proceeding in six stages, which

---

[24] Schein, *op. cit.*, 123–24.
[25] For an analysis of Schein's definition, see Bennis, *op. cit.*, 99.
[26] Schein, *op. cit.*, 9.

interact with and overlap each other. The first stage is the initial contact with the client organization, which establishes the beginning of a relationship. The second stage consists of defining the relationship and making both a formal and a psychological contract. It is at this point that the consultant determines whether or not he can help the organization resolve its problems and, from a personal standpoint, he wants to do so. The third stage is selecting a setting and a method of work. The method of work should be as congruent as possible with the values of the parties involved in process consultation. The fourth stage consists of data gathering and diagnosis. This process may include direct observation, interviews, or questionnaires. The fifth stage is intervention, in which four kinds of intervention are possible: (1) agenda setting, (2) feedback of observations or other data, (3) coaching or counseling, and (4) structural suggestions. The sixth stage consists of reducing involvement with the client.[27]

Schein spent a considerable amount of time studying communication, member roles and functions in groups, group problem solving, group norms and growth. He also studied leadership and authority, and intergroup cooperation and competition as variables which affect process consultation. He concluded:

The work of the process consultant with groups in the organization can be thought of as one key step in an organization program. Often it is the first step, in that it brings to managers an awareness of process, which in turn makes it possible for them to think in more developmental terms. Equally often it is a necessary step in the middle of an organization development program in building strength and linking together individuals from different functions.[28]

The key to process consultation is the ability to establish a helping relationship, knowing what kinds of processes to look for in organizations, and intervening in such a way that organization processes are improved.

PAUL LAWRENCE (1922–) AND JAY W. LORSCH (1932–)

Paul Lawrence and Jay W. Lorsch defined an organization as the coordination of different activities of group members to carry out planned transactions.[29] To them, OD is a way to change the organization from its current state to a better-developed state. They identified several developmental issues faced by all organizations. A foremost issue is *organizational-environment interface.* Interface refers to the

---

[27] *Ibid.*, 78.
[28] *Ibid.*, 8.
[29] Lawrence and Lorsch, *op. cit.*

process of developing internal relationships or the nature of the trans-actions between the organization and its wider environment.[30]

The first organization-environment interface is made up of those transactions which cross organizational boundaries. One of the issues affecting the organization's performance is the stability of its environ-ment. The awareness of the organization members of environmental goals and needs and their ability to reflect and to relate to those goals and needs are other major issues.

The second critical interface is group-to-group relations. The issues can be framed as questions: Are the groups clearly defined or differ-entiated? Are they also well integrated? Are there conflict relation-ships? What are the lines of communication and patterns of decision making?

The third interface is individual-and-organization relations. Here the crucial issues (some of which are parallel to group-to-group issues) are motivation, communication of organizational goals, and correla-tion of organizational goals with individual needs.

When diagnosing the issues, three areas should be looked at:

1. *Perceptions*—the information the system takes in about its environment.

2. *Values*—the set of conscious beliefs about what is right and wrong, important and unimportant.

3. *Motives*—the underlying drives or needs which develop un-consciously as the individual (or organization) experiences success and failure in mastering the environment. The overall diagnosis is con-cerned with a systems approach, which looks at the interdependent components.

The key developmental problem in organizational-environment interface is not just one of initial strategy formation as occurs at the birth of an organization; it is also that of maintaining a continuing evaluation of the changes in the organization's environment. Lawrence and Lorsch's main focus is on how the quality of organization and en-vironment transactions can be perpetuated and enhanced.

Like other theorists who are also consultants, their main objective in OD work is to persuade the managers to accept the diagnosis and then to act upon it. Perhaps the most effective way to diagnose problems and plan change is to bring OD specialists into the organization and have them work with the managerial staff on a day-to-day basis.

Lawrence and Lorsch pointed out that there are two crucial aspects in diagnosing organizational problems: (1) the nature of the data gathered and (2) the manner in which the data are interpreted and

[30] *Ibid.*

fed back to the members of the system or organization. Some data will be outside the context of the change action and therefore have no bearing on it. Moreover, many consultants do not adequately communicate their findings and recommendations to the organization. Data can be presented to the client system in two ways: (1) raw data can be discussed with the members of top management, who are asked to make the diagnosis of their own problems, or (2) the consultant can present his own diagnosis without sharing his data. The drawback to the first approach is that management may not be able to extrapolate solutions from the data. The second approach has inherent in it the problem of getting management to see why the change agent defines problems as he does.

A considerable amount of time and effort should be expended by the consultant both in interviewing and in utilizing questionnaires. Later he should analyze these data and use them as a basis for developing a conceptual framework. These results and findings should then be communicated to managers with the assumption that they will work out any structural changes that are required. However, Lawrence and Lorsch were emphatic that the action taken by management should not be unrelated to or separate from the diagnosis provided by the consultant.[31]

By placing greater emphasis on diagnosis, Lawrence and Lorsch believed that they could develop an approach to organizational change and development better tailored to a specific situation. The consultant, they concluded, should design interventions which fit the particular problems of the organization, rather than relying on general pre-packaged programs. By emphasizing diagnosis and data feedback, the members of the management group are left with tools which they can continue to apply to similar problems in the future. Too often the consultant takes his conceptual scheme and strategies with him when he leaves, and the organization must seek help for each new set of problems.

Lawrence and Lorsch also concluded that an individual's relationship to an organization depends upon (1) its nature, (2) the task at hand, and (3) the value orientation of the organization and the difference between that orientation and the individual's. The social structure, the predispositions of the members, and the external environment of the organization are additional influential factors.

OTHER THEORISTS

Matthew B. Miles assessed the health of an organization on the basis of whether standards were ached in the areas of task accomplishment

[31] *Ibid.*, 14.

and internal integration.[32] Daniel Katz and his coauthors wrote of the motivational basis or organizational behavior. They identified six motivational patterns or reasons for such behavior: (1) conformity, (2) organization rewards, (3) individual rewards, (4) intrinsic satisfaction from role performance, (5) internalization of organizational values, and (6) involvement in primary-group relationships.[33] In their opinion change agents are in error when they either disregard organizational realities or confuse individual change with modification in organizational variables.

Ronald Lippitt, Jeanne Watson, and Bruce Westley explored the dimensions of the consultant's role.[34] Successful consultation with an organization ends with at least three kinds of learning: (1) coping with the problem, (2) clarifying future problems, and (3) learning new procedures and types of structure to help the organization maintain a healthy state of changeability.

Jack R. Gibb has written extensively about the role of the consultant in organizational change.[35] Gibb's effective consulting process is based on a data-gathering enterprise in which problems are defined, data are gathered, and actions are planned on the basis of the best current appraisal of the data.

Richard Walton highlighted the role of third parties on the effects of conflict resolution in organizations.[36] Walton defined social negotiations as an awareness of the conflict, the wish to solve common problems, the urge to change, the attitudes of trust, and the desire to be responsible for achieving consensus or acceptance within their groups.

Helping a Group with Planned Change: A Case Study[37]
RICHARD BECKHARD

This article reports an attempt by a consultant to assist a client system in an industrial setting to diagnose management communications and to plan systematically a change in relations among the key executives, the department heads, and their different departments. The events to be described took place over a period of about a year, and indicate the trend toward a change which took place and is taking place in this particular management group.

[32] Mathew B. Miles, ed., *Innovation in Education*.

[33] Daniel Katz et al., *Productivity, Supervision and Morale in an Office Situation*.

[34] Ronald Lippitt, Jeane Watson, and Bruce Westley, *The Dynamics of Planned Change*.

[35] In Jack R. Gibb and Ronald Lippitt, eds., "Consulting with Groups and Organizations," *Journal of Social Issues*, Vol. 15, No. 2 (1959), 1–74.

[36] Walton, *op. cit.*

[37] By Richard Beckhard. Reprinted from *Journal of Social Issues*, Vol. 15, No. 2 (1959), by permission of the Society for the Psychological Study of Social Issues.

THE CLIENT SYSTEM

The Vernon Company is a small company of about 200 employees. They manufacture chemical products which go into household cleaners. The president of the company has held his office for ten years. He believes strongly in the importance of effective human relations and in keeping up-to-date with modern management theory and practices. The vice-president of sales has been with the company for fifteen years and is largely responsible for its tremendous growth since World War II. Two other department heads make up the executive committee: a vice-president in charge of production, research, and engineering, and a comptroller.

Reporting to these four men are eleven department heads. With the exception of two regional sales managers, the entire group works together in a small headquarters office and members are in daily contact with each other. Because it is a small organization strong "family feeling" has developed. They have developed a high degree of awareness of each other and of each other's way of work.

THE STATUS OF SOME OF THE RELATIONSHIPS PRIOR TO THE CHANGE EFFORT

Since the change goal was an improvement of various relationships in the work situation, it will be useful to look briefly at some relationships that existed at the beginning of the change effort.

The president and the sales vice-president, who are very different people with differing backgrounds, had tremendous difficulty in communicating with each other. There was considerable competition between the two men in executive meetings and a tendency to reject each other's ideas.

The vice-president of production and research had, when he moved into that position, made one of his subordinates director of the laboratory. This man, who is an excellent research man, proved to be an inadequate administrator. The laboratory was not producing new ideas, or new applications of existing products, fast enough to meet the sales department's needs and requirements.

The regional sales managers felt that the home office sales people were overdemanding in their requirements and lacked understanding of field problems. There was open conflict between one of these men and the vice-president of sales.

The following is illustrative of relationship problems that existed. As an outgrowth of a permissive management policy, each supervisor freely interpreted office procedures in a way he deemed functional to his department. For example, if one supervisor wanted to give his sec-

retary an afternoon off because she had worked overtime the previous week, he had freedom to do this. Discipline was fairly lax in terms of morning arrival time. Coffee breaks were overextended. A few supervisors who were enforcing the policies literally were both frustrated and unhappy with the other supervisors who tended not to enforce them and were even more unhappy with a system which allowed this flexibility.

It should be remembered that the specific illustrations of difficulties did not reflect low morale or an inefficient operation. On the contrary, the management group was quite cohesive and highly committed to the organization's goals. This very cohesiveness caused what might be minor irritation in another setting to become items of high importance, since they were seen as threats to the cohesiveness of the group.

ASSUMPTIONS UNDERLYING THE CONSULTANT'S STRATEGY

Following is a more or less chronological account from the first contact by the client system to the point of replanning. Before describing the step by step process, it might be helpful to the reader to understand the assumptions which the consultant brought to the relationship.

The first assumption was that there are several developmental phases in a client-consultant relationship which more or less follow in sequence and are repeated. One way of thinking about the phases is that there are two parallel and simultaneous agenda on which the client and the client system must work on the problem, and the work on the relationship.

A further set of assumptions underlining the change agent's strategy was that this type of change problem was essentially a learning problem and that for the persons involved in the client system to change in their behavior toward each other and for relationships therefore to improve, it was essential that the individuals in the system learn some new diagnostic skills, some new behaviors and some better ways of getting information about the effects of their own behavior on other members of the system. The aim of the consultant then was to help set up conditions which would optimize learning. These conditions would include establishing a training climate, interpersonal exposure, some personal feedback, and some opportunities for individuals to experiment with new behaviors.

A third assumption was that a major function of the consultant was to help the client collect appropriate and correct information about feelings in the situation and then to help create a training or learning situation in which those concerned could, in a supportive climate, look at this information and work jointly on ways of dealing with it.

STEP 1: INITIAL CONTACT BY CLIENT SYSTEM

The president of the organization knew the consultant from other affiliations and initiated the request for help. He saw the problem as one of improving communication between himself and the sales vice-president since both needed to find ways of listening to each other better and solving problems together with less emotionality. He also felt that the executive committee was overdependent on him and that it was not taking the initiative which he would like to see it take in acting as a leadership group. He had some questions about the effectiveness of a junior management board which he had set up and to which all of the members of the management group belonged, exclusive of the executive committee. This board acted in an advisory capacity to the executive group. It was seen by the president as a way of getting more participation from the junior executives and more feeling of involvement in the management of the company.

STEP 2: DEFINING THE PROBLEM AND ESTABLISHING THE RELATIONSHIP

The president felt that there was need for some formal training of the management group on communications, improving meetings, and leadership skills. He felt initially that what was needed was some sort of training program, perhaps a series of monthly management conferences, or some weekend workshops for the top management group.

As the president discussed his problem, it became clear to the consultant that it was necessary to collect much additional data before planning any activity. The consultant team proposed a fact-finding step to ascertain how the various members of the client system saw the "work world" and where they saw difficulties in communication, relationships, and problem-solving. The president agreed to this fact-finding step. Members of the consulting team held individual interviews and collected attitude and perception data at four levels in the organization: the president, the vice-president, the department heads, and a sample of supervisors reporting to the department heads. These data were tabulated and classified into four categories: decision-making, authority, communications, and meetings.

After the data were put together in crude form, the consultant met with the president and "fed back" the information to him, using quotes from the interviews. The president then convened a meeting of his executive committee. The consultant fed back the same data to them without editorial comment. The president then held a discussion with his vice-presidents on the implications of the data. Subsequent meetings were held with all the department heads by area.

The consultant made no attempt to interpret the data except in terms of clarification and suggested no action at this time.

338

STEP 3: PLANNING FIRST ACTION STEP

After the data had been fed back to all concerned, the consultant met again with the president and the executive committee to rediagnose the problem and to make specific plans for the first action step. It was decided to convene a three-day weekend meeting of the executive group and the junior management group at an isolated location removed from the work setting. At this time the data collected in the interviews would be fed back again in an organized form as the basis for setting up problems on which the group could work during the conference.

A meeting plan was developed using the data as a basis. Some appropriate theory was developed which, it was hoped, would help the client group to understand some of the reasons for concerns they expressed as well as pointing out to them some possible ways of dealing with them.

The general plan for the three-day conference included three types of activities: (1) presentations of organization behavior and communications theory; (2) problem-solving sessions dealing with relationship problems that existed within the group; and (3) demonstration-helping sessions in which the total group worked on some back-home operational problem.

To indicate how the plan actually worked, we will describe the activities of the first day.

The conference opened with a presentation of charts containing a summary of the material which the participants had produced. The consultant asked the group to analyze and discuss the meaning of the various items on the board. This discussion took most of the morning of the first day. At the end of the morning, one of the consultants presented a lecturette on some ways of looking at organizations. He included some organization behavior theory that would help the group to see the relationships among structure, functions, and roles.

In the afternoon, the consultants, who by then had created a fairly high degree of dependency on the part of the participants, changed roles and suggested that they would act as resources if needed but that the task for the afternoon was to identify some of the problems mentioned in the data and begin to work on them. The group accepted the task and very quickly identified one relationship problem that had been part of the original data: the problem of the director of research in his relationships with his laboratory people, the vice-president, the president, and the other departments. This provided a common "case" for the group.

For example it became apparent that the vice-president of research and engineering had been over-protecting the research director, and

339

was doing the same thing in the meeting. This behavior was called to the vice-president's attention by a number of members of the group who used the vice-president's presentation of the research director's problem as an illustration. This "feedback" came as quite a shock to the research vice-president but he was able to absorb it and use it in his subsequent behavior.

The three days were spent in a series of such problem-solving sessions interspersed with theory presentations. On the second evening, the entire group served as consultants on a particular program which the sales department was contemplating and one on which they wished help from other departments. This was a fairly dramatic session with the whole group bringing its resources to bear on a corporate problem which directly affected only one department but which had consequence for all of them.

One assumption underlying the conference design was that unless whatever learnings came out during the conference could be made consciously transferable to the back-home situation, the group would not be getting maximum value from the conference. Accordingly, the third morning was spent meeting in vertical "family groups."

In the latter half of the morning, the groups came together and reported those items on which they wanted help from other departments. The group then discussed further steps in the development of its own working together. Several action steps were taken. (1) Each area planned to have weekly staff meetings of its whole group for the next few months. (2) It was agreed that four to six months later there should be another quick sampling of how things were going through a series of group interviews, and a brief conference with the total group. (3) It was felt that for a period of a couple of years the group should meet as a total group at least once a year and perhaps twice. (4) The junior management group was to study its own functions and report back in the fall.

STEP 4: ASSESSMENT OF EFFECTS

It had been agreed that there would be no further contact between the client system and the consultant until people had had a chance to apply some of the findings of the conference to their work settings. The consultant team did predict, on the basis of the conference itself, that some of the following relationship changes might be observable.

1. The president and the sales vice-president, who had had considerable interaction during the meeting and who had given each other quite a bit of feedback, might be able to listen a little more effectively to each other.

340

2. The overcontrolling behavior of the vice-president of produc-tion and research might be eased.

3. A somewhat more realistic self-image might be developed on the part of the junior management group.

4. Communications between heads of areas and the people re-porting to them might be improved.

It was agreed that these predictions would be checked with subse-quent data.

STEP 5: REPLANNING AND REESTABLISHING THE RELATIONSHIP

Approximately four months after the first conference the client group again contacted the consultant team and said that they were ready to explore next steps. A number of changes had been noticed in terms of relationships. Some specific problems of the first conference had been dealt with to everyone's satisfaction. Some problems, par-ticularly the relationship between junior and senior management, showed little change. People were ready to review their progress and see "where we go from here."

The consultant felt that it would again be desirable to collect infor-mation on perceptions and feelings from various parts of the system and that it would also be important to have the maximum amount of participation on the part of the members of the management group in the further planning of their work toward this general change and improvement. He therefore arranged a two-day meeting in which he met with the total training group in two subgroups for a group inter-view. In addition he held individual interviews with a number of key people.

At these two meetings, the groups identified those items on which some progress had been made and also identified the key concerns which had emerged during the intervening few months.

The following day, the total group met with the consultant. The consultant put in agenda form the various issues which had been identi-fied the previous day in the interview groups. The group tackled the problems, taking some action where action was indicated. Some of the specific actions of that day were:

1. Revising of the job descriptions for the junior group, redefining their responsibilities and the boundaries of their authority.

2. Setting up a study of the wage and salary program.

3. Establishing new communications procedures between the junior and senior management group.

4. Deciding to meet as a total group every three months without a consultant for a one-day maangement conference.

5. *Planning to have a consultant meet periodically with the executive committee and be available during those visits to meet with any individual of the total group who wished to talk with him.*

The reader will note here a marked change in the relationship between the client system and the consultant. The client is moving toward a more independent status. He recognizes the consultant's possible contribution but wishes to be able to move forward without this help wherever he can. At the same time he does not want to cut off the help.

There were several rather marked differences in the tone and activities between this conference and the first one. The reader will note that in the first conference the general theme was diagnosing the relationships between the parts of the system and trying to find some way of giving and accepting feedback. The giving and accepting of feedback had been developed as a group standard. The theme of the second conference was learning to solve problems better. Out of this second meeting came joint planning and establishment of procedures for implementing the planning. Now the group could be more self-determining. It selected its own procedural development with the three monthly confeernces. It identified the need for maintaining the group as a group. And it also defined a different role for the consultant.

SUMMARY

A few comments relative to the assumptions made prior to consultation in this particular case may be useful in thinking about the consulting process.

1. *It is necessary to establish a relationship with the several parts of the system before any effective problem-solving can be started.*

2. *It is important to establish a climate and procedures for feedback both between the helper and the client system and among the parts of the client system if effective change is to take place.*

3. *The consultant must continuously assess the readiness and the capacity of the client system to change.*

4. *Because a change situation of this kind is primarily a learning situation, it is incumbent on the consultant to create a series of conditions in which the client system can learn.*

5. *The consultant must be critical of his own motivations in terms of types of material presented or help offered. He must be sure that the material is designed to meet both perceived and real client needs, not only the consultant's perception of client needs.*

6. *The consultant should be aware at all times that in a healthy*

342

change relationship the client should always be able to reject the ideas, the help, and the relationship.

7. It is desirable to create conditions where the consultants can withdraw, at least temporarily, so that the group can become independent and can grow.

8. It is equally important after an initial change effort that some procedural planning be done for reestablishing the relationship: evaluating the interim action, and evaluating the consultant's role.

9. It is desirable for the consultant to be prepared to accept and help develop new role relationships as the client system gets stronger so that it can move from a dependent relationship to a more independent and finally an interdependent state.

SUMMARY

Warren Bennis has appraised OD efforts from a broad perspective, and his critical comments are rare among OD literature. He lists the following areas of unfinished OD business:

1. Some consultants stress the truth-love model (trust, truth, love, collaboration) to the exclusion of power and the politics of change (conflict, distrust, violence). This emphasis renders OD impotent in diffuse power structures such as cities, large-scale national organizations, and the urban ghetto.

2. Because OD costs money, the systems which are reaping the benefits are the ones with large financial resources. Blake and Mouton label this rich-get-richer phenomenon "corporate Darwinism."

3. "Climate" and interpersonal relationships are often emphasized to the exclusion of structural, political, legal, and technological problems.[38]

Despite criticism of the method, organization development is believed by its proponents to be the kind of planned change which can help us cope with our bureaucratic institutions. OD, they are convinced, is an excellent approach to changing organizations for several reasons. Most importantly, it takes into account the human factor in production. Moreover, the change involves the client system, which has the advantage of self-induced motivation, increasing the client system's opportunity to engage in problem-solving behavior and to learn the effects of that behavior. OD involves procedures that help organizations diagnose their own problems. There are documented cases in which OD programs have not only promoted improved organization functioning but also produced individual changes in attitudes, values, communicative skills, and behavior.

[38] Bennis, *op. cit.*, 77–82.

Yet students who feel the urge to embrace OD principles as the absolute answer and solution to every problem should take a look at the record. It does not always work. Paul C. Buchanan has made a comparative study of successful and unsuccessful OD efforts. By examining similarities and differences among those cases which had favorable outcomes, he attempted to pinpoint the issues that are "crucial" to the process. He concluded that

1. The focus of improvement should be on individual performances in the organization.

2. Linkage should exist between the initial point of change and other persons and organizations with which the client has important interdependency.

3. There should be linkage between the initial point of change and other persons and subsystems in the client's organization. Buchanan concludes that the profession of organization development is slowly adding knowledge to the general theory of practice.[39]

Apparently it is going to be the responsibility of professionals in the field to educate and then develop the next generation of OD practitioners. Few universities have the expertise to do so.

Chapter 12
SUGGESTED READING

Argyris, Chris. *Integrating the Individual and the Organization.* New York, John Wiley & Sons, Inc., 1964.
———. *Understanding Organizational Behavior.* Homewood, Ill., Dorsey Press, Inc., 1960.
Beckhard, Richard. *Organization Development: Strategies and Models.* Reading, Mass., Addison-Wesley Publishing Co., 1969.
———, ed., *Conferences for Learning, Planning, and Action.* Washington, D.C., National Training Laboratories Institute for Applied Behavioral Science, 1962.
Bennis, Warren G. *Changing Organizations: Essays on the Development and Evaluation of Human Organizations.* New York, McGraw-Hill Book Company, 1966.
———. *Organization Development: Its Nature, Origins, and Prospects.* Reading, Mass., Addison-Wesley Publishing Co., Inc., 1969.
———, Kenneth D. Benne, and Robert Chin, eds. *The Planning of Change.* New York, Holt, Rinehart & Winston, Inc., 1969.
Blake, Robert R., and Jane S. Mouton. *Building A Dynamic Corporation Through Grid Organization Development.* Reading, Mass., Addison-Wesley Publishing Co., 1969.

[39] Paul C. Buchanan, "Crucial Issues in Organization Development," in Watson, *Basic Reader in Human Relations Training,* 51–67.

——, and ——. "Initiating Organization Development," *Training Director's Journal,* Vol. 19 (October, 1965).

Bradford, Leland P., ed. *Group Development.* Washington, D.C., National Training Laboratories Institute For Applied Behavioral Science, 1969.

Davis, Keith, ed. *Human Relations and Organizational Behavior: Readings and Comments,* 4th ed. New York, McGraw-Hill Book Company, 1972.

——, and W. G. Scott, eds., *Readings in Human Relations: A Focus in Executive Training.* New York, McGraw-Hill Book Company, 1969.

Drucker, Peter. *Managing for Results.* New York, Harper & Row, Publishers, Inc., 1971.

——. *The Practice of Management.* New York, Harper & Row, Publishers, Inc., 1971.

Eddy, William B., et al., eds. *Behavioral Science and the Manager's Role.* Washington, D.C., National Training Laboratories Institute for Applied Behavioral Science, 1969.

Episcopal Church. *Basic Reader in Human Relations Training.* 7 vols. New York, Episcopal Church, 1970.

Epstein, Jack H., and Robert Warren. "The Role of Behavioral Science in Organizations," *Personnel Journal,* Vol. 47 (October, 1968).

Fordyce, Jack L., and Raymond Weil. *Managing with People: A Manager's Handbook of Organization Development Methods.* Reading, Mass., Addison-Wesley Publishing Co., 1971.

Gibb, Jack R., and Ronald Lippitt, eds., "Consulting with Groups in Organizations," *Journal of Social Issues,* Vol. 15 (1959).

Ginsberg, Eli, et al. *Effecting Change in Large Organizations.* New York, Columbia University Press, 1957.

Guest, Robert H. *Organization Change: The Effect of Successful Leadership.* Homewood, Ill., Dorsey Press, Inc., 1962.

Hage, Jerald, and Michael Aiken. *Social Change in Complex Organizations.* New York, Random House, Inc., 1970.

Katz, Daniel, et al. *Productivity, Supervision and Morale in an Office Situation.* Ann Arbor, Institute for Social Research, University of Michigan, 1950.

Lawrence, Paul R., and Jay W. Lorsch. *Developing Organizations: Diagnosis and Action.* Reading, Mass., Addison-Wesley Publishing Co., 1969.

Lippitt, Ronald, Jeane Watson, and Bruce Westley. *The Dynamics of Planned Change: A Comparative Study of Principles and Techniques.* New York, Harcourt, Brace & World, Inc., 1958.

McGregor, Douglas. *The Human Side of Enterprise.* New York, McGraw-Hill Book Company, 1960.

Maslow, Abraham H. *Eupsychian Management: A Journal.* Homewood, Ill., Dorsey Press, Inc., 1965.

Miles, Matthew B. *Innovation in Education.* New York, Teachers College Press, Columbia University, 1964.

Nylen, Donald, J. Robert Mitchell, and Anthony Stout. *Handbook of Staff Development and Human Relations Training: Materials Developed for*

Use in Africa. Washington, D.C., National Training Laboratories Institute for Applied Behavioral Science, 1967.

Peter, Laurence, and Raymond Hull. *The Peter Principle.* New York, William Morrow & Co., Inc., 1969.

Schein, Edgar H. *Process Consultation: Its Role in Organization Development.* Reading, Mass., Addison-Wesley Publishing Co., 1969.

———, and Warren G. Bennis. *Personal and Organization Change Through Group Methods.* New York, John Wiley & Sons, Inc., 1965.

Schmuck, Richard A., and Matthew B. Miles, eds. *Organization Development in Schools.* Palo Alto, Calif., National Press Books, 1971.

Tannenbaum, Robert, Irving R. Weschler, and Fred Massarik. *Leadership and Organization.* New York, McGraw-Hill Book Company, 1961.

Terry, George R. *Principles of Management.* Homewood, Ill., Richard D. Irwin Inc., 1972.

Townsend, Robert. *Up the Organization: How to Stop the Corporation from Stifling People and Strangling Profits.* New York, Alfred A. Knopf, Inc., 1970.

Walton, Richard E. *Interpersonal Peacemaking: Confrontations and Third-Party Consultation.* Reading, Mass., Addison-Wesley Publishing Co., 1969.

Watson, Goodwin. *Change in School Systems.* Washington, D.C., National Training Laboratories Institute for Applied Behavioral Science, 1967.

———. *Concepts For Social Change.* Washington, D.C., National Training Laboratories Institute For Applied Behavioral Science, 1969.

Part Four   **NEW TECHNIQUES**

White makes a subtly derogatory remark about Mrs.
White, disguised as an anecdote, and ends: "Isn't that
right, sweetheart?" Mrs. White tends to agree for two
ostensibly Adult reasons: (a) because the anecdote itself
is, in the main, accurately reported, and to disagree
about what is presented as a peripheral detail (but is really
the essential point of the transaction) would be pedantic;
(b) because it would be surly to disagree with a man who
calls one "sweetheart" in public.—ERIC BERNE

At the Western Regional Meeting of the American Group Psychotherapy Association in November, 1957, Eric Berne presented a paper
entitled "Transactional Analysis: A New and Effective Method of
Group Therapy."[1] That paper became the basis for a new and rapidly
growing technique in human relations training—transactional analysis
(TA). Transactional analysis is a therapeutic approach designed to
provide the client with an understanding of his personality as it is
shaped in social situations, or "transactions." Believing that the life
roles which we assume are not limited by chronological age, transactional analysts focus on behavior common to children and adults.
The five main concepts basic to TA are: (1) *Child,* (2) *Parent,* (3)
Adult, (4) *game,* and (5) *stroke.*

The *Child* may be defined as the stage of personality development
which accentuates the "recordings of internal events (feelings) in
response to external events (mostly mother and father) between birth
and age five."[2] According to TA theory, each of us starts out with the
Child, and as we grow, we develop the Parent and Adult ego states. To
distinguish clearly between Parent and Child, it should be remembered that much of the recording in the Child is preverbal recording—
that is, it is recorded before the person has adequate command of
language. Hence, the Child is mainly associated with internal feelings
or nonverbal events.

---

[1] Eric Berne, "Transactional Analysis: A New and Effective Method of Group
Therapy," *American Journal of Psychotherapy,* Vol. 12 (1958), 735–43.
[2] Thomas A. Harris, *I'm O.K.—You're O.K.: A Practical Guide to Transactional
Analysis,* 19.

The *Parent* is the stage of personality development which accentuates the "recording (within us) of imposed unquestioned, external events perceived by a person between birth and age five. The mother and father (persons) become internalized in the Parent as recordings of what the child observed them to say and do."[3] In other words, Parent is a social concept of dominance internalized by the individual at an early age. The fact is that many recordings in the Parent are unquestioned and can either be favorable or unfavorable, depending on the situation.

The *Adult* is the stage of personality development which accentuates the "recording of data acquired and computed through exploration and testing."[4] The Adult is frequently thought of as a built-in computer whose functions are to evaluate data gathered from or presented by the Parent, the Child, or the environment and to respond appropriately to these data. Transactional analysts believe that the Adult should be in control at all times once a person has completed five years of life. This does not mean that the Parent and Child are no longer viable; however, it does mean that a person operating in the Parent or the Child ego state (definitions of self) must be aware that he is in such an ego state and must accept or reject it.

By the time we are grown, according to TA theory, all three ego states operate interchangeably and frequently in rapid succession. Crucial to interpersonal interaction is the belief that each of us chooses to operate out of a particular ego state.

A *game* is an ongoing series of complimentary ulterior transactions progressing to a well-defined, predictable outcome. Berne concluded that every game is basically dishonest.

A *stroke* can be a physical touch, a single word, such as, "Hi," or a glancing nod. A stroke can be "positive," such as a pat on the back, or "negative," such as a harsh look. Finally, a stroke can be "crooked," that is, made up of contradictory messages. A stroke is regarded as the fundamental unit of social action; it is the recognition of another's presence. Two or more mutual strokes constitute a *transaction.*

Transactions are the basic units of social intercourse. They take place among the separate ego states of each person rather than between persons. Each transaction is comprised of a *transactional stimulus* (in which one person acknowledges in some way the presence of others) and the *transactional response* (in which another person does or says something related to the initial stimulus).[5] In technical terms TA is

[3] *Ibid.*, 25.
[4] *Ibid.*, 29.
[5] Eric Berne, *Games People Play*, 29.

concerned with determining which ego state implemented the transactional stimulus and which one executed the transactional response.

Most people store strokes and "replay" them for themselves at future times. For instance, during times of stress we may recall positive strokes. However, when a person continues to depend on stored strokes instead of current transactions, he remains emotionally withdrawn.

Young children need many strokes in order to survive. At a very early age children accept whatever kinds of strokes they receive—positive, negative, or crooked. Therefore, children who grow up receiving mainly negative strokes continue to crave them during adolescence and adulthood. Juvenile delinquents, alcoholics, and drug addicts are people who keep receiving the negative strokes they have been conditioned to believe they need.

TA is concerned with four kinds of analysis. *Structural analysis*, the analysis of individual personality, seeks to answer the following questions: Who am I? Why do I act the way I do? How did I get this way? It is a method of analyzing a person's thoughts, feelings, and behavior based on the phenomena of ego states. *Transactional analysis* is the analysis of what people do and say to one another. *Game analysis* is the analysis of ulterior transactions leading to a "payoff." *Script analysis* is the analysis of specific life dramas that people compulsively play out.

TA defines Parent, Adult, and Child ego states in a more personal sense than do the id, ego, and superego concepts of Freudian psychoanalysis. Berne noted that Parent, Adult, and Child states represent psychological, historical, and behavioral realities. In discussing life scripts and script analysis, Berne credited the research of Freud with helping him arrive at this aspect of TA: ". . . a script is an ongoing life plan formed in early childhood under parental pressure. It is the psychological force which propels the person toward his destiny, regardless of whether he fights it or says it is his own free will."[6] This life script, or plan, fulfills a major human need, namely, that of structuring long periods of time. In the script, each person feels "O.K." or "not O.K." In Berne's words, "Time structuring is an objective term for the existential problem of what to do after saying Hello."[7] Stated another way, time structuring allows us to play our roles within a predetermined framework.

Psychotherapists using TA try to identify and alter dangerous or tragic scripts. To do so they use diagramed outlines of the patient's childhood messages as they are reconstructed from current transactions.

[6] Eric Berne, *What Do You Say After You Say Hello?*, 32.
[7] *Ibid.*, 26.

TA IN ACTION

In studying ego states, it is helpful to resort to structural analysis, which has as its purpose the separation of one feeling-and-behavior pattern from another.[8] Analysis of unsuccessful transactions is the principal business of psychotherapists using TA. It is important to remember that in transactions the Parent acts, talks, and responds like a parental figure; the Adult is, metaphorically speaking, similar to a computer as it estimates probabilities; and the Child, considered the most vulnerable ego state, will behave much like a youngster between the ages of two and five.[9]

Figure 4A shows a basic structural diagram of the personality; Figure 4B is an abbreviated form. Figure 4C contains subdivisions which show that the Parent has both Mother and Father components and also that the Child incorporates aspects of the Parent-Adult-Child (P-A-C). Figure 4D is more refined in its descriptive connotations. Figure 5A illustrates six ego states involved when two people, husband and wife, confront one another.

The first rule of communication in TA is that when stimulus and response on the P-A-C transactional diagram make parallel lines the transaction is "complementary" (see Figures 5A and 5B).[10] Comple-

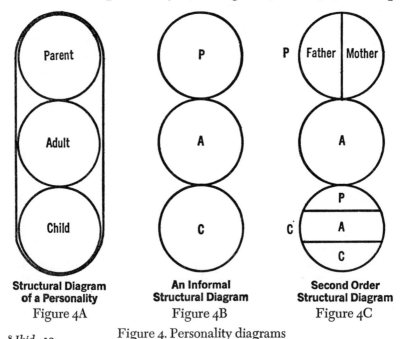

Structural Diagram of a Personality	An Informal Structural Diagram	Second Order Structural Diagram
Figure 4A	Figure 4B	Figure 4C

Figure 4. Personality diagrams

[8] *Ibid.*, 13.
[9] *Ibid.*, 14–16.
[10] Harris, *op. cit.*, 70.

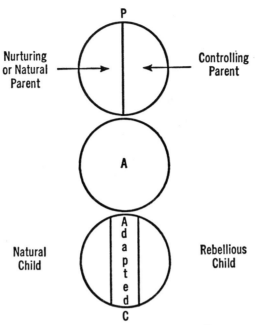

P

Nurturing or Natural Parent

Controlling Parent

A

Natural Child

Adapted

Rebellious Child

C

Descriptive Aspects of the Personality

Figure 4D

SOURCE (Figures 4A–D): Eric Berne, *What Do You Say After You Say Hello?* (New York, Grove Press, Inc., 1972), 12–13. Used by permission.

mentary transactions maintain open channels of communication and are usually gratifying:

> MARY *(Parent to Child): "Let's talk about something pleasant. I know you've had a hard day at the office."*
> BILL *(Child to Parent): "Thanks, dear, nobody but you cares about me."*

The second TA rule of communication is that when stimulus and response cross on the P-A-C transactional diagram communication stops (see Figures 6A and 6B). These are referred to as "uncomplementary," or "crossed," transactions and constitute an unhealthy relationship.[11] More specifically, the trouble arises in this situation because an unexpected response is made to the stimulus, thus activating an inappropriate ego state, which in turn causes the lines of communication to become crossed:

> BILL *(Adult to Adult): "We haven't been very happy together for a*

11 *Ibid.,* 81.

353

Figure 5. Transaction diagrams

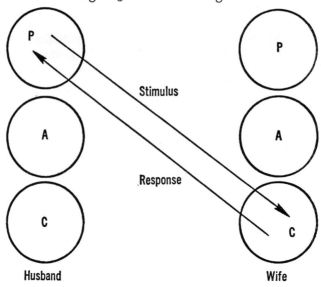

Husband   **Wife**

A Complementary Transaction PC-CP
Figure 5A

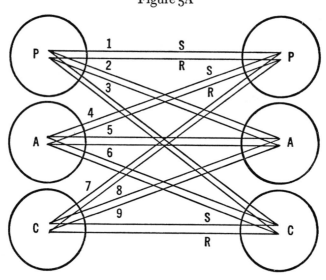

A Relationship Diagram
Showing Nine Possible Complementary Transactions
Figure 5B

SOURCE: Eric Berne, *What Do You Say After You Say Hello?* (New York, Grove Press, Inc., 1972), 16. Used by permission.

Figure 6. Crossed Transactions

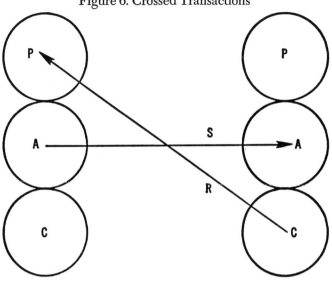

Crossed Transaction Type I AA-CP

Figure 6A

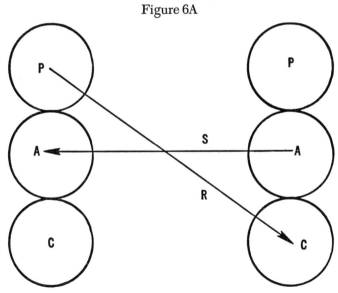

Crossed Transaction Type II AA-PC

Figure 6B

SOURCE: Eric Berne, *What Do You Say After You Say Hello?* (New York, Grove Press, Inc., 1972), 16. Used by permission.

355

*long time. I realize that now, and I think it's time we try to look
at reasons for our fights and, if possible, change our behavior."*
MARY *(Critical Parent addressing Child): "You're always messing
things up. You never listen to me. I've given you the best years
of my life, and this is how you repay me."*

Another example of crossed transactions can be sketched as follows:
An intended Adult-Adult transaction, "Where are the car keys?" might
be responded to in a Child-Parent fashion: "You always blame me
when you can't find things."[12]

The treatment of individuals by TA is hailed by TA proponents as a
most efficient method because it follows the principle of scientific
economy (sometimes known as Occam's Razor) by making two assumptions: (1) that human beings can change from one ego state to
another and (2) that, if A says something and B says something shortly
thereafter, it can be verified whether or not what B said was a response
to what A said.[13]

Finally, transactional analysts stress that change begins with a bi-
lateral contract between the therapist and the client. This approach,
they state, preserves the self-determination of a client and allows him
to know when he has achieved what he sought therapy for. Theorists
Berne, Thomas A. Harris, Muriel James, Dorothy Jongeward, John
Powell, and Claude M. Steiner have done much to refine TA as a technique for improving human relationships.

While Berne was the pioneer of the TA movement, several others
contributed to it development. In addition to those cited in subsequent pages, David Kupfer, the first president of the International
Transactional Analysis Association (ITAA), developed many of the
clinical techniques of TA and helped organize the TA teaching
program.

ERIC BERNE (1910–70)

As noted earlier, Eric Berne developed the concept of TA. In doing so,
he built upon the research in psychotherapy of Rene Spitz, Wilder
Penfield, Paul Federn, and Eduardo Weiss.[14] From Spitz he gained an
appreciation of the effect on infants of maternal deprivation. From
Penfield he adopted the hypothesis that psychological reality is based
on complete and discrete ego states. From the research of Federn and
Weiss he concluded that ego states at early age levels tend to be maintained in the individual's adult personality.

[12] Berne, *Games People Play*, 30.
[13] Berne, *What Do You Say After You Say Hello?*, 17–19.
[14] See Eric Berne, *Transactional Analysis in Psychotherapy and Principles of Group Treatment*.

Central to Berne's concept of TA are the four life positions. The first position, "I'm not O.K., you're O.K.," is initially assumed by all children. Basically it is a "get a stroke" position. The child has a negative self-concept and needs reassurance which he cannot give to himself.

The next position, "I'm not O.K., you're not O.K.," is caused by the absence of stroking during the early years of life. In effect the little person is saying, "I'm not O.K., and neither are you because you don't stroke me. In fact, you punish me even more than you did before I could walk."

The third position, "I'm O.K., you're not O.K.," is the position assumed by the child who has suffered brutal mental or physical pain at the hands of significant adults. It is a life-saving position in that it allows for the individual to accept the negative strokes of persons who control an aspect of his life. Unfortunately, this position also allows the individual to treat others cruelly.

The fourth and final position, "I'm O.K., you're O.K.," differs from the preceding three positions in that it is arrived at through conscious effort. It is the position of hope. In this position the Adult is in control at all times.

The therapeutic process of TA, suggested by Berne but, he says, amenable to reordering, consists of (1) the initial interview, (2) structural analysis, (3) transactional analysis, (4) game analysis, (5) script analysis, (6) redecision, and (7) the terminal interview. Perhaps the most important step in the above sequence is redecision, which occurs when the patient breaks through self-degradation and focuses on the goals of happiness and fulfillment.

TA as presented by Berne has several advantages over Freudian theory or Gestalt therapy. First, and probably most obvious, the total approach is provided in simple layman's terms. In this manner, there is less chance of meaning being lost in translation. Such terms as *Child*, *Parent*, *Adult*, *game*, and *stroke* are easily defined and comfortably used by both the therapist and the patient.

Second, the client and the therapist play games which every individual has played at least once in his lifetime. This method minimizes the client's embarrassment in seeking therapy. In addition, reasons and solutions are presented so that the client can identify the game as well as predict the outcome. He can also see how he reacts to certain confrontations. In this area TA has been particularly beneficial with clients in drug and alcohol rehabilitation programs, as shown by Claude Steiner's work with alcoholics, discussed later in this chapter.

On the other hand, there are some obvious disadvantages to Berne's method of therapy. The most obvious advantage of TA is also a distinct disadvantage. The very simplicity of the terminology limits the depth

357

to which TA can probe. In other words, some games and ego states are obvious and require little effort to detect; however, deep psychological problems cannot be diagnosed or "healed" by the clients. Furthermore, some clients would prefer to become proficient in playing games as an intellectual exercise and thus do little to achieve good mental health.

An individual who is to be helped by TA must first be made aware that a game is in fact being played and, second, must choose the particular game he wants to play. It is important to note that overt resistance or acceptance to play a game can be a game in itself. Moreover, the ultimate decision for improvement must be made by the client.

THOMAS A. HARRIS (1913–)

Thomas A. Harris commenced his study of psychiatry in 1942 while on active duty with the United States Navy. He later was appointed chief of the Psychiatric Branch of the Bureau of Medicine. Since his retirement from the navy he has continued to teach, consult with clients, and conduct research. In 1960 he began working closely with Eric Berne, and the two maintained a close association until Berne's death in 1970.

Harris has made several significant contributions to psychology in general and to TA specifically. Foremost among these is his clarification of the basic concepts of Parent, Adult, and Child as components of TA. Harris succeeded in making TA more intelligible and readable for both laymen and professionals. He removed the mysterious jargon and scientific verbiage which has engulfed most other psychological theories. With Berne he developed a logical, understandable, and comprehensive theory for the actions and reactions of men, women, and children in all walks of life and degrees of sanity.

Harris emphasizes that the "I'm O.K., you're O.K." position is within the reach of the average person. The readability of Harris' writings may well reduce the workload of analysts by allowing persons with minor problems to help themselves or, at the very least, to understand and accept themselves.

Harris has graphically portrayed and positively documented the ways in which TA can be effectively used in child rearing and marital problems. Furthermore, he believes that TA should not be restricted to the therapeutic practitioner. Thus, parents who are having problems with their children and married couples who are on the verge of divorce can frequently equip themselves to handle their crises effectively.

Harris supports Berne's theory of the three distinct personalities, or ego states, in each person's makeup, and he has refined the states in the following ways: Everything the Child sees his parents do and everything he hears his parents say is recorded in the Parent. While these external events are being acted out in the Parent, the internal events are being recorded in the Child. Since he has no vocabulary during his early experiences, these internal events are the feelings the child has in response to what he sees and hears.

Whether Parent data are a burden or a boon depends on how appropriate they are to the present and how the data has been "updated" by the Adult. The Adult is considered the *thought concept* of life, while the Parent is the *taught concept* and the Child is the *felt concept* of life.

Harris contributed heavily toward expanding Berne's concept of the four life positions and entitled his book *I'm O.K.—You're O.K.* Harris wrote that very early in life the Child draws the conclusion that I'm not O.K." and that the parents are O.K. "I'm O.K." means "I'm two feet tall, I'm helpless, I'm defenseless, I'm dirty, nothing I do is right, parents have all the answers, I'm clumsy and I have no words with which to make you understand how I feel." "You're O.K." means "You are six feet tall, you're powerful, you're always right, you're smart, you have life-or-death control over me, and you can hit me and hurt me, and it's still O.K."

In the first position the person feels himself at the mercy of others. He feels a great need for recognition and positive stroking. If this stroking disappears and the child receives negative strokes, he concludes, "I'm not O.K., you're not O.K." In this position the Adult stops developing, since this state needs positive strokes to develop. A child who is brutalized by his parents will often switch to the third position, "I'm O.K., you're not O.K." It is believed that this feeling of "I'm O.K." comes from self-stroking.

The fourth position, "I'm O.K., you're O.K.," is different from the first three. The first three positions are unconscious and are determined very early in life. By the third year of life one of these first three positions is fixed in every person. These positions are arrived at on the basis of data from the Parent and Child and are based on emotion and impressions. In contrast, the fourth position is a conscious and verbal decision and is based on thought, faith, and action. The decision for this position is made by the Adult by "turning off" the recordings of the Parent and the Child.

According to Harris, most people operate from the "I'm not O.K., you're O.K." position. The goal of TA is to convince the patient that he has freedom of choice and the freedom to change at will. This freedom grows from knowing the truth about what is in the Parent and what is in the Child and how these data feed into present-day transactions. When the Parent or the Child dominates, the outcome is predictable.

However, when the Adult is in charge, the outcome is not always predictable. There is a possibility of failure or of success, but most important is the possibility of change.

In addition to child rearing and marriage counseling, Harris applies the P-A-C system to problems of mental retardation, violence, student revolt, racial prejudice, creativity, religion, and international relations. The treatment of individuals in groups is the method of choice used by transactional analysts. The content of group transactions is related mostly to the current problems of the group members. What happened yesterday or last week is much more important than what happened years ago.

Unfortunately, Harris' clear-cut and readable explanation of TA has produced negative side effects. Several questions have been raised about TA: Could it make players better manipulators of other persons? By thoroughly explaining Parent, Adult, Child, and games, has Harris invited the reader to ignore interpersonal problems and focus on the game of "Game Calling"? Has Harris made a specialized psychological tool available to the pseudoprofessional for his use or abuse?

Harris' critics point out that his approach to TA focuses on behavioral rather than attitudinal change. Harris places little emphasis on attitudes except to say that a person in the "I'm O.K., you're O.K." position can consciously choose to accept or reject any given attitude.

MURIEL JAMES (1917–) AND DOROTHY JONGEWARD (1925–)

Muriel James and Dorothy Jongeward have worked extensively in TA and follow the teachings and writings of Berne and Perls. In their widely acclaimed book *Born to Win* they are primarily concerned with TA theory and its application to the daily life of the average person. However, they use Gestalt-oriented experiments to supplement TA theory and methods. They point out that Berne's theory gives a rational method for analyzing and understanding behavior, while Gestalt therapy offers a useful method for discovering the "pieces" of the personality. Both methods, they conclude, are concerned with finding awareness, self-responsibility, and genuineness, and both are concerned with the here-and-now.[15]

They stress that we are not totally at the mercy of our heredity or environment and that we can modify them if we choose. A "winner" is an individual who responds authentically by being credible, trustworthy, responsive, and genuine, while a loser is an individual who fails to respond authentically. Few persons are ever wholly winners or losers, and those who decide to become winners discover that they can

[15] Muriel James and Dorothy Jongeward, *Born to Win: Transactional Analysis with Gestalt Experiments*, 25.

rely more and more on their own judgment. Life for winners is based not on *getting more* but on *being more*. To a winner time is precious. He lives it here and now. A winner learns to know his feelings and his limitations and is not afraid of them. A winner can be spontaneous. He can change his plans when the situation calls for such change. A winner cares about the world and its peoples. He is not isolated from the general problems of society. Above all, he does what he can to make the world a better place.

Many experiences contribute to making people losers. Such experiences prevent progress toward self-actualization. A loser tends to live in the past and laments: "If only something would happen." He waits for a magical rescue. A loser spends much of his time playacting—he pretends, manipulates, and perpetuates old roles from childhood. Like the frog-prince in the fairy tale, he is spellbound and lives life being something he is not meant to be.

James and Jongeward point out that learning about oneself can be a frightening and frustrating experience: to learn the worst or best about oneself means to face the decision whether to change. TA can be a practical frame of reference from which one can evaluate his decisions and behavior and change what it is desirable to change. In this vein James and Jongeward conclude that mental and physical health is probably related to the way a person has been recognized or touched. One can learn how to develop more positive patterns of recognition or touch by consciously filtering through his Adult state information and data supplied by the Parent and the Child.

James and Jongeward note that each person has a "psychological script" for his life which is rooted in the messages that he receives from his parents, constructive, destructive, or nonproductive and thus program him for a positive life or for a tragic ending. The aware person can determine the course of his own life plan and rewrite it in accordance with his needs.

The persons we are least likely to know are our parents. Parents are normally seen in a distorted way as either meeting or failing to meet childhood wants. Sometimes when a person becomes aware of who his parents are or were, he becomes critical and may have to learn to understand, accept, and forgive them. If his own Parent ego state is incomplete, the Adult ego state can take over the task of parenting.

James and Jongeward view the Child as the foundation of a person's self-image. Thus the feelings of being a winner or a loser stem from the Child ego state. Each individual has an identity as both a person and a sexual being. The messages received as a child about one's name, how one feels about being a boy or a girl, and how one feels about the opposite sex affect the identity of the individual as being O.K. or not O.K.

James and Jongeward conclude that the Adult ego state objectively deals with reality and is influenced by education and experience. Inner conflict or self-defeating interaction between the inner Child and the Parent can be resolved by the Adult ego state. To help the process along, the Adult must gain knowledge about the Child and Parent ego states. A fully functioning Adult allows appropriate expression of all ego states because each has its contribution to make to a total personality.

The message is clear in *Born to Win:* courage is required to experience the freedom which comes from autonomy. Courage is also required to accept intimacy, take a stand in an unpopular cause, choose authenticity over approval, and accept responsibility for choice. In short, courage is required to accept one's uniqueness. The path of an ethical person who is aware, spontaneous, and able to be intimate is not easy, but such a person is likely to discover that he was "born to win." And a winner is glad to be alive.

JOHN POWELL (1925–)

In his book *Why Am I Afraid To Tell You Who I Am?* John Powell concludes that none of us wants to be a phony but that the fears and risks involved in honest self-communication seem so intense that most of us seek refuge in roles, masks, and games. After a while it is difficult for us to distinguish between what we really are at any given moment and what we pretend to be. Powell believes that TA is the means by which we can discover our "real selves."

Like Sidney Jourard, Powell maintains that a person needs to share himself with another person really to know himself. This sharing opens minds, fills one with a new awareness, deepens feelings, and gives meaning to life. However, as Powell points out, our greatest problem is communicating ourselves to others. He uses the pastimes, rituals, and games of Berne to illustrate what he calls the "five levels of communication."

The outer, or fifth, level of communication is the "cliché conversation." At this level everyone is safe, for there is no sharing. This is the level at which the rituals of Berne take place. The conversation is: "Hi. Hi. How are you? Fine, thank you, I'll be seeing you. So long." The other person senses the superficiality and obliges by giving the standard answers.

The fourth level is the "reporting facts about others" level. At this level we expose almost nothing of ourselves. We tell others what so-and-so has done or said. We seek shelter in gossip items and conversation pieces, giving nothing of ourselves and inviting nothing from others.

At the third level, called "my idea and judgments," there is some communication and risk taking in telling of ideas and decisions. However, we watch others closely and retreat if they narrow their eyes or show some other form of disapproval. Even worse, we may resort to saying things we do not mean because we sense that that is what the other person wants to hear. At this level we might say such things as, "I think you are intelligent," or, "I think you are beautiful."

The second level is described as "my feelings of emotions." This is the "gut level," where we follow up the third level statement, "I think you are intelligent," with such statements as "I'm proud to be your friend," "I'm jealous," or "I'm suspicious." At this level there is mutual openness and honesty and it takes the rawest kind of courage. Without this level of communication, Powell concludes, we cannot grow, nor can we help anyone else to grow.

The first level is the "peak communication" level. This level will never be a permanent experience, but there will be moments when encounter attains perfect communication and the two persons involved will feel an almost perfect and mutual empathy. All deep and authenitc friendships and marriages will experience, from time to time, this complete and personal communication.

Powell also focuses on the psychological and physical changes in our bodies which protect the ego states of the Parent, Adult, and Child. He writes:

. . . *repressed emotions are the most common cause of fatigue and actual sickness. . . . Repressed emotions may find their outlet in the "acting out" of headaches, skin-rashes, allergies, asthma, common colds, aching backs or limbs, but they can also be acted out in the tension of tightened muscles, the slamming of doors, the clenching of fists, the rise of blood pressure, the grinding of teeth, tears, temper tantrums, acts of violence. We do not bury our emotions dead; they remain in our subconscious minds and intestines, to hurt and trouble us. It is not only much more conducive to an authentic relationship to report our true feelings, but it is equally essential to our integrity and health.*[16]

Powell lists many games that are played to mask and distort the truth about oneself. Such games are often played for the wrongful purpose of "using people." The person who loves things and uses people is not likely to achieve happiness or human fulfillment.

CLAUDE M. STEINER (1935–)

Rejecting traditional medical approaches to treating alcoholics, Claude M. Steiner pioneered the use of TA as a new approach to the problem

[16] John Powell, *Why Am I Afraid to Tell You Who I Am?*, 75.

of alcoholism. His book *Games Alcoholics Play: The Analysis of Life Scripts* illustrates this approach.

Steiner defies the focus of his work as "an extension of the theory and practice of TA into the specific areas of scripts."[17] A script is a life plan, decided on by the child before age six or seven. Like Berne, Steiner contends that a life script can be altered.

Steiner notes that various psychological theories have tried to account for alcoholism on the basis of personality traits such as dependency, oral fixation, and feelings of inferiority. He believes, however, that the alcoholic, because of certain situations that characterize his childhood environment, has, according to script theory, made conscious (willed) decisions that will eventually lead to an alcoholic life course.[18]

Steiner proposes that, since alcoholism is a script and not, as thought by some, "an incurable disease," an alcoholic can make a conscious decision to abandon his alcoholic life script. The aim of therapy is to help the alcoholic abandon that script and accept a nonalcoholic script. This means that the alcoholic can either adopt a new life script or be "script-free." Being script-free means not being a participant in a particular activity. Steiner takes issue with the stance of Alcoholics Anonymous that "once an alcoholic, always an alcoholic." He suggests instead that a former alcoholic who has abandoned his alcoholic life script for over a year can be considered cured and no longer an alcoholic.

Steiner has observed that alcoholics may be classified into three basic categories according to the transactions in which they engage: "Drunk and Proud," "Lush," and "Wino." The Drunk and Proud player assumes the structural position "I'm not O.K., you're O.K." and plays the game to achieve a guilt-free expression of aggression. Accordingly, Drunk and Proud is a three-handed game between the alcoholic and a player who alternates between being persecutor and patsy. There is no rescuer in this game. The advantages to the alcoholic in playing this game are numerous. On the psychological level he is able to express aggression and also avoid blame. The alcoholic then puts himself in a position of being disapproved of and allowing the disapprover to appear virtuous and blameless; however, upon close examination he is neither virtuous nor blameless but foolish and full of blame. The payoff for the Drunk and Proud player is that he receives positive strokes from the drinking companion and receives positive stroking from the patsy. At the same time he receives negative stroking from the persecutor.

The game Lush is most often played, according to Steiner, by middle-aged married suburban housewives, downtrodden working

17 Claude Steiner, *Games Alcoholics Play: The Analysis of Life Scripts*, xiii.
18 *Ibid.*, xviii.

white-collar employees, and aging male homosexuals. The game is played in response to sexual deprivation or, in TA terminology, to lack of stroking. The structural analysis of the game indicates that most often it is three-handed, consisting of the alcoholic, the rescuer, and the patsy. While Drunk and Proud is a two-person game, Lush involves many people as the alcoholic attempts to gain the needed strokes. Thus, unlike the Drunk and Proud player who drinks away from home, the Lush player typically drinks at home but will often leave the house to seek stroking or sexual gratification. The advantages of playing Lush are twofold: the player is able to acquire the needed strokes, and he is able to avoid blame for his own shortcomings.

The game of Wino is the most destructive alcoholic life script. It assumes the structural position "I'm not O.K., you're O.K." There are only two players in this game—the alcoholic and his connection. The only payoff in the game is oral gratification. The game of Wino is played for keeps, for body tissues and organs are destroyed in the transactions.

It is Steiner's contention that, for successful therapy to be undertaken, certain conditions must be agreed upon by both therapist and client. There must be mutual consent for treatment by both parties— that is, an offer of therapy with clearly defined goals and acceptance of the offer by the client of his own free will. The goals of the therapy should be to bring about the confrontation of drinking and the adaptation by the client to a suitable life script. This can be brought about through group sessions and individual counseling.

Steiner's approach seems relevant for treating other social problems.

Sweetheart[19]

ERIC BERNE

Thesis. *This is seen in its fullest flower in the early stages of marital group therapy, when the parties feel defensive; it can also be observed on social occasions. White makes a subtly derogatory remark about Mrs. White, disguised as an anecdote, and ends: "Isn't that right, sweetheart?" Mrs. White tends to agree for two ostensibly Adult reasons: (a) because the anecdote itself is, in the main, accurately reported, and to disagree about what is presented as a peripheral detail (but is really the essential point of the transaction) would seem pedantic; (b) because it would seem surly to disagree with a man who calls one "sweetheart" in public. The psychological reason for her agreement, however, is her depressive position. She married him precisely because she knew he*

[19] Reprinted from Eric Berne, *Games People Play: The Psychology of Human Relationships,* by permission of Grove Press, Inc. Copyright © 1964 by Eric Berne.

would perform this service for her: exposing her deficiencies and thus saving her from the embarassment of having to expose them herself. Her parents accommodated her the same way when she was little.

Next to "Courtroom," this is the most common game played in marital groups. The more tense the situation, and the closer the game is to exposure, the more bitterly is the word "sweetheart" enunciated, until the underlying resentment becomes obvious. On careful consideration it can be seen that this is a relative of "Schlemiel," since the significant move is Mrs. White's implicit forgiveness for White's resentment, of which she is trying hard not to be aware. Hence anti-"Sweetheart" is played analogously to anti-"Schemiel": "You can tell derogatory anecdotes about me, but please don't call me 'sweetheart.'" This antithesis carries with it the same perils as does anti-"Schlemiel." A more sophisticated and less dangerous antithesis is to reply: "Yes honey!"

In another form the wife, instead of agreeing, responds with a similar "Sweetheart" type anecdote about the husband, saying in effect, "You have a dirty face too, dear."

Sometimes the endearments are not actually pronounced but a careful listener can hear them even when they are unspoken. This is "Sweetheart," Silent Type.

Games Managers Play[20]
LOUIS FRIED

The insights into social relationships suggested by Dr. Eric Berne's Games People Play indicate that a similar look at the world of management might be stimulating. The games identified in this sphere have been analyzed in a clinical manner to describe the players' overt activities and their covert or internally rationalized motives for their actions.

THE "STONE TABLETS" POLICY

The player assumes that past policy decisions should not be questioned regardless of their applicability to current conditions. He feels that if top management wanted to change the "commandments," it would do so.

The Payoff. The player obtains a feeling of security from the stability of these policies "engraved in stone." He also attributes omniscience to management, investing it with godlike (or father-image) characteristics. This permits him to evade responsibility for errors so long as he obeys policy.

[20] By Louis Fried. Reprinted from *Management Review*, November–December, 1967, by permission of the editor.

THE CRASH PROGRAM

This is a multiplayer game with two basic types: the Crasher (who initiates the crash program) and the Crashee (who has to perform the work of the program). The Crasher has often procrastinated to the point where only a special effort can solve the problem. This may be a deliberate effort to set himself up in a position to make a heroic contribution to the firm.

The Crash Program is related to another game called "Beat the Budget" in that it provides an opportunity for the manager of an understaffed function to raise an alarm that will permit him to indiscriminately ignore previous budget constraints. Instead of reporting that his function could not properly operate at the original level, he operates within the budget until his situation is critical and then demands the Crash Program.

The Crashee, too, can use the program to make a heroic contribution. He can also use the program as an excuse for games like Workhorse.

The Payoff. *The Crasher can benefit from the notice of his superiors or by giving vent to his sadistic impulses. He also can free himself from constraint or convince himself that he can, by this effort, make up for previous negligence or error. Unfortunately, the Crash Program almost always costs more than the properly planned activity would have cost.*

The Crashee may use the program to make an impression on his superior. He may also use it against the Crasher by faking his effort. This way he doubles his payoff by looking like a heroic worker while sabotaging the program to strike back at the Crasher's sadism.

HOT POTATO (HOPO)

This is the well-known game of passing the buck. It is often played in conjunction with Stone Tablets, Delayed Reaction Decision, or Consensus. HOPO flourishes in any area of weak authority or where conflicting lines of authority exist.

HOPO has a subgame called Recrimination in which, rather than just passing the hot potato, the players actively accuse each other of being at fault. Recrimination is not only a good smoke screen but, by using a technique of misdirection, can also consume a great deal of time. This dulls the original keen interest in locating the real source of a problem. There is also some chance that, given enough time, the problem will disappear.

The Payoff. *The player obviously hopes to advance by selectively taking credit for successes while avoiding the blame for failures.*

367

CONSENSUS

The executive interviews members of his staff on a question and as many of his superiors as he can safely approach. He then publishes the results of his survey as a "consensus" decision.

The Payoff. *The player is able to hide from responsibility behind a communal "we decided" when stating policy or decisions.*

THE DELAYED REACTION DECISION

This game requires two players, a superior and a subordinate. The superior delays making decisions until circumstances force his subordinate to act. The superior can then adopt the decisions if the results are good or blame the subordinate if the results are bad.

The subordinate plays his version, which might be titled, "You get your job." At the sign of a delay by his superior, the subordinate forces events and creates an atmosphere in which action appears necessary. He then acts and gambles on the outcome.

The Payoff. *The payoff to the superior is obviously a chance to stay out of trouble by sidestepping responsibiilty. Numerous executives of limited talent maintain a hold on top positions through skillful use of this game.*

The payoff for the subordinate is multivalued. He may be seeking an outlet for masochistic impulses, in which case he will specialize in wrong decisions. On the other hand, he may be trying to make himself indispensable to a weak superior. This particular subordinate's end of the game could be titled "Eager Beaver."

WORKHORSE

The player of this game works at least six days a week and never less than nine hours per day. He finds excuses to come to work on holidays and never takes a vacation. He makes sure to be at work before his superior arrives and after he leaves. He triple-checks everything he does.

The Payoff. *Workhorse is not played for advancement. The Eager Beaver may play a game that looks like Workhorse, but he, being consciously after advancement, merely tries to create an impression without working.*

The actual Workhorse player really works. The game is played for payoffs that vary with the motivation. Generally, however, the Workhorse player is a frightened under-achiever. He occupies a position beyond his normal capability and must therefore work much harder than average to do his job. The payoff for this player is survival in the firm.

368

BEAT THE BUDGET

The object of this game is to manipulate the budget to accomplish a given purpose. Techniques are extremely varied. Subgames range from Martyr to Empire.

The Martyr player *seeks advancement by demonstrating his ability to save the firm's money. This performance may lead to total disregard for accomplishing his stated purpose in a satisfactory manner. Martyr players try to find methods that are "cheaper but just as good" rather than do the originally defined task. This may—and usually does—result in unsatisfactory or inadequate performance. However, until such results are discovered, the player is a hero. When the results are discovered, he may play Martyr and claim credit for saving the firm's money.*

Bright Boy. *This player takes advantages of the timing relationship between budgets and short-run projects by using a method of flexible budgeting. The essence of the game is to budget after project is completed. When the budget is exceeded on major projects, then Bright Boy can make his excuses palatable by pointing to his excellent past record of project budget comparisons.*

The Empire player *spends to the limit of his budget and beyond if circumstances will permit. If he approaches the end of a budget period with funds unspent, he finds some way to dispose of these funds. Empire players are probably greater gamblers than Martyrs. The Empire player tries to assure himself successively larger budgets by his technique. The Empire game was a favorite during the cost-plus-fixed-fee government contract days and is still popular in R&D-oriented firms.*

The Payoff. *Martyr and Empire represent two different routes to advancement. In fact, the Martyr may even go so far as to suggest elimination of his own job in the hope of advancing.*

Bright Boy, *on the other hand, is usually a game of survival rather than of advancement.*

MUSICAL CHAIRS

This is an executive game for one player. The basic method is to use reorganization as an excuse for poor organizational performance. If a functional area of the firm has problems that do not seem to permit a rapid solution, then the player moves his supervisors into positions with which they are entirely unfamiliar. Naturally, each supervisor must learn the duties of his new position. This learning process takes time, during which the original problem cannot be cured. With luck, the problem may disappear.

But sometimes the transplanted supervisors create more problems by

369

taking the move seriously and trying to modify the new areas before they're thoroughly familiar with them. On the other hand, there's always the remote possibility that some supervisor may solve the problem.

The Payoff. Chairs is played to gain time and, to a lesser degree, on the long-shot hope it may solve a problem. It's ordinarily used only when an executive can think of no immediate solution to problems.

INTRAMURAL POLITICS (INTRAPOL)

This is the big game and all member of management (willing or otherwise) must play it. The previously mentioned games are all used in addition to these briefly described by their titless Rumor, Crown Prince, Inside Track, Three-Way Parlay, and Gang-Up.

The Payoff. INTRAPOL is generally played for advancement but may be played for survival. The heavy players are often identifiable by nervous characteristics, club trophies and handy supplies of dyspepsia preventives.

SUMMARY

Transactional analysis has some positive aspects, the foremost being that it is specific rather than academic. Furthermore, TA allows a person to change rather than merely adjust. For, after all, it should not be the primary purpose of interpersonal relations programs to determine who is to blame for past behavior or which parent was responsible for destructive early decisions affecting one's Parent, Adult, or Child ego states. What should matter is the options available for change. TA is realistic in that it confronts the individual with his responsibility for the future. It also assists in the establishment of self-control, self-direction, and the discovery of freedom of choice. The language used in TA can easily be understood. It is much easier to relate to a parent, an adult, or a child than it is to an id, an ego, or a superego. Therefore, TA gives the client a tool to use in self-analysis and an opportunity for relatively fast treatment.

Critics of TA, on the other hand, claim that it borders on group psychotherapy and thus usurps the role of psychiatry. Probably the chief disadvantage of TA is that anyone can claim to be a TA expert and thereby lead or teach transactional groups. Without a doubt TA is a useful technique in "opening up" people. But, like Humpty Dumpty after the fall, who puts the pieces back together again?

It may be of interest to note that most TA authors write as though they were concerned Parents, encouraging—even chiding—their child-like readers to abandon Child scripts. An even more critical aspect of TA is its potential racist overtones. Most TA writers give the impression

370

that the only significant games and scripts are those which revolve around white, middle-class life-styles.

In summary, transactional analysis is a fairly uncomplicated, easy-to-understand, rational approach to comprehending and changing human behavior. There is much evidence to substantiate Berne's claim that the Parent, Adult, and Child ego states have universal application. Certainly the preconscious life script appears to be universal. Whether TA will be the final key to improving interpersonal relationships is doubtful, but it has become *one* of the keys. It seems likely that TA will be a method in wide use for many years to come.

Chapter 13
SUGGESTED READING

Berne, Eric. *Games People Play.* New York, Grove Press, 1958.
———. "Transactional Analysis: A New and Effective Method of Group Therapy," *American Journal of Psychotherapy,* Vol. 12 (1958).
———. *Principles of Group Treatment.* New York, Oxford University Press, 1966.
———. *Transactional Analysis in Psychotherapy.* New York, Grove Press, 1961.
———. *What Do You Say After You Say Hello?* New York, Grove Press, 1972.
Harris, Thomas A. *I'm OK—You're OK.* New York, Harper and Row, Publishers, Inc., 1969.
James, Muriel, and Dorothy Jongeward. *Born to Win: Transactional Analysis with Gestalt Experiments.* Reading, Mass., Addison-Wesley Publishing Co., 1971.
Lamott, Kenneth. "The Four Possible Life Positions: 1. I'm Not OK—You're OK, 2. I'm Not OK—You're Not OK, 3. I'm OK—You're Not OK, 4. I'm OK—You're OK," *The New York Times Magazine,* November 19, 1972.
McCormick, Paul, and Leonard Campos. *Introduce Yourself to Transactional Analysis: A TA Handbook.* Berkeley, Calif., Transactional Publications, 1969.
Powell, John. *Why Am I Afraid to Tell You Who I Am?* Chicago, Argus Communications Co., 1969.
Shepard, Martin, and Marjorie Lee. *Games Analysts Play.* New York, G. P. Putnam's Sons, 1970.
Steiner, Claude M. *Games Alcoholics Play: The Analysis of Life Scripts.* New York, Grove Press, 1971.

*At the end of the game, the group gathered. Who had
the most money? The minister. He collected large sums
of money and gave little away. Next were the storekeepers; the wealthiest a man who catered solely to the
rich. The policeman had the next largest amount. He
accepted money from the poor who wanted to stay
out of jail.*—JAMES EGBERT

There is a growing interest in adult "games," which include a wide
range of foci: war games, sports games, and human relations training
games. Games are an integral part of American culture. They characterize Americans' frustrations and their efforts to solve problems or to
beat a system. Some training games are designed to reduce the element
of chance and create opportunities for individual strategy, while other
games are designed to create a social or psychological awakening to
problems of human relations.[1]

KINDS OF GAMES

Games reflect the norms, rules, mores, frustrations, and strategies of
life. They allow a player to experience vicariously what life could be,
should be, or actually is. Generally speaking, games can be classified
into three groups. The first are the mass-consumer packaged games,
such as Monopoly or chess. In an earlier time they were also referred
to as parlor games. Second are the noncommercial, minimally structured games, examples being the spontaneous games of children and
even some of the games adults play. Third are the simulation games,
which were developed for the sole purpose of teaching specific concepts to its players.

Parlor games are usually board games or strategy games. Board
games (also known as *track games*) progress along a prescribed route
toward a specific goal, and obstacles and challenges are met along the

---

[1] See Don Rottenberg, "Can You Come Over for Mob Strategy Tonight—Or Will It
Be a Game of Adultery?" *Today's Health*, August, 1971, 47.

way. Strategy games, such as chess, leave the decisions about routes or directions to the individual players. As such these games can be psychologically revealing about the player's aspirations, politics, society, work, and even dreams. Most board games usually require a certain amount of skill. Many games, such as Monopoly, have remained in their original format. Others have retained the original goals or purposes but have changed in board design and rules.

The second kind of games includes the less formally structured ones. The spontaneous games played by children today are similar to those played centuries ago. Generally, they are passed on through generations verbally from child to child without adult intervention. The rules and rituals of the games are similar from generation to generation and from country to country. Such games require varying amounts of skill and coordination and are characterized by varying degrees of chance. In some instances they help a child to find his place among his peers, to observe his position in relation to the rest of the world without suffering severe psychological damage, and to experience some of life's emotions and incidents through play. Many educators believe that such games are essential for the emotional development of children. The games that adults teach children to play also help prepare them for life. Examples of children's games include follow the leader, hopscotch, jacks, and musical chairs. However, these games are more structured in nature. That is, the adults usually have specific purposes for playing the games, and the games are played within a certain time frame.

The third kind of games includes those specifically labeled "simulation games." These games fall into two groups. In one group the rules, regulations, and norms are preestablished, and the game is explained to the players before they begin. The players know what is expected of them, and afterward they hold an elaborate follow-up discussion. The second group of simulation games includes those games in which the players are not told what they are to do. During the follow-up discussion, however, the players are told what they have been doing and why they were doing it. Participants learn whether they achieved the goal of the game and also discuss how they felt about playing the game.

Simulation gaming has been defined as the creation of realistic games designed to give the players life-like problem-solving experience related to their past, present, or future work.[2] Simulation gaming takes real-life situations, replicates some of the stresses, frustrations, and problems, and puts them in a format that can be reenacted. According to Richard D. Duke, simulation gaming provides genuine understand-

[2] F. P. Venditti, *Program Directors for Solving Multi-Ethnic Problems: A Simulation Game for Elementary and High School Teachers.*

ing of social problems because the rules and strategies of the games must reflect life-like situations.[3]

WAR GAMES

The origin of war games has not been firmly established, but they probably began in the sixth century in China, when the warlord Sun Tzu conducted mock military operations by scribbling in the sand and analyzing all facets of a theoretical military encounter. Sun Tzu examined the most effective moves that could be made against all the moves his enemy might make.

The Germans used such games as *Kriegspiel* during the eighteenth century to train professional soldiers in military tactics. During World Wars I and II war games were extensively used to develop and evaluate actual operational plans. In 1928, John Von Neumann designed a formalized mathematical game theory. Von Neumann's theory was later improved upon by Oskar Morgenstern, J. C. McKinsey, J. D. Williams, Melvin Dresher, and Norman Dalkey.

Over the years war games have become increasingly popular among military forces around the world. They have been used in peacetime as training devices, and in times of conflict they have been used to test strategy and permit contingency planning.[4] A quote from Fleet Admiral Chester W. Nimitz suggests that such games were very effective in World War II: "The war with Japan had been re-enacted in the game rooms . . . by so many people in so many different ways that nothing that happened during the war was a surprise—absolutely nothing except the Kamikaze tactics toward the end of the war.[5]

The strategies of modern warfare present numberless complex problems which at first glance seem to defy analytical solution. Modern technology has provided military forces with communication, mobility, and firepower capabilities which stagger the imagination. Military problems are further complicated by continuous advances in technology and the evolutionary nature of man and of war itself.

War games of varying degrees of complexity—from tin soldiers moved about on a terrain board to sophisticated model building and digital-computer simulations—have been used successfully to train personnel, determine optimal strategic and tactical force compositions, develop tactical doctrine and organizations, identify logistical support requirements, and evaluate and select optimal mixes of weapons systems.

Psychological conditioning of personnel for war may also be accom-

[3] Richard D. Duke, *Gaming-Simulations in the Teaching of Urban Sociology.*
[4] John R. Raser, *Simulation and Society: An Exploration of Scientific Gaming,* 46.
[5] Quoted in Elliot Carlson, *Learning Through Games,* 5.

374

plished through war games. Although substantiating empirical data are not yet available, most psychologists agree that this conditioning process begins during early years of childhood with such games as cowboys and Indians and games played with toy replicas of implements of war. Conditioned response is further developed through such war games as field training exercises and command-post exercises.

Despite their usefulness, a primary disadvantage of war games has been their limited transfer value. This is due to the difficulties involved in achieving realism and also to the problem of having to identify the desired parameters and variables to produce the best results. The advantages of war games include their experimental variability and relative low cost; they also enable the military chiefs to make medium-to-long-range forecasts and to develop conditioned behavior and, in some instances, creative responses. From a human relations perspective, however, peace games are socially more productive.

INTERNATIONAL RELATIONS GAMES

The purpose of simulating international relations is to develop a successful means of teaching international relations and, even more importantly, to provide a vehicle for research and experimentation in the field of international relations. It is interesting to note that

the first serious attempt to build a computer simulation of a political system was made at the University of Oklahoma by Oliver Benson, who constructed a "simple diplomatic game." Benson's game was a model that geared together war potential, aggressiveness, atomic capability, coalition membership, possession of bases abroad, geographic location, and trade among eighteen countries. In cycling this model on the computer, he derived "actions and counteractions" that would change the state-of-the-system power relationships in ways that conform to international relations theory.[6]

In this context simulation appears to be a valuable tool to help new members of the diplomatic corps learn to recognize and react to crisis situations. By playing such games, these persons have an opportunity to create scenarios which will prepare them for such situations. For example, an American B-52 bomber armed with nuclear weapons aboard crashes in a Communist-bloc nation. This scenario is then programmed to include messages, data, and opportunities for diplomatic maneuvers. When one considers that millions of people have been killed in wars because diplomats have failed to recognize and react appropriately to crises, game simulations of international relations should not be dismissed as unimportant.

[6]Raser, *op. cit.*, 56–57.

Table 7. Social-Studies Games

SOCIAL STUDIES		ELEMENTS COMMON TO SOCIAL STUDIES AND TO GAMES			FORMAL GAMES	
Subject	Topic	Players	Objectives	Typical Resources	Example	Type
History	Civil War	Loyalists vs. Rebels in Civil War	Gain support of neutrals	Military power, propaganda		Strategy (sequential player actions that are mutually responsive and stress need for predicting opponent's moves)
		High, low vs. middle in High-low poker	Gain support of opposite	Card suites, betting (persuasive) strategy	High-low poker (2 winners)	
	Coloniza-tion	Colonizers vs. Colonizers	Control colonial region	Power, decision, speed, determin-ation		Showdown (simultaneous player actions depending little on uncertainties of opponent's moves)
		Climbers vs. Climbers	Control "mountain"	Power, decision, speed, determin-ation	King of the Mountain	
Geography	Raw Materials Produc-tion	Producer vs. Producer	Capture market	Location closest to market		Strategy
		Player vs. Player	Capture ball	Closest to ball	Soccer	
	Trade Routes	Civilization vs. Geography	Get closest to market	Mobility		Showdown
		Players vs. Position	Get closest to objective	Movement	Shuffle-board	
Civics	Legisla-tive Processes	Elected Reps. vs. Elected Reps.	Vote or kill legislation in spite of blocs	Votes on right issue at right timing		Strategy
		Players	Score goals, deny opponents goals	Players at right place at right time	Basketball, football	
	Elections	Candidates vs. Candidates	Win	Outdistanc-ing oppo-nents		Showdown
		Racers vs. Racers	Win	Run faster	Races	
Economics	Union-Manage-ment Collective Bargaining	Union vs. Manage-ment	Increased share of profits	Strike vs. lockout		Strategy
		Teams	Goals	Massed power	Rugby	
	Competi-tive Invest-ment	Investors vs. Investors	Profit	Capital, calculation, luck		Showdown
		Players	"Play" profit	Capital, calculation, luck	"Monopoly"	

SOURCE: *Serious Games* by Clark C. Abt. Copyright © 1970 by Abt Associates, Inc. Reprinted by permission of The Viking Press, Inc.

EDUCATIONAL GAMES

In 1956 the American Management Association developed a management training game utilizing computers. In contrast to previous games, the computers allowed for greater complexity, and within a short time other groups began developing computer-designed simulation games for their own purposes. Games were soon in demand for use in education, as well as in business and government management trainee programs. Some were simple, two-person games designed to produce a winner and a loser, while others were designed to produce no winners or all winners. Some games were designed to produce interaction between one individual and another or between a group of persons and a computer. Participants played against a prearranged program in the computer or competed against one another or against some stated standard of performance.

By the mid-1960's research had caught up with the overzealous claims of game manufacturers. It was clear that games were not a foolproof means of gaining social insight. By the late 1960's skepticism began to replace unqualified optimism. The games did seem to teach, but research had not yet determined exactly what they taught or why and how they worked. The effects of gaming seemed to go beyond what was testable with available instruments.[7]

From the early emphasis on management training, simulation gaming is beginning to supplement traditional instruction in classrooms, ranging from elementary to postgraduate school. Special games have been developed for use in the social studies—history, economics, geography, political science, sociology, and anthropoolgy—as well as in mathematics and science. These games appear to have met with some success:

Students who are not motivated to learn in school are frequently highly motivated in their other activities. Even the youngest children play with a vengeance cops-and-robbers, hide-and-seek, cowboys-and-Indians, and other competitive games. The differences in these two environments, at least in the degree of attention and interest in participating, are partially explained by the great drama in the play environment and the frequent lack of drama in the school environment. This "drama" involves conflicts of uncertain outcome among actors with whom the child can identify; in playing games, children "become" the characters they represent, and engage vicariously in the conflicts their roles afford. The application of these exciting elements to activities in the school can stimulate the child to learn new intellectual concepts.[8]

[7] Sarane S. Boocock and G. O. Schild, eds., *Simulation Games in Learning*, 115.
[8] Clark C. Abt, *Serious Games*, 16–17.

One of the first simulation games was Inter-Nation Simulation (INS), devised at Northwestern University by Harold Guetzkow and his associates. Developed as a computer simulation for college students in international relations, the game has been modified for use by high school students without the use of a computer. In this game five fictional nations, each represented by three or more student participants who serve as decision makers, live through a compressed time period. The players are in complete control of the destiny of their countries. Following predetermined rules of behavior, the players decide the fates of their nations. Each nation has a mythical history, specific strengths and weaknesses, and specific domestic and foreign needs. The players are free to use their resources as they please. They can go to war if they desire, but it becomes painfully clear that they must live with that decision. Leaders can be deposed or exiled if things go poorly; they can support international organizations; they can sign alliances; they can isolate themselves. The game can be completed in as little as six hours or as long as forty-eight hours, depending upon the teacher's goals. While most teachers try to instill humanistic values in the players, it is important to note that some of the simulations end in nuclear war.[9]

Most participants are enthusiastic about the INS game. Most feel that they have gained an increased empathy for the plight of small nations and a better understanding of the feelings that nationalism produces. Most participants say that they gained an awareness of the complexity involved in international relations as well as an increased understanding of the problems of decision making and the need for accurate information before making decisions.[10]

There are several other well-received simulation games in the area of the social studies. One such game is Dangerous Parallel, a crisis game based on the events of the Korean War. Two games, Napoli and Game of Democracy, simulate the democratic legislative process. Still another game, Crisis, simulates an international mining crisis, while Propaganda Game revolves around various propaganda techniques. Geography students play Euro-Card, a game about Europe. Consumer, Community Disaster, and Family Game are designed to familiarize the players with the everyday happenings and unusual circumstances affecting people in all walks of life. Equations and On-Sets are mathematics games emphasizing the development of logic and reasoning power. Games about animal hunting growing out of Jerome Bruner's curriculum project "Man: A Course of Study" are available for elementary school students. Secondary history students can play Disunia,

[9] Harold Guetzkow, ed., *Simulation In Social Science: Readings*, 82–92.
[10] Carlson, *op. cit.*, 70.

378

a game about revolutionary America, or Game of Empire, about the British Empire in the eighteenth century.[11]

Life Career is a game of particular value to adolescents trying to make important decisions about their personal lives. A product of Johns Hopkins University research and development, the game attempts to simulate the current job, education, and marriage situations in America. The players try to develop the most "satisfying" life for fictitious students. Each hypothetical student has different backgrounds, abilities, interests, and needs. A complete history of the hypothetical student is given to each player as he begins to make decisions for his student. Scores are recorded in four areas: education, job, family life, and leisure. High scores indicate reasonable success in each area.

James S. Coleman, professor of social relations in Johns Hopkins University, is a foremost theorist of simulation games. Coleman has developed several simulation games for Johns Hopkins and for the Baltimore public school system. He first became interested in using simulation games to teach high school students while conducting a study of adolescents in Illinois.[12] In this study Coleman concluded that the high schools in his survey did not reward students in a constructive manner for academic achievement. Thus from his knowledge of the uses and successes of strategy and management simulation games he designed simulation games that can be played by high school students. The major objective of the games is to enable students to receive positive rewards for academic achievement.

As a beginning Coleman made certain assumptions about simulation games: (1) an individual learns more by experiencing and relating to certain actions and reactions to interaction than by being in a sterile classroom environment; (2) certain characteristics of human behavior and of our society are learned only through experience; and (3) simulation games, in order to be effective, should have certain characteristics. One of these characteristics is that the game should allow the player to see the consequences of his actions, whether he wins or loses. A second characteristic is that a game has an element of chance, as well as a requirement for skill. This allows the less able student to become as involved as the more able student. A third desirable characteristic is that the game should enable the student to see that he has some control over his future. This can be achieved when the student realizes that his decisions in a controlled and predictable environment can have some application in future real-life situations.

According to Coleman, a well-structured game has a wide range and variety of rules and skill requirements. The less able and the more

[11] Boocock and Schild, *op. cit.*, 276–79.
[12] James S. Coleman, "Learning Through Games," *NEA Journal*, Vol. 56 (1967), 69.

able students can thus get the most out of their potential without thwarting their ability and with a minimum of frustration. Finally, the game should have some kind of follow-up to allow the students a broader scope, or view, of the game process in a learning situation. If the game has a specific principle or goal, a follow-up also helps all the students see and understand such principles. A well-designed game will help students see certain aspects of society or human behavior which they will sometime encounter.

Coleman listed several advantages in playing simulation games. If Coleman is correct in his assumptions, one of these advantages is that the individual will be able to see and understand many of the consequences of the decision making he will face as an adult. Another advantage is that a game has the quality of helping the student maintain his interest and attention because he is actively participating in the game rather than passively sitting and trying to learn. The antiquated role of the teacher as the sole dispenser of knowledge diminishes because the student's own interactions, during and after the game, enable him to see how much he has or has not learned. With the role of the teacher diminished, the student will rely more on his own resources.

Coleman cautioned teachers about several drawbacks of games. First, if the students do not wish to observe the rules of the game, the effectiveness of the game will be greatly reduced. Second, both the environment and the conditions of a game are controlled and predictable. Often this is not the case in real-life situations. Third, a student can become so involved in a game that he will lose proper perspective. Sometimes, when many game values and norms are preset, the student does not really have an understanding of how these values and norms came into being; they are stated, and the student simply accepts them. Later, when he must decide which values and norms he should or should not accept, he will find it difficult to make his decision. Thus, if the game is to be an effective teaching aid, the teacher must know the game well enough to explain it with confidence and must know at what point during the game the students have demonstrated their maximum learning potential in terms of it. Coleman joined a long line of those who warn teachers to view simulation games as a means for teaching and not an end to teaching.

SOCIAL GAMES

Social games fall into six broad categories: social-consciousness, political, therapeutic, sexual-liberation, environmental-conservation, and children's games. Broadly defined, *social game* is one in which certain social processes are explicitly mirrored in the structure and functioning of the game. This is exemplified in the simulation game called Ghetto, which affords the players a view of life from the perspective of low-income persons.[13] Other games focus on psychological conditions. One of these is Group Therapy, designed to help persons loosen up and become open and honest with each other. Some experts question the attraction of such "instant therapy." On the other hand, proponents point out that the games are an obvious extension of the current search for open communication. These games exploit psychoanalytic theories and techniques and the popularity of sensitivity training, psychodrama, encounter groups, nude psychology, and other forms of therapeutic group interaction.[14]

The theory underlying sensitivity groups has been discussed in previous chapters. A well-led therapy group can offer a "safe" catharsis for "hang-ups," because the proceedings are controlled by a trained leader. The greatest weakness of simulation games, and specifically the psychological games, lies in the fact that there is no qualified leader—only a host who reads instructions. Most professional psychologists and psychiatrists agree on the need for a leader in group therapy. In games people may naïvely voice thoughts and feelings about each other with no assurance that the recipients of the information are emotionally prepared to handle it. This situation can be particularly dangerous when two or more persons in the group have similar problems and attempt to "treat" one another during the course of the game. In such encounters a professional therapist should be present to control the situation.

But social games that have an external focus have proved useful. Examples are Smog and Dirty Water, which deal with air and water pollution. The inventor of Smog created the game for frustrated youths who are dedicated to cleaning up the environment but are too naïve to cope with political realities.[15] The players of Smog learn that it is neither wise nor possible to restrict industry indiscriminately. Both games are also designed to influence industrial leaders who fail to realize that combating pollution can often increase profits in the long run by making workers happier, increasing their productiivty, and slowing despoilment of valuable natural resources.

STARPOWER

Starpower is an interpersonal simulation game that emphasizes conflict among members of a stagnant three-tiered (upper-, middle-, lower-class) society. To progress upward in the society, the players must gain

[13] "Ghetto," *Newsweek*, December 7, 1970, 61.

[14] Barbara Ford, "Games That Play With Your Psyche," *Science Digest*, March, 1970, 26.

[15] Daniel Zwerdlin, "On a Dirty Day You Can Play Forever," *New Republic*, August 29, 1970, 11.

wealth by trading. The medium of exchange is poker chips, which, singly or in combination, are worth set amounts. After a few rounds of trading the group with the most wealth, or points, makes the rules for the rest of the society. The purpose of the game is to stimulate discussions about the uses of power. The stated goal of each player is to accumulate the most wealth.

In the initial briefing four rules are set forth for the players:

1. Players must hold hands to trade.
2. Persons who do not wish to trade must fold their arms.
3. Chips must be hidden, not disclosed.
4. Players can trade with any circle, square, or triangle (circles represent the lower class, squares the middle class, and triangles the upper class).

Bargaining sessions last seven minutes. At the end of each session scores are taken by adding up the value of each player's chips. The scores are cumulative at the end of each round. The top scorers in the two lower groups are allowed to progress upward, replacing the lowest scorer in each respective higher group. There must always be a one-for-one exchange.

Power is concentrated in the upper class by virtue of its superior wealth and control over the rules of the game. The middle class is not powerless but tends to maintain an essentially laissez-faire attitude. The lower class derives its power from moral authority and the threat of violence. One of the weaknesses of the game is that there are no police to enforce the rules. When the upper class attempts to impose an unfair tax on the group, the middle and lower classes frequently refuse to pay it, and there is no way to enforce the legal taxation.

One of the most valuable by-products of this game is the insight players can gain about feelings of powerlessness. It is a frustrating experience to be placed in the lowest group, and for those players who grew up in an upper- or middle-class environment the experience is usually very enlightening. Indeed, being placed in a position of power-lessness has a considerable effect on almost all players.

The most interesting phenomenon which usually takes place is the change in goals. Prestige and power associated with superior wealth remain the goal for the middle and upper classes; however, political power becomes the goal of the lower class as its members realize that, no matter what strategy they use, they are not likely to be able to improve their position significantly without political coalitions.

Another interesting development in the course of the game is the emergence of leaders. Those who have been acknowledged as leaders of the group before the game frequently do not maintain their positions

382

of authority when they are placed in the lower group.

While it is unwise to assert unqualifiedly the usefulness of Starpower for identification and assessment of potential leaders, tentative hypotheses can certainly be formulated about how they behave in a simulated task situation.

The Poverty Game[16]
JAMES EGBERT

Children learn by play. So do adults. . . . There are still adults who believe that children should listen quietly as their teacher tells them what to believe and how to act. However, most church-school teachers know that children learn best while they play with blocks, water, trucks, or paint. Regretfully, we still want older children, youth, and adults to work. We forget that everyone learns through play, as they act out, participate in, and simulate life.

With this understanding, educators have begun to develop classroom games. We are just beginning to explore their vast possibilities in learning. Simulation games are exciting and stimulating for both student and teacher. A class can engage in learning experiences once impossible. Games are miniature models of life. They teach participants to deal with reality. Games produce immediate, vital, lasting education.

THE GAME

Supplies: A collection of magazines, a quantity of Elmer's Glue, scissors, a packet of bright construction paper, an assortment of dull faded construction paper, scrap paper, foil paper, vividly colored tissue paper, pipe cleaners, dirty yarn, soda straws, clean yarn, cigarette butts, etc. Numbered envelopes containing pieces of construction paper marked one cent, two cents, three cents, four cents, five cents, according to the needs described below.

Preparation: Divide your group into the following categories: citizens (the majority of your group), storekeepers, a policeman, welfare workers, a clergyman, an organizer of the poor, a group of observers, and a game supervisor to keep the game moving.

Citizens indiscriminately receive money on this scale: in a group of ten, three have no money, two have three cents, two have six cents, one has ten cents, one has twelve cents, and one has seventeen cents. A larger group would have more wealth but a wider distribution of poverty. For instance, in a group of twenty participants: six have no

[16] By James Egbert. Reprinted from *Colloquy* by permission of the United Church Press.

money, four have three cents, two have ten cents, four have six cents, one has twelve cents, one has fifteen cents, and one has twenty cents. The welfare workers receive half-cents to give as welfare payments and the storekeepers money for change.

PLAN OF ACTION

1. The citizens are told they must produce a collage in twenty minutes. They are given sealed money envelopes and told that supplies are sold at various stores. At the end of the time period, every citizen must have a collage to hang on the wall.

2. Storekeepers sell materials the workers need. In a Glue Store, one dab of Elmer's Glue costs one cent; in an Equipment Store, scissors are three cents; in a Paper Store, a small sheet of colored tissue paper is two cents, construction paper is three cents, and scrap materials may be any price. A Junk Store has such items as pictures torn from magazines, chicken feathers, and wilted flowers. Storekeepers may overcharge, sell damaged merchandise, or bargain with customers. They should encourage wealthy customers to spend money. The poor should be mistreated. Near the end of the time limit, storekeepers can increase or reduce prices. They can send a policeman to collect an I.O.U. A citizen can be jailed for not paying.

3. The police patrol the area. They spy on the poor and harass them. They especially watch for cheating and stealing. They rough up offenders. They ridicule poor people and side with the wealthy. They make arrests and place offenders in a "jail" for one to five minutes.

4. The welfare worker has a few half-cent pieces. He assists the poor, but requires them to fill out long forms and wait for long periods before receiving help. He asks personal questions like: "What will you do with your money? How much money did you get? Have you tried to get money somewhere else?" He gives one-quarter and half-cent allowances.

5. The clergyman gives out very little money. He talks about the poor people's relationship to the church and gives money only if people promise to attend church. He asks several rich people for money for the poor.

6. The supervisor is the director of the game. He must know who is assuming what role and who has money. He acts as a catalyst and is very pushy and insulting. He demands that the poor produce more work but is very critical of their work. He rejects even the finished products, saying they could have been better.

7. The organizer of the poor attempts to unite them. He can organize sit-ins, demonstrations, boycotts, or whatever. He may achieve

384

his goal in either a constructive or destructive way. The police are very much opposed to such activity and act accordingly.

8. The observers have a list of citizens and how much money each has received. They record the comments and interaction of the group for later discussion.

At the end of the game, all collages are displayed. The participants may jeer or cheer. The supervisor should ask the feelings of the participants and compare them to real life situations. They should note who has money at the end of the game.

AN EDITOR OBSERVES THE GAME PLAYED

I played The Poverty Game at Faith Presbyterian Church in Medford, New Jersey. The leader, equipped with supplies, explained the objectives of the game. He divided us according to plan, privately briefing those who had special roles. Each person was to play his part seriously —and honestly. We had one variation in the game—and I think it was effective. All who had no money wore black masks. (One was the labor organizer.)

We began. The leader, acting as supervisor, kept the action going by making various suggestions to players. He told the welfare worker to keep her "wards" coming back each day, told the minister to give long preachy sermons, told the storekeeper to make the poor wait and attend to the rich.

At the end of the game, the group gathered. Who had the most money? The minister. He collected large sums of money and gave little away. Next were the storekeepers, the wealthiest a man who catered solely to the rich. The policeman had the next largest amount. He accepted money from the poor who wanted to stay out of jail.

Each participant spoke of his experience. Frustration was the name of the game. The most frustrated was the man trying to organize the poor—and thus help them. The poor, especially the black poor, were frustrated because they were unable to buy collage materials. They borrowed money but had to pay such a large interest rate that their materials were usually repossessed. One man's anger and frustration drove him to steal supplies. He was thrown in jail. Others spoke of the difficulty of being believed or trusted—an experience alien to most of us. Some of the poor were hired by the rich to make their collages. They worked long hours and were paid so little they could not afford collages of their own. The poor who committed crimes were punished more severely than others.

We all gained some understanding of the dynamics of poverty, and the anger, frustration, and hopelessness it brings. We discussed these

385

*feelings and their power to dehumanize, to drive, or to depress people.
We asked how the church might respond to them. Even those initially
pessimistic about the game's value agreed that people can learn by
playing.*

SUMMARY: TO PLAY OR NOT TO PLAY

The advantages of simulation gaming are impressive. From the perspective of human relations, the most important advantage is the interest and enthusiasm they create. Some games that focus on self-
discipline and self-judgment offer the players a chance to practice
decision making and to accept responsibility for their actions. Although
simulations must perforce simplify reality, they offer a degree of realism that can be complex, as can be seen in the labored decisions that
participants are many times forced to make. The empathy that participants gain in some games is certainly a step toward erasing destructive prejudice and discrimination in schools and communities.

Many games provide learning situations for both the slow and the
gifted. When used in classrooms, they can serve as points of departure
for class discussions. They can help anchor abstract ideas to concrete
and realistic situations and thus increase the players' confidence in
their ability to relate to world, national, state, and local issues—and to
do so as individuals. In sum, games can teach facts, processes, and
alternative strategies.

Alice Kaplan Gordon has listed other benefits games offer: interaction and peer learning, awareness of the techniques of competition
and cooperation, perception of self and problem solving, and socialization techniques.[17] A useful by-product of simulation games is the
emergence of leaders. As Gordon observes, the brightest students are
not necessarily the "winners" of simulation games. One reason for this
seeming anomaly is that games offer more leadership roles than are
normally available in classroom activities. The slow student is willing
to risk more because it is "only a game" and, therefore, he may perform
differently from the way he would under real-life circumstances.

In contrast to role playing, game playing involves more people and
usually lasts for a longer period of time. But simulation games have
limitations that make it mandatory to select with care those to be used
in the classroom. It is important to remember that, no matter how
sophisticated they are, games are artificial. They are not reality; they
simulate reality by singling out and emphasizing specific variables.
Some games are poorly designed and are a waste of time. Worst of all,
winning may be overemphasized in games designed to accelerate
learning.

[17] Alice Kaplan Gordon, *Games for Growth.*

386

Research has not yet determined that games are superior to traditional teaching techniques. Simulation games are not easy to direct, and inadequately prepared leaders may destroy the effectiveness of the game. On the whole, however, properly selected and conducted, simulation games are a valuable tool for human relations practitioners, particularly when used to supplement other learning situations.

Chapter 14
SUGGESTED READING

Abt, Clark C. *Serious Games.* New York, Viking Press, Inc., 1970.

Barton, Richard F. *A Primer on Simulation and Gaming.* Englewood Cliffs, N.J., Prentice-Hall, Inc., 1970.

Benson, Dennis. *Gaming.* Nashville, Abingdon Press, 1971.

Boocock, Sarane S., and G. O. Schild, eds. *Simultation Games in Learning.* Beverly Hills, Calif., Sage Publications, 1968.

Carlson, Elliot. *Learning Through Games: A New Approach to Problem Solving.* Washington, D.C., Public Affairs Press, 1969.

Coleman, James S. "Games as Vehicles for Social Theory," *American Behavioral Scientist,* Vol. 12 (July–August, 1969).

———. "Introduction: In Defense of Games," *American Behavioral Scientist,* Vol. 10 (October, 1966).

———. *Simulation Games and Social Theory.* Occasional Paper. John Hopkins University, 1968.

Cruickshank, Donald E. "Simulation: New Direction in Teacher Preparation," *Phi Delta Kappan,* Vol. 48 (September, 1966).

Dill, William R., and Neil Droppelt. "The Acquisition of Experience in a Complex Management Game," *Management Science,* Vol. 10 (October, 1963).

Duke, Richard D. *Gaming-Simulations in the Teaching of Urban Sociology.* East Lansing, Michigan State University, 1970.

Ford, Barbara. "Games That Play With Your Psyche," *Science Digest,* March, 1970.

Gordon, Alice Kaplan. *Games for Growth.* Chicago, Science Research Associates, Inc., 1971.

Griffin, Sidney F. *The Crisis Game: Simulating International Conflict.* New York, Doubleday & Company, Inc., 1965.

Guetzkow, Harold, ed. *Simulation in Social Science.* Engelwood Cliffs, N.J., Prentice-Hall, Inc., 1962.

Hausrath, Alfred H. *Venture Simulation in War, Business, and Politics.* New York, McGraw-Hill Book Company, 1971.

Hermann, Charles F. *Crisis in Foreign Policy: A Simulation Analysis.* Indianapolis, The Bobbs-Merrill Company, 1969.

Klietsch, Ronald G. *An Introduction to Learning Games and Instructional Simulations.* St. Paul, Minn., Instructional Simulations & Games Company, 1969.

Maleiver, Bruce L. *The Encounter Game.* New York, Stein and Day, 1973.

McKenney, James, and William R. Dill. "Influences on Learning in Simulation Games," *American Behavioral Scientist,* Vol. 10 (October, 1966).

Meier, Robert C., William T. Newell, and Harold L. Pozer. *Simulation in Business and Economics.* Engelwood Cliffs, N.J., Prentice-Hall, Inc., 1969.

Postman, Neil, and Charles Weingartner. *Teaching as a Subversive Activity.* New York, Delacorte Press, 1969.

Raser, John R. *Simulation and Society: An Exploration of Scientific Gaming.* Boston, Allyn & Bacon, Inc., 1969.

Rottenberg, Don. "Can You Come Over for Mob Strategy Tonight—Or Will It Be a Game of Adultery?" *Today's Health,* August, 1971.

Shubik, Martin. *Game Theory and Related Approaches to Social Behavior.* New York, John Wiley & Sons, Inc., 1964.

Twelker, Paul A. *Instructional Simulation Systems.* Corvallis, Oreg., Continuing Education Publications, Oregon State University, 1969.

Venditti, F. P. *Program Directors for Solving Multi-Ethnic Problems: A Simulation Game for Elementary and High School Teachers.* Knoxville, University of Tennessee, 1970.

Vesugi, Thomas K., and W. Vinacke. "Strategy in a Feminine Game," *Sociometry,* Vol. 26 (March, 1963).

Werner, Roland, and Joan T. Werner. *Bibliography of Simulations: Social Systems and Education.* LaJolla, Calif., Western Behavioral Sciences Institute, 1969.

Youngers, John C., and John F. Aceti. *Simulation Games and Activities for Social Studies.* Dansville, N.Y., The Instructor Publications, 1969.

Zuckerman, David W., and Robert E. Horn. *The Guide to Simulation Games for Education and Training,* 2d. ed. Lexington, Mass., Information Resources, Inc., 1973.

Zwerdlin, Daniel. "On a Dirty Day You Can Play Forever," *New Republic,* August 29, 1970.

*The poor also need mediators, or third parties, in their
dealings with institutions or agencies. A rent strike,
grievance meeting, or even a phone call to the landlord
is not always easily accomplished. The time period
between perceiving a problem and taking action toward
its resolution is often characterized by anxiety and
turmoil.—*DAVID HEYMANN

By now it should be clear that the problems confronting professional
change agents are both varied and awesome. A quick summary of the
seemingly insurmountable and rapidly worsening problems the nation
faces can all but immobilize the best-meaning among us. Yet, even
though we have been shocked awake by the world's imperfections,
standing wide-eyed in horror is an inadequate stance to assume. If we
are to move toward effective social change, we must forsake the posture
of untrained, traumatized innocents. The options are clear: we can
either hire out as mourners or try to become actively involved in abating and preventing social problems. We must become the realists about
whom Malcolm Boyd wrote:

*Shallow activism must . . . be changed into a considerably deeper
and more sophisticated sense of involvement. This calls for listening to
people outside one's own ingrown and myopic clique as well as sober
examination of self-righteousness in one's motives and actions. . . . A
realist throws away rose-colored glasses, straightens his shoulder and
looks freely about him in all directions. He wants to see whatever there
is to see, in relation to other people and things as well as to himself. A
realist alone comprehends hope. Optimism is as antithetical to authentic hope as pessimism. Hope is rooted in realism.*[1]

Commitment to social change does not mean *disorder*, but a *new*
order. Change agents do not remain detached, objective, and neutral.

[1] Malcolm Boyd, *Human Like Me, Jesus,* 128.

Far from it, for they are, first of all, human beings—with their own sets of values, attitudes, beliefs, fears, and dreams.

HOW TO GO DOWN FIGHTING

Peter Berger has suggested that there are autonomous responses to the social environment: (1) one may attempt to transform it, (2) one may withdraw from it, or (3) one may attempt to manipulate it.[2] For change agents transformation and manipulation are the relevant alternatives. According to Berger, transformation of social structures is possible because society not only forms individuals but also is formed by them. The survival of a social system requires the acceptance of its individual members. People are not and cannot be forced to perform all the cooperative acts required for the smooth functioning of a social system. Cooperation is ensured through the process of socialization; social controls are internalized. The status quo is maintained when individuals operate on a commonly shared definition of reality. Social change begins with a redefinition of reality.

The civil-rights movement began when black and white citizens began to question the social definition of the black and his "place" in society. That social definition was buttressed not only by social custom but also by law. When Mrs. Rosa Parks refused to move to the back of an Alabama bus she was breaking the law, and she was arrested. In a situation like this, part of the function of a charismatic leader is to appeal to a "law higher than man-made law." Saul Alinsky gave the following example of John L. Lewis' justification for the illegal activities of striking union members: "A man's right to a job transcends the right of private property."[3] In the civil-rights movement, a similar justification was made by Martin Luther King, Jr., who justified civil disobedience in terms of broad democratic, moral, and religious values.

The civil-rights movement relied heavily on tactics of nonviolent confrontation—sit-ins, marches, economic boycotts. These tactics have since been used for many purposes, such as peace movements and ecology campaigns. They have become popular partly because they call for large numbers of people but do not require large numbers of dollars. Public confrontation has been used primarily by the hard-core poor and the temporarily poor (students). Another advantage of such strategies is that they do not require political sophistication on the part of every participant. Individuals who participate in a public demonstration need not be professionals in the field of social change. The leaders, however, must be skilled and well disciplined, or energy will be dissipated in useless or even counterproductive activities.

[2] Peter Berger, *Invitation to Sociology: A Humanistic Perspective*, 121–31.
[3] Marion Sanders, *The Professional Radical: Conversations with Saul Alinsky*, 16.

Among the hard-core poor one significant advantage of confrontation tactics is that they do not require skill in the manipulation of bureaucratic institutions. Poor people do not have to waste time on theoretical debates about whether they should try to work within or outside the system. The essence of their problem is that they are unable to get inside the system, whether or not they want to. When the poor attempt to influence bureaucratic institutions, their inability to play organization games of survival is usually even more crippling than their lack of financial resources.

In their article "Bureaucracy and the Lower Class," Gordon Sjoberg, Richard Brymer, and Buford Farris discuss the inability of members of the lower class to manipulate social-welfare institutions. Middle-class persons generally learn how to get special concessions by utilizing "backstage" maneuvers. The lower-class person tends to be intimidated by bureaucratic institutions and is often unaware of his rights and privileges in relation to those institutions. Because of his lack of knowledge about how organizations work, he is inept at manipulating them. This lack of organizational sophistication not only keeps him from shaping social welfare institutions to fit his needs but also keeps him from effectively utilizing the programs that are available to him.[4]

The techniques commonly used by the powerful to control the powerless are externally imposed and include moralizing, rhetoric, and coercion. It thus becomes increasingly important for citizens to participate actively in the shaping of their futures. Human relations practitioners begin "where people are at" and from this starting point help people find the ways and the strength to move individually and collectively to "where they want to be."[5]

The low status of the poor, a status which generally is a severe handicap in their social functioning, can sometimes operate as a perverse kind of asset. Having little to lose in terms of prestige, some poor persons challenge oppressive agency administrators. Much has been written about the superior organizational skills of members of the middle class. However, Saul Alinsky, who advocated a different kind of "organizing," saw the middle class as very difficult to organize. His definition of organization called for action on a minute-to-minute basis —even if it meant being rude and making a scene. A successfully socialized middle-class person has a deeply ingrained aversion to being rude or making a scene. Alinsky illustrated his point with this story:

To give you an example, I was flying into New York from San Fran-

[4] Gordon Sjoberg, Richard Brymer, and Buford Farris, "Bureaucracy and the Lower Class," *Sociology and Social Research*, Vol. 50 (April, 1966), 331.
[5] Julie Hover, Betty Levy, and Susan R. Sacks, "Training for Political Awareness and Commitment," *Social Change*, Vol. 1 (1971), 5.

cisco during an air traffic jam-up. We were due at five-thirty but didn't make it until about eleven o'clock that night. We'd only eaten one meal all day. The hotel we went to had kept the dining room open but they'd run out of entrees. So I found myself with a grilled cheese sandwich and a cup of coffee. Some people sitting near me ordered griddle cakes. The waitress brought them but not the syrup and butter. Every time they said "Miss," she would say "Wait a minute," and the cakes were getting colder and colder. I tapped one of them on the shoulder and asked if they wanted the butter and syrup. He said, yes, we would appreciate it. So in a loud voice I yelled across the floor, "Hey, get off your goddam ass and bring the butter and syrup right now." Which she did. These people were so horrified that they kept telling the waitress they didn't know me, had nothing to do with me, that they were not responsible for the scene. Of course while they were saying this they ate their butter and syrup on the griddle cakes.[6]

The unwillingness of "respectable" middle-class citizens and community leaders to employ certain kinds of tactics explains the paradox discussed by William Kornhauser.[7] He observed that those elements in a community that do *not* have power often win controversies. His conclusion was based on a study of the referendums held on fluoridation in many American communities during the 1950's. The powerful and prestigious persons were generally for fluoridation, but fluoridation was rejected over 50 per cent of the time. The profluoridation forces did not go all out in fighting for fluoridation because they did not want to alienate large numbers of persons. The antifluoridation group, on the other hand, was composed of people who had, in general, less education, lower occupational status, and lower incomes. They did not have commitments or responsibilities in the community and were not subjected to the restraints experienced by those who had economic and political interests. Because they normally did not participate in community organization, they did not have any experience with, or commitment to, the normal rules of the game. Kornhauser quoted James Coleman's analysis of the effects of social isolation:

People who feel apart and unidentified are quickest to overstep the bounds of legitimate methods and carry the dispute into disruptive channels. When there are few or none who are identified, then there are essentially no norms to restrain the opposing sides. . . . Conversely, if most people and organizations in the community are identified with the community as a whole, then the potentially disruptive effects of the

[6] Sanders, *op. cit.*, 89–90.
[7] William Kornhauser, "Power and Participation in the Local Community," in *Perspectives on the American Community* (ed. by Roland Warren), 489–94.

dispute are felt by all; there are conscious attempts at reconciliation.[8]

Poor and alienated members of society frequently gravitate toward "extremist," "disruptive" tactics because "legitimate" channels are often closed to them. The use of legitimate methods requires access to and skill in the manipulation of existing social institutions. Generally, middle-class persons are able to work within the bounds of social systems. Furthermore, the penalty imposed on a middle-class person who refuses to work within those bounds tends to be rather harsh. Thus, middle-class persons are restrained by more than an aversion to making a scene.

Most persons remain in the middle class, respectable and employed, by working through the "proper channels." This is especially important if their job involves working with leaders of the community who are poor and alienated, since such leaders are, as noted above, quick to overstep organizational boundaries. Social workers, as links between the haves and the have-nots, must deal with the conflicts inherent in serving a population that is drastically different from, and essentially at the mercy of, the constituency which financially supports the social-welfare institution.

Lydia Rapaport has stated that social workers tend to identify ideologically with the problems and needs of the economically and socially disadvantaged groups which they largely serve.[9] One factor that counteracts this tendency, however, is professional socialization. In many schools social-work education stresses the idea that the social worker should "empathize" but not "identify with" the client, claiming that a certain degree of emotional detachment is necessary if objective judgments are to be made. Social workers who "overidentify" with their clients are described as emotionally and professionally immature:

If he [the social worker] seeks to "take the role of the client" in the sense of understanding the latter's belief and value system, he will ultimately have to challenge or at least question some of the rules that govern the operation of the system of which he is a part. For if he understands why clients act the way they do, he is likely to recognize that they have valid reasons for objecting to his conception of reality or more specifically, to some of the bureaucratic regulations.[10]

The dilemma of the social-service worker was articulated in a letter written to VISTA program director Sargent Shriver by two volunteers

[8] *Ibid.*, 495.

[9] Lydia Rapaport, "In Defense of Social Work: An Examination of Stress in the Profession," in *Perspective on Social Welfare* (ed. by Paul Weinberger), 446.

[10] Sjoberg et al., *op. cit.*, 329.

who were fired from the program because of their involvement in organizing a waitress strike:

The VISTA volunteer on the job occupies a most difficult and precarious position in his relation to institutions and organizations with and for which he works. . . . On the one hand, the Volunteer works for and receives a subsistence allowance from the VISTA organization. . . . But on the other hand, the Volunteer is assigned to work on a project for a sponsoring agency and is directed to accept guidance for actual "work in the field" from that agency through a VISTA supervisor. The third dimension of role conflict is the commitment of the Volunteer to the poor and their organizations. Thus the Volunteer must walk a tight wire between three or more organizations, all of which are often claiming the right to direct our steps.[11]

One of the volunteers who wrote the letter quoted above decided, after losing his job with VISTA, to stay in the community as an independent worker. He said that he felt that he had been terminated not for neglecting his job of fighting poverty but for doing his job too effectively and "rocking the boat." (The boat had been rocked so hard that the governor of the state involved had gone to Washington about the matter, and VISTA administrators had concluded that the two volunteers would have to be sacrificed to save the rest of the program.)

Organizational maintenance must be a primary goal of the administrator, whether the program is privately or publicly funded. This was dramatically illustrated in 1963 by Community Progress Incorporated (CPI), of New Haven, Connecticut, which was at that time funded by the Public Affairs Program of the Ford Foundation. CPI was one of the Ford Foundation's "gray-area" projects intended to take on three "tough and diverse jobs":
—*of trying to mesh the policies and operations of separate public and private jurisdictions;*
—*of working with disadvantaged minority groups, particularly the Negro community;*
—*of looking beyond old and fixed ways of doing things, to invent and evaluate new approaches in education, housing, employment, legal services, and welfare.*[12]

The project sounded very bold and innovative. However, from the beginning New Haven's community-action program was promoted and protected by city hall, and CPI quickly became dependent upon the city's power structure. When CPI, with the cooperation of the New

[11] Quoted in William Crook and Ross Thomas, *Warriors for the Poor.*
[12] Daniel P. Moynihan, *Maximum Feasible Misunderstanding,* 36.

Haven County Bar Association, set up a program of legal aid for the poor, its intention was to supply legal help to poor families—that is, to provide advice on simple matters and to make referrals on more complex cases. However, one of the two lawyers (a concerned liberal) interpreted her role more broadly than CPI had intended. Believing that as a lawyer her first duty was to the cause of justice rather than to her employer, she sought to provide legal advice for complex cases rather than to refer them. The result was continuing friction between her and the agency director.

The problem came to a head in February, 1963, when three young black men were accused of assaulting and raping a white nurse. Two of the accused pleaded guilty. The third pleaded innocent, and his mother asked CPI's legal aid for help, believing that the public defender was not only inexperienced but also unsympathetic toward her son. The director of CPI refused the request. All three men were convicted and sentenced, and the concerned liberal attorney resigned. The program went on, with the continuing support of the mayor and the community.[13]

Neil Gilbert has summarized the dilemma faced by the professional in antipoverty programs.[14] He may try to play a politically neutral role as a "middleman" between the "distributors" and the "consumers" of social services. In such a role coordination and cooperation are stressed, and federal funds are not used to disrupt the activities of local agencies. This is a difficult role to maintain because the interests of the poor frequently do not coincide with those of the welfare system. The practitioner's dilemma is clear: if the middleman attempts to avoid overloading the system by placing a lid on demand, he has sold out to the system. If he chooses to support his client's demands, he is labeled an agitator by his agency.

In the preceding examples the social practitioners lost when they decided to act as advocates of the poor. Both were examples of might against right, and might won out both times. This pattern has been repeated many times in social-welfare programs across the country. Even when entire agencies take on the advocacy role, the result is usually the same. Daniel Moynihan described the typical four-stage sequence for client-advocating agencies:

First, a period of organizing, with much publicity and great expectations everywhere. Second, the beginning of operations, with the onset of conflict between the agency and local government institutions, with even greater publicity. Third, a period of counterattack from local

[13] Peter Marris and Martin Rein, *Dilemmas of Social Reform*, 157, 171–73.
[14] Neil Gilbert, *Clients of Constituents*, 26–27.

395

government, not infrequently accompanied by conflict and difficulties, including accounting troubles, within the agency itself. Fourth, victory for the established institutions, or at best, stalemate, accompanied by bitterness and charges of betrayal. . . . Whereupon it would emerge that the community action agency, which had talked so much, been so much in the headlines, promised so much in the way of change in the fundamentals of things, was powerless.[15]

Moynihan believes that most poverty warriors have been rather naïve in thinking that American taxpayers will willingly subsidize Saul Alinsky–type tactics against established social institutions.

Given the fact that the establishment does not seem eager to finance its own destruction (or even significant alteration), one possible alternative is to become an independent organizer or an organizer for an antiestablishment organization. This approach is basically the same as that used by the radical labor leaders of the 1930's and 1940's. According to Alan McSurely, establishment-oriented groups teach their organizers to (1) maintain objectivity and view people as "cases," (2) develop commitment to their professional groups, (3) set up one-way communication links with their "cases," (4) try to develop a consensus within existing political forces, and (5) develop new service programs to placate the clients.[16] The style of antiestablishment organizing advocated by McSurely involves (1) treatment of persons as persons rather than as "cases," (2) complete personal commitment, (3) honest communication, and (4) the goal of building strong new leadership and independent political forces.

Some of the problems encountered by McSurely's antiestablishment organizers have been described by Paul Bullock. One problem is the difficulty of developing a community organization which actually represents the entire community. It is unlikely that more than a small percentage of community residents will ever become actively involved in the organization, which means that there is a good chance that the views of many citizens will be unrepresented or misrepresented. The persons whose views are most likely to be heard are the atypical ones who are inclined to speak out about their problems. The residents who gravitate toward leadership positions tend to be upwardly mobile persons who are relatively sophisticated about available opportunities for advancement and are motivated to take advantage of them. There is thus a danger that the organization will be dominated by individuals who are inclined to use the organization to serve personal rather than community ends.[17]

[15] Moynihan, *op. cit.*, 131, 135.
[16] Alan McSurely, *Hangups*, 1–3.
[17] Paul Bullock, "Morality and Tactics in Community Organizing," in *Poverty: Views*

396

Another problem faced by the antiestablishment organizer is the defeatist, cynical attitude prevalent in low-income neighborhoods. Low-income life does little to nurture the hope and cooperative spirit required for successful community organization. When the organizer arrives, he is viewed with suspicion. Ghetto dwellers tend to assume either that the organizer is a patsy who can be exploited by them or that he has arrived to take advantage of someone else. The slum dweller is not likely to share the ideology of a new-leftist organizer. The immediate interest of the poor person is to have more money, not to promote the community or to restructure society.

The issues on which a successful community organizer will focus will usually be practical, immediate problems. If the people choose their own direction, the push will generally be toward reform measures that will fit easily within the framework of the prevailing social systems. Even if the organizer has more radical goals, he must adjust to reality as that reality is defined by his clients.

The need to tailor his personal vision to fit the actual goals of a poor community is not the harshest reality with which the organizer must deal. McSurely concluded that most of the organizer's "hangups" or negative attitudes are caused by fear.[18] Legal and physical harassment are but two reasons for this fear. Put it all together, and we can come up with one reason why there are not many radical community organizers: operating on their own, out in the open, using public confrontation tactics, radical organizers are very visible, very vulnerable, very unprotected. A person can get hurt that way. Moreover, there is no guarantee that mourners will flock to the funeral. For the would-be change agent, "fighting the system" is an alternative, but we should not be surprised when the system fights back.

HOW TO COME UP FIGHTING

A social practitioner can opt to "work within the system." Most people do. The question is: How effectively can one work for social change within the existing framework? Obviously, the answer depends on one's analysis of the existing framework. Jack Minnis decided, "those who control the economy of the nation are the *only ones* who have the power to change things. . . . I am now convinced that the nature of power in this society is such that it is a dangerous delusion to suppose those who wield it can be pressured to use it in ways they do not choose to and that, inevitably, they will choose to use it to the detriment of the people."[19]

from the Left (ed. by Jeremy Larner and Irving Howe), 140–48.

[18] McSurely, *op. cit.*, 15.

[19] Jack Minnis, *The Care and Feeding of Power Structures Revisited*, 6.

While C. Wright Mills would probably not agree, much of his work is based on the assumption that power in this country is centralized in the hands of a few. Mills discussed the liberal image of the American system of power as a moving balance of many competing interests. He dismissed the gutter fights of American politics as methods used by contestants on the middle level of power. The real decision makers, he concluded, are above and beyond it all.[20]

Floyd Hunter's essay "Community Power Structure: A Study of Decision Makers" is generally regarded as the classic documentation of the elitist power structure operating on the local level.[21] Hunter identified a number of power pyramids but described the major economic interests of the economy as "overwhelmingly represented" in the policy-making elite. Like Mills, Hunter saw the top decision makers as puppeteers who operate behind the public scene. Hunter believed that businessmen comprise the power elite in Regional City *as they do in other cities.*

An elitist interpretation of the social system furnishes a convenient explanation for those who believe that things are in a mess but do not want to blame the community as a whole. Aaron Wildavsky admitted that resources which can be used to affect public decisions are unequally distributed, but he maintained that effective resources are widely dispersed so that no one has all of them and few have none. Wildavsky also pointed out that persons who have control over resources use them sparingly or not at all and with varying degrees of effectiveness. His conclusion was that no person or group is powerful in all or even most of the significant areas of community life. The general pattern is for different individuals and groups to make decisions in different issue areas.[22]

Although Hunter's work is sometimes interpreted to mean that businessmen have a total monopoly on power, his diagram of the community decision-making system designates high-level government employees and top-ranking members of civic and professional associations as "upper limits power personnel."

Munger's discussion of public decision making in Syracuse underscored the significance of the power of government employees and social-welfare and professional groups: the initiators of public action are most freueqntly professional members of governmental agencies.

[20] C. Wright Mills, *Power, Politics, and People*, 25–31.

[21] Floyd Hunter, "Community Power Structure and Social Welfare," in *Social Perspectives on Behavior* (ed. by Herman Stein and Richard Cloward), 397–418.

[22] Aaron Wildavsky, "Why American Cities are Pluralist," in *Politics in the Metropolis* (ed. by Thomas Dye and Brett Hawkins), 346–56.

Wildavsky's analysis was confirmed by Frank Munger's description of the Syracuse, New York, metropolitan area:

First, the myth that significant decisions in Syracuse emanate from one source does not stand up under close scrutiny. Second, there tend to be as many decision centers as there are important decision areas, which means that the decision-making power is fragmented among the institutions, agencies, and individuals which cluster about these areas. Third, in reality there appear to be many kinds of community power, with one kind differing from another in so many fundamental ways as to make a meaningful comparison impossible.[23]

Professionals provide the expertise which turns ideas into viable plans of action. The plan of action is then promoted, primarily through the mass media. Although publicity is nominally aimed at the general public, it is usually directed toward the specific groups believed to hold the power of decision. The message will generally be aimed at public officials and dominant economic groups. On many issues, however, the support of the major institutionalized social-welfare and professional groups is so important that they are in fact the primary targets of the message.

All organizations, as subsystems of the larger society, are affected and constrained by forces in the larger society. Even so, there is much evidence to indicate that social-welfare bureaucracies, with their control of vast institutional resources, operate with a considerable measure of autonomy. Governmental social-service agencies neither depend on nor are controlled by their clients. Such agencies may gain so much power that they are not really controlled by either taxpayers or elected officials.

Seymour Lipset studied the techniques used by conservative civil servants to block the progress of progressive socialistic and social-welfare governments. He specifically documented the experience of the social-democratic movement which gained control of the British government toward the end of World War II.[24] The newly elected socialist cabinet minister anticipated resistance to their plans on the part of the civil service. They entered office prepared to get rid of all high-ranking civil servants who showed opposition to their plans, and many civil servants expected to be discharged or demoted. To keep their positions, the civil servants went to great lengths to ingratiate

[23] Frank Munger, "Community Power and Metropolitan Decision-making," in *Strategies of Community Organization* (ed. by Frank Cox et al.), 363.

[24] Symour Lipset, "Bureaucracy and Social Reform," in *Complex Organizations* (ed. by Amitai Etzioni), 262–63.

themselves with the new officials. They were "outwardly obsequious, flattered their ministers, and in general did everything they could to convince the cabinet that they were cooperative." The new ministers were delighted and began to trust and depend on the experienced civil servants.

As soon as the civil servants realized that they were in no danger of being discharged they went back to conducting their departments as they had always done, a procedure most of them reasoned to be much easier than changing the system. Most of the top-ranking officials were members of the upper social class, and they felt that the reforms advocated by the socialist ministers were radical and would not work. Lipset listed three methods used by civil servants to modify government policies: (1) the continuation by government departments of traditional, and from the socialist point of view, "reactionary" modes of procedure; (2) changes in the intent of new laws and regulations through administrative practices; and (3) direct and indirect methods of influencing cabinet members to adopt policies advocated by top-level civil servants.[25]

Eventually the dependence of the cabinet ministers on civil servants who were preventing implementation of reform precipitated such conflict between the ministers and nonofficeholding members of their party that the ministers were forced to replace experienced administrators with new personnel who were more sympathetic. At this point departmental policies began to come into line with the goals of the elected officials. The fact that such changes could be made by administrators who were motivated to do so points up the influence of personal attitudes and social background on organizational behavior. The fact that the will of the electorate and the goals of the elected officials were not carried into action until sympathetic administrators were appointed demonstrates Lipset's observation that the members of the administrative bureaucracy constitute one of the major "houses" of government, and as such have the power to initiate, amend, and veto actions proposed by other branches.

Bureaucratic autonomy on the local level was discussed by Edward Banfield and James Wilson in *City Politics*. They pointed out that top officials in local governmental hierarchies must make policy decisions which affect their power base and are essentially political in nature. Even in strong-mayor cities the mayor's ability to control his administrative subordinates is limited. Banfield and Wilson offered this illustration:

In New York, when Mayor Wagner said something about sending

[25] *Ibid.*, 263.

police patrols into housing projects, he received a polite but firm reminder from his subordinate, the police commissioner, that he, the mayor, had nothing to say in the matter. "Needless to say," the police commissioner wrote him, "I, as Police Commissioner, having sole responsibility under the law for the disposition of the police force, will go on making my determinations according to professional police judgment and with reference to the best interests of the citizen as a whole."[26]

The fact that government bureaucracies are not completely under the thumb of clients, the general taxpaying public, or elected officials does not preclude the possibility that public administrators are the puppets of community decision makers.

Many local agencies are controlled by rules and regulations decided at the state or federal level. The agency's freedom of action may be considerably restricted by such rules. Furthermore, the rules may be so contradictory, so numerous, so complicated, and so changeable that only a few knowledgeable members of an agency know the latitude of action available to the agency. An example of this kind of control is the public-assistance program, which operates on a local level but within the framework of state and federal laws and regulations. In her study of the Massachusetts public-assistance programs Martha Derthick found local programs largely impervious to local influences.[27] Such programs were not seen to be much affected by client complaints, worker attitudes, or values of the larger community.

In the communities Derthick studied it was evident that if popularly elected government officials had been responsible for administration of public assistance, the rules would have been more restrictive, and more effort would have been made to differentiate between the "deserving" and the "undeserving" poor. Before the intervention of the state and the federal government in the welfare function, the local welfare boards had been very powerful. But at the time she made her study, the views of local elected officials and members of the welfare boards were largely irrelevant.

Intercity differences in administration of public administration were noticeable, and those inconsistencies were directly traceable to differences in executive direction—in the kinds of goals defined by the director of each agency and in the methods used to achieve them. In one agency, whose director was strongly committed to the concept of social service, the organization tended to be client-oriented and internally permissive. In another agency, which was not visibly different

26 Edward Banfield and James Wilson, *City Politics*, 218.
27 Martha Derthick, "Intercity Differences in Administration of the Public Assistance Program: The Case of Massachusetts," in *City Politics and Public Policy* (ed. by James Wilson), 254–55.

in terms of social and political environment, the director was rule-oriented and authoritarian, and workers were considerably more limited in the services they could provide to clients.

Such examples demonstrate not only the degree of autonomy sometimes enjoyed by social-service bureaucrats but also the skewing of power within them. In some instances the attitudes of individual social practitioners are not a significant variable. The fact that social-service bureaucracies have power does not mean that this power is placed in the hands of its personnel. The average practitioner has little to offer but dedication and limited expertise, and few large organizations are going to be awed by such resources. Successful work within an organization requires considerable skill in manipulating rules and people.

LEADING IN THE SHEEP

Murray G. Ross defines community organization as a process by which a community: (1) identifies its needs or objectives, (2) orders (or ranks) these needs or objectives, (3) develops the confidence and will to work at achieving these needs or objectives, (4) finds the resources (internal and external) to deal with these needs or objectives, (5) takes action in respect to them, and in so doing extends and develops cooperative and collaborative attitudes and practices in the community.[28]

Effective community organization rests upon the following humanistic value assumptions:

1. Dignity and worth are inherent in each individual.
2. Each individual has potential for social growth.
3. Each individual has the right and responsibility to participate in planning and managing his own life.

The human relations practitioner should be attuned to four basic variables affecting efforts to improve the quality of community life: discontent, leadership, involvement, and communication.

Deep-seated feelings of discontent with respect to specific aspects of community life are frequently the beginning of associations and organizations which unite diverse populations. Whether discontent will be a positive community factor depends upon the ability of group members to focus upon major areas of discontent and achieve unity of leadership.

To be effective, a leader must have the acceptance of and identification with the community or group. Of course, it helps if the leader is knowledgeable about external and internal resources, but more than knowledge is needed. A leader must be able to involve most (ideally, all) group members in the decision-making process.

[28] Murray G. Ross, *Community Organization: Theory Principles and Practices.*

Involvement includes gaining knowledge of the facts, circumstances, and potential solutions relevant to the community problem. Emotional as well as intellectual behavior is a means through which group members become involved, and both kinds of behavior are important.

Finally, communication is essential for the identification of the problem, selection of possible courses of action, and the securing of support from members of the community. Previous life experiences, cultural differences, and individual biases are but a few of the factors which must be overcome before group members can achieve consensus.

Much of a community organizer's work consists of getting members of a community to identify and deal with such feelings as powerlessness, apathy, and despair.

TO MANIPULATE OR NOT TO MANIPULATE

In *The Machiavellians*, Stanley Guterman describes Machiavellianism as an "amoral, manipulative attitude toward other individuals, combined with a cynical view of men's motives and of their character."[29] Guterman's evidence suggests that we can differentiate between Machiavellians and non-Machiavellians and that this difference in moral character can be traced to differences in family background. Guterman's study of variations in the family milieu is based on Freud's explanation of the formation of the superego.

According to Freud, in making a child conform to their standards, parents force him to renounce instinctual gratification. The child's natural response is anger. However, the child who does not want to lose parental love does not express his anger openly. Instead, he turns his aggressive feelings inward in the form of guilt. On the basis of this theory Guterman hypothesizes that the strength of an individual's superego is affected by: (1) the strictness of his parents and (2) the amount of love they gave him when he was young. On the basis of his own research Guterman concludes that parents who are emotionally close to their children and strict in their discipline without being harsh and punitive are likely to produce children with strong superegos. Machiavellianism is often associated with low rapport between the parents and their children—inconsistency in home discipline and greater use of physical punishment.

Friendships established by Machiavellians tend to be less imtimate than those established by non-Machiavellians, and this is explained by the Machiavellian's unwillingness to invest strong emotions in his ties with others. It seems reasonable that Machiavellian tactics come more easily to some persons than to others. For persons in whom such values

[29] Stanley Guterman, *The Machiavellians*, 3.

403

as honesty and straightforwardness are deeply ingrained, the use of such tactics may be very difficult or impossible. However, looking around at social injustices, we can build a strong case that most Americans behave as Machiavellians at some time in their lives. It seems, therefore, that Machiavellianism can be used as a strategy by many persons who would not be characterized as amoral in their general outlook.

Machiavellian tactics may even be used at times by human relations practitioners. The reasons why such tactics might well be adopted have been best explained by Niccolò Machiavelli himself. The first is the difficulty and danger of attempting reform:

It must be considered that there is nothing more difficult to carry out, nor more doubtful of success, nor more dangerous to handle, than to initiate a new order of things. For the reformer has enemies in all those who profit by the old order, and only lukewarm defenders in all those who would profit by the new order, this lukewarmness arising partly from fear of their adversaries, who have the law in their favor; and partly from the incredulity of mankind, who do not truly believe in anything new until they have had actual experience of it.

The second reason is the danger of honesty and virtue, in contrast with the effectiveness of subterfuge:

It is not, therefore, necessary for a prince to have [virtuous] qualities, but it is very necessary to seem to have them. I would even be bold to say that to possess them and always to observe them is dangerous, but to appear to possess them is useful. Thus it is well to seem merciful, faithful, humane, sincere, religious, and also to be so; but you must have the mind so disposed that when it is needful to be otherwise you may change to the opposite qualities. . . . For how we live is so far removed from how we ought to live, that he who abandons what is done for what ought to be done, will rather learn to bring about his own ruin than his preservation.[30]

It could be argued that the behavior necessary for survival in the cut-throat world of sixteenth-century Italy would be inappropriate in twentieth-century America. The problem of justification of means cannot be morally avoided. The human relations professional is always in the process of change. As one goal is achieved, he is moving on to the next. He may be described in epitaphs in terms of his achievements, but his life is defined more by his means than by the ends that he occasionally reaches. Thus the change agent must come to terms with the

---

[30] Niccolo Machiavelli, *The Prince and the Discourses,* 21, 65, 56.

morality of the means he adopts. Saul Alinsky, discussing means and ends, said that the "man of action" understands that

in action one does not always have the luxury of a decision which is consistent both with one's individual conscience and the good of mankind. The choice must always be for the latter. Action is for mass salvation and not for the individual's idea of his own personal salvation. He who sacrifices the mass good for his personal conscience has a perverted conception of what is meant by "personal salvation."[31]

Alinsky also believed that the most unethical of all means is the nonuse of any means—doing nothing. Yet it is usually those who act rather than those who refuse to act who are expected to explain themselves. Similarly, change agents often feel a need to rationalize their manipulation of others. All human beings are both manipulating and manipulated in the natural course of life. It is generally overlooked that persons are responsible not only for their manipulation of others but also for the ways in which they allow themselves to be manipulated. Probably most evil acts are performed not by persons who see themselves as manipulators but by persons who view themselves as martyrs —victims of external forces. Peter Berger called this facet of individual moral responsibiilty "bad faith."[32] Bad faith involves pretending that behavior is forced when in fact it is voluntary. Often this occurs in connection with a social role: "I have to do this because I am a ——— (policeman, teacher, judge, administrator, etc.)." Such a statement willfully ignores the reality that each person has the option of rejecting or stepping outside his role. "I can't" is usually a preface to a socially acceptable alibi which allows the individual to present himself as a helpless victim of circumstances.

Since any society is a network of social roles and derives its stability from the willingness of individual members to accept these roles as absolutes, such self-deceit usually is not socially defined as deceit. To act out a role as if it were in fact the only possible way to act, to define oneself in terms of one's role, to believe completely in the role one is playing—all are essentially fraudulent acts, but all are required by society, and all of them fall under the socially accepted definition of "sincerity."

In *Modern Organization*, Amitai Etzioni discussed three methods of

[31] Saul Alinsky, "Of Means and Ends," in Cox et al., *Strategies of Community Organization*, 199.

[32] Berger, *op. cit.*, 142.

organizational control: physical, material, and symbolic.[33] Physical controls are seldom used against paid employees, regardless of their offenses. The organization's control of material resources, such as the employee's salary, is often felt by employees to be the primary determinant of their behavior ("Well, I would do that, but I've got three children to support"). However, the fear of loss of income is generally exaggerated. Many employees, such as government workers who are covered by civil-service provisions, are not usually in much danger of losing their jobs. As Ira Sharkansky has pointed out, public administrators must deal with statutory restrictions on their right to hire and fire employees:

Unlike the managers of private firms, the heads of many public agencies cannot readily discipline a subordinate who does not accept instructions. Civil service sanction procedures are lengthy and threaten to disrupt morale within an agency when they are invoked against an employee. Many administrators feel that it costs more in heartache to attempt dismissal proceedings than it would be worth in greater efficiency. . . . Because of the publicity involved, as well as the difficult procedures necessary to dismiss an employee who has civil service protection, a superior may not be able to fire his obstreperous subordinate or even to transfer him to a "harmless" assignment.[34]

In most social-service bureaucracies, the dominant factors impinging on role performance are social or symbolic rather than economic. Although the importance of the work group to the individual was first documented in studies of the factory worker, more recent research has indicated that the importance of informal work groups is probably even greater for persons in the higher ranks. The management-level person is more likely to have experienced social and geographical mobility, therefore cutting himself off from his parents, his place of birth, and his former friends. Consequently, he tends to rely more heavily on social relationships established at his place of work.

To the extent that work associates become a significant reference group for the individual, one would expect him to attempt to elicit their approval. As discussed earlier, Maslow's theory of the hierarchy of human needs postulates that needs are ranked in the following order, the person seeking satisfaction for the next higher needs as soon as the previous needs are satisfied: (1) physiological needs, (2) safety needs, (3) love needs, (4) esteem needs, and (5) needs for self-actualization. Under this theory the degree of need for work-group approval is af-

---

[33] Amitai Etzioni, *Modern Organizations*, 59.

[34] Ira Sharkansky, *Public Administration: Policy-Making in Government Agencies*, 44.

fected by the degree to which the individual's love and esteem needs are being satisfied by relationships outside of the work situation.

A certain measure of approval and respect from peers, superiors, and subordinates is necessary for effective functioning within any organization. This approval generally requires a fairly high degree of behavioral conformity on the part of the interacting individuals. Gordon Tullock concluded that the successful organizational politician

must be trusted by other persons, particularly by his superiors.... If he should develop a deviant personality, he would be unlikely to inspire much confidence in others. The rational politician will, therefore, make every effort to conform to the image of the "proper" person that is held by the membership of the organization man. He must become an "organization man."[35]

The individual may play his organizational roles either sincerely or cynically. Erving Goffman has used the term *sincere* to describe "individuals who believe in the impression fostered by their own performance."[36] On the other hand, the cynical performer realizes that he is putting on an act and is not taken in by it. The "politician," as described by Tullock, plays his role with cynical detachment. This kind of conformity masks an inner determination to manipulate the organization for personal ends. Tullock's description of the politics of bureaucracy sounds very much like Machiavelli's: "The successful politician is unlikely to adhere to the highest standards of ethics, but he must make a show of doing so."[37] According to Tullock, the politician cannot indulge in authentic interpersonal relationships with work associates. He must undermine his peers so that they will not rise above him, conceal from them the difference between his actual behavior and that demanded by their common superior.

The behavior of such an organizational politician might be described as *instrumental* rather than *expressive*. His behavior is designed to achieve personal goals; the information which he voluntarily supplies about himself is supplied for a purpose and may be fraudulent. Yet by such means he may win the esteem and approval of his organizational associates.

Posing in the nude and appearing in full costume—or false costume— is certain to elicit differing responses. Thus it would seem that each individual should evaluate his audience's response in terms of the manner in which he presents himself to them. Self-esteem based on false data is essentially different from esteem based on a more accurate

[35] Gordon Tullock, *The Politics of Bureaucracy*, 37.
[36] Erving Goffman, *The Presentation of Self in Everyday Life*, 17–18.
[37] Tullock, *op. cit.*, 38.

picture of his "real" self. Some critics would argue that any kind of esteem is better than no estem at all, but it seems that reality-based esteem is the most emotionally satisfying. If this is true, the need of persons to be "what they really are" is a factor encouraging open non-manipulative interpersonal relationships.

Ethical humanism is concerned with improving human relations. John Anton outlined the following principles of ethical humanism: (1) it aims at the fullest possible development of every human being, (2) it seeks to use science creatively rather than destructively, (3) it affirms the dignity of man and his right to the greatest possible freedom of development compatible with the rights of others, (4) it insists that personal liberty must be combined with social responsibility, and (5) it is a way of life aimed at maximum possible fulfillment through the cultivation of ethical and creative living.[38]

GOOD GUYS DON'T ALWAYS FINISH LAST

When individuals conspire together to bring about social change, honest and open interpersonal relationships are possible. Trust and interdependence evolve naturally from shared values and shared goals. The foundation of the human relations approach to organization is free communication, cooperation, and mutual respect among all members of the organization. In the ideal organization, as described by Warren Bennis, communication among members is full, free, and unaffected by rank or power.[39] Decisions are based on consensus rather than upon coercion or compromise. Influence is based on technical competence and knowledge rather than on hierarchical power. The organizational atmosphere encourages emotional expression as well as task performance. Conflict between the organization and the individual is accepted as inevitable and is mediated on rational grounds.

However, Bennis questioned the ability of human beings to work collaboratively in structures where relationships are based on full communication. He illustrated some problems inherent in open structures by quoting the command reputedly given by a movie producer to his staff: "I want you all to tell me what's wrong with our operation even if it means losing your job!" Yet without open communication, Bennis predicted, traditional hierarchical bureaucracies will fail because of their inability to adapt to rapid environmental changes. It is conceivable that bureaucracies as we know them are disappearing, but there is little evidence to support this contention. Gerald Caiden observed

[38] John P. Anton, "Human Excellence," in *Moral Problems in Contemporary Society* (ed. by Paul Kurtz), 128.
[39] Warren Bennis, *Changing Organizations*, 19.

408

that large-scale organizations, instead of disappearing, seem to be adapting themselves to changing conditions.[40]

Bennis and others are probably correct in believing that the value system which dominates modern organizations tends to produce inauthentic relationships which are coercive, false, static, unhelpful, and basically incomplete. Organizational relationships in traditional bureaucracies clearly do not allow the natural and free expression of feelings. Indeed, most organizations are breeding grounds for mistrust, intergroup conflict, ultraconformity, and rigidity.

It would be accurate to say that few organizations allow the individual to "be himself" or to express his "real self." The "self" can be viewed as a composite of many selves; the personality can be viewed as a learned repertoire of roles. According to Orville Brim, Jr., there is no "core personality" underneath the individual's behavior and feelings.[41] Even so, persons do subjectively experience differences in the "realness" of their behavior in different situations.

Goffman believes that all social interaction is composed of performances, with each person composing and playing the part of his chosen character.[42] He differentiates, however, between behavior in the "front stage" and "backstage" behavior. Western society, he has concluded, is characterized by the use of one language of behavior for informal or backstage interaction and another language of behavior for occasions when a performance is being presented. When he is "backstage," the individual can relax; he can drop his front, try speaking his mind, and step out of character. The higher an individual's social status, the smaller the number of persons with whom he can be familiar, the less time he spends backstage, and the more likely it is that he will be required to be polite as opposed to authentic.

Organizational life requires that the bureaucrat maintain a proper front. To counter this suppression of interaction, informal social groups form within the organization, allowing a greater latitude of behavior within the confines of the group. However, most organizational interaction calls for well-disciplined performance of various roles. The ease or difficulty with which the individual performs these roles will be affected by the degree to which his values are congruent with the behavior required of him.

The change-oriented individual is likely to find that his personal beliefs are not the mirror image of prevailing attitudes in the organiza-

---

[40] Gerald Caiden, *Administrative Reform*, 179.

[41] Orville Brim, Jr., "Personality Development as Role Learning," in *Personality Development in Children* (ed. by Ira Iscoe and Harold Stevenson), 141.

[42] Goffman, *op. cit.*, 56.

tion which employs him. One possible response to this realization is that he immediately clarifies with those around him the exact nature and extent of the difference between reality and his vision of how things ought to be. The general result of such a "confession" is that his associates label him as "strange" and "different." There is a predictable sequence of events which normally occurs when such a person deviates noticeably from the group norm. First, the group will direct an increasing amount of communication toward him, trying to change his attitude. If this fails, one after another will abandon him as hopeless. Communication to him will decrease. In the end he will be ignored or excluded.

Some change agents elect initially to blend into the organization in a relatively inconspicuous way, saying little and listening a lot. By presenting an unthreatening front, they are more likely to be able to gather the kind of information that will be helpful in planning for change. The value of protective coloration has long been recognized. Saint Paul recommended this strategy in his First Letter to the Corinthians:

> I am a free man, nobody's slave; but I make myself everybody's slave in order to win as many as possible. While working with the Jews, I live like a Jew in order to win them; and even though I myself am not subject to the Law of Moses, I live as though I were, when working with those who are, in order to win them. In the same way, when with the Gentiles I live like a Gentile, outside the Jewish law, in order to win Gentiles. This does not mean that I don't obey God's law, for I am really under Christ's law. Among the weak in faith I become weak like one of them in order to win them. So I become all things to all men, that I may save some of them by any means possible [I Cor. 9:19–23].

Saint Paul was evidently willing to sacrifice the luxury of spontaneous self-expression in order to influence the minds of men in disparate social groups. A recent discussion of conformity as a deliberate strategy comes from *The Organization Man*:

> The man who drives a Buick Special and lives in a ranch-type house just like hundreds of other ranch-type houses can assert himself as effectively and courageously against his particular society as the Bohemian against his particular society. He usually does not, it is true, but if he does, the surface uniformities can serve quite well as protective coloration. The organization people who are best able to control their environment rather than be controlled by it are well aware that they are not too easily distinguishable from others in the outward

410

obeisances paid to the good opinion of others. And that is one of the reasons they do control. They disarm society.[43]

This is Machiavellian role playing directed toward the goal of social reform. Such rational manipulation of social variables is a natural extension of normal conduct in a *Gesellschaft* (impersonal-oriented) society, the main difference being the special goals of the reformer. In the *Gesellschaft* society, as described by Ferdinand Tönnies, the prototype for social relations is barter and exchange.[44] Rational will predominates, and the individual evaluates his actions in terms of their efficiency in achieving his ends. From this follows an amoral, manipulative outlook, in which other persons are viewed as means for achieving one's own objectives.

A *Gemeinschaft* (personal-oriented) society, in contrast, is characterized by (1) an attitude of love among persons, (2) mutual understanding and consensus with respect to values and attitudes, and (3) a strong, organized community life. The individual in this kind of society does not try to use people. His behavior is determined by his emotions, his habits, and his sense of duty.

Encounter-group or sensitivity-group sessions which submerge the participants in marathon sessions of intense interaction can be viewed as an attempt to duplicate the extensity, intensity, and concord of *Gemeinschaft* society. Understanding and spontaneous self-expression of the *Gemeinschaft* society become the goals that training groups attempt to achieve. They also try to help group members move from fear to trust, from restricted to open communication, from externally imposed behavior to self-determination, and from dependence to interdependence.

The TORI theory, formulated by Jack and Lorraine Gibb, is based on the assumption that the deepest needs of man are to trust and to be trusted, to be in intimate communication, to actualize one's inner self, and to be genuinely interdependent.[45] Basic to properly conducted sensitivity training is the requirement that participants learn to interact as "persons" rather than as "roles." The long-range goal is a total program of environmental change, in which organizational structures, management practices, building designs, and personnel policies are changed to provide an institutional environment which promotes personal growth.

Until the new organizational form predicted by Bennis emerges and replaces the current hierarchical bureaucracy, it seems likely that inter-

[43] William H. Whyte, Jr., *The Organization Man*, 7–8.
[44] Ferdinand Tönnies, *Gemeinschaft and Gesellschaft*.
[45] Jack Gibb and Lorraine Gibb, "The Role of Freedom in a TORI Group," in *Encounter* (ed. by Arthur Burton).

personal skills, such as honesty and self-expression, will transfer to "backstage" relationships with family and friends where they can be usefully applied. The interpersonal skills of role playing and self-control will continue to be necessary for organizational interaction on the "front stage."

In *Mirrors and Masks: The Search for Identity*, Anselm Strauss discussed the need for a sense of personal continuity.[46] One strategy is to minimize identity change by seeking membership in organizations that are compatible with one's present identity. The roles that one plays in different organizations can also be manipulated so that their demands become more or less consonant. One can also gather supporters who confirm one's current self-image. Strauss observed that the more swiftly a society is changing the more necessary it becomes for a person to be able to select group memberships in order to maintain a sense of personal continuity.

Human relations professionals, like other persons, must rely fairly heavily on the reinforcement of those who share or accept their definition of reality. Such reinforcement is likely to come from family, friends, fellow professionals, and interested observers. Maximum mutual support probably comes out of relationships that are characterized by trust, understanding, open and complete communication, spontaneous self-expression, and affection. Credibility for human relations will come when human relations practitioners respond as professionals. In one respect the practicing psychologist offers a suitable model for the human relations practitioner who would be truly professional:

A psychologist does not claim either directly or by implication professional qualifications that exceed his actual qualifications, nor does he misrepresent his affiliation with any institution, organization, or individual, nor lead others to assume he has affiliations that he does not have. The psychologist is responsible for correcting others who misrepresent his professional qualifications or affiliations.[47]

The responsibility of psychotherapists to clients also suggests appropriate behavior for human relations practitioners:

. . . every therapist is required by law to remain responsible once he has undertaken a professional relationship. He must maintain records and remain available to the individual unless he formally discontinues his responsibility, stating his reasons and recommendations in writing.

[46] Anselm Strauss, *Mirrors and Masks: The Search for Identity*, 141–44.

[47] Quoted in National Training Laboratories Institute, *Standards for the Use of Laboratory Method* (Washington, D.C., National Training Laboratory for the Behavioral Sciences, 1969), 15.

Even after this declaration he remains legally responsible to the individual for what has already transpired.[48]

In his relationships in the "outside world"—the world of the "front stage"—the human relations professional should be guided by humanistic values. When these values, such as honesty and a conviction that all children are deserving of equal education opportunities, come into conflict he should make the choice in terms of his own moral priorities and the immediate situation. As Alinsky pointed out, the real question is not, "Does the end justify the means?" but "Does *this particular* end justify *this particular* means?"[49]

The Machiavellian reformer faces the constant danger of being conquered by the means which he is attempting to manipulate. There is always the danger that we will become what we pretend to be. Tullock discussed the possibility that an individual who enters a bureaucracy with altruistic motives will lose track of his original goals in the process of moving upward:

It is conceivable that he may want to rise to the top solely in order that he may use the resulting power for "good." The extent that this actually happens is an open question, but it is certainly true that there are people who enter upon their careers with this motivation, and who keep it in their minds during most of their careers. The very process of moving up, however, may serve to warp their judgment so that those who actually do attain superior positions may be rather uncertain as to what they conceive to be "good."[50]

It is for this reason that the reformer must always choose deliberate deception over self-deception. Only by remembering that he is pretending can he avoid what he pretends to be. Even by following this advice, he may not be able to survive in the bureaucracy (when he wrote *The Prince*, Machiavelli was unemployed and out of favor with the ruling regime). However, by being honest with himself, the reformer has a better chance to retain mastery over his own tactics than to be mastered by them.

The Client's Stake In Mediation[51]
DAVID HEYMANN

The poor also need mediators, or third parties, in their dealings with

[48] Ralph Cranshaw, "How Sensitive is Sensitivity Training?" *American Journal of Psychiatry*, 1969, 139.
[49] Alinsky, *op. cit.*, 208.
[50] Tullock, *op. cit.*, 29.
[51] Taken from David Heymann, "Social Worker in the Antipoverty Program," in *The Practice of Group Work* (ed. by William Schwartz and Serapio R. Zalba), 169–72.

institutions or agencies. A rent strike, grievance meeting, or even a phone call to the landlord is not always easily accomplished. The time period between perceiving a problem and taking action toward its resolution is often characterized by anxiety and turmoil. Frequently the ghetto resident is faced with pressures and obstacles that inhibit his problem-solving activity. Legal procedures, the filing of complaints, and formal meetings are unfamiliar activities, and talking with neighbors about common problems may be a new and awkward experience for many people.

The social worker can be quite useful in these areas by enabling tenants to talk with each other as well as with institutional representatives with whom they must deal. In the following excerpt the worker supports an angry and fearful tenant in speaking to the building superintendent concerning apartment repairs:

I said that I knew Mr. M. [superintendent] was not the easiest guy to get along with, but when I was gone she would have no one to do it for her, and it might be easier then, if she could try now. Mrs. B., an extremely nervous and weak woman, was unable to speak.

I said that if she wanted I would go with her and talk to him. There was another pause, and she finally said that she would go talk to him, and it was good that I could go with her because she would feel much less nervous.

We went to visit Mr. M. three times, each time finding him not at home. At first, Mrs. B. sent her child to knock at the door, but by the third time she knocked herself, although a little timidly. Finally Mr. M. answered and invited us in. Mrs. B. stood there speechless and Mr. M. began fidgeting with a piece of paper. I said that Mrs. B. had come to explain to him some of the repairs that she wanted made in her apartment. Mrs. B. then started to speak fluently in Spanish, explaining the things that had been promised but were not done. As she spoke, Mrs. B. seemed to gain strength; she took him to her apartment and angrily showed him all the violations, holes, falling plaster, and leaking pipes....

In this example the worker does not take the problem away from the client but asks her to try to deal with it with the support of his presence. Mrs. B. is able to express her anger and becomes more free to act than previously. Tenants need a worker who can understand the ambivalent feelings of fear and anger and yet is able to move with them as they assert themselves. Conflicts between tenants, a person's fear of speaking in a group, or general feelings of hopelessness and despair must be brought out and dealt with by the worker. Only in this way can the obstacles toward movement be identified and challenged:

414

Mrs. L. said that she had, at first, been very afraid to participate in the rent strike because her family had told her you don't do those things in this country. But by my support of her, and frequent visiting with the tenants, she had gradually come to realize that she did have rights, and that if everyone stuck together she would not feel so afraid. She spoke about how she had slowly realized that the landlord was cheating her and didn't really care about her; how alone she had felt; and how good it was to find that her neighbors were with her in doing something about this terrible situation.

As the people begin to support each other, the worker can help them recognize both their common strengths and the obstacles that lie in their path. And as the process evolves, the clients grow in their ability to move into negotiation with other systems. In this process the worker-mediator must learn to play his third-party role consistently, maintaining his interest in the communication between clients and other systems. In the following the worker holds his role up to scrutiny of the tenants before they move into meeting with the landlord:

I explained that at the meeting between tenants and landlord I would be in the middle, between both sides. Mrs. N., a tenant, thought that was a good idea since "my husband flies off the handle, and the landlord also gets mad. Maybe with you there, we can get something done."

Mrs. N. recognizes the worker as a person who, because of his function, can aid tenants and landlord in controlling their angry feelings, and this service is seen as a helpful tool in negotiation. The ghetto resident usually has the feeling that no matter what he says, he will not be heard. The social worker can be of great use in helping a person master his feelings of helplessness—not only by helping him speak but by guaranteeing an active but objective stance in pursuing the free flow of communication. A tenant, after a heated meeting with the building superintendent, illustrates this concept when he tells the worker "I am happy the meeting went so good, and it was because you stayed on both sides, and didn't take sides."

The worker will find that as both parties begin to trust him and understand his role, he will be freer to move about:

I said to the tenants that they must wonder how I worked, since I seemed to be talking to everyone, on all sides, all the time. I said it must seem strange that I expected them to confide in me, and yet talked to the landlord, tenants who weren't on rent strike, and welfare investigators. Everyone thought about this, and finally Mr. Q. said he didn't care what I did or who I talked to because he knew I helped the tenants.

415

I have referred to the building superintendent as an institutional representative with whom clients must deal directly. School teachers, hospital aides, child care workers, and others have similar positions within their agency systems. They are closest to the client; they are most often the lowest in status in their institutional hierarchies; and their function is to provide the actual service of the agency.

Because they supply the direct service and are within immediate reach of the client, these institutional representatives bear the full force of the client's angry feelings toward the agency. They are most often blamed by higher agency members for service level problems. The literature on bureaucracy documents the fact that the communication tends to be increasingly negative as it moves down the staff hierarchy....

SUMMARY

By being honest with himself, a human relations practitioner retains the ability to be honest with others. The belief that complicated and contradictory role playing for humanistic reasons can successfully bring about social change is certainly not new. Less well intentioned persons have managed to survive in hostile environments. One question might nag an individual at each step in his climb to success: "What if I am wrong in my beliefs?" There is no justification for a specific change if it will create conditions more deplorable than the present ones. Thus, human relations practitioners must operate on something more than hunches or good feelings. Training for humane living is indeed foreign to most of us. But it is worth dedicating a lifetime to its pursuit.

Chapter 15
SUGGESTED READING

Aguliera, Donna C. *Crisis Intervention Theory and Methodology.* Saint Louis, C. V. Mosby Company, 1970.

Alberts, David S. *A Plan for Measuring the Performance of Social Programs.* New York, Frederick A. Praeger, Inc., 1970.

Alinsky, Saul D. *Rules for Radicals.* New York, Vintage Books, Inc., 1971.

Argyris, Chris. *Understanding Organizational Behavior.* Homewood, Ill., Dorsey Press, Inc., 1960.

Banfield, Edward, and James Wilson. *City Politics.* New York, Random House, Inc., 1963.

Barnlund, Dean, and Franklyn Hairman. *The Dynamics of Discussion.* Boston, Houghton Mifflin Company, 1960.

Beckhard, Richard. *How to Plan Workshops and Conferences.* New York, Association Press, 1956.

Bennis, Warren. *Changing Organizations.* New York, McGraw-Hill Book Company, 1966.

Berger, Peter. *Invitation to Sociology: A Humanistic Perspective.* New York, Doubleday & Company, Inc., 1963.

Blau, Peter, and Richard Scott. *Formal Organizations: A Comparative Approach.* San Francisco, Chandler Publishing Company, 1962.

Borgardus, Emory S. *Leaders and Leadership.* New York, Appleton-Century-Crofts, Inc., 1934.

Boyd, Malcolm. *Human Like Me, Jesus.* New York, Simon & Schuster, Inc., 1971.

Brager, George. *Changing Services for Changing Clients.* New York, Columbia University Press, 1969.

Brill, Naomi I. *Working with People: The Helping Process.* Philadelphia, J. B. Lippincott Company, 1973.

Burton, Arthur, ed. *Encounter.* San Francisco, Jossey-Bass, Inc., 1969.

Caiden, Gerald. *Administrative Reform.* Chicago, Aldine Publishing Company, 1969.

Cox, John E., Jack Rothman, and John Troopman, eds. *Strategies of Community Organization.* Itasca, Ill., F. E. Peacock Publishers, Inc., 1970.

Crook, William, and Ross Thomas. *Warriors for the Poor.* New York, William Morrow & Company, Inc., 1969.

Dye, Thomas, and Brett Hawkins, eds. *Politics in the Metropolis.* Columbus, Ohio, Charles E. Merrill Publishing Company, 1967.

Dyer, William G. *The Sensitive Manipulator: The Change Agent Who Builds With Others.* Provo, Utah, Brigham Young University Press, 1972.

Etzioni, Amitai. *Modern Organizations.* Englewood Cliffs, N.J., Prentice-Hall, Inc., 1964.

———, ed. *Complex Organizations: A Sociological Reader.* New York, Holt, Rinehart & Winston, Inc., 1961.

Gilbert, Neil, *Clients or Constituents.* San Francisco, Jossey-Bass, Inc., 1970.

Goffman, Erving. *The Presentation of Self in Everyday Life.* Garden City, N.Y,. Doubleday & Company, Inc., 1959.

Gorlow, Leon, and Walter Katovsky, eds. *Readings in the Psychology of Adjustment.* New York, McGraw-Hill Book Company, 1959.

Guterman, Stanley. *The Machiavellians.* Lincoln, University of Nebraska Press, 1970.

Hornstein, Harvey A., Barbara Bunker, W. Burke, Marion Gindes, and Roy Lewicki. *Social Intervention: A Behavioral Science Approach.* New York, The Free Press, 1971.

Iscoe, Ira, and Harold Stevenson, eds. *Personality Development in Children.* Austin, University of Texas Press, 1970.

Karrass, Chester L. *The Negotiating Game.* New York, The World Publishing Company, 1970.

King, Clarence. *Working with People in Community Action.* New York, Association Press, 1965.

Kurtz, Paul. *Moral Problems in Contemporary Society: Essays in Humanistic Ethics.* Englewood Cliffs, N.J., Prentice-Hall, Inc., 1969.

417

Larner, Jeremy, and Irving Howe, eds. *Poverty: Views from the Left*. New York, William Morrow & Company, Inc., 1968.

Machiavelli, Niccolò. *The Prince and The Discourses*. New York, Random House, Inc., 1940.

Maier, Norman. *Problem-Solving Discussions and Conferences: Leadership Methods and Skills*. New York, McGraw-Hill Book Company, 1964.

Marris, Peter, and Martin Rein. *Dilemmas of Social Reform*. New York, Atherton Press, 1967.

McSurely, Alan. *Hangups*. Louisville, Kentucky, Southern Conference Educational Fund, 1967.

Middleman, Ruth R. *The Non-Verbal Method in Working with Groups*. New York, Association Press, 1968.

Mills, C. Wright. *Power, Politics, and People*. New York, Oxford University Press, 1963.

Minnis, Jack. *The Care and Feeding of Power Structures Revisited*. Louisville, Kentucky, Southern Conference Educational Fund, 1967.

Moynihan, Daniel. *Maximum Feasible Misunderstanding*. New York, The Free Press, 1969.

Organizer's Manual Collective. *The Organizer's Manual*. New York, Bantam Books, Inc., 1971.

Oxnam, G. Bromley. *Personalities in Social Reform*. New York, Abingdon-Cokesbury Press, 1950.

Packard, Vance. *The Pyramid Climbers*. New York, McGraw-Hill Book Company, 1962.

Presthus, Robert. *The Organizational Society*. New York, Alfred A. Knopf, Inc., 1962.

Ross, Murray G. *Community Organization: Theory, Principles and Practices*. New York, Harper & Row Publishers, Inc., 1957.

Rothman, Jack, ed. *Promoting Social Justice in the Multigroup Society: A Casebook for Group Relations Practitioners*. New York, Association Press, 1971.

Sanders, Marion. *The Professional Radical: Conversations with Saul Alinsky*. Evanston, Harper & Row, Publishers, Inc., 1965.

Schwartz, William, and Serapio R. Zalba, eds. *The Practice of Group Work*. New York, Columbia University Press, 1971.

Sharkansky, Ira. *Public Administration: Policy-Making in Government Agencies*. Chicago, Markham Publishing Company, 1970.

Sherif, Carolyn, et al. *Attitudes and Attitude Change*. Philadelphia, W. B. Saunders Company, 1965.

Stein, Herman, and Richard Cloward, eds. *Social Perspective on Behavior*. New York, The Free Press, 1958.

Strauss, Anslem. *Mirrors and Masks: The Search for Identity*. Glencoe, Ill., The Free Press, 1959.

Taylor, Jack W. *How to Select and Develop Leaders*. New York, McGraw-Hill Book Company, 1962.

Tönnies, Ferdinand. *Gemeinschaft and Gesellschaft*. 1st ed., 1887, translated and ed. by C. P. Loomis as *Fundamental Concepts of Sociology.* New York, American Book Company, 1940.

Tullock, Gordon. *The Politics of Bureaucracy.* Washington, D.C., Public Affairs Press, 1965.

Warren, Roland. *Truth, Love, and Social Change.* Chicago, Rand-McNally & Company, 1971.

———, ed. *Perspectives on the American Community.* Chicago, Rand-Mc-Nally & Company, 1966.

Watson, Goodwin, ed. *Concepts for Social Change.* Washington, D.C., National Training Laboratories Institute for Applied Behavioral Science, 1967.

Weinberger, Paul E., ed. *Perspectives on Social Welfare.* New York, The Macmillan Company, 1969.

Whyte, William H., Jr. *The Organization Man.* New York, Doubleday & Company, Inc., 1956.

Wilson, James, ed. *City Politics and Public Policy.* New York, John Wiley & Sons, Inc., 1968.

Wolf, Alexander, and Emanuel K. Schwartz. *Psychoanalysis in Groups.* New York, Grune & Stratton, Inc., 1962.

Zaleznik, Abraham. *Human Dilemmas of Leadership.* New York, Harper & Row, Publishers, Inc., 1966.

Zimbardo, Phillip G., and Ebbe B. Ebbeson. *Influencing Attitudes and Changing Behavior.* Reading, Mass., Addison-Wesley Publishing Company, 1969.

Appendix A MY BELIEFS AND BEHAVIOR

Respond to the following statements according to whether you believe they are generally false to generally true by putting a check mark at the right of the word you choose.

1. I act the way I feel.

   usually—often—sometimes—occasionally—rarely—never—

2. I like to touch other people.

   usually—often—sometimes—occasionally—rarely—never—

3. I find it easy to listen to other people.

   usually—often—sometimes—occasionally—rarely—never—

4. I tell others how I feel.

   usually—often—sometimes—occasionally—rarely—never—

5. I feel self-conscious about my body.

   usually—often—sometimes—occasionally—rarely—never—

6. I like to look another person in the eye.

   usually—often—sometimes—occasionally—rarely—never—

7. I am glad to be the sex I am.

   usually—often—sometimes—occasionally—rarely—never—

8. I find it hard to understand people I don't like.

   usually—often—sometimes—occasionally—rarely—never—

9. People only like attractive people.

   usually—often—sometimes—occasionally—rarely—never—

10. Sex is only for marriage.

    usually—often—sometimes—occasionally—rarely—never—

11. It's all right for a man to cry in public.

    usually—often—sometimes—occasionally—rarely—never—

12. Women feel emotions more deeply than men do.

    usually—often—sometimes—occasionally—rarely—never—

13. I feel that younger people appreciate and enjoy their maleness and femaleness.

    usually—often—sometimes—occasionally—rarely—never—

14. I feel that old people appreciate and enjoy their maleness and femaleness.

    usually—often—sometimes—occasionally—rarely—never—

15. I like to touch myself.

    usually—often—sometimes—occasionally—rarely—never—

16. Other people like to be with me.

    usually—often—sometimes—occasionally—rarely—never—

17. People misunderstand me.

    usually—often—sometimes—occasionally—rarely—never—

18. I express affection easily.

    usually—often—sometimes—occasionally—rarely—never—

19. I have the capacity to express myself as man or woman.

    usually—often—sometimes—occasionally—rarely—never—

20. I am aware of communication between myself and others that is not always expressed in talking.

    usually—often—sometimes—occasionally—rarely—never—

21. I respond to affection easily.

    usually—often—sometimes—occasionally—rarely—never—

22. I like to express myself in ways other than talking.

    usually—often—sometimes—occasionally—rarely—never—

23. I freely respond to my creative urges.

    usually—often—sometimes—occasionally—rarely—never—

Appendix B IRRITATING LISTENING HABITS

Below are listed fifty listening habits that are distinctly irritating to people. Some of these habits seem unconscious, some purposeful, some trivial, some important, some remediable, some deeply rooted in the personality of the person. (1) Place an X before the habits listed that irritate you when they are practiced by others. (2) Place an I before the habits of which you believe yourself guilty.

___ 1. He doesn't give me a chance to talk. I never get a chance to tell my problem.

___ 2. She interrupts me when I talk.

___ 3. He never looks at me when I talk. I don't know whether he's listening or not.

___ 4. She makes me feel that I'm wasting her time. She doodles and draws pictures all the time.

___ 5. He continually fidgets with a pencil, a paper, or something, looking at it and examining it as if studying it rather than listening to me.

___ 6. She paces back and forth as if impatient with the way I am telling my story.

___ 7. He has such a poker face and manner that I never know whether he's listening or whether he understands me.

___ 8. She treats me like a child, ignoring me while taking several incoming phone calls.

___ 9. He never smiles; I'm afraid to talk to him.

___10. She asks questions as if she doubted everything I say.

___11. He always gets me off the subject with his questions and comments.

___12. Whenever I make a suggestion, she throws cold water on it. I've quit making suggestions.

___13. He always tries to get ahead of me by prestating my point or prefinishing my sentence.

___14. She rephrases what I say in such a way that she puts words into my mouth that I didn't mean.

___15. He talks me around into a corner and makes me feel like a fool.

___16. She frequently answers a question with another question—and usually it's one I can't answer. It embarrasses me.

___17. Occasionally he asks a question about what I have just told him that shows he wasn't listening. For example, just after I finish telling him about a problem he might then ask, "Let's see, what was it you wanted to talk to me about?"

___18. She always takes notes when I am talking. I get so worried about what she is writing, and so worried about how I am saying things, that I forget what I was saying.

___19. He argues with everything I say—even before I have a chance to state my case.

___20. Everything I say reminds her of an experience she has had or an event that she has heard about recently. I get frustrated when she continually interrupts to say, "That reminds me. . . ."

___21. He sits there picking hangnails or clipping fingernails or cleaning his nails or cleaning his glasses, etc. I know he can't do that and listen too.

___22. He rummages through the papers on his desk or through his desk drawers instead of listening.

___23. She twitches and turns constantly, just waiting for me to stop so that she can take over.

___24. When I have a good idea, he says, "Oh, yes, I've been thinking about that for some time."

___25. Whenever I talk to him, he swings around and looks out the window.

___26. She smiles all the time, even when I am telling her about a serious problem of mine.

___27. She stares at me as if trying to outstare me.

___28. He looks at me as if appraising me. I begin to wonder if I have a smudge on my face, or a tear in my coat, etc.

___29. He looks me in the eye too much—unnaturally long at a time. It's just not normal.

___30. She overdoes trying to show me she's following what I'm saying —too many nods of her head, or "Mm-hm's, and, "Uh-huh's."

___31. He inserts humorous remarks when I am trying to be serious.

___32. After apparently listening, she may say, "It looks to me as though your problem is . . . ," and what she suggests usually isn't my problem at all.

___33. She has bad breath and sits too close to me. It gets nauseating.

___34. He blows smoke in my face. It almost makes me dizzy at times.

___35. She asks personal questions when other people are in the same office or room with us.

___36. He frequently looks at his watch or the clock while I am talking.

___37. She closes her eyes, rests her head on her hand, as if resting.

___38. He doesn't put down what he is doing when I am in and turn his attention to me completely.

___39. She doesn't seem to take personal interest in me. She is completely withdrawn and distant.

___40. He always makes some remark which indicates that he is doing me a favor in seeing me.

___41. She acts as if I should know how to solve the problem.—she does!

___42. He is always rushed for time and makes comments about his "busy day." He won't sit still.

___43. He walks away when I am talking and often stands with his back to me.

___44. He passes the buck on problems. "We'll have to think about it," he'll say.

___45. He says he has to go to another meeting, but only after we talk a while.

___46. He acts as if he knows it all, frequently incidents in which he was the hero.

___47. She says something and then denies it at the next meeting we have.

___48. She tries to avoid seeing me—as if she doesn't want to talk to me about any problems.

___49. If several people are in the room, she looks at someone other than the person who is talking.

___50. He asks questions that demand agreement with him. For example, he makes a statement and then says, "Don't you think so?" or, "Don't you agree?"

Try to recall your typical attitudes and behavior in groups (staff meetings, committees, etc.) and mark all the scales for your usual behavior. Then select three or four that you would most like to change. Draw an arrow showing which direction you would like to move.

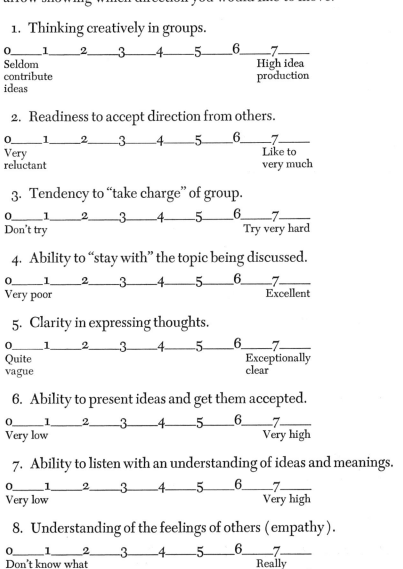

1. Thinking creatively in groups.

0____1____2____3____4____5____6____7____
Seldom
contribute
ideas

High idea
production

2. Readiness to accept direction from others.

0____1____2____3____4____5____6____7____
Very
reluctant

Like to
very much

3. Tendency to "take charge" of group.

0____1____2____3____4____5____6____7____
Don't try

Try very hard

4. Ability to "stay with" the topic being discussed.

0____1____2____3____4____5____6____7____
Very poor

Excellent

5. Clarity in expressing thoughts.

0____1____2____3____4____5____6____7____
Quite
vague

Exceptionally
clear

6. Ability to present ideas and get them accepted.

0____1____2____3____4____5____6____7____
Very low

Very high

7. Ability to listen with an understanding of ideas and meanings.

0____1____2____3____4____5____6____7____
Very low

Very high

8. Understanding of the feelings of others (empathy).

0____1____2____3____4____5____6____7____
Don't know what
they feel

Really
understand

9. Understanding why I do what I do (insight).

0____1____2____3____4____5____6____7____
Don't   Really
know   understand

10. Express emotions.

0____1____2____3____4____5____6____7____
Conceal   Reveal
everything   everything

11. Tendency to comment upon or evaluate behavior of others.

0____1____2____3____4____5____6____7____
Highly   Very
critical   accepting

12. Reactions to comments about or evaluations of my own behavior.

0____1____2____3____4____5____6____7____
Ignore   Take them
them   very seriously

13. Acceptance of opinions in opposition to my own.

0____1____2____3____4____5____6____7____
Low   High

14. Expressions of conflict and antagonism in the group.

0____1____2____3____4____5____6____7____
Can't stand   Like them
them   very much

15. Expressions of affection and warmth.

0____1____2____3____4____5____6____7____
Can't stand   Like them
them   very much

16. Behavior toward others.

0____1____2____3____4____5____6____7____
Cool   Warm

17. Tendency to trust others.

0____1____2____3____4____5____6____7____
Quite   Extremely
suspicious   trusting

Place a check mark along each scale, showing about where you would rate this group at this time.

TASK FUNCTIONS

1. How clear are the goals in this group?

0	1	2	3	4	5	6	7
Utter confusion		Hidden agenda	Average		Fairly clear now	Clear focus, shared by all	

2. How strongly involved do we feel in what this group is doing?

0	1	2	3	4	5	6	7
Couldn't care less		Not much interest	Average		Interested	Deeply involved concern	

3. How well do we diagnose our group problems?

0	1	2	3	4	5	6	7
Avoid; try to disregard		Slight attention	Average		Considerable attention	Face frankly, analyze with care; successful diagnoses	

4. How appropriate are our group norms and procedures for our group goals?

0	1	2	3	4	5	6	7
Defeating our purpose		Not much help	Average		Often fitting, useful	The best possible means to our ends	

5. How well do we integrate contributions from various members?

0	1	2	3	4	5	6	7
Each goes it alone, says his say, disregards others; no summary or integration		Slight attention to others' ideas	Average		Considerable attention to using others ideas	Each speaks, builds directly on contributions from others, relates, ties together	

6. How do we usually make decisions?

0	1	2	3	4	5	6	7
We don't	Self authorized	Only a few contribute	Average		Most members contribute a great deal	Everyone contributes fully and creatively	

MAINTENANCE FUNCTIONS

1. How much do members enjoy working with the others in this group?

0	1	2	3	4	5	6	7
All hate it; ready to quit		Discontented	Average; some pleased, some don't care, some displeased		Rather pleased; some enjoyment	All love it; real joy; strong cohesion	

2. How much encouragement, support, and appreciation do we give to one another as we work?

0	1	2	3	4	5	6	7
None		Seldom give support	Average; some appreciated, some ignored, some criticized		Often give support	Abundant for every member even when we disagree	

3. How freely are our personal and group feelings (both affectionate and hostile) expressed?

0	1	2	3	4	5	6	7
No feelings expressed; all work-oriented		Seldom express feelings; only negative or only positive ones	Average; expressed when unusually strong		Often express feelings, both positive and negative	Both personal and group feelings expressed	

4. How constructively are we able to use disagreements and conflicts in this group?

0	1	2	3	4	5	6	7
Avoid or repress them, or so bad they threaten to break up the group		Seldom examine conflicts	Average; smooth them over, change the subject; occasional constructive exploration		Often explore conflicts	Welcome them, explore them, find them most valuable	

432

5. How sensitive and responsive are we to the feelings of others which are not being overtly expressed?

0	1	2	3	4	5	6	7
Blind, insensitive, unconcerned, inert, ruthless		Seldom notice them	Average; only occasional response to such feelings		Often respond to them	Fully aware, very sensitive, very responsive	

6. How frequently do we give feedback which other members can connect directly with specific behaviors?

0	1	2	3	4	5	6	7
Never give any, or give only "right" judgments		Rather seldom	Average		Fairly	Very frequently given and well received	

7. How many members are experiencing new understanding of themselves, seeing new facets of others, experiencing changes in outlook and perspective, developing a sense of growth and self-realization?

0	1	2	3	4	5	6	7
None		A few	About half		Most	All	

433

Appendix E   EMPATHY EXERCISE

Purpose: To increase the ability to empathize.

Procedure:

Introduction: Empathy is the capacity to tune in on another person's feelings and behavior in a given situation. It is the imaginative projection of one's own consciousness into another being. Empathy is implied in an old Indian prayer: "O Lord, help me not to judge my neighbor until I have walked a mile in his mocassins." In contrast to sympathy, empathy is the capacity not only to tune in on another person's feelings, but also to feel the same way.

Directions:

A. The trainer asks each person to identify privately another person in the group with whom he is having difficulty relating. Then each person jots down on a piece of paper his response to the following questions:

1. What is this person doing and saying that bothers you?
2. What assumptions does this person make that cause him to act this way?
3. What do his assumptions demand that he do or not do?
4. What does he see as the gain or risk in acting this way?
5. What are his feelings in this situation?
6. What are the risks for him in changing this pattern of behavior?
7. What possible gain might there be for him in changing?

B. Divide into triads:
   A is consultant.
   B is consultee.
   C is observer.

   (Walk through the exercise with one of the triads to clarify each person's task.)

   The consultant's task is to enable the person to work on his problem in relating to the person with whom he is trying to empathize. The observer's task is to note questions asked and the response evoked and then to use this feedback to help the consultant and consultee to reflect on their relationship.

C. Timing:
   A consults with *B*—five minutes
   Feedback from *C* and pull learning—ten minutes

434

A continues to consult with B—five minutes
Feedback and pull learnings—ten minutes
D. Switch roles:
   B is consultant
   C is consultee
   A is observer
   (Same timing)
E. Switch roles again:
   C is consultant
   A is consultee
   B is observer
   (Same timing)
F. Move into clusters for remaining time to share learning.

435

Imagine that through some weird set of events it has become apparent that the entire world is about to be subjected to a violent nuclear holocaust which will spell an end to all human life on this planet. Scientists have, however, devised a special protection chamber which, although small in size, is absolutely guaranteed to keep its occupants alive through this event. The chamber will hold ten persons, who already have been selected. They are:

1. An accountant.
2. The accountant's pregnant wife.
3. A Mexican-American liberal-arts coed.
4. A black professional football player.
5. An intelligent woman movie star.
6. An alcoholic medical student.
7. A famous novelist.
8. A homosexual biochemist.
9. A seventy-year-old Indian clergyman.
10. An armed policeman.

At the very last minute the scientists announce that, contrary to their previous calculations, only seven persons can be safely life-supported in the capsule.

Which of the people listed above should be deleted from the list? Only seven can be the sole survivors of the human race.

You decide the three who will not survive.

I. Defining a community problem

    A. What does the difficulty seem to be?
        1. Who sees this as a problem?
        2. Who is affected by it?
        3. How are they affected?
        4. What are your feelings about the situation?

    B. What significant events or incidents illustrate the problem?
        1. Who does what?
        2. What seems to happen?

    C. What is your role in the situation? How are you involved? With whom? As you refer to other people, specify what the relationships are between you and them.

    D. What are you trying to do about the problem?

    E. What do you think you might try to do about the problem?

    F. What other significant factors affect the problem (within the community, outside, intercommunity, historical factors, etc.)?

II. Clarifying goals as an aspect of the problem definition

    A. What differences exist in the goals toward which individuals and groups are working with reference to this problem?
        1. What seem to be the goals of individuals in the community who are directly affected by the problem?
        2. What seem to be the goals of groups and organizations in the community that are affected by it?
        3. What are the goals of other problem-related individuals, groups, or organizations which are not currently involved in working on the problem?
            a. Those inside the community?
            b. Those outside the community?
        4. What are your own personal goals as they relate to the problem?
        5. What are the goals of your colleagues or your work group?
            a. In what ways do they differ from your goals?
        6. What are the goals of your organization?
            a. In what ways do they differ from those of your colleagues?

       b. In what ways do they differ from those of your work group?

       c. In what ways do they differ from your own?

B. Types of goals that are operative:

  1. What are the immediate operational goals in the problem situation?

  2. What are the intermediate or long-range goals operative in this situation?

C. What are the priorities among the goals?

III. Clarifying norms or standards as an aspect of problem definition, and as a basis for developing an effective action program

A. What are the norms or standards held by people affected by the problem?

B. What are the norms or standards of groups and organizations affected by the problem?

C. What are the norms or standards in the community which relate to the problem?

D. What are the norms or standards of groups and organizations attempting to do something about the problem?

E. Among the norms or standards identified above, which ones tend to support action on the problem and which ones tend to impede action?

F. In what way could you attempt to modify the norms or standards which tend to impede action on the problem?

IV. Clarifying your role as an aspect of the problem definition and as a basis for developing an effective action program

A. What do the people affected by the problem define as your role?

B. What do groups and organizations affected by the problem define as your role?

C. What does the community at large expect from you in relation to this problem?

D. What do groups and organizations trying to do something about the problem tend to see as your role?

    E. What do you define as your role?
      1. In practice?
      2. Ideally?

    F. What are the major role conflicts that you see emerging out of the problem in relation to the questions raised above?

    G. In what way could your role be defined in this problem so that conflict would be reduced?

V. Clarifying power, authority, and influence as an aspect of problem definition and as a basis for developing an effective action program

    A. What influence or authority do you have in relation to groups or organizations directly affected by the problem?

    B. What influence or authority do the individuals or groups affected by the problem perceive that you have with reference to it?

    C. What influence or authority does the community at large perceive that you have in relation to this problem?

    D. What authority or influence do organizations and groups who may also be trying to do something about the problem perceive that you have?

    E. How are individuals, groups, or organizations with authority or influence aligned with reference to the problem?

    F. How can influential individuals, groups, and organizations be encouraged to bring their authority or influence to bear on the problem?

    G. How can people who believe themselves powerless to affect the decision be involved in a constructive manner?

VI. Initiating and legitimatizing proposed action

    A. Which individuals, groups, and organizations have the legal or socially defined right to initiate action for the solution of the problem?
      1. What role and influence do you have with these individuals, groups, and organizations?

    B. Are the initiators able to give their full approval or sponsorship to your proposed action for the solution of the problem?

1. What appropriate means do the initiators see as available for the solution of this problem?

C. Which ideas for action proposed by the initiators may be viewed as compatible with your projected solutions?
   1. What is the basis for their opposition or neutrality, if it exists?
   2. In what ways does it appear possible for you to gain their support?

VII. Organizing for action

Assuming that a problem has been identified and defined, that some action is proposed, one then confronts the problem of organizing for action. At this stage, it is likely that very few people understand the problem or see the need for action and that fewer still are committed to any kind of action. Some way must be found to help people explore the problem, the need for action, and the ways in which some kind of alternative solution to the problem might be accepted. The following questions might be helpful:

A. What kind of organization seems to be needed to move ahead from the initiation and legitimization stage to the involvement of people in the community in the implementation of action?
   1. How well is the problem understood by people generally?
   2. What specific resources are needed to carry out the proposed action successfully?
   3. What structure is needed to facilitate the proposed
      a. Having some existing organization or group of organizations take responsibility for action? If so, which?
      b. Creating some new temporary organization? If so, what?
      c. Creating some more or less continuing organization to guide the action? If so, what?

B. What kinds of procedures need to be established to facilitate the proposed action?
   1. Mobilization of needed resources?
   2. Strategies for the development and modification of plans of work?
   3. Continuing communication?
   4. Participative decision making?
   5. Appropriate and mutually supportive relationships with

other groups and organizations?
6. Continuing evaluation and realistic assessment of resources needed, accomplishments, processes?

C. How will the action program be launched in the community?

VIII. Evaluating action programs

A. Kinds of data to be collected
1. To what extent have the goals of the action program been achieved?
2. What was the relative effectiveness of the methods and procedures used?
3. What was the relative effectiveness of the way resources were used?
4. In what ways can we account for the success or lack of success in the program?
5. What should be done differently if the program were to be repeated?

445

446

The paper on which this book is printed bears the watermark of the University of Oklahoma Press and has an effective life of at least three hundred years.